Y0-AAY-554

BUS157 $1595

The practice of supervision
Achieving results through people

Consulting Editor in Management
John M. Ivancevich   *University of Houston*

Andrew J. DuBrin
Rochester Institute of Technology

The practice of supervision

*Achieving results
through people*

1980

Business Publications, Inc.   *Dallas, Texas   75243*
Irwin-Dorsey Limited   *Georgetown, Ontario   L7G 4B3*

© BUSINESS PUBLICATIONS, INC., 1980

All rights reserved. No part of this publication may be reproduced, stored in a retrieval system, or transmitted, in any form or by any means, electronic, mechanical, photocopying, recording, or otherwise, without the prior written permission of the publisher.

ISBN 0-256-02272-0
Library of Congress Catalog Card No. 79–53355

Printed in the United States of America

1 2 3 4 5 6 7 8 9 0 MP 7 6 5 4 3 2 1 0

*To my students and other people
whose work I have supervised*

Preface

Why would an author write a book about supervision when so many good ones are already on the market? Five objectives or purposes underlie the writing of *The Practice of Supervision*.

1. To provide valid information about the human aspects of supervision that will be of direct help to both future and practicing supervisors and middle managers. Most texts with the term management in the title provide information primarily useful to people who are, or will be, perched at high places in large organizations.

2. To present current information about achieving results through people. To achieve this objective, modern topics are discussed. Among them are interpreting games played by employees, coping with office politics, managing your job-related tensions, resolving conflict, and dealing with job discrimination.

3. To provide a comprehensive overview of the traditional supervisory topics, but involving modern people in modern situations. Too many books about supervision are in essence books about factory supervision. This book includes factory, office, business, industrial, institutional, and a variety of miscellaneous settings in discussing supervision.

4. To provide a format not only useful but interesting to supervisors and prospective supervisors. Most of the ideas presented in the text are illustrated with case examples or conversations between people. Some of the information found in this text is based on the trade (nontechnical and popular), rather than the scientific literature in management.

5. To place an emphasis on achieving insight into the human aspects of supervising people and dealing with the organization. To achieve this objective, the reader is made aware of the human

and subjective aspects of seemingly objective topics such as MBO, cost control, and decision making. In addition, the reader is given the opportunity to complete several self-examination exercises that provide clues to his or her personal makeup.

This book is intended for use primarily by three groups: practicing supervisors, prospective supervisors, and other managers whose subordinates are involved directly in performing operative work (usually referred to as middle managers or lower-middle managers).

Our definition of a supervisor is a first-level manager—somebody who achieves results with and through individual workers. The term manager refers to any person who is responsible for the work of subordinates. A president is a top-level manager or executive; a regional vice president is a high-level middle manager; a supervisor is a first-level manager. The lower the level of management, the more directly the manager interacts with subordinates. This book is written for those people who spend a substantial portion of their work days solving human problems.

By carefully reading this book and implementing many of its suggestions, a supervisor or higher-level manager should be able to increase productivity and contribute to employee morale and job satisfaction. Insights on improving supervisory practice are provided, chapter by chapter, topic by topic. For example, if you improve communications with employees (as described in Chapter 9) in your department, productivity might increase along with morale and job satisfaction.

An important feature of this book are cases and self-insight exercises at the end of chapters, along with case examples and illustrative conversations contained within the chapters. The cases and exercises give you a chance to try out the concepts and techniques presented in the chapter. The case examples and illustrative conversations help explain what a concept means in practice. For instance instead of only talking about the concept of helping your boss succeed, I present a case history of how one chief manufacturing engineer helped his immediate superior succeed.

An additional value of the cases is that they provide practice in accomplishing results through people—the most important responsibility of supervisors and higher-level managers.

Acknowledgments

Writing a textbook is a collective effort. The ideas of hundreds of people are incorporated in this book. An attempt has been made to give credit to all the sources used by way of citations through footnotes and Suggested Readings in the text. The many uncredited ideas in this book are case examples and insights I have gathered in working with and supervising people. Among these people are present and past subordinates of mine, college students, workshop participants, and hundreds of supervisors who have attended talks of mine.

Several outside reviewers helped shape the final form of this manuscript. Thanks are due my consulting editor, John M. Ivancevich of the University of Houston, W. Clay Hamner of Duke University, Barbara Hanley of The University of Minnesota, and Robert M. Rompf of Michigan State University. John D. Minch of Carbillo College deserves special credit for the scope and depth of his suggestions. K. Lois Smith, my manuscript typist, once again turned in a journeywoman's effort.

My wife Marcia, our daughter Melanie, and my sons Drew and Douglas receive my appreciation for their interest in my writing.

December 1979 **Andrew J. DuBrin**

Contents

part three
BASIC SUPERVISORY FUNCTIONS

part four
SUPERVISORY SKILLS AND TECHNIQUES

part five
SPECIAL CHALLENGES AND DEMANDS

part six
HELPING YOURSELF SUCCEED

part one

Understanding the supervisor's job

The supervisor's job

LEARNING OBJECTIVES

After reading and thinking through the material in this chapter, you should be able to:

1. Define the term *supervisor*.
2. Understand the difference between the work of a supervisor and other managerial workers.
3. Explain why supervisory jobs are even more difficult today than in the past.
4. Recognize the major responsibilities of a supervisor.
5. List and define in your own words at least six different supervisory functions.
6. Explain the framework for accomplishing results and illustrate its use.

A management consultant asked the personnel manager of a large insurance company, "How does your business keep running so smoothly? Each visit here I learn of another shake-up in top management. Vice presidents come and go as if they were big league baseball managers. Yet I hear that your policyholders don't complain too much about service."

"I think I can answer your question," replied the personnel manager. "Our day-to-day work gets done by our office supervisors and their workers. It doesn't matter who the players are at the top of the company. The game is still the same down below. Most of our supervisors have been with us a long time. They make sure the work gets done without worrying about the politics in the executive suite."

Although comments made by this personnel manager may be overdramatic, they do illustrate an important fact of work life:

Organizations cannot be properly run without competent first-level managers. Supervisors are the key to success in any firm. Because of the widespread recognition of this fact, supervisors are usually held accountable for whatever goes wrong in a work organization.

WHO IS A SUPERVISOR?

A supervisor is a first-level manager responsible for directing the job activities of one or more subordinates so that work objectives are accomplished. He or she directs the work activities of people who themselves are individual performers—not managers. Our definition of a supervisor stands in contrast to the position taken by many management experts that all managers should be classified as supervisors. According to the latter line of reasoning, a company president is a top-level supervisor. So is the president of the United States and the prime minister of Canada. The person in charge of the mailroom, however, is a first-level supervisor. Whatever definition of supervisor you accept, one vital ingredient holds true. A supervisor is a person who accomplishes work with and through other people who are subordinates.

Different supervisory titles

A number of different job titles are used to label the work of supervisors. Often these differences in job titles reflect genuine differences in the nature of the job. For instance, an *assistant foreman* is usually an understudy to the foreman or forewoman. This person handles a few supervisory problems on a daily basis but becomes a full-fledged supervisor when the department foreman or forewoman is away from the department.

Among the titles used for first level managers (in addition to supervisor) are foreman, forewoman, foreperson (very rarely in written form), group leader, first-line manager, direct manager, working supervisor, lead man, lead woman, setup person, hourly rated supervisor, and checker.[1] Titles such as administrator, sec-

---

[1] Paul Pigors and Charles A. Myers, *Personnel Administration: A Point of View and a Method,* 8th ed. (New York: McGraw-Hill, 1977), p. 118.

tion head, department head, and vice president are usually re-served for higher-level managers. The managerial job title, "chairman" or "chairperson" is particularly confusing. Many chairpersons are top level executives who outrank the president of the organization. Other chairpersons are supervisors. The chairperson of a college department is really a first-level super-visor in charge of the work activities of professors.

Different supervisory jobs

As implied by the diversity of job titles for a supervisor, the basic job performed by a supervisor varies greatly in complexity. A supervisor in a small post office might need limited technical knowledge and face few changes in the work routine. A labora-tory supervisor might need high technical competence in order to assist subordinates who are all professionals or technicians.

Some supervisors are expected to prepare a budget, visit cus-tomers, contribute to long-range planning, solve technical prob-lems, and resolve labor disputes. Another person might be called a supervisor, yet may spend almost all of the workday checking to see that others are working properly. Such supervisory posi-tions are becoming increasingly rare. As job duties vary, so does supervisory pay. Many supervisors working in factories earn less money than some of their subordinates. The latter often increase their income through incentive bonuses and overtime pay—two privileges left behind by people when they become members of management. At the other extreme are supervisors who partici-pate in the profit sharing of the firm and earn a substantially above-average income.

THE NEW SUPERVISORY CHALLENGE[2]

The job of a supervisor has always been both challenging and frustrating. First-level managers are frequently asked to accom-plish results through people, many of whom are less than en-

---

[2] This section of the chapter is based on the thoughts contained in David S. Brown, "Rethinking the Supervisory Role," *Supervisory Management*, November 1977, pp. 2–10. © 1977 by AMACOM, a division of American Management Associations. All rights reserved.

thusiastic about achieving company goals. In addition, supervisors are often asked to make do with aging equipment. To complicate the supervisory dilemma, supervisors generally do not participate in many of the financial rewards and privileges enjoyed by higher ranking managers. As supervisors face the 1980s, they are confronted by forces that make the supervisory job even more challenging than in the past. Four factors are particularly significant: the complexity of work; the decline of the work ethic; the increased number of people whose jobs are difficult to supervise; and the rising expectations of workers.

Increasing complexity of work. A visitor to a modern high school in the United States or Canada would be impressed by the technical complexity of many of the career-oriented (the "vocational" courses of old) courses. High school students learn to program and debug computers and repair jet engines. Similarly, on the job young people are performing tasks much more complex than their parents performed at the peak of their careers. Jobs have become so specialized in all fields that most supervisors have difficulty in providing expert technical advice to more than a few operations under their jurisdiction. In the words of David S. Brown, a professor of management:[3]

> Those who become highly proficient in the performing of a task earn the right to free themselves from the close and watchful attention of their supervisors. Furthermore, often the supervisor is incapable of providing the guidance that was once given. More often, he chooses to regard the individual's work area as private domain only to be entered when things go wrong. Some supervisors manage to keep well-enough informed so that they will know what to do in the event of the subordinate's illness or resignation, but they make a point, for good reason, of staying well enough out of the way.

Decline of the work ethic. In recent years there appears to have been a lessening of the belief that hard work is a good thing in itself. Fewer people, particularly among production and clerical workers, believe that hard work is a way of achieving dignity and self-respect. Many young people decrease their effort when working at jobs they consider undesirable for physical or psycho-

---

[3] Ibid., p. 7.

logical reasons. Many of those people who have not shown a complete disregard for the work ethic are still choosy about the type of work they are willing to perform.

In the extreme, the changing work ethic has been blamed for the rising number of imported manufactured goods in the United States and Canada. If North America's production workers were more productive, goods would cost less. Consequently countries such as Japan—where the work ethic is still strong—would not be at such a competitive advantage in the United States and Canada. In Chapter 8, we will describe a positive strategy the supervisor can use in coping with those people whose work ethic is weak.

Increased number of difficult-to-supervise jobs. "How do you like your new job?" asked the mail clerk's friend. She replied, "Fabulous. I buzz around the building all day pushing my little mail cart. Nobody is looking over my shoulder. I can stop for coffee or a cigarette any time I want. I almost never see my boss." This freedom-loving mail clerk is not alone. An increasing number of jobs in our complex technological society are difficult to supervise because the job holder is not physically confined to one department. Among the many people difficult to supervise because of their mobility are expediters, messengers, coordinators, sales representatives, police officers, social workers, photographers, news reporters, garbage collectors, and service representatives. People assigned to special projects are also difficult to supervise because they work for at least two supervisors, the project head and their regular manager.

As mentioned above, jobs of high technical complexity are also difficult to supervise because the job holder is often more knowledgeable than the superior. New processes and equipment also contribute to difficult-to-supervise jobs. As new tools are introduced new practices develop. Those who are involved with the new system tend to develop their own guidelines and procedures. People who believe they have mastered a new technique or piece of equipment tend to resist supervision, at least about the technical aspects of their job.

Rising expectations. Another significant factor affecting the supervisory job is the rising expectations of employees. People want more and more of their needs satisfied on the job. Workers are making demands upon managers at all levels, as summarized by a Department of Health, Education, and Welfare report:[4]

> What the workers want most, as more than 100 studies in the past 20 years show, is to become masters of their immediate environments and to feel that their work and they themselves are important—the twin ingredients of self-esteem. Workers recognize that some of the dirty jobs can be transformed only into the merely tolerable, but the most oppressive features of work are felt to be avoidable: constant supervision and coercion, lack of variety, monotony, meaningless tasks, and isolation. An increasing number of workers want more autonomy in tackling their tasks, greater opportunity for increasing their skills, rewards that are directly connected to the intrinsic aspects of work, and greater participation in the design of work and formulation of their tasks.

SUPERVISORY RESPONSIBILITIES

A relevant way of understanding the supervisor's job is to examine the multiple responsibilities of a supervisor. Different groups in the organization have different expectations of what they would like the supervisor to accomplish. Figure 1–1 illustrates the five key groups to whom a supervisor is usually responsible.[5] The union is represented by a dotted line because not every supervisor deals with a labor or professional union. This particular formulation of supervisory responsibilities was chosen because of its realism. Another formulation might add such groups as the government, stockholders, customers, and the general community. In virtually all organizations, however, top management (or the public relations or personnel department) interfaces with outside groups.

Supervisor's responsibility to higher management

A major role or responsibility of a supervisor is to the immediate superior who represents higher management. The supervisor is the "person in the middle" or *linking pin* between employees

---

[4] *Work in America,* Department of Health, Education and Welfare, as quoted in Brown, "Supervisory Role," p. 5.

[5] This section of the chapter closely follows Archie B. Carroll and Ted F. Anthony, "An Overview of the Supervisor's Job," *Personnel Journal,* May 1976, pp. 228–31, 249. Reprinted with permission of *Personnel Journal,* copyright May 1976.

FIGURE 1–1
The supervisor's main responsibilities

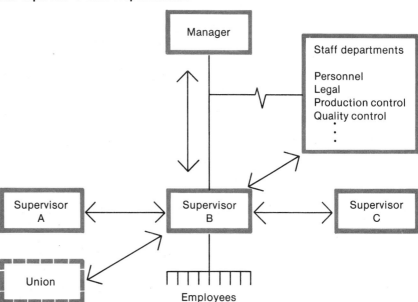

Source: Archie B. Carroll and Ted F. Anthony, "An Overview of the Supervisor's Job." Reprinted with permission of *Personnel Journal*, copyright May 1976.

and higher management. Supervisors receive directives from management, through their immediate managers, and then are assigned the task of implementing that directive. A supervisor might be told that an order from higher management says production costs will be decreased 5 percent. It is the supervisor's job to ensure that costs are cut 5 percent in the specific department. The supervisor might also be told how to implement this directive, say, by pushing for a decrease in the production of parts so defective that they must be scrapped.

The expectations management has of the supervisor in turn become the functions (or activities) to be performed by the supervisor. The functions performed by a supervisor will be discussed in more detail later in this chapter. Among the many responsibilities supervisors have to higher management are to (a) make production decisions (for instance, start jobs, stop jobs, take unsafe tools out of production, ask for more or less work depending on load conditions); (b) keep control of costs; and (c) maintain high morale and productivity.

In order to meet the expectations of higher management, the supervisor must interact with other groups. Each role demand (responsibility) is usually met by coordination with somebody else. If Jim, an office supervisor, is told by his manager to hire five temporary clerks, he will probably call upon the personnel department for assistance. If Sara, a mill supervisor, is told by her manager to decrease accident frequency, she will probably hold a meeting with her department to discuss the problem. Or she might issue a firm order that everybody must wear safety goggles at all times when working in an area requiring them. In either case, Sara must interact with her subordinates to meet her responsibilities to management.

Supervisor's responsibilities to employees

Much of a supervisor's job involves the carrying out responsibilities to employees. Proper discharge of these responsibilities is the primary way in which supervisors meet the demands placed on them by management. Employees place leadership expectations on supervisors. As Archie B. Carroll and Ted F. Anthony summarize the situation:

> They expect him or her to provide them with direction and support. They expect him or her to be their representative to higher management. They expect him or her to look after their needs—social needs and personal needs as well as work-related needs. Perhaps employees should not expect all of this from their leaders—but nevertheless many of them do—and the supervisor must deal with these expectations.[6]

Supervisors have so many different expectations from their subordinates and so many different obligations toward them that it would be difficult to cover all of them. Differences in subordinates, jobs, work organizations, and cultures are among the many different factors that influence which responsibilities supervisors have toward their subordinates. A man in charge of a group of hard-core unemployed trainees would have to provide his subordinates more emotional support than would a woman in charge of a group of experienced dress cutters. A representa-

---

[6] Ibid., p. 231.

tive sample of supervisory responsibility toward subordinates is as follows:

1. Establish a warm and trusting working climate within the department. In other words, be considerate and open with employees.

2. When employee problems occur, handle them promptly. An employee might need a personal day off in order to travel out of town to attend a best friend's wedding. The supervisor should take care of this problem before it causes the employee to be distracted from the job.

3. Be fair in relationships with employees. Although one worker in the department may be more likable than some others, it is important to make work assignments strictly on the basis of job competence or other organizational requirements.

4. Provide all employees with a clear explanation of all matters connected with their job. Sometimes employees need an explanation over seemingly self-apparent work rules. One receptionist went to the rest room while she held a customer on "hold." When reprimanded she said that she thought a person had the freedom to go to the rest room "whenever nature called."

5. Train employees in job-related skills. Despite the presence of professionally staffed training departments, most employees still need on-the-job training.

6. Counsel with employees when legitimate needs for counseling exist. Although supervisors are not expected to function as personal counselors, it is often important to listen to employee problems and then recommend that they seek outside help. To illustrate, after listening to a subordinate's tale of woe about financial problems, a supervisor might suggest that the person visit the employee credit union to obtain help.

7. Discuss contemplated changes before they take place. By doing so, a supervisor is often able to overcome employee resistance to change.

8. Help in the orientation of new workers. Although most employees receive some kind of orientation program from the company (or other type of organization), it is important that the supervisor familiarize the new employee with major personnel policies, work regulations, safety regulations, and so forth.

9. Coordinate and schedule work in ways that minimize

peaks and valleys in the work load. Such action helps avert the troublesome problem of employees being overworked or underworked.

10. Develop a satisfactory level of morale within the group. The term *morale* refers to a positive attitude and feeling about a number of things such as quality of supervision and attitudes toward co-workers and superiors.

11. Support employees when they are being treated arbitrarily from above. Supervisors gain respect to the extent that they can perform this delicate act. Supervisors cannot go against orders from above, but they can see to it that upper management take another look at a situation in which it appears an employee has been treated unfairly.

Supervisor's responsibilities to co-workers

As shown in Figure 1–1, supervisors do have responsibilities toward other supervisors. If supervisors act too independently, teamwork is not possible. Perhaps the supervisor's responsibilities toward co-workers are not as extensive or as important as those responsibilities toward higher management and employees. Yet, coordination with other departments is essential. Carroll and Anthony summarize these responsibilities:[7]

"Coordinate whatever work flow or paperwork that needs to be exchanged among supervisors." It is important to answer memos from other supervisors and to provide your input into reports.

"Communicate with other departments about mutual needs and problems." If you as a supervisor notice a morale problem in your department, it could be worth checking to see if other departments are experiencing a similar problem. It could be a companywide concern.

"Give them support as members of the same management team." Suppose several other supervisors want to make a request to top management that the company hold more open meetings with supervisors. It would be to your advantage to go along with their recommendation.

---

[7] Ibid., p. 231. The examples in this list are provided by the present author.

"Coordinate policy interpretations with other departments to assure consistency and uniformity." For example, you might check with other departments to see that they too are (or are not) docking people for coming to work one hour late on days of a heavy snowstorm.

Supervisor's responsibilities to staff departments

The role of modern supervisors demands that they spend considerable time coordinating efforts with a variety of staff groups. Relationships with staff groups are not unlike relationships with co-workers. However, an important distinction can be drawn. Members of the staff groups are usually specialists who claim expertise in a particular area, whereas supervisors are more likely to be generalists. Thus there is an opportunity for conflict and friction. The staff groups mentioned for illustrative purposes in Figure 1–1 are personnel, legal, production control, and quality control. Coordinated activities also take place with departments such as medical, training, labor relations, and safety. Supervisors who fulfill their obligations should:[8]

"Comply with reasonable requests for information from staff managers." Some requests may seem more reasonable than others. Occupational Safety and Health Act (OSHA) regulations sent through the personnel department at times may seem picayune to supervisors trying to maintain production quotas.

"Utilize whatever standardized reporting forms are necessary in the judgment of staff managers." Although a particular form may seem irrelevant to a supervisor, that particular information may be valuable to a staff specialist. For instance, somebody from personnel research may be conducting a study to determine if biorhythms of the supervisor may be related to employee accident frequency. (The hypothesis could be that a grouchy supervisor fosters accidents.) Although the form may seem whimsical to the supervisor, it could lead to information that will decrease accident frequency.

---

[8] Ibid.

"Listen to the counsel of staff managers pertaining to matters which fall into their expertise." An industrial engineer might recommend a work method that seems to work against common sense, yet if tried out could prove to be a cost saver.

"Consult with staff managers for their expertise on problems." An insightful supervisor knows when to ask for help, yet does not ask staff departments to take over any regular duties. If a cannery supervisor notices that the tomato soup coming out of vats is darker than usual, the food technology department should be consulted immediately.

"Coordinate with staff managers and specialists where task requirements deem it necessary." There should be no cause for embarassment if a production supervisor has trouble explaining to an employee how to operate a numeric control machine. An industrial engineer, or similar person, should be consulted for assistance.

Supervisory responsibilities to the union

When a labor contract exists, the responsibilities of supervisors become more explicit. Carroll and Anthony state that "if a labor contract exists, and it usually will with a union present, then the supervisor has a responsibility to the worker, the union, and management to see that the spirit as well as the letter of the agreement is heeded and fairly applied."[9] Specifically the supervisor should:

"Become knowledgeable about every aspect of the labor agreement." The supervisor should at least be aware that some clause of the contract relates to a particular action such as whether or not the supervisor can suspend an employee for abusive language.

"Attempt to maintain a conciliatory atmosphere in the relationship with the union." A supervisor does not have to have a pro-union attitude, but a cordial working relationship is important.

---

[9] Ibid., pp. 231 and 249. As above, examples in the list are provided by the present author.

"Respect the terms of the agreement even though he or she may personally disagree with it." Similarly, a supervisor may not agree with all the terms of a house mortgage, but after the agreement has been signed, it must be obeyed.

"Effectively administer the grievance machinery of the labor contract." In some companies supervisors spend a substantial portion of their time taking care of grievances. With improper handling, grievances can consume even more time.

Treat employees fairly and show no preference for either union or nonunion members.

"Represent management for that is where his or her first loyalty lies." Although supervisors rarely have all the privileges of higher management, they *are* members of management.

SUPERVISORY FUNCTIONS OR ACTIVITIES

Another relevant way of understanding the supervisory role is to examine the functions or activities actually performed by supervisors. This is the traditional or typical way of analyzing managerial jobs. A frequently used classification of management functions is that of planning, controlling, organizing, and directing or leading. We prefer to use an analysis of supervisory functions based upon an extensive field study of the performance activities of 452 managers, about 40 percent of whom were supervisors.[10] Part of this study asked the managers to allocate their time over eight different management functions. The following list defines these functions and adds a few explanatory statements.[11]

1. *Planning:* "Determining goals, policies, and courses of action. Work scheduling, budgeting, setting up procedures, setting goals or standards, preparing agendas, programming." When a supervisor helps determine what work activities the department will undertake in the next week, that supervisor is planning. The

---

[10] The information presented in this section of the chapter closely follows Thomas A. Mahoney, Thomas H. Jerdee, and Stephen J. Carroll, "The Job(s) of Management," *Industrial Relations,* February 1965, pp. 97–110.

[11] Ibid., p. 100.

higher the level of management, the more planning that person does. Supervisors tend to be engaged in very short-range planning, while top executives plan for the longer range.

2. *Investigating:* "Collecting and preparing information, usually in the form of records, reports, and accounts. Inventorying, measuring output, preparing financial statements, recordkeeping, performing research, job analysis." When a supervisor keeps a running record of a spare parts inventory, this individual is investigating.

3. *Coordinating:* "Exchanging information with people in the organization other than subordinates in order to relate and adjust programs. Advising other departments, expediting, liaison with other managers, arranging meetings, informing superiors, seeking other departments' cooperation." When a supervisor requests a meeting with another department to discuss a work hold-up created by this department, the supervisor is coordinating.

4. *Evaluating:* "Assessment and appraisal of proposals or of reported or observed performance. Employee appraisals, judging output records, judging financial reports, product inspection, approving requests, judging proposals and suggestions." An example of evaluating is when a supervisor says to a subordinate, "This report you just turned in won't do. It needs more information." Evaluating can be considered part of controlling—measuring performance and taking corrective action if performance falls below standard.

5. *Directing* (sometimes called supervising or leading): "Directing, leading, and developing subordinates. Counseling subordinates, training subordinates, explaining work rules, assigning work, disciplining, handling complaints of subordinates." When a supervisor encourages a subordinate, this could be considered a form of leading. Much of this text deals with the supervisory function of directing in its broadest definition. The specific chapter about leadership deals with leadership as a process of personally influencing subordinates.

6. *Staffing:* "Maintaining the work force of a unit or several units. College recruiting, employment interviewing, selecting employees, placing employees, promoting employees, transferring employees." At one time supervisors did most of the staffing for their departments. Personnel departments now assist supervisors with many of these functions.

7. *Negotiating:* "Purchasing, selling, or contracting for goods or services. Tax negotiations, contracting suppliers, dealing with sales representatives, advertising products, collective bargaining, selling to dealers or customers." Should a supervisor be assigned the responsibility of approving the sale of a new piece of equipment for the department, the supervisor would be negotiating.

8. *Representing:* "Advancing general organizational interests through speeches, consultation, and contracts with individuals or groups outside the organization. Public speeches, community drives, news releases, attending conventions, business club meetings." Supervisors spend a small amount of time representing. Supervisors who talk about their companies while attending a Rotary Club meeting are representing.

An experienced supervisor reading the above list of functions will readily detect that a vital supervisory function is missing. Although most organizations do not mention it in their annual reports, supervisors (and other managers) spend an undetermined amount of time fighting fires—dealing with unplanned for situations. One supervisor described the fire-fighting function in this way: "Jack, the superintendent comes rushing into my department and tells me to drop everything in order to ship 100 units for another customer. I told Jack that our plan called for working on that order the following month. He told me to scrap the plan; that if we didn't take care of our biggest customer there would be no need for making any more plans. Every week I take care of another emergency."

Some fire fighting is preventable. If supervisors and higher level managers do a careful job of planning and controlling, it is possible to prevent some fires from having to be fought. In one printing shop, a supervisor might be forced to make frantic telephone calls to suppliers in order to purchase paper needed for a special customer requirement. In another printing shop, better planning and controlling might prevent such a fire-fighting episode.

First, the latter shop maintains an up-to-date list of suppliers to contact for special printing requirements. Second, they exercise careful inventory controls. When the stock runs low on a particular item, they reorder immediately. A supervisor in this print shop would not have to fight fires in relation to running short on paper to meet special customer requirements.

Work patterns and management level. How much of each function a manager performs is heavily influenced by the job level. As mentioned above, upper management does more planning than does first-level management. Supervisors also spend much more time in direct contact with subordinates than do members of upper management. Thus in Table 1–1 we see that

TABLE 1–1.
Percentage of workday spent on various performance functions by two levels of management

	Level of management	
Performance	Supervisors (N = 173)	Upper management (N = 145)
Planning	13	28
Investigating	8	12
Coordinating	11	20
Evaluating	10	12
Directing	54	18
Staffing	—	—
Negotiating	3	8
Representing	1	2
Fire fighting	?	?
	100	100

Source: Based on data presented in Thomas A. Mahoney, Thomas H. Jerdee, and Stephen J. Carroll, "The Jobs of Management," *Industrial Relations,* February 1965, p. 105.

supervisors (in that particular study) spend about 50 percent of their time leading, while members of top management spend about 18 percent of their time in such activity. According to this one study, upper management spends more time in coordination than do supervisors. Members of upper management, for example, spend much of their day in group meetings with other department heads.

CHARACTERISTICS OF EFFECTIVE SUPERVISORS

Probably 10,000 studies have been conducted about the underlying characteristics that contribute to effectiveness as a leader or manager. One conclusion frequently reached by researchers is that the answer "depends upon the situation." A supervisor in a logging camp may need a different set of personal characteristics than a supervisor in a beauty parlor. The situation includes such factors as the people to be supervised, the job to be performed, the company, and the cultural background of the people. Despite these vast differences in situations, some generalizations can be drawn about the characteristics that help a supervisor function effectively in a variety of situations.

What is effectiveness? Effectiveness, from the standpoint of this text, means that a supervisor accomplishes results that are desired by the organization. Simultaneously the supervisor accomplishes these results without sacrificing job satisfaction or morale. An effective supervisor has a concern for both production and people—a statement you will read and hear many times in the formal study of supervision and leadership. Seven characteristics are particularly significant in helping supervisors do their jobs effectively. Another way of stating the same idea is to say in order to carry out the nine performance functions described above, seven broad characteristics are very helpful.

Sound human relations skills. A materials manager at an electrical company stated bluntly, "Being able to work with people is the most important characteristic a first-line supervisor can have. I can buy technological expertise, but it's hard to find someone with good basic communications skills."[12]

Perhaps this statement is oversimplified (and even offensive to a good technician), but it does point to the importance of the ability to work well with people as a supervisory characteristic. Working well with people does not necessarily mean that a supervisor is overly lenient with them. It means that the supervisor relates to people in such a manner to capture their trust and cooperation. It would be difficult to argue that any managerial job did not require sound human relations skills. Virtually every supervisory training program includes a session or two on improving relationships with people.

Technical competence. The closer a manager is to working with the technical aspects of an organization, the more techni-

---

[12] Thomas DeLong, "What Do Middle Managers Really Want from First-Line Supervisors?" *Supervisory Management,* September 1977, pp. 9–12.

cally competent the person must be. Supervisors who are not technically competent—those who do not understand the actual work performed by a department—run the risk of not establishing rapport with their subordinates. Technical competence is a very important supervisory characteristic when relating to talented or technically sophisticated subordinates. The supervisor of a medical team is usually a highly competent physician. Similarly, the supervisor of a group of tool and die makers needs technical competence to be credible.

Strong work motivation and high energy. Most supervisory jobs are demanding both physically and mentally. A successful incumbent must be willing to work hard and long in order to achieve success. Many supervisors are initially selected for their positions because of the enthusiasm they display for achieving good work results. Another fundamental reason strong work motivation is required for effectiveness is that a person has to be willing to accept the heavy responsibility that being a supervisor entails. Even if a person does not aspire to rise to the top of the organization, the individual must be strongly oriented toward work to be effective as a first-level manager.

Good problem-solving ability. Supervisors and higher level managers do not have to brilliant, but evidence suggests that they should stand up well in problem-solving ability in comparison to group members. A supervisor who prefers abstract problem solving to dealing with tangible problems may develop work interests other than those important to the group. For instance, a supervisor who is highly competent in solving complex problems may prefer such activities to dealing with the more routine aspects of the job.

Good work habits. A disorganized, unplanning, impulsive supervisor is an ineffective supervisor. With the increasing paperwork requirements of the job, a supervisor has to be all the more organized and attentive to details. Some management experts believe that good work habits are more important than the right personality characteristics in making for an effective manager. Good work habits become increasingly important as a manager gains in administrative responsibility.

Ability to size up people and situations. Insight into people and situations involving people is an essential supervisory characteristic. A supervisor with good insights is able to make better work assignments and do a better job of training and developing subordinates. The insightful supervisor intuitively makes a careful assessment of the strengths and weaknesses of subordinates. An example of insensitivity (or poor insight) into situations and people would be to hold a departmental meeting late in the afternoon before a major religious or national holiday. Why try to capture people's attention when they are thinking about something else? A meeting about an emergency, however, would be an exception to this example of insensitivity.

Self-confidence. An effective leader is usually a self-confident individual. Research has shown this to be true in a wide variety of leadership situations from high school athletics to the shop floor. A self-confident supervisor helps subordinates overcome their feelings of concern about being able to accomplish the tough requirements of a job. A self-confident supervisor also conveys the impression to subordinates of knowing how to handle the task of supervising the group. A distinction should be drawn between self-confidence and arrogance. A person too high in self-confidence may give subordinates the impression of being brash and unfeeling or, worse, covering up for feelings of insecurity.

A FRAMEWORK FOR ACCOMPLISHING RESULTS

A supervisor is paid to accomplish results for the employer. Whether the results involve accomplishments with things or with people, the supervisor should use a systematic approach. A basic framework for accomplishing results is presented here and serves as a unifying theme for this book. No matter what function the supervisor is performing, nor what responsibility is being carried out, a logical and systematic approach is called for. Plan-conscious and orderly supervisors have a higher probability of accomplishing results than their counterparts who rely heavily on intuition and impulse and neglect the basics of problem solving.

Identify problem. As shown in Figure 1–2, accomplishing results begins with recognizing that a problem exists (or that certain

FIGURE 1–2
A Framework for accomplishing results

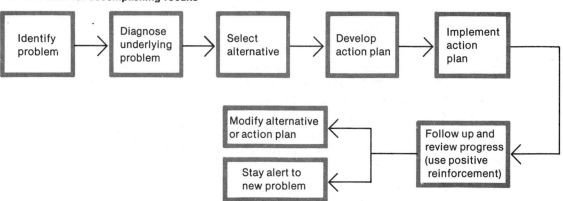

results need to be accomplished). Nick, a custodial supervisor at a large manufacturing plant, begins to receive a number of complaints from department heads that his custodial staff is performing poorly. Nick has been informed that basic janitorial work such as floor mopping and emptying wastebaskets has been performed improperly, or sometimes not performed at all.

Diagnose the underlying problem. Nick speaks to his custodial workers about the complaints. Several of the workers mention that they try to do a good job, but it is easy to forget small items such as emptying a wastebasket or not wiping up a floor stain because the job is so boring. Nick tentatively accepts this analysis as reflecting the true nature of the problem. (Nick also recognizes that it might be possible to select personnel for whom custodial work is not boring.)

Specify and weigh alternatives. Nick jots down a number of potential solutions to the problem of worker boredom leading to poor results. To arrive at an optimum solution to the problem, Nick confers with his boss and a member of the personnel department. The proposed alternative solutions are:

1. Fire the custodial workers who are the worst offenders and try to replace them with more competent custodial help.
2. Tell the complaining department heads that their housekeeping standards are unrealistically high.
3. Conduct a training program for custodial workers.

4. Appoint an assistant custodial supervisor who will follow the custodial workers around on their nightly chores.
5. Award prizes for employees in his department who produce "complaint-free" work.
6. Improve the quality of the custodial worker's job so that it proves to be less boring.

Nick examines some of the positive and negative aspects to each alternative. Among Nick's most important considerations are money and the need for obtaining approvals from other departments. For instance, if Nick fires a few workers and asks for replacements, he will be involved in long negotiating sessions with personnel and upper management. Nick also wants to choose an alternative that does not create more problems than it solves. Challenging that housekeeping standards of other department heads are unrealistic would fall into this category.

Select an alternative.   Nick, in agreement with his boss, decides that alternative number six is worth a try. He hopes to make the custodial job more appealing by two specific methods. First, Nick will rotate assignments between factory and office cleaning. Second, each custodial worker will be given a sign-off sheet that will be used to identify who was responsible for cleaning a certain area. After cleaning each department, the custodial worker will leave a note stating, "This office was cleaned by *name of custodial worker.*" Nick assumes that his subordinates would take more pride in their work if they were identified as the person responsible for cleaning.

Develop action plan.   An action plan describes in detail what steps must be taken to implement the alternative. Nick held a meeting with his workers and also spoke to each one individually about the new plan. A new rotation work schedule was established, and all workers in the department were given an explanation of how to use the sign-off sheet.

Conduct follow-up and review sessions.   Nick checked with each of his workers every two weeks to see how the new plan was operating. He asked the custodial people about their reactions to the new procedure and whether or not it was helping their efficiency. Of more importance, Nick and his secretary kept a careful diary of the number of complaints about office or factory housekeeping.

During the follow-up and review sessions, the supervisor rewards behavior that is moving in the desired direction. When Nick learns that complaints about housekeeping have decreased, he informs his employees about this accomplishment. In addition to providing *feedback,* Nick gives them *positive reinforcement* (PR). He encourages the constructive behavior they have exhibited by praising them, giving them recognition, or perhaps promising them that a salary increase might be forthcoming. Providing positive reinforcement for constructive behavior is one of the most powerful actions a supervisor can take to improve the functioning of a department. Frequent mention will therefore be made of PR in the forthcoming chapters.

Stay alert for new problems. Nick's plan worked as well or better than expected. Complaints about poor housekeeping dwindled down to a negligible amount. Nevertheless, Nick did not close his mind to the possibility of problems reoccurring in the future.

Modify alternative or action plan. Intended solutions to problems do not always work. Had Nick's plan not improved the quality of custodial care he would have to select another alternative or modify his action plan for the alternative he chose. Perhaps rotating assignments could be eliminated and the "pride slips" be retained. Or the jobs might have been enriched by giving workers total responsibility for one area. Instead of one person mopping and another dusting and waxing, each worker could perform all the operations necessary to clean an office or portion of the factory. As things worked out, Nick did not have to modify the alternative or the action plan.

HOW THIS BOOK WILL HELP YOU

If you—as a present or potential supervisor—carefully study the information in this book and incorporate many of its suggestions into your mode of doing things, you should attain five objectives (and more importantly derive five benefits). People vary so widely in learning ability, personality, and life circumstances that some people will attain some of these objectives and not others. For example, you might be so shy with people at this stage in your career that you would be unwilling to confront employees with their game playing—one suggestion made in this book. Or you might not be interested in working in a manufacturing environment. Therefore the information in this book about accident prevention might not be of interest to you. Possibly you are locked into a family business and therefore have limited interest in the career-planning techniques discussed toward the end of the book.

Improved supervisory skills

Ideally, reading this book carefully will give you information and insights that will make you a more effective supervisor. If you study and apply the ideas presented in this text, you should be able to improve your skills in such vital areas as encouraging production from employees and communicating more effectively with people. Among the many other skills discussed are techniques for coping with delicate employee problems, such as drug and alcohol dependence.

Better understanding of job-related human behavior and organizations. A major objective of this text is to help you achieve a deeper understanding of people at work and how organizations operate. Every reader of this book has some understanding of how people and organizations behave, but an improved understanding can lead to an improved ability to deal even more effectively with situations. Among the topics explored are why many employees find comfort in belonging to a labor union and why bureaucracies exist.

Awareness of relevant information. Being familiar with relevant general knowledge about the world of work is part of being acclimated to and creating a positive impression in any place of work. By reading this book you will become conversant with many of the buzz words of modern organizations, such as leadership style, positive reinforcement, action plan, and participative management.

Managing of job problems. Every supervisor inevitably runs into human problems on the job. Reading about these problems and prescriptions for coping with them could save you considerable inner turmoil. Among the many vital managerial skills you might acquire by studying this text are handling conflict between employees, simple methods of cost control, and methods of preventing accidents. Reading this book, alone, will not help you manage job problems. You must practice the new ideas in a job setting.

Personal development. A person who is able to apply the information contained in this book should become a more effective supervisor and a bigger contributor to the organization. Equally important, the diligent reader should be able to achieve substantial gains in personal development. Among the key topics in personal development presented in this text are career management, better management of time, and improved job creativity.

SUMMARY OF KEY POINTS

- ☐ A supervisor is a first-level manager responsible for directing the job activities of one or more subordinates so that work objectives are accomplished.
- ☐ People who perform supervisory work have a variety of job titles and conduct work activities that vary in complexity and job content.
- ☐ Today's supervisory jobs are more challenging than ever because (1) jobs are more complex, (2) the work ethic has shown a decline among many employees, (3) many jobs are difficult to supervise, (4) workers have rising job expectations.
- ☐ A supervisor's primary responsibilities are to higher management, employees, co-workers, staff departments, and, lastly, the union.
- ☐ The basic supervisory functions are planning, investigating, evaluating, directing, staffing, negotiating, representing, and fire fighting (dealing with unplanned for events).
- ☐ It is a subject of debate whether or not effective supervisors in different situations have similar characteristics. Yet, certain traits and behaviors are important for supervisory effectiveness. These are sound human relations skills, technical competence, strong motivation and high energy, good problem-solving ability, good work habits, ability to size up people and situations, and self-confidence.
- ☐ The general framework for accomplishing results through people is composed of seven stages: identify the problem; diagnose the underlying problem; specify and weigh alternatives;

select an alternative; develop an action plan; conduct follow-up and review sessions; stay alert for new problems. If the first solution selected to the problem does not work, it will be necessary to modify the alternative or action plan chosen.

☐ If this text is studied carefully and the ideas applied in practice, you will probably increase your knowledge and skills as a supervisor.

GUIDELINES FOR SUPERVISORY PRACTICE

1. Recognize that some frustrations are inevitable in the life of a supervisor. The job is demanding and challenging. The work is complex; some employees have unrealistic expectations; others are under-motivated.

2. To function effectively as a supervisor, realize that you have to satisfy the demands of higher management, employees, co-workers, staff departments, and sometimes labor unions.

3. Your effectiveness as a supervisor will increase if you build strength in the areas of human relations skills, technical competence, motivation and energy, problem-solving ability, work habits, insight into people and situations, and self-confidence.

4. When faced with a problem involving people, use a systematic approach for its resolution. We recommend the Framework for Accomplishing Results as one such approach.

QUESTIONS FOR DISCUSSION AND REVIEW

1. In what way has this chapter influenced your attitude toward being (or becoming) a supervisor?

2. If supervisors have such a tough job, why are they paid a smaller salary than members of higher management or professional workers?

3. How much status and prestige does the job of a first-level supervisor carry? Explain your answer.

4. Define the term *supervisor*. Explain the difference between a supervisor and an executive.

5. Give several synonyms for the job title "supervisor."

6. Do all supervisors manage production or clerical workers? Explain.

7. What is the new supervisory challenge?

8. Do you think many production workers these days want to become supervisors? Explain.

9. What is the decline of the work ethic?

10. What are a supervisor's main responsibilities?

11. Which of a supervisor's responsibilities would you think create the biggest headache?

12. In what way is a supervisor a "linking pin"?

13. In what way is a supervisor responsible to staff departments?
14. Define, in your own words, the basic supervisory functions or activities.
15. Why do supervisors spend so much time directing or leading subordinates?
16. Name and define five different characteristics or traits that tend to be associated with effectiveness as a supervisor?
17. What characteristics of an effective supervisor do you currently possess? Which ones are you lacking?
18. Summarize the Framework for Accomplishing Results described in this chapter. Do you think the framework will work? Why or why not?

A supervisory problem: The clear-cut job

Chad, a 24-year-old male, is a community college graduate with several years of varied work experience. To earn his way in life he has held such jobs as busboy, construction worker, messenger, car washer, lawn care expert, and bartender. Chad believes he is now ready for full-time employment leading to a future in management. He applies for a job as a supervisor in a fruit and vegetable cannery. Chad, much to his delight, is hired at a satisfactory starting salary.

The first day on the job Chad says to his boss: "Mike, I would like a written job description. According to my studies, a supervisor spends a lot of time performing different functions and also is responsible to many different groups. What are the expectations of my job?"

"Cut out the fancy talk," replies Mike. "Your job is clear-cut. Get those damn cans filled with peas and corn and ship them down the line to the packing department. Shape up any employee who gives you trouble. See me next week if you have any problems. I'll be out of town for a few days."

1. *What should Chad do about this situation?*
2. *Do you think Chad should be concerned that he took the wrong job?*
3. *What challenges lie ahead for Chad?*

SOME SUGGESTED READING

Barker, Kenneth, J.; Coggins, Patrick E.; Krygier, Roman J., Jr.; and Smith, Dwaine, H. "Attitudes of Foremen in the Petroleum and Automotive Industries." *Sloan Management Review,* Fall 1974, pp. 57–68.

Benson, Carl A. "New Supervisors: From the Top of the Heap to the Bottom of the Heap." *Personnel Journal,* April 1976, pp. 176–78.

Bittel, Lester R. *What Every Supervisor Should Know.* 3d ed. New York: McGraw-Hill, 1974.

Brown, David S. "Rethinking the Supervisor Role." *Supervisory Management,* November 1977, pp. 2–10.

Carroll, Archie B., and Anthony, Ted F. "An Overview of the Supervisor's Job." *Personnel Journal,* May 1976, pp. 228–31, 249.

DeLong, Thomas. "What Do Middle Managers Really Want from First-Line Supervisors?" *Supervisory Management,* September 1977, pp. 8–12.

DuBrin, Andrew J. *Human Relations: A Job-Oriented Approach.* Reston, Va.: Reston, 1978.

Gellerman, Saul W. "Supervision: Substance and Style." *Harvard Business Review,* March–April 1976, pp. 89–98.

Kay, Brian R. "Prescription and Perception of the Supervisory Role: A Rolecentric Interpretation." *Occupational Psychology,* July 1963, pp 219–27.

Mintzberg, Henry. "The Manager's Job: Folklore and Fact." *Harvard Business Review,* July–August 1975, pp. 49–61.

Van Dersal, William R. *The Successful Supervisor in Government and Business.* 3d ed. New York: Harper & Row, 1974.

Wikstrom, Walter S. *Management at the Foreman's Level.* New York: National Industrial Conference Board, 1967.

part two

Understanding the human environment

People one at a time

2

LEARNING OBJECTIVES

After reading and thinking through the material in this chapter, you should be able to:

1. Explain how a supervisor's job is affected by individual differences among people.
2. Describe in general form the Framework for Understanding Individual Behavior.
3. Describe how perception influences job behavior.
4. Explain why our perceptions are often inaccurate.
5. Explain the difference between classical and operant conditioning.
6. Discuss how people learn a complicated set of skills.
7. Give a specific example of how needs and motives influence job behavior.
8. Illustrate several ways in which values and beliefs influence job behavior.
9. Discuss how job stress might have both beneficial and detrimental consequences in a job setting.

"To tell you the truth," said one supervisor to another over an after-work beer, "if it weren't for people, my job would be a breeze. It's hard to find any two people alike. One guy working for me will be a pleasure. He'll get everything done on time with no mistakes and I won't have to prod him along. Another guy working for me will be so much of a bother that the department would be better off without him. Some people are fun to work with. Other people are about as much fun as a case of athlete's foot. I wish I knew the answer."

The veteran supervisor who made these comments has cogently pointed to one of the major challenges and rewards of a supervisor's job—individual differences among people. Even

33

when jobs are highly automated, individual differences in the makeup of people account for variations in performance. One worker who has memory lapses because a highly automated job is boring can create a production slowdown or a safety hazard for the entire department, whereas another worker may find the highly automated job to be a comfortable routine, thus allowing the production system to work at maximum efficiency.

In this chapter we will explore some of the major factors influencing individual behavior on the job. Among these factors are perception, learning, motives and needs, values, and reactions to frustration and stress. A supervisor who has an awareness of these major facets of human behavior should be able to do a better job of managing individual differences than a supervisor lacking such knowledge. One chapter about the basics of individual behavior does not present an adequate substitute for a more complete study of human psychology. Our thrust, however, is to show how basic facts about human behavior are related to job behavior.

A FRAMEWORK FOR UNDERSTANDING INDIVIDUAL BEHAVIOR

To deal effectively with individuals in a work environment you need a framework for understanding human beings. Even if the framework you choose is not the most sophisticated available, it is better than no framework at all. A framework provides you with a starting point for arriving at conclusions about people, but it should not be an intellectual straitjacket that prevents you from making spontaneous observations.

To use a marketing analogy, a good general strategy is to price your product below that of the competition. Since most purchasers are price conscious, if you offer the same or better product at a lower price, you will get the business. This is generally sound strategy but there are exceptions. Wine, perfume, cold medicines, and vitamins offered at higher prices than competitive products of comparable value sometimes sell better. People somehow expect "good" perfume, cold medicines, and vitamins to be high priced. These people believe that a high price indicates high quality. If you blindly employed the strategy of pricing your products low, you would be at a disadvantage in this situation. In general, the low-price strategy would work effectively.

The Framework for Understanding Individual Behavior has been developed over time by specialists in human behavior.[1] Shown in Figure 2–1, the framework can be brought to life by

FIGURE 2–1
A framework for understanding individual behavior

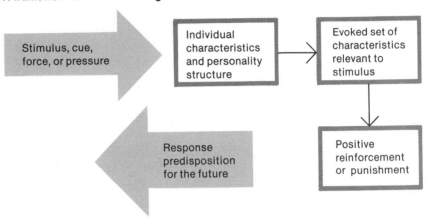

applying it to a case history of a supervisor who tackled a challenging assignment. Later in the chapter we will give separate attention to key elements in the framework and other basic considerations about people one at a time.

Stimulus, cue, force, or pressure. Gabe, a production supervisor in a multiproduct manufacturing company, received a phone call from John Wadsworth, the vice president of product planning.

Wadsworth: Hello Gabe, this is John Wadsworth from product planning. I have some important information for you. I've already cleared our conversation with your boss. We want you to serve on the new product planning committee. It's a new development in the company. We want a diagonal slice of the organization to help in the planning of new products. We figure a person like yourself could provide some valuable input into the manufacturing feasibility of some of our new product ideas. If you serve on the

---

[1] This framework stems most directly from two sources: Henry L. Tosi and Stephen J. Carroll, *Management: Contingencies, Structure, and Process* (Chicago: St. Clair Press, 1976), pp. 58–60, Andrew J. DuBrin, *Human Relations: A Job-Oriented Approach* (Reston, Va.: Reston, 1978), pp. 5–8. The Tosi and Carroll model is based on James G. March and Herbert A. Simon, *Organizations* (New York: Wiley, 1958).

committee you'll be in contact with people from every major function in the company. You'll have a good chance to display your talents in places where it counts. Could we have your answer by the middle of next week?

Gabe: My gosh, it's an honor to be asked to serve on a companywide task force. I've never tackled any assignment outside my department before. And we're right in the middle of the start-up of a new product. I wonder if my department could spare my being away for so much time each week. Would it be possible to meet with you and discuss the details of this assignment?

Wadsworth: Okay, let's meet in my office tomorrow morning at ten.

Gave has thus received a stimulus, cue, force, or pressure from the environment in the form of a phone call from a company executive.

Individual characteristics and personality structure. What Gabe will do next in this situation depends heavily upon certain things about him as a person. Each stimulus or environmental force, brings forth (or awakens) different aspects of our personal makeup. A stimulus, or force, evokes only those elements that the individual associates with the stimulus, or force in question.

For instance, Gabe's *self-concept* includes many different elements. He prides himself in being a good bowler and a good father, but these aspects of his self-concept will not come into play in his decision whether or not to tackle the assignment. Also, these aspects of his self-concept will not influence to any measurable extent how well Gabe would perform if he should undertake the assignment.

Gabe's *past experiences* will contribute selectively to Gabe's acceptance or rejection of this assignment and to how he performs. Many aspects of his past experience will be called to mind by the stimulus of the new product committee assignment, in addition to his history of relating to an authority figure like Wadsworth. If Wadsworth reminds him of an unfriendly high school teacher or a stern and uncompromising early boss in his life, Gabe may be reluctant to serve on a committee with him. Gabe, or anybody else, may not be consciously aware of the profound influence of past experience on present decisions. Thus they serve as an automatic, semiconscious influence.

Evoked set of characteristics relevant to stimulus. As Gabe discusses the assignment with the vice president of product planning, many elements of his personal makeup come into play. For example, his *level of drive* toward accomplishing worthwhile tasks is higher than average. Gabe wants to succeed in his career. His level of drive impels him toward a decision such as "Yes, Wadsworth, I'll tackle this assignment and do my best." Gabe's past experience with creative work will also exert a relevant influence. Twice during his days as a nonexempt employee he won small suggestion awards in his company. He thus has some past experience in creative thinking. (Gabe rightfully believes that a person assigned to a new product planning committee should be capable of creative thinking.)

Before Gabe could proceed to take on the assignment, other aspects of his functioning were evoked. He considered himself to be a supervisor of above-average intelligence or problem-solving ability. Gabe also felt that his skills in dealing with people were solid enough to work smoothly with a wide range of people, many of whom might have more formal education than himself.

Many of Gabe's *needs* and *motives* were also evoked by Wadsworth's invitation to join the select committee. A need is a deficit within an individual, such as a craving for water or recognition. A motive is a need or desire coupled with the intention to attain an appropriate goal. Gabe has long felt that he wanted more recognition than he is currently achieving in his job as production supervisor. As he recently told his wife, "I want to be somebody special in the company."

Response.   As already hinted, Gabe did say yes to the offer. During his meeting with Wadsworth, he agreed to serve on the committee providing he could find a suitable way to cover for his absence from the department. Gabe then conferred with his own manager. Between the two of them, he figured out a simple plan to keep the department running smoothly during the time in which Gabe would be away on his committee assignment. Shelia, a standout performer in Gabe's department, would serve as acting supervisor (in addition to her regular duties) during Gabe's absences.

Also included in the response category is Gabe's performance on the committee. He offered several concrete suggestions about what he thought would be the manufacturing feasibility of several proposed products. For one product, a computerized cash register, Gabe noted that much of the work would have to be subcontracted because the present work force had no experience with miniaturized parts. For another proposed product, novelty telephones, Gabe noted that it would be easy to retrain part of the work force to perform such work. He reasoned that many company employees already had experience in medium-size electronic subassemblies.

Positive reinforcement or punishment. In this situation Gabe received almost all positive reinforcement. Performing the task well was a reward in itself; it helped to strengthen Gabe's self-confidence. A special reward Gabe received was his delight in knowing that he could make a positive contribution to a team effort involving a high-level company concern—the development of new products. Perhaps the major reward forthcoming to Gabe was the recognition he received as a member of the new product planning committee. Friends would make comments to Gabe such as "How's the atmosphere up there in the executive suite?" or "Do you have time for a cup of coffee with us ordinary guys?" If Gabe had failed miserably in the assignment, he would have perceived it as punishment.

Response predisposition for the future. As a consequence of the substantial positive reinforcement received by Gabe, he is now predisposed to take on new responsibilities offered him by the company. Realizing now that he can work effectively with executives and highly trained specialists, Gabe has reevaluated his career goals. He has spoken to the personnel department about enrolling in company-sponsored management development programs. Gabe is now inclined favorably to tackle any assignment that will enhance his credentials for becoming a superintendent (the next level of management in his company's manufacturing organization).

If Gabe had not experienced positive reinforcement during his committee assignment, he would not have been so eager to take on new responsibilities in the future. Nonreinforcement would have occurred if the other committee members were noncommittal about Gabe's contribution to the committee. The probability of Gabe wanting to take on another committee assignment would have been small had Gabe been *punished* while serving on the new product committee. Punishment might have taken the form of Wadsworth asking that Gabe be removed from the committee because of lack of contribution. If Gabe had been transferred away from his department to a less-desirable job while serving on the committee, this too would have been perceived as punishment.

HOW PERCEPTION INFLUENCES JOB BEHAVIOR

Perception deals with the various ways in which people interpret things in the external world and how they act on the basis of these interpretations. The process of perception can be technically defined as the "organization of sensory information into meaningful experiences."[2] Those aspects of perception most directly relevant to the supervisor deal with how people interpret various cues and stimuli in the job environment and how they act as a consequence of these interpretations. Perception also deals with a study of the mechanisms that underlie perception such as the structure of the eyes, ears, nose, and skin.

A supervisor is most likely to encounter perceptual problems when the stimulus or cue to be perceived has an emotional meaning to employees, co-workers or superiors. Assume that Brian, an office supervisor, announces to the members of his department, "Look folks, the new typewriter we ordered has arrived. We are using it to replace the oldest typewriter in the office. It has a five-year guarantee." Most people in the office will interpret this message at face value and Brian will not experience a communications problem. (Communication and perception form a system. Our perception influences the messages we receive and the messages we send.) Most people will mutter to themselves, something to the effect, "Yes, that's a new typewriter for the office. We probably needed a new one."

Brian might have experienced problems in human perception if he had communicated this message to his employees: "Folks, I would like you to meet Brenda. She's an office temporary who is here to help us out this week." Announcing the presence of an office temporary would trigger several different perceptions, de-

---

[2] Definition found in glossary of *Understanding Psychology* (DelMar, Calif.: CRM Books, 1974), p. 426.

pending upon many motives, needs, and knowledge of department employees. Among the possible interpretations are these:

> An office temporary? I wonder if this means the company is going to cut down the regular work force and use temporaries to help us through peak loads.

> This seems to be a sure sign that business has picked up. The front office would never authorize extra help unless business were booming. Things look good for getting a decent raise this year.

> I wonder if Brian has brought in a temporary worker to show us we had better get hustling or we could be replaced? I've heard a lot of these so-called temporaries usually wind up with a full-time job if they like the temporary assignment.

Characteristics about the person influencing perception

As suggested by Brian's experiences, factors within people influence their perception of the external environment. Seven factors influence perception in general and also in a job situation. One or more of these factors may influence perception at a given time and some of these factors are generally more influential than others.[3]

Physiological and anatomical condition. Basic body physiology and anatomy exert some influence on job perception and behavior. A supervisor will have to speak loudly when giving directions to a hearing-impaired employee, and not use color-coded signals when dealing with a color-blind employee. A frail person might perceive lifting a 45-pound box to be an arduous task, while a physically strong person would perceive the task as a pleasant exercise.

Family influences. A profound influence on the perception and behavior of most people is their family background, both present and past. A person reared in a family where parents have strong authority is likely to perceive a directive from a boss as a normal way of life. A person raised in a family where authority and power are shared with parents and children may have a more

---

[3] The first three items in list are based on Edgar F. Huse and James L. Bowditch, *Behavior in Organizations: A Systems Approach to Managing* (Reading, Mass.: Addison-Wesley, 1973), p. 89.

difficult time perceiving orders as legitimate. That particular employee may have a stronger need for freedom from supervision.

Cultural influences. A person's cultural background is another major influence on that individual's perception of stimuli in the job environment. For instance, a young woman whose cultural values influence her to perceive work as a necessary evil or as punishment might have a negative attitude toward an extra assignment. Another young woman whose cultural values influence her to perceive work as a privilege and a prime reason for living will take a different view of the stimulus of additional work. In contrast she may express enthusiasm for the project while her less work-oriented counterpart may show passive resistance (drag her heels).

Motives, needs, and goals. A major determinant of people's perception is their motivation at the time with respect to the object or experience to be perceived (the stimulus or cue). A man who believes his family is deprived because they lack a color television will take an active interest in a suggestion system that offers cash awards. He may fantasize translating his suggestion idea into a cash award that is big enough to purchase a color television set. Another man who is not currently interested in acquiring new possessions or who has a low need for recognition may barely notice the suggestion system box. Employees who are harboring guilt about having stolen office supplies may perceive a routine audit of department supplies as an investigation directed at them. Much more will be said about the influence of needs, motives, and goals on behavior later in this chapter and again in Chapter 8.

Past experiences. How a man or woman perceives a stimulus today is heavily influenced by what happened when that stimulus was presented in the past. This basic perceptual fact is illustrated by the threadbare joke about the man who will never again volunteer for an assignment because of one experience. While in the army he volunteered for an assignment only to wind up cleaning latrines. An older woman may perceive a young worker assigned to the department as a threat because in the past she was shown up by an energetic young worker. An employee who demands clarification on the smallest work rules, such as the limits to lunch hour, may be reacting to a past event:

His last employer fired him for chronically returning late from lunch.

Personality characteristics. How a person perceives an event is also influenced by that individual's stable traits and characteristics, or personality. An optimistic, adventuresome individual might perceive a new boss as a welcome challenge—as another influential person to impress with a display of job competence. A pessimistic, cautious individual might perceive the same new boss as a threat—as another influential person who might think critically of every day job performance. Similarly, an impulsive production inspector might perceive one defect in a sample as an indication that the department has a major quality problem. A more reflective, or less impulsive, production inspector might perceive the same defect as simply an indication that more sampling is necessary: Something may or may not be wrong with the quality of goods produced in the department.

Devices people use to deal with sensory information

Under ideal circumstances the employee perceives information as it is intended to be communicated or as it exists in reality. A junior accountant examining a set of figures will hopefully arrive at a conclusion that will satisfy both her boss and generally accepted accounting principles. Hopefully, the night maintenance worker who sees water on the floor will perceive it as a probable leak, not as simply the product of a careless person spilling a bucket of water. Hopefully, a union steward offered a promotion to a supervisory position will perceive it as an act of good faith on the part of management, not as a plot to get him out of the union. In reality, people use a number of devices to help them simplify their perception of external events.[4]

Denial. If the sensory information is particularly painful to us, we often deny to ourselves and others that the information ever existed. A secretary was confronted with the fact that use of the office copying machine to make copies of personal Christmas card lists was against company regulations. Even though the

---

[4] Our list, but not our examples, is based on W. Clay Hamner and Dennis W. Organ, *Organizational Behavior: An Applied Psychological Approach* (Dallas: Business Publications, 1978), pp. 99–100. © 1978 by Business Publications, Inc.

secretary had typed the company policy manual just six months previous to the confrontation, the response was, "I never saw that regulation." Similarly, many people use denial when reading the message from the surgeon general printed on each pack of American-made cigarettes.

Stereotyping. A common method of simplifying the perceptual process is to evaluate an individual or thing on the basis of our perception of the group or class to which that person or object belongs. One production employee said he preferred not to accept a transfer to the quality control department, giving as his reason, "I don't want to work for a nitpicker." One supervisor told the purchasing department that they were making a mistake by purchasing components made in Korea. She gave as her reason, "All Korean-made products are junk merchandise." More will be said about stereotyping in Chapter 17 about discrimination.

Halo effect. A tendency exists to characterize everything we know about a person because of one recognizable favorable or unfavorable trait. When a company does not insist upon the use of objective measures of performance, it is not uncommon for a supervisor to give a favorable performance rating to people who dress well or smile frequently. The fine appearance or warm smile of these people has created a halo around them. Employees often create a negative halo about a supervisor simply because that supervisor is gruff or stern in manner of speech.

Expectancy. If a person perceives or expects that another individual will behave in a particular way, that person often lives up to such an expectancy. A supervisor who perceives an employee as being competent will actually help that person become competent by giving him or her subtle signs of encouragement. Unfortunately, if you expect somebody to fail, that person will often live down to your expectation. How a supervisor's prophecy about an employee can become self-fulfilling will be discussed again in Chapter 8 about motivation.

Projection. Another shortcut in the perceptual process is to project our own bad faults onto others instead of making an objective appraisal of the situation. A manager might listen to a supervisor's request for one additional clerk because of what the supervisor perceives as a heavy workload within her department. The manager might mutter, "Who does she think she is trying to build an empire for herself?" In reality, the manager might be the empire builder and is projecting this undesirable characteristic on to the supervisor.

Selective perception. This mechanism is used when a person draws an unjustified conclusion from an unclear situation. Upon his return from a weekend of hunting, a tool and die maker might see his supervisor's car leaving his block. Once in the door he confronts his wife with the *fact* that she and his boss are having an affair. Perhaps the tool and die maker in question is looking for an excuse to have a fight with his wife (or his supervisor). Since human psychology is always complex, it could also be concluded that he is thinking of having an affair himself!

Perceptual defense. Once we hold a perception of something or somebody, we tend to cling to that perception by making things that we see, hear, smell, or touch consistent with that belief. All of the previous perceptual shortcuts are involved in perceptual defense. Supervisors and individual performers are not the only ones who engage in perceptual defense. The president of an American camera company insisted for ten years that Japanese competitors were not a serious threat to his company's high-priced line of cameras. At this writing the American company has been out of business for ten years, and the former president owns and operates a hardware store.

HOW PEOPLE LEARN

Much of human learning takes place on the job simply because people spend such a large proportion of their lives in a job setting. A supervisor who understands the basics of human learning can more readily help employees learn than a supervisor who is insensitive to the learning process. An exception are those gifted supervisors who intuitively act as good teachers and coaches. Learning is best defined as a relatively permanent change in behavior based on practice or experience. A person does not learn how to grow physically, hear sounds, or see light. These are innate, inborn patterns of behavior. But a person does learn how to wire a circuit board, program a computer, cut hair, fix flat tires, or balance a checkbook. Unless new learning takes place, almost no person would be able to perform his or her job in a satisfactory manner.

Learning of simple habits and reflexes: Classical conditioning

The learning experiments with salivating dogs conducted by the Russian physiologist Ivan Pavlov have been widely quoted. The principles of classical conditioning stemming from his experiments help us understand the most elementary type of learning—how people acquire uncomplicated habits and reflexes.[5] Since most of work behavior involves more than reflexes and simple habits, classical conditioning itself is not of major consequence to the supervisor. Yet its basic principles and concepts are included in more complicated forms of learning.

Classical conditioning works in this manner. Clyde, a physically normal individual, takes an entry level, unskilled job in a factory. His first day on the job, a bell rings in his department at 11:45 A.M. Suddenly every other worker stops working and opens a lunch box or heads out to the company cafeteria. Clyde says to himself, "The bell must mean it's time for lunch." By the third day on the job, Clyde develops stomach pangs and begins to salivate as soon as the bell rings. Prior to this job Clyde was in the habit of eating lunch at 1:00 P.M. and did not begin to have stomach pangs until that time.

Looking at the essentials of classical conditioning, here is what happened to Clyde: Since the food naturally and automatically elicits (brings forth) stomach pangs and salivation, it is referred to as the *unconditioned stimulus* (UCS). Salivating to the food in Clyde's lunch box or in the cafeteria occurs automatically without any learning. It is therefore called the *unconditioned response* (UCR). The sound of the department bell was originally neutral with respect to the salivary or hunger pang response, since it did not naturally elicit the UCR. Conditioning has taken place when the previously neutral stimulus (the department bell in Clyde's case) acquires the capacity to bring forth hunger pangs and salivation. The previously neutral stimulus is now called the *conditioned stimulus* (CS), and the hunger pangs and salivation to the sound of the bell are known as *conditioned responses* (CR).

---

[5] One recommended brief discussion of classical conditioning is Audrey Haber and Richard P. Runyon, *Fundamentals of Psychology* (Reading, Mass.: Addison-Wesley, 1974), pp. 81–92.

Two other important conditiong concepts are also of major importance. Should the department bell ring frequently when it is not time for lunch, Clyde's hunger pangs and salivation responses will gradually cease or *extinguish*. (An important expectation is that time alone or the empty feeling in his stomach can also serve as a stimulus to Clyde). As Clyde goes through life, he will learn not to salivate or experience hunger pangs to every bell that sounds like the one used in his department. At first he may *generalize* his learning by salivating to many different bells and experiencing hunger pangs in response to a variety of bells. After a while, Clyde will *discriminate* and only make such responses to the bell in his department (or any other bell that signals food time).

Classical conditioning helps to explain such elementary job behaviors as how people learn to avoid being conked on the head by cranes and low-hanging pipes and how we learn to step to the side of an aisle when we hear the buzz of a forklift truck behind us. It also explains how people learn to avoid being burned twice by a hot pipe or shocked twice by inscrting a screwdriver into an electric outlet.

Learning through positive reinforcement:
Operant conditioning

Positive reinforcement was mentioned in our Framework for Accomplishing Results as a way of motivating people to repeat constructive behavior. It will be described in Chapter 8 as a major approach to motivating employees. *Positive reinforcement* (PR) applies equally well to the subjects of motivation and learning. PR helps people learn new skills. Once a skill is learned, PR is useful in inducing people to repeat that skill. You cannot motivate people to perform a task they do not know how to perform. But you can motivate a person to want to learn how to perform that task. Motivation and learning are thus separate but closely related basic human processes. A manager whose job involves dealing with people is continually facing the problem of helping people learn and motivating them to repeat the learned behaviors.

Operant conditioning is learning what takes place as a consequence of behavior. In other words, a person's actions are instrumental in determining whether or not learning takes place. A supervisor asked a darkroom technician how he learned to jiggle the trays of photo chemicals while the prints were being processed. The technician replied, "I just tried it once and it seemed to help solve the problem of white spots appearing on the finished prints." In this case, the *operant* is the jiggling of the trays. The technician adopted jiggling as a standard practice because he received positive reinforcement—the disappearance of troublesome white spots on the prints—for his initial effort.

Operant conditioning differs from classical conditioning in one major respect. In classical conditioning, we can specify the unconditioned stimulus (such as food or water) which elicits the response (such as stomach contractions or salivation). In operant conditioning, somehow the individual tries out a behavior or action. If it leads to a reward, that behavior tends to be repeated. Much human learning proceeds on this basis. Learning how to ride a bicycle, drive a car on ice, surf in the ocean, or order wine in a restaurant is largely attributed to operant conditioning. Through this process we acquire skills that we did not previously know we possessed. Whenever a spontaneous behavior leads to positive reinforcement it will tend to be repeated.

Spontaneous behavior will also tend to be repeated when it leads to relief from an uncomfortable situation, so-called *negative reinforcement.* A teenager wearing cutoff jeans while riding a motorcycle might suddenly shriek in pain when bare calves touch against an exposed part of the engine. The teenager on future rides might then wear full-length jeans (as undoubtedly recommended by the manufacterer of the motorcycle) and no longer get burned. Negative reinforcement has taken place because something aversive (the burning sensation) has been removed by means of a new behavior (wearing full-length jeans).

In practice, learning through operant conditioning proceeds as a sequence of interrelated events, as illustrated in Figure 2–2.[6] Craig Peters, a sales representative, receives a memo from his supervisor to prepare a monthly report of customer inventories on the company's line of ski equipment. The memo is the con-

---

[6] This illustration is based on James L. Gibson, John M. Ivancevich, and James H. Donnelly, Jr., *Organizations: Behavior, Structure, Processes,* rev. ed. (Dallas: Business Publications, 1976), p. 112. © 1976 by Business Publications, Inc.

FIGURE 2-2
An example of operant conditioning in practice

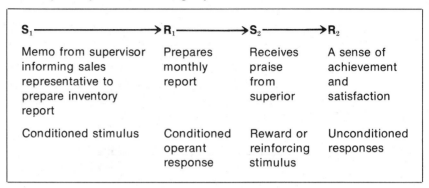

ditioned stimulus. Peters' conditioned operant response is to prepare the report. The operant response is referred to as conditioned because Peters did not spontaneously think of preparing the report. His boss generously praises the first report for its thoroughness and clarity. Such praise acts as a reward—Peters has received positive reinforcement. His response is a sense of achievement and self-satisfaction. His unconditioned responses to this reward are feelings of achievement and self-satisfaction.

Specific rules for the application of positive reinforcement to motivation will be presented in Chapter 8. In Chapter 14, we will discuss how principles of learning might be applied to the training and coaching of subordinates. Operant conditioning is an important part of any supervisor's job, whether he or she applies these principles systematically or intuitively.

Learning complicated skills: Modeling and shaping

When you acquire a complicated skill such as speaking in front of a group, photography, preparing a budget, or coaching a subordinate, you learn much more than just a single stimulus-response relationship. You learn about a large number of these relationships and you also learn how to put them together in a cohesive, smooth-flowing pattern. Two important processes that help in learning complicated skills are modeling (or imitation) and shaping (learning through approximations until the total skill is learned).[7]

Modeling occurs when you learn a skill by observing another person perform that skill. Many apprentices learn part of their trade just by watching a journeyman practice his or her trade. Carefully observing professional athletes on television can improve your own game in that particular sport if you have the right physical equipment and motivation. Modeling or imitation often brings forth behaviors people did not previously seem to have in their repetoire. A cogent example is reported in the book *Changing Supervisor Behavior:*[8]

> . . . a long-time foreman with a reputation for heavy-handed, authoritarian manner was transferred to a section run by a young, well-educated manager. The new manager treated the foreman with a great deal of respect and deference for his knowledge and experience. The foreman was initially uncomfortable in this new relationship because his previous managers, unlike his new manager, had almost never seriously sought his opinion on important matters relating to production operations. Now, the foreman is not only pleased that his opinions are valued and often put into effect, but he has begun to ask *his* subordinates, the line employees, for their views on a number of job-related matters. As the manager has done to him, the foreman also makes it a point to thank his employees for their ideas and lets them know when he implements their suggestions.

Shaping involves the reinforcement of a series of small steps that build up to the final or desired behavior. It is another way in which complicated skills are learned. At each successful step of the way the learner receives some positive reinforcement. Unless the learner receives positive reinforcement at each step of the way, that person will probably not acquire the total skill. As the learner improves in ability to perform the task, more skill is required to receive the reward.

A young man might be shaped into an automobile mechanic through a series of small skills beginning with changing tires. He receives a series of rewards as he moves along the path from a garage helper to a mechanic who can diagnose an engine malfunction and repair the problem. Among the forms of positive

---

[7] *Understanding Psychology*, p. 143.

[8] Arnold P. Goldstein and Melvin Sorcher, *Changing Supervisor Behavior* (Emsford, N.Y.: Pergamon, 1974), p. 26.

reinforcement he received along the way were approval for acquired skills, pay increments, and the feeling of pride as new minor skills were learned. The negative reinforcement he received was fewer bruised knuckles. When these series of small skills are put together in a complicated pattern of responses, the man has been converted from a fledgling garage assistant to a full-fledged mechanic. Shaping is a concept that applies to both learning and motivation. It will therefore be reintroduced in a later chapter.

HOW MOTIVES AND NEEDS INFLUENCE JOB BEHAVIOR[9]

As briefly mentioned in our Framework for Understanding Individual Behavior, needs and motives exert an important influence on people's actions in a job situation. For several decades, need theories have been used to explain work motivation. In simplest form, people work to satisfy needs. You will thus work hard to satisfy needs of yours that are currently not being satisfied. The two most popular need theories will be described here because they are historically significant and the forerunners of systems of improving worker motivation such as positive reinforcement and job enrichment.

Maslow's self-actualizing model of people

Abraham Maslow reasoned that human beings have an internal need pushing them on toward self-actualization (fulfillment) and personal superiority.[10] However, before these higher-level needs are activated, certain lower-level needs must be satisfied. A poor person thus thinks of finding a job as a way of obtaining the necessities of life. Once these are obtained, that person may think of achieving recognition and self-fulfillment on the job. When a person is generally satisfied at one level, that person looks for satisfaction at a higher level.

---

[9] Portions of this section of the chapter are reproduced from DuBrin, *Human Relations*, pp. 26–31. Reprinted with permission.

[10] Virtually every text in organizational behavior, human relations, or introduction to management has a discussion of Maslow's need hierarchy. An original source is Abraham H. Maslow, *Motivation and Personality* (New York: Harper & Row, 1954), p. 13 cf.

A major misinterpretation of Maslow's theory is that people behave as they do because of their quest to satisfy one particular need. In reality, many different motives are dominant at any one time. A draftsman may satisfy a number of needs (for instance, recognition, esteem, and self-satisfaction) by developing a design that works in practice.

Maslow arranged human needs into a five-level hierarchy. Each level refers to a group of needs—not one need for each level. These need levels are described next in ascending order.

Physiological needs refer to bodily needs, such as the requirements for food, water, shelter, and sleep. In general, most jobs provide ample opportunity to satisfy physiological needs. Nevertheless, some people go to work hungry or in need of sleep. Until that person gets a satisfying meal or takes a nap, this individual will not be concerned about finding an outlet on the job for creative impulses.

Safety needs include actual physical safety as a feeling of being safe from both physical and emotional injury. Many jobs frustrate a person's need for safety (police officer, taxicab driver). Therefore, many people would be motivated by the propsects of a safe environment. People who do very unsafe things for a living (such as racing-car drivers and tightrope walkers) find thrills and recognition more important than safety. Many people are an exception to Maslow's need hierarchy.

Love needs are essentially social or belonging needs. Unlike the two previous levels of needs, they center around a person's interaction with other people. Many people have a strong urge to be part of a group and to be accepted by that group. Peer acceptance is important in school and on the job. Many people are unhappy with their jobs unless they have the opportunity to work in close contact with others.

Esteem needs represent an individual's demands to be seen as a person of worth by others—and to himself or herself. Esteem needs are also called *ego* needs, pointing to the fact that people want to be seen as competent and capable. A job that is seen by yourself and others as being worthwhile provides a good opportunity to satisfy esteem needs.

Self-actualizing needs are the highest levels of needs, including the need for self-fulfillment and personal development. True self-actualization is an ideal to strive for, rather than something that automatically stems from occupying a challenging position. A self-actualized person is somebody who has become what he or she is capable of becoming. Few of us reach all our potential, even when we are so motivated.

Not every self-actualized person is a nationally or internationally prominent individual. A woman of average intelligence who attains an associate's degree and later becomes the owner-operator of an antique store might be self-actualized. Her potential and desire may both have been realized by self-employment as an antique dealer.

Maslow's need hierarchy appears to be a convenient way of classifying needs, but it has limited utility in explaining work behavior. Its primary value has been the fact that it highlights the importance of human needs in a work setting. When a manager wants to motivate another individual, the manager must offer that individual a reward that will satisfy an important need. Another criticism of the hierarchy approach is that career advancement may be the true factor underlying changes in need deficiencies.[11] Researchers found in one study that, as managers advance in organizations, their needs for safety decrease. Simultaneously, they experience an increase in their needs for affiliation with other people, achievement, and self-actualization.

Herzberg's two-factor theory

Over two decades ago Frederick Herzberg reported research suggesting that some elements of a job give people a chance to satisfy higher-level needs.[12] Such job elements are called *satisfiers* or *motivators*. Although individuals and groups vary somewhat in the particular job elements that they find satisfying or motivating, they generally refer to the *content* (guts of) the job. Specifically, they are achievement, recognition, challenging work, responsibility, and the opportunity for advancement. Following this theory, if you want to motivate most people, provide

---

[11] Douglas T. Hall and K. E. Nougaim, "An Examination of Maslow's Need Hierarchy in an Organizational Setting," *Organizational Behavior and Human Performance*, February 1968, pp. 12–35.

[12] Herzberg is also quoted in the general sources noted in footnote 10. An original source is Frederick Herzberg, *Work and the Nature of Man* (Cleveland: World Publishing Co., 1966).

them with the opportunity to do interesting work or receive a promotion.

In contrast, some job elements appeal more to lower-level needs; they tend to be noticed primarily by their absence. For instance, you may grumble about having to work in a hot, cramped office with no windows. Because of it you may experience job dissatisfaction or even be demotivated. But a cool, un-crowded office with a view of the ocean will probably not increase your level of job satisfaction or motivation.

Herzberg and his associates also noted that dissatisfiers relate mostly to the *context* (the job setting or external elements). Specifically, they are company policy and administration, super-vision, physical working conditions, relationships with others on the job, status, job security, salary, and personal life.

The motivation-hygiene theory of Herzberg has had a con-siderable impact upon practicing managers. Job enrichment owes its origins to the thinking of Herzberg. Nevertheless, a large body of research evidence has accumulated which indicates that Herzberg's ideas are not as universally correct as originally thought. Abraham K. Korman observes that Herzberg erred by assuming that most, if not all, individuals are at the higher-level needs. A complex, challenging, variable, and autonomous job is motivating for all people who are *operating at higher-level needs.* Although many factory workers and clerical workers are operating at higher-level needs, many are not.

Whatever need theory of motivation you find useful, it is es-sential to recognize that needs are dynamic, not static. The same individual may have a different need hierarchy at different stages in a lifetime. A man preoccupied with softball may want a non-challenging job so that he can reserve most of his energy for softball competition. Later in life this same man may be search-ing for self-fulfillment on the job and thus be motivated by chal-lenging work.

HOW VALUES AND BELIEFS INFLUENCE JOB BEHAVIOR

Another group of factors influencing how a person behaves on the job is that person's values and beliefs. A value refers to the importance a person attaches to something. If you believe that religion is one of the most important parts of your life, your

"I find this work truly fulfilling in many ways—there's the exercise, the sense of accomplishment, and, most important, the opportunity to make lots of noise."

Reprinted by permission The Wall Street Journal.

religious values are strong. If you pay very little attention to conserving energy, energy conservation is a weak value of yours. Beliefs exert a similar influence on job behavior. If you believe that the company wants to take advantage of you, you might demand that an informal statement made by your manager be put in writing.

The meaning of work.   An important value influencing job behavior is the significance an employee attaches to work. An employee who regards work as a necessary evil or as punishment will be difficult to motivate. An approach to dealing with employees who place a low value on work (those with a weak work ethic) will be described in Chapter 8. In contrast, a person who regards work as the central theme in life may prove to be a vigorous worker on the job. The work-addicted person may want to spend more hours on the job than company or union policy allow. Such workaholics are more likely to be found among the ranks of managers and professional people than among hourly and clerical workers.

Values lead to goals and objectives.   Robert M. Fulmer notes that the worker's background composed of job experiences, education, cultural influences, and personality lead to the formation of values.[13] "Through the lens of those values, the individual will perceive his or her needs." Needs, in turn, lead to the setting of goals and objectives, and career plans. As this process continues, the worker carves out a role for himself or herself that is consistent with those values.

> Margot, an intelligent woman with an industrial engineering degree is an example of how values can lead to the setting of goals on the job. Margot had long been interested in occupying leadership positions. (She valued being dominant over other people). She became the only woman in her high school graduating class to become an industrial engineer. Upon taking her first job in industry, she told the employment interviewer that she wanted to become a high-ranking executive in the manufacturing field. She has geared her life toward accomplishing that goal.
>
> Today, Margot is the highest-ranking woman in manufacturing (a second-level manager) in her company—a well-known manufacturer of office machines. Margot now says, "I won't rest until I become an officer of this company. I may be the highest-ranking woman in manufacturing, but I'm still too far down in the company to exert the influence I would like."

Conflict of values.   When the demands made by the organization or a superior clash with basic values of the individual, that

---

[13] Robert M. Fulmer, *Practical Human Relations* (Homewood, Ill.: Richard D. Irwin, 1977), p. 264. © 1977 by Richard D. Irwin, Inc.

person suffers from *person-role conflict.* [14] The individual wants to obey orders, but does not want to perform an act that seems inconsistent with his or her values. A situation such as this might occur when an employee is asked to produce a product that he or she feels is unsafe or of no value to society.

A saleswoman in a retail furniture store resigned, giving her boss this explanation: "I'm leaving because I don't think we're doing right by our customers. We sell mostly to poor people who can't get credit elsewhere. The furniture we sell them is shoddy, overpriced merchandise. But that's only half the problem. We're really in the finance business, but we don't admit it to our customers. If people paid cash or obtained bank financing for the furniture they bought from us, we would make no profits. Most of our profits come from interest paid by our customers. I'm very disturbed about what we're doing to people."

HOW STRESS, TENSION, AND ANXIETY INFLUENCE JOB BEHAVIOR

To understand individuals in a work environment, including oneself, it is necessary to be aware of potentially negative aspects of behavior. In virtually every work organization employees and managers are exposed to a variety of stresses. For many people such stress is a good thing. Most people require some stress in order to perform at their best. Many employees say, "I'm at my best under pressure. If there isn't any pressure on me I tend to goof off a little." Yet too much stress may have harmful consequences to the person and to the organization. An industrial physician has summarized the relationship between stress and job performance in this manner:

> We all need stress. The goal is not a state of nirvana where the executive is suspended in an emotional nothingness. But we have to distinguish between satisfying and unsatisfying stress. It is satisfying when you are running around achieving goals. It is unsatisfying when everything gets out of control. That's when people develop symptoms such as headaches, diarrhea, and heart palpitations. [15]

---

[14] Stephen J. Carroll and Henry L. Tosi, *Organizational Behavior* (Chicago: St. Clair Press, 1977), p. 114.

[15] Quoted in Lee Smith, "What Kills Executives," *Dun's Review,* March 1976, p. 37.

Generalizations about how much stress is harmful are difficult to reach. Some sources of stress will have adverse consequences for most people. Among these are losing one's job, going through a divorce, or receiving conflicting directions from two bosses. Some forms of stress tend not to be harmful. Among them are engaging in reasonable competition, being criticized by a boss, or losing a set of keys.

Stress is a force acting on the individual, such as being laid off or being turned down for a job you felt you deserved. Stress generally produces tension, a condition resulting from the mobilization of inner resources to meet a threat. Our muscles become more taut when we are tense, our heart beats more rapidly, and our rate of breathing increases. Feelings of strain and uneasiness are associated with tension. Standing next to a power saw would induce tension in most people unfamiliar with such equipment. Tension also involves an impulse to action—in this case an impulse to get away from the saw.

Anxiety is closely associated with tension and is sometimes a by-product of tension. It is defined as a generalized feeling of fear and apprehension usually resulting from a perceived threat. The threat, in turn, is accompanied by feelings of uneasiness. Skilled craftsworkers who are in jobs well below their skill levels may experience anxiety although they cannot specifically pinpoint why they feel anxious.

Sources of stress. The potential sources of stress listed in Figure 2–3 point to the variety of circumstances and conditions that can produce tension and anxiety among individual performers, supervisors, and managers. Few people are immune from stress in their jobs. It is convenient to regard job stresses as consisting of those imposed by the organization and those self-imposed by the individual. For instance, if supervisors are under stress because they have not achieved their goals of being promoted to middle-management positions, one might argue that they brought the stress on themselves. Should the organization guarantee every supervisor a promotion to middle management?

It is beyond the scope of this chapter to discuss the many potential sources of stress in a job environment. Some of them will be discussed in another context at various places in the text. Nevertheless, it is important for the supervisor or potential

FIGURE 2–3
How stress, tension, and anxiety influence job behavior

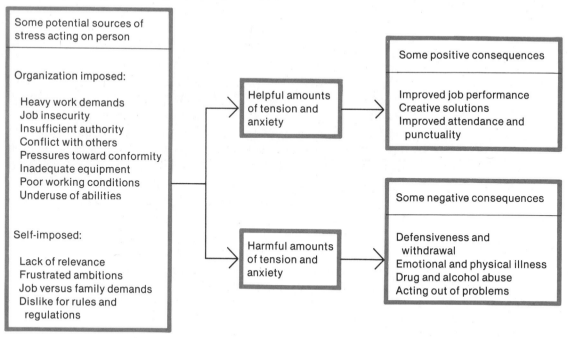

supervisor to recognize that stress is almost inevitable in a work environment. Because stress is inevitable, a supervisor must also deal with its consequences.

Positive consequences of tension and anxiety. As shown in Figure 2–3, stress may produce helpful amounts of tension and anxiety. In other words, the tension and anxiety produced by the stress leads to positive consequences for the individual and the organization. A man worrying about his job may work hard to improve his performance (and thereby have less to worry about). A woman in conflict with another may become more creative in order to show their mutual boss who is the more competent person. A person forced to work with inadequate equipment may improve work attendance in order to qualify for a transfer to a department with better equipment. A skillful supervisor would try to maintain an amount of stress on employees that would be just enough to obtain positive consequences. The potential stress of heavy work demands is a case in point. If workers are not kept busy enough, the quality of their work may suffer as a by-product of lethargy. With too much stress, work may suffer. With an appropriately heavy work load, performance stands a good chance of increasing.

Negative consequences of tension and anxiety. Stress also leads to harmful amounts of tension and anxiety which in turn leads to some negative consequences for the individual and the organization. Several of these consequences will be discussed at various places in the text. Chapter 19, on self-management, will include a discussion of how supervisors can handle their own job-related tensions.

Defensiveness and withdrawal is one class of behaviors that may take place in response to severe stress. An individual who believes that work is meaningless may become less attentive and be absent more frequently. Employees who are worried about losing their jobs often become defensive about their mistakes and increasingly cautious about taking risks: They often become afraid to be blamed for anything that might go wrong.

Emotional and physical illness is the most widely studied class of behaviors that may occur in response to stress. Much of the field of abnormal psychology and psychiatry deals with this topic. When the stress is great enough, some people become uncontrollably tense to the point of requiring care by a mental health specialist. Stress also produces such legitimate physical symptoms as back pain and skin disorders, in addition to the well-known stress reactions such as ulcers, migraine headaches, and colitis.

A physician employed full time in the manufacturing department of a large company made this comment about the relationship between job stress and employee health: "You can tell when the pressure is up on the shop floor. My staff of nurses and I are besieged with all kinds of mental and physical complaints. People come in here (the plant medical department) complaining of things like low back pain, blurred vision, upset stomachs, and heart palpitations. When one part of the plant was going to be automated, we had an outbreak of people who developed low back pain. A layoff produces more visits to the medical department than does the flu."

SUMMARY OF KEY POINTS

☐ The Framework for Understanding Individual Behavior is designed to help explain why people act as they do. People's behavior is triggered by a stimulus, cue, force, or pressure. How a person responds is in large measure determined by factors such as personality, self-concept, and past experiences. Which characteristics are evoked is influenced by which ones are relevant to the particular stimulus. Once a person responds to the situation, that person receives positive reinforcement or punishment. When behavior receives reinforcement, it tends to be repeated in the future.

☐ Perception—the organization of sensory information into meaningful experiences—influences job behavior. Perception is influenced by factors within the person such as motives, needs, and goals. It is also influenced by characteristics of the stimulus such as distinctiveness, intensity, and frequency.

☐ People take many shortcuts to perceptions, such as denial, stereotyping, the halo effect, expectancy, projection, and perceptual defense.

☐ Classical conditioning is the most elementary form of learning. It occurs when a previously neutral stimulus is associated with a natural (unconditioned) stimulus. Eventually the neutral stimulus brings forth the unconditioned response. For example a factory whistle blown just prior to a lunch break induces employees to salivate.

☐ Operant conditioning occurs when a person's spontaneous actions are rewarded or punished, resulting in an increase or a decrease in the behavior. Much of human learning occurs through operant conditioning.

☐ Complicated sets of skills are frequently learned by modeling or imitation. Such skill repetoires are also learned by behavior shaping, a form of learning in which approximations to the final skill are rewarded. Eventually only the final skill is rewarded.

☐ A good deal of job behavior can be attributed to the effort of people to satisfy needs and motives. Two cornerstone need theories of job behavior are Maslow's self-actualizing model of people and Herzberg's two-factor theory. In general, people strive to satisfy higher-level needs only after lower-level needs are satisfied.

☐ Values and beliefs influence job behavior in several ways: the meaning you attach to work often influences your motivation; people's values lead to goals and objectives; and work assignments may conflict with personal values causing stress and inaction.

☐ Stress and its resultant tension and anxiety have a variety of effects on job behavior, some positive and some negative. Under the best conditions, the optimum amount of stress leads to improved job performance. Harmful or dissatisfying stress can lead to such consequences as defensiveness and withdrawal, emotional and physical illness, drug and alcohol abuse, or acting out of problems including assaulting others.

GUIDELINES FOR SUPERVISORY PRACTICE

1. A challenging part of any supervisory job is dealing with individual differences among people. You cannot possibly develop a full understanding of all your employees. However, you should be sensitive to the fact that people will respond differently to the same event depending on their past experiences and personal characteristics.

2. Your response or lack of response to an employee's actions will influence the individual's response predisposition for the future. If you encourage an action, it will tend to be repeated; if you ignore or punish it, the reaction will tend not to be repeated.

3. Recognize that there is a good chance that your actions and statements will not be perceived by employees the way you want them to be perceived. It is therefore important to get feedback on how your statements and actions were perceived.

4. If you keep in mind the basic ways in which people learn, it may be easier to teach employees new skills. A very practical way of imparting skills is for you to serve as a model and give frequent feedback on how well subordinates are learning.

5. In teaching an employee a complicated skill, give feedback, encouragement, and praise for any steps made in the right direction.

6. A practical way of motivating people is to find out what they want, and then give them a chance to attain what they want by accomplishing work goals.

7. Be careful not to place people under too much stress. Many negative consequences to the organization and the individual may result, such as behavior and emotional problems.

8. Be careful not to place people under too little stress. Under these conditions people may become lethargic. Performance may suffer as a result.

QUESTIONS FOR DISCUSSION AND REVIEW

1. What makes people so different from one another?

2. How might a supervisor make use of the Framework for Understanding Individual Behavior?

3. Identify three stimuli, cues, pressures, or forces acting on you at this moment.

4. What kind of positive reinforcement have you received lately? What effect has it had on you?

5. What are three different perceptions people might have about a supervisor? Why do these differences in perceptions probably exist?

6. How do you think poor and wealthy people differ in their perception of money? Why do these differences in perception exist?

7. Suppose an 18-year-old man with no work experience and a 50-year-old man with 25 years of supervisory experience took this course. How would their perceptions of this course probably differ?

8. In what way do goldfish and human beings differ in the way they learn? What are some similarities?

9. What methods of learning are you using to acquire information in this course?

10. What is the difference between shaping and modeling (or imitation)?

11. How do needs and motives influence the amount of effort you put forth on the job?

12. What are your two most active psychological needs these days? How do you know they are active?

13. It is not unknown for human beings to cannibalize one another when shut off from other sources of food (such as being lost on a mountain). What do these incidents tell us about human motivation?

14. According to Herzberg's two-factor theory what would be the best way to motivate a supervisor?

15. Give examples of two people you think are self-actualized. Why did you reach such a conclusion?

16. If a person had strong religious values, how might those values influence job behavior?

17. What meaning do you attach to work?

18. How are individual differences in capability influenced by highly automated jobs?

19. In what way are you different from most people?

A supervisory problem: Is this any way to run a restaurant?

You work as a restaurant manager for a large chain of quality restaurants. The owner says to you one day, "Let's do something good for society. We'll find 25 people recently released from prison, or on parole, who are likely to have a difficult time finding employment. We'll put them to work in one of our restaurants. You'll be the manager in this new restaurant. Your only employees will be these ex-convicts.

You ask, "Which ex-cons shall we hire?" Your boss answers, "The first 25 to show up for the job. First come, first hired. I don't care about their sex, age, race, appearance, size, schooling, or their reasons for conviction. Just put them on the payroll, train them, and run a first-class, profitable restaurant."

1. *What will be your biggest challenge in this assignment?*
2. *What type of individual differences are you likely to find among employees?*
3. *Is this any way to run a restaurant? Explain.*

SOME SUGGESTED READING

Boshear, Elmer H., and Smith, Robert D.   *Understanding People: Models and Concepts.* La Jolla, Calif.: University Associates, 1977.

Carvell, Fred J.   *Human Relations in Business.* 2d ed. New York: The Macmillan Co., 1975.

Diggins, Dean, and Huber, Jack.   *The Human Personality.* Little, Brown, 1976.

DuBrin, Andrew J.   *Fundamentals of Organizational Behavior: An Applied Perspective.* 2d ed. Elmsford, N.Y.: Pergamon, 1978.

Frew, David R.   *Management of Stress: Using TM at Work.* Chicago: Nelson-Hall, 1977.

Hamner, W. Clay, and Organ, Dennis W.   *Organizational Behavior: An Applied Psychological Approach.* Dallas: Business Publications, Inc., 1978.

Huse, Edgar F., and Bowditch, James L.   *Behavior in Organizations: A Systems Approach to Managing.* 2d ed. Reading, Mass.: Addison-Wesley, 1977.

London, Perry.   *Beginning Psychology.* Rev. ed. Homewood, Ill.: Dorsey Press, 1978.

McLean, Alan, (ed.)   *Occupational Stress.* Springfield, Ill.: Charles C Thomas, 1974.

Moore, Lewis S.   "Motivation through Positive Reinforcement." *Supervisory Management,* October 1976, pp. 2–9.

Sarason, Irwin G.   *Abnormal Psychology: The Problems of Maladaptive Behavior.* 2d ed. Englewood Cliffs, N.J.: Prentice-Hall, 1976.

Smith, Maury.   *A Practical Guide to Value Clarification.* La Jolla, Calif.: University Associates, 1977.

People in work groups

3

LEARNING OBJECTIVES

After reading and thinking through the material in this chapter you should be able to:

1. Explain what a group is and is not.
2. Discuss five major benefits employees often derive from belonging to a work group.
3. Describe the difference between a formal and an informal work group. Also give your own example of each.
4. Identify and define two types of formal groups.
5. Give an analysis of factors that contribute to the effectiveness of work groups.
6. Provide several strategies that will help a supervisor win the support of the group.

Groups are an inescapable part of a supervisor's job. A supervisor spends most of the day dealing with members of a work group. Often the interaction is with a group member who reports to the supervisor. Yet the supervisor is also a member of a group that reports to the next level of management. Every supervisor thus belongs to at least two work groups. In addition, many supervisors become members of temporary work groups such as task forces of project teams. It is not unusual for a supervisor to also belong to a company-related group such as a softball team or bridge club.

Groups are the basic building blocks of the larger organization. Almost all work that gets accomplished is a product of group effort.

Part of the mystery of a group is that it has an identity of its own that transcends that of its members. You might make a

64

humorous comment to five people individually and get five blank stares. That same humorous comment told to those five people arranged into a group might produce a loud guffaw. A group can often accomplish tasks that could not be accomplished by combining the individual contributions of its members. This is the main reason organizations use groups to get work accomplished. For instance, an individual working alone could hardly build a regrigerator.

Our study of groups begins with a basic definition: A group is a "collection of individuals who regularly interact with each other, who are psychologically aware of each other, and who perceive themselves to be a group."[1] A husband and wife team of truckdrivers would thus constitute a group. So would the safety committee of an iron foundry. However, ten people waiting in line in a hospital cafeteria would not be a real group. Although they might talk to each other, their interaction would not be on a planned or recurring basis.

In the previous chapter we described certain general properties about individuals. Here we will do the same for groups. In the next chapter the emphasis will be upon total organizations, which are basically a collection of small groups. Groups will enter into consideration at many other places in this book. For instance, a later chapter about office politics implies that a variety of tactics must be used to compete successfully with other group members.

WHAT EMPLOYEES DERIVE FROM GROUP MEMBERSHIP

A place of work arranges its activities into small groups for the purpose of getting work accomplished. So far, nobody has arrived at a workable alternative to departments or teams. Prehistoric men and women, undoubtedly, organized their hunting forays into small groups. Posthistoric men and women, if science fiction books and movies are correct, will also organize their space-faring adventures into small groups. Employees themselves derive benefits from working in groups. For most employees, group effort is a natural way of life. A supervisor who

---

[1] Henry L. Tosi and Stephen J. Carroll, *Management: Contingencies, Structure, and Process* (Chicago: St. Clair Press, 1976), p. 97.

understands why people enjoy (what they find reinforcing about) working in groups may be able to capitalize upon the productive forces of the group.

Learning job-related skills

Many things an employee learns on the job are taught by the supervisor or the training department. Yet a good deal of learning is acquired through association with peers. An analysis of work groups in many different settings revealed three primary methods by which people learn from each other in a work group.[2]

Direct instruction. Group members frequently tell a new member how to do something. Such information may be invaluable for the neophyte in getting adjusted to the organization. A recently hired group member may ask an experienced employee, "How do I get a Xerox copy made of this purchase order?" or "How do I get my paycheck if I am out sick on payday?" Not knowing basic information can be stressful to the new (or old) employee. Often an employee will ask instructions of another for help because the worker is too embarrassed to ask the supervisor for help.

Direct instruction may not be sufficient for a person to learn a new skill, but it does get a person started in the right direction. A librarian might be told by another librarian how to operate a microfilm reader. With a little initial instruction (such as, "Here is how you turn on the machine") and much trial and error (operant conditioning), the skill will be acquired in time.

Feedback on progress. The group serves a vital function in giving the learner information on what that person is doing right or wrong in conducting the job. In other words, co-workers will tell you how well you are performing your job. Equally important, the group can provide reinforcement by rewarding correct behaviors and punishing incorrect ones. Both functions are helpful in helping a person improve job skills.

A waiter explains how informational feedback and feedback through rewards and punishments helped in the learning experience:

---

[2] An authoritative source here is J. Richard Hackman, "Group Influences on Individuals," in *Handbook of Industrial and Organizational Psychology,* ed. Marvin D. Dunnette (Chicago: Rand McNally, 1976), pp. 1485–88.

This was my first job in a posh restaurant. Pierre, one of the other wait-ers, told me the dining room supervisor would have a fit if he overheard me chatting with customers about the weather. We were supposed to be strictly professional. Once I waved a party on over to one of my tables. At closing time, I heard a lot from the other waiters about that trick. I was told I would get no cooperation from them if I pulled that stunt again. We're supposed to wait and let the hostess do all the seating. They said if they caught me again, they might mess up an order on my tray.

Modeling.   As discussed in the previous chapter, much of the learning of complicated skills often takes place by imitating the actions of an experienced and competent person. Watching an-other group member perform a difficult task is a natural method of learning in organizations. Unless you work in a group such modeling is difficult to achieve. J. Richard Hackman has sum-marized the value of modeling in these words:[3]

> One of the most pervasive ways a group can be helpful to individual members in role and skill learning is through the provision of models. The need for models apparently is very great, especially for complex tasks and roles, some of which may be impossible to learn adequately in the absence of a concrete model.

Learning standards of conduct (norms)

Group membership helps the employee learn what is *really* expected in terms of job performance. A supervisor might say, "We want full production from everybody." In practice, most of the workers slack off just a bit. The official coffee break may be 10 minutes in the morning and afternoon, but group norms or standards allow two 15-minute breaks per day. A norm is thus defined as a standard that is shared by members of the group.[4]

Group norms also exist for such matters as which types of clothing are acceptable at work, whether or not to carry lunch to work, and proper methods of addressing the boss. Suppose an employee wonders whether to call his boss's boss "Ms. Gordon," "Miss Gordon," "Mrs. Gordon," or "Jane." He is more likely to

---

[3] Ibid., p. 1486.

[4] James L. Gibson, John M. Ivancevich, and James H. Donnelly, Jr., *Organizations: Behavior, Structure, Processes* (Dallas: Business Publications, 1976), p. 158. © 1976 by Business Publications, Inc.

observe what others do than to ask his boss "What name should I call your boss?"

Some employees are more dependent than others upon group norms. People who conform the most to group standards of conduct tend to be less intelligent and self-sufficient than nonconformers. One study concluded that the person most likely to remain independent and to resist group pressure tends to be:[5]

1. Intelligent, as measured by mental ability tests (conformists, however, are not necessarily unintelligent).
2. Original in his or her thinking.
3. Self-confident and not particularly bothered by feelings of anxiety or inferiority.
4. Reasonably tolerant, responsible, and dominant, and not overly dependent upon other people.

Aside from personality characteristics, many characteristics about the situation can influence the importance of group norms. People are more likely to use group norms as a guide to personal conduct under these conditions:[6]

The situation is ambiguous. When people are not certain of what is expected of them, they become somewhat dependent upon whatever norms of conduct might be available. To avoid this situation, it is important for a supervisor to state clearly what is expected of employees.

The necessity of going along with the group for accomplishing goals. Six people on a product team are willing to adhere to group norms of conduct when it becomes apparent that they are technologically dependent upon one another. For instance, team members are willing to adhere to rules and regulations with regard to computer usage if they need computer time to complete a project.

The appropriateness of the goals being offered the individual. When the goals of the group mesh with the needs, motives, and desires of the individual, the person will probably go along with group norms. In a department operating on an incentive system for production beyond the standard, the group norm

---

[5] These studies are summarized in David Krech, Richard S. Crutchfield, and Norman Livson, *Elements of Psychology; A Briefer Course* (New York: Alfred A. Knopf, 1970), pp. 479–82.

[6] Research about this topic is summarized in Abraham K. Korman, *Organizational Behavior* (Englewood Cliffs, N.J.: Prentice-Hall, 1977), p. 81.

might call for 15 percent bonus pay. Most members will agree to such a norm because they desire bonus pay.

Satisfaction of psychological needs

Many people receive most of their work-related satisfactions from interacting with members of their department. As one seamstrsss said to a researcher, "What I dislike most about vacations is that I don't have the chance to talk with the other workers in the department. My husband doesn't talk much to me and the kids hardly need me anymore since they've become teenagers."

Most workers apparently dislike positions that involve a minimum of group contact. Some sales representatives, insurance claim adjusters, field auditors, and the like find these positions unsatisfactory because they involve a minimum of contact with an enduring work group. Specifically, groups can provide these kinds of psychological satisfactions to members:[7]

An outlet for affiliation needs. People have a natural need to affiliate with others and the group provides such an outlet. The friendships people develop on the job are meaningful to them. When people work with friends their job satisfaction increases. A supervisor must recognize, however, that when people become too friendly on the job, they may become lax in their work standards.

A source of emotional support to group members. Work groups, just like social groups, provide members with reassurance and support. When a group member of a tightly knit (cohesive) group feels emotionally down, the person can rely on the group for some temporary bolstering. As one production worker expressed it, "After I get a chewing out from my foreman, I tell the guys about it during lunch break. They usually tell me not to take it so hard cause Bill chews out everybody. Just kidding about it makes me feel better."

A means of coping with a common enemy. One of the powerful appeals of labor unions is that employees feel union membership gives them more clout in bringing their complaints to management. When a group is faced with a common enemy, the

---

[7] This discussion is based on a similar discussion in Andrew J. DuBrin, *Fundamentals of Organizational Behavior: An Applied Perspective,* 2d ed. (Elmsford, N.Y.: Pergamon, 1978), pp. 185–86.

members typically band together and become more united in their actions. Suppose a shipping department is in conflict with an order department over the issue of timely shipments. Members of both departments are likely to develop more loyalty to their own department and even exaggerate the negative characteristics of the other department.

Reduction of tension

Group membership has the mental advantage of reducing tension for many people.[8] The emotional support provided by the group helps you control tension. A study conducted by Stanley E. Seashore of 228 industrial work groups in a machinery company showed that tension and anxiety were least pronounced in the highly cohesive groups.[9]

It is a common practice in work groups for members to share problems (both personal and job related) with each other. When faced with a major problem, having a sympathetic listener often reduces tension. The advice offered by a co-worker might lead to a solution to your problem, further reducing your tension. One woman was becoming increasingly tense about funding her child's college education. A co-worker suggested that she apply for a long-term tuition loan offered by a local bank. The troubled woman was able to secure such a loan and her level of tension was reduced.

A means to obtain ends

People often join groups as a means of achieving certain ends that they want outside of the group.[10] One study conducted many years ago showed that college women often joined sororities in order to increase their prestige in the college community. Workers at professional and employee levels may join

---

[8] The discussions about reduction of tension and a means to attain ends are quoted directly from Andrew J. DuBrin, *Human Relations: A Job-Oriented Approach* (Reston, Va.: Reston, 1978), pp. 163, 165–66.

[9] Stanley E. Seashore, *Group Cohesiveness in the Industrial Work Group* (Ann Arbor, Mich.: Survey Research Center, University of Michigan, 1954).

[10] Marvin E. Shaw, *Group Dynamics: The Psychology of Small Group Behavior* (New York: McGraw-Hill, 1971).

labor unions in order to obtain higher wages and improved working conditions. In both examples, the ends (prestige or more money) are more important to the individuals than is group membership itself.

Industrial work groups may also serve as a vehicle for group members attaining an end outside of the group. The career-minded person will often volunteer for a committee assignment in order to be "discovered" by a member of top management. As described in Chapter 16, certain groups are advantageous to your career because they make you *visible* to influential people. Many a junior executive has distinguished himself or herself while on loan to the Community Chest fund-raising campaign. A favorable report goes back to the company that loaned the executive to the campaign, enhancing his or her reputation.

PROBLEMS SOMETIMES CREATED BY GROUPS

Despite their many virtues, work groups sometimes create problems for employees and management. The informal group structure tends to create more of these problems than does the formal structure. Almost every advantage of group membership described above could also be a disadvantage in some situations. To illustrate, people might find such satisfaction in relating to their co-workers that they tend to waste time. Here we will concentrate on four problems that are by-products of group effort.

Shirking of individual responsibility. For those employees who are not well motivated toward work, group assignments are sometimes an invitation to goof off. An undermotivated member can sometimes squeeze by without contributing a fair share to the group effort. The responsibility shirker risks being ostracized by the group, but may be willing to pay this price rather than work hard. A way for the supervisor to minimize such shirking of responsibility is to carefully draw assignments and use both individual and group objectives.

Pressures toward conformity. The most frequent criticism of group effort is that the individual may be forced to act and think like other group members. The individual might even be forced to slow down production to meet the average imposed by the informal group. In some situations conformity can be detrimental to all concerned.

As a case in point, one bricklayer in five might believe that a method of laying bricks inside a silo is unsafe. After learning that co-workers think that the method is safe, the bricklayer may say, "If the other members of the group disagree with me, I'm probably wrong. Why be an odd ball? I'll say the wall will stand up under pressure."

Such an act of conformity has two negative consequences. First, the conforming bricklayer may be right. This method of laying the brick may be unsafe and lives might be saved if it is brought to the attention of the construction supervisor. Second, this individual is not contributing his judgment, based on years of experience, to the group effort.

Pressures toward mediocrity. A potential hazard of being well accepted by your work group—whether you are a supervisor or an employee—is that it could hold back your performance. Eventually this holding back of performance could hold back your career. Your allegiance to the group could make it difficult for you to advance into management or perform your job in a superior manner. To avoid falling out of favor with the group, some people will avoid superior performance; thus they will not be given special recognition by management.

Breeding of conflict. At their worst, groups breed conflict in an organization. Intergroup conflict occurs when group members develop the attitude that their work group is more important than the organization as a whole. Rivalries develop, and "beating the other department" becomes more important than trying to reach goals important to the organization. In one company a rivalry developed between the quality control and final assembly departments. After a while, quality control became tighter and tighter in their interpretation of what constituted a quality defect. At one point the final assembly department accused the quality control department of damaging the product in order to call it defective.

FORMAL GROUPS

Organizations can be divided into two major types of groups, the formal and informal. A supervisor must be knowledgeable about both types of groups in order to carry out the mission of a department. First we will examine the more readily understood of the two major types of groups, the formal group. As illustrated in Figure 3–1, a formal group often takes the form of a department in an organization. The fact that an activity or group of people is termed *a department* makes it a formal group.

FIGURE 3–1
Typical formal groups within a major division of a large manufacturing corporation

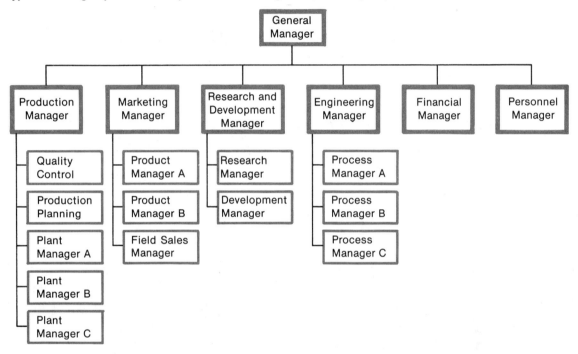

A formal group is one deliberately formed by the organization to accomplish specific tasks and achieve objectives. Formal groups are often designated by an organization chart. At other times a written memo may suffice to indicate that a formal group has been developed. If a supervisor reads a memo listing him or her as belonging to a safety committee, that person has involuntarily become a member of a formal group—the safety committee.

Two types of formal groups. The life span of a formal group is a major factor in understanding how the group functions. Some formal groups are relatively permanent while others are relatively temporary. Formal groups such as a department are required for the daily operation of the organization. They tend to remain in operation until a reorganization. Examples of permanent formal groups include the finished goods department, the cost accounting department, the training department, and the legal department. A department may undergo complete turnover in one year, yet its function remains the same. Methods used by the department may also change, but the basic purpose of a permanent formal group remains the same. A billing department may become computerized, yet its basic function—sending out bills—has not changed.

Temporary formal groups include task forces, projects, and committees. A task force to study the problem of labor unrest will probably be dissolved once the labor problem is thoroughly studied. A committee is basically a temporary task force. The committee members are assigned a project that they work on in addition to their normal duties. Once the committee has completed its assignment, its recommendations are passed along to the official who sanctioned the committee.

INFORMAL GROUPS

A supervisor who studies only the organization chart will fall short of understanding group formation within the department. Formal groups tell us what arrangements are the necessary minimum to get the organization's work accomplished. Yet they do not tell us the whole story of how group relationships develop on the job. Partly out of a desire for friendship and partly out of the necessity of getting work accomplished, people arrange themselves into a variety of informal groups.

A supervisor must be cognizant of informal groups because employees almost inevitably create some informal groups. Several of the reasons for such group formation have already been specified in our discussion of why people join groups. Three examples will help explain the concept of an informal group:

Four hospital aides working on the same ward meet once a week for lunch in the hospital cafeteria. The purpose of their get-together is to discuss the tedium of their jobs. During lunch they exchange stories of the demands placed on them by patients. A typical comment made by one of the aides, "Did you know that one of the cancer patients insisted that I clip his toenails? You should have heard what I told him."

Four accountants form a jogging club that meets three days per week at lunchtime to run one mile.

Four supervisors from different parts of the plant commute to work every day when they are all working the same shift. Often discussing snowmobiles and hunting, they also discuss company business while commuting to work.

The third example illustrates that an informal group can be partly social and partly job related. When the four supervisors discuss common concerns, such as how to motivate apparently lazy employees, the company benefits. An exchange of such information can lead to the development of sound supervisory strategies. It could also be argued that the mutual gripe club formed by the four hospital aides also helps the hospital. Because the aides are releasing pent-up feelings to each other, they might not take these angry feelings out on the patients.

Filling in the gaps. An informal group's social function is readily understood. How an informal group supplements the formal group structure to the advantage of the organization is less widely understood. Without such informal arrangements, many organizations would fail or would be seriously hampered in getting their work accomplished. Informal group arrangements often take care of minor emergencies that are not adequately planned for by the company. The Jumper Cable Patrol that exists in a plant in London, Ontario, is one such helpful informal arrangement. Buck, a supervisor in that company, explains the operation of the patrol:

> As you might suspect, winters can be quite cold in London. The executives can afford very expensive cars that will start in almost any weather. But many of the plant personnel have cars that sometimes go dead sitting out there in the parking lot. The company has never seen fit to be equipped with a tow truck to run a free road service for the employees. Our solution has been to form a little club called the Jumper Cable Patrol. Two of us at a time sit out in the parking lot. All members of the club carry battery jumper cables in their cars. On a rotating basis of about two days a month, we donate an hour or so to helping out stuck employees. We figure it out so there's about an hour of coverage after quitting

time. We cruise around the parking lot, two in a car, to see if anybody needs help. The payment we get for our services is a warm smile from the folks we help. We're not expecting payment from the company.

The gap filled in by the Jumper Cable Patrol is that of preventing employees from experiencing discomfort that could have consequences for job behavior. Employees who are preoccupied with whether or not their car will start on a given subfreezing day might be preoccupied enough to get themselves into an industrial accident. Also, a person who spends three hours trying to get help for an unstartable car may very well call in sick the following day.

WHY SOME GROUPS SUCCEED AND OTHERS FAIL[11]

Some work groups are more effective than others. Group effectiveness refers in general to the dual consideration of productivity and morale. A group that both meets its work goals and keeps members satisfied can be considered an effective group. Although the evidence is not conclusive, it appears that there are identifiable reasons why some groups succeed and others fail. A supervisor plays an important role in determining whether or not these conditions for group success are present. A supervisor is a key member of the work group.

Technical competence of employees. However obvious this fact, the technical competence of employees is often overlooked when studying the psychology of groups. A precondition for group success is that group members are competent in the broad sense of the term. Job competence stems from such factors as adequate technical knowledge, proper training, sufficient problem-solving ability, and a high enough level of motivation. Asked why a department was one of the highest producing in the plant, the supervisor responded, "Simple enough. We've got the best people."

Proper leadership. A fact about work groups is that they are more likely to achieve their goals under the proper type of lead-

---

[11] Our discussion of why some groups succeed and others fail closely follows the discussion in DuBrin, *Human Relations*, pp. 158–61. However, the present discussion includes a wider range of factors.

ership. The nature of the work performed by the group and the type of employees heavily influence which approach to leadership is best (as discussed in Chapter 10). A supervisor in charge of a group of newcomers to the work force would probably need to give them much reassurance and support. A supervisor in charge of a group of experienced and competent skilled workers would not need to give them so much encouragement.

One firm generalization about the proper type of leadership for a small group is that the leader should give group members an accurate statement of what is expected of them and what they should expect. People in work groups need definite guidelines for performing their task and usually require assistance from the leader. What we have said does not imply that the more dogmatic the leader, the more productive the group or the more satisfied the group members. Based on years of research conducted by the University of Michigan, it has been concluded that an effective leader of a small group typically engages in behaviors such as the following:[12]

☐ Listens carefully and patiently.
☐ Has patience with progress made by the group, particularly on slow problems.
☐ Gives the group members ample opportunity to express their thoughts.
☐ Is careful not to impose a decision on the group.
☐ Frequently puts contributions in the form of questions or states them speculatively.

Right mix of people.   A group functions best when the mix of people is a good one for getting the job accomplished. Supervisors determine infrequently which people are invited to join or leave their work groups. Yet knowledge of this basic idea of group functioning can be helpful in making recommendations about the employees needed to help produce an effective team. Obtaining the right mix of people is more crucial when cooperation among the team members is called for. When people work independently of each other, such as a group of bookkeepers, obtaining the right mix of skills is less important.

The importance of the right mix of skills and capabilities to the success of a group can be readily visualized in the context of

---

[12] Rensis Likert, *New Patterns of Management* (New York: McGraw-Hill, 1961).

a house construction team. A supervisor of such a group would want to make certain that a variety of skills, such as carpentry, plumbing, electrical, and masonry were present in the group. The team would also need a mixture of physical sizes. Inevitably there would be some "bull work," whereby a physically large and strong person would be an asset. People who were small and nimble would also be needed for purposes such as erecting the framework for the roof. At one period in the airplane industry, midgets found ready employment. People of their size were needed to crawl into inaccessible parts of aircraft such as nose cones.

High degree of cooperation. As just suggested, when group members are dependent upon each other, you need a high degree of cooperation to make the group truly effective. To get the job done properly, a house construction team would have to cooperate fully with each other. If the wallboard is put into place before the electrician has finished the internal wiring, it will have to be ripped out. Thus the tradespeople have to cooperate if the house is to be constructed properly and on time.

Another important measure of group effectiveness—employee satisfaction—is generally high when a high degree of cooperation exists. Most employees prefer serenity and cooperation to argumentativeness and intense competition on the job. Many workers feel they have enough stress in life without experiencing more of it because co-workers refuse to cooperate.

Cohesiveness. When group members are attracted to each other and they stick together, we say the group is cohesive. Effective groups are usually cohesive groups. When there is mutual dislike, distrust, and dissension in the group, both productivity and morale are likely to suffer. Successful athletic teams such as the Dallas Cowboys or the Cincinnati Reds are highly cohesive groups, particularly during their winning years.

So long as the cohesive group is on the side of management, the group will be productive. When a cohesive group is angry at management, the result can conceivably be sabotage. Larry, a photo lab technician, describes how group cohesiveness can work against the interests of management:

I was assigned to the night shift operation of this photo lab. The five other fellows and gals working with me and I became good buddies. Management began to hassle us about things like housekeeping and what we were allowed to do on rest breaks. We had installed a cot that we used for napping during our lunch break. Management said the cot had to go. We decided as a group to make some "mistakes" in processing the film until management saw things our way.

One night we made the developer solution too weak which meant that the film we processed that night went back to the customers way underexposed. When our supervisor heard about that mistake, he became very upset. But still management hassled us about little things. Another night we accidentally used fixer instead of developer in the film developing tanks. We ruined all the film that night. When the supervisor found out what happened he demanded to know who caused the problem. We all gave him an innocent "who, me?" stare.

Emotional support to members. An effective work group provides emotional support to its members. Group members rely on each other to help them out over the inevitable rough spots that take place in most job environments. A particularly effective team of supervisors working in an industrial pump company developed a pattern of encouraging each other during troublesome times.

Fred, an inspection supervisor described the support in these terms:

> Although we have a fine company that can afford to hire pretty decent people, we still get some lulus working for us. When I get hot under the collar about one of these characters who just won't put in an honest day's work, I rap about the problem with one of the other supervisors. The problem doesn't go away because of our conversation, but I do feel better about it. Sometimes you get a good idea about handling the problem from talking to another supervisor with the same problem.

Mutual trust and confidence. A group that gives emotional support to its members also has trust and confidence in each other. Effective work groups score high on mutual beliefs and trust. When groups perform dangerous tasks, mutual trust and confidence are of paramount importance. Imagine the apprehension experienced by scuba divers who did not trust the capabilities of the people above water who were responsible for elevating them to the top and who regulated their oxygen supply! A team of heavy equipment operators must also have high trust and confidence in the technical capabilities and integrity of each other. An organizational psychologist has noted that only when groups achieve mutual trust and confidence are they more effective than individuals in solving problems and making decisions.[13]

The right size. Obviously an effective work group must be of the right size. Effective departments headed by one supervisor may vary in size from 3 employees to 60 employees. What is the right size for one type of task may be the wrong size for successfully completing another task. Five may be the right number of people for a company art department. But five people may be too small a number to accomplish the work required of an electroplating department.

A case in point of the importance of the right size for a work group was a neighborhood bakery operated by the owner and six employees. As business volume increased, three more people were hired. Customer service suffered a setback. Employees began to physically get in each others way. The close working conditions led to much conflict among employees. Too many bakery employees spoiled the bakery.

A general guideline is that from five to seven people are the desired maximum when considerable interaction among the people in the group is needed. When a lot of work has to be accomplished and people are not highly dependent upon one another, the group size may be increased without worrying about a loss of effectiveness.

GETTING THE GROUP ON YOUR SIDE[14]

A supervisor must work well with employees and the group as an entity in itself. The importance of the supervisor cultivating the group increases as the group becomes more cohesive. A number of suggestions for achieving a good relationship with a group can be made based on experience and a knowledge of the leadership role. A supervisor who wants to cultivate a good rela-

---

[13] Edgar H. Schein, *Organizational Psychology*, 2d ed. (Englewood Cliffs, N.J.: Prentice-Hall, 1970), p. 95.

[14] Some of the information in this section stems from Andrew J. DuBrin, *Winning at Office Politics* (New York: Van Nostrand Reinhold, 1978).

tionship with subordinates should give careful consideration to these suggestions.

Keep communication channels open.   Many minor problems between supervisor and subordinate fester into major problems. Early intervention in these problems would have prevented them from becoming such a disruptive force. In order to work through little problems, it is important for a supervisor to keep open channels of communication with the group. To the extent that few problems exist between the supervisor and the group, the group tends to be on the side of the supervisor.

An open communication channel serves as an early warning signal about problems. One supervisor made it a practice to have lunch once a month with seven subordinates. It was called the Anything Goes Lunch. One problem the group brought up was that the supervisor was being negligent in ordering office supplies for them. This simple problem was resolved before it escalated into ill will between the supervisor and the group.

Respect and accept the informal leader.   Most work groups have one member who is perceived by other group members as having leadership qualities. Often this informal leader acts as the group spokesperson in matters of importance to the group. Another important function served by the informal leader is that this person is influential in swinging group opinion. A leader who respects the role of the informal leader stands a good chance of establishing and maintaining the support of the group. On the other hand, a supervisor who acts resentful of this role may lose the confidence and support of the group.

Supervisors must proceed delicately in trying to cultivate the informal leader. If it appears that they are trying to bribe the informal leader to sway the group toward supervision, the process may backfire:

> Gus, a supervisor in an automobile body shop, noticed that the mechanics and helpers were leaving their work stations earlier and earlier in order to wash up prior to quitting time. He mentioned the problem several times, but the early leaving persisted. Gus then took aside Hector, the man he thought to be the most influential group member. Gus told Hector that if he were able to get the group to cooperate about not leaving their work stations so early, he would recommend Hector for a salary increase. Hector then told the group that Gus was trying to bribe him to keep the workers in line. The relationship between Gus and the group further deteriorated.

Practice equality.   A supervisor does not have to like all subordinates equally well. But supervisors should try to make assignments on the basis of merit, otherwise they run the risk of being accused of favoritism. Equality thus means that each department member has an equal chance of obtaining whatever rewards the supervisor has to offer providing that person performs well. Being branded as unfair or playing favorites is a primary factor contributing to a supervisor losing the support of the group. A practice such as awarding most of the overtime work to one or two employees quickly leads to charges of favoritism.

Follow through on commitments.   Supervisors who are negligent in following through on commitments to their employees stand a good chance of losing support of the group. Commitments to employees include a variety of major and minor matters, such as conducting performance reviews on time, ordering supplies for the department, helping employees process benefit forms such as medical claims, and inquiring about job transfer or promotion possibilities. Following through on commitments is a simple administrative practice that, in my opinion, helps supervisors to be seen as effective leaders whether or not they have dynamic or charismatic personalities.

Dispense group rewards.   A key strategy in getting the group on your side if you are a supervisor is to reward the group as a whole when such rewards are deserved. Assume a supervisor receives a compliment from higher management that he or she has done an outstanding job. The supervisor in question should share this praise with the group since most accomplishments of a manager reflect a group effort. Biff, a supervisor in a company that provides components for automobiles, explains a remarkably simple yet effective use of a group reward:

> I've been a supervisor for ten years and it took me seven years to hit upon my favorite method of winning the fellows and gals over to my side. One season the fellows and gals had worked their _____ off to meet a large quota established by upper management. As a reward for all that hard work, one morning I brought in two dozen donuts. I told the gang that the donuts were a bonus because they had pulled together so hard to make the department look good. You would have thought I bought everyone a color television. I could really see what a difference this little act of appreciation on my part made. It helped me develop an even better working relationship with my employees.

Be sensitive to human relationships. Many supervisors have made the mistake of trying to be too rational or efficient in their approaches to managing people. If you try to be too scientific in your approach to management, the result could be so mechanistic that you could lose the support of the group. A newly appointed manager of one branch of a chain of home improvement service centers fell into this trap.

Shortly after arriving on the scene the manager decided to reorganize the branch. In doing so, the old cliques of people that worked together as teammates on projects were broken up. The result was the group became alienated from the new manager and productivity and morale suffered.

Support the group. A time-tested supervisory practice that helps bring a group closer to supervisors is for them to defend their groups to higher management. Support of this nature can take many forms. Among the most important is for the supervisor to act as an intermediary in bringing demands made by the group to higher management. Assume that a group of production workers thought the company should provide protective clothing because of a corrosive new chemical now used in the department. However these workers realize that in the past no employees were issued protective clothing unless it were required by legislation. If the supervisor bargained successfully with management for protective clothing for this group, this action would solidify future relationships with the group. A supervisor who supports the group often receives support in return.

SUMMARY OF KEY POINTS

☐ A group has an identity of its own that transcends that of its members. A group is defined as a collection of individuals who regularly interact with each other, who are psychologically aware of each other, and who perceive themselves to be a group.

☐ Among the benefits employees derive from belonging to a work group are learning job-related skills, learning standards of conduct, satisfaction of psychological needs, reduction of tension, and a means to attain ends.

☐ Groups foster employee learning by three primary means: (1) direct instruction, (2) feedback on progress, (3) modeling or imitation.

☐ A formal group is one deliberately formed by the organization to accomplish specific tasks and objectives. Formal groups can be relatively permanent or temporary.

☐ An informal group is a natural grouping of people in work situations that evolves to take care of people's desires for friendship and companionship. An informal group often helps the organization by supplementing the formal organization structure.

☐ Among the characteristics of an effective work group are: technically competent employees, proper leadership, right mix of people with respect to talents and personal characteristics among the members, cohesiveness of members, emotional support to members, mutual trust and confidence, a workable size for the task at hand.

☐ A supervisor who wants to gain the support of a group might use these strategies: Keep channels of communication open with group members. Respect and accept the informal leader. Practice equality—do not play favorites. Follow through on commitments. Dispense group rewards. Be sensitive to human relationships. Support the group in its demands to higher management.

GUIDELINES FOR SUPERVISORY PRACTICE

1. Recognize that it is quite natural for an employee to want to be "one of the gang." Therefore they may identify more strongly with the work group than with management.

2. To do your job effectively, you have to deal with both the formal and informal groups. If the informal group is on your side, it can help get work accomplished.

3. To increase group productivity, you have to give subordinates a clear picture of what you want accomplished. In addition, you should show an interest in their welfare.

4. Getting the group on your side is an important part of your job. Among the ways to achieve this objective are: Keep communication channels open. Respect and accept the informal leader. Practice equality—do not play favorites. Follow through on commitments. Dispense group rewards. Be sensitive to human relationships. Help the group achieve its legitimate requests from higher management.

1. Suppose you and six strangers were stuck in an elevator. The seven of you worked together to plan an escape. Explain whether or not you people would be considered a group?

2. Should a supervisor act like any other employee in the department? Why or why not?

3. What benefits have you personally derived from working in a group?

4. If so much learning takes place in a work group, why do most companies have training departments?

5. What group norms are present in the classroom in which you are taking this course?

6. Think of somebody you know who prefers to work alone rather than in a group. What personality characteristics does this individual seem to possess?

7. Name three formal groups in which you are currently a member. Explain why you classify each as a formal group.

8. Give three examples of informal groups you have observed in a work setting.

9. Do you think you would prefer working in a permanent or a temporary formal work group? Give the reasons for your answer.

10. How do the Dallas Cowboys (or any other very successful athletic team in particular) fit the various characteristics of a successful group described in this chapter?

11. Think of a supervisor you know who lost the support of a work group. What went wrong?

12. How big do you think a group can get in terms of numbers of people before it no longer seems like a group? Explain your reasoning.

A supervisory problem: Everybody does it around here

You are the supervisor of three dry cleaning stores. Each outlet is operated by one store clerk plus the managerial assistance you provide. During two impromptu visits to your locations you uncover two violations of the same company policy. In one store you discover that the clerk in charge has borrowed a dress belonging to a customer. When confronted with the problem she says, "Hey, don't pick on me, the woman who worked here before me did the same thing. She told me management didn't care so long as we returned the clothing clean and in good shape. I never have held up a customer's dress for more than a day."

You advise your clerk that such an action is against company rules. But you decide to postpone disciplinary action until you think about the problem some more. The next day you discover that the clerk in charge of one of your other stores has borrowed a customer's leather jacket. You bring the discretion to his attention. He replies, "I haven't done anything wrong. It's all part of the game around here. Borrowing fancy clothes from customers is one of the fringe benefits of working for a dry cleaners. Everybody does it around here. With the amount of money we are paid, we sure need some fringe benefits."

1. *Why is this supervisory problem included in a chapter about people in work groups?*
2. *How would you handle the situation?*
3. *If such borrowing of customer clothing is common practice, do you think you should put a halt to such behavior? Why or why not?*

SOME SUGGESTED READING

Hackman, J. Richard. "Group Influences on Individuals." In *Handbook of Industrial and Organizational Psychology.* Edited by Marvin D. Dunnette. Chicago: Rand McNally, 1976, pp. 1455–1525.

Homans, George. *The Human Group.* New York: Harcourt, Brace & World, 1950.

House, William C. "Effects of Group Cohesiveness on Organization Performance." *Personnel Journal,* January 1966, pp. 28–33.

Lau, James B. *Behavior in Organizations: An Experiential Approach.* Rev. ed. Homewood, Ill.: Richard D. Irwin, Inc., 1979.

Leavitt, Harold J. *Managerial Psychology.* Chicago: University of Chicago Press, 1972.

Maier, Norman R. F. *Problem Solving and Creativity in Individuals and Groups.* Monterey, Calif.: Brooks/Cole, 1970.

Roy, David. "Quota Restriction and Goldbricking in a Machine Shop." *American Journal of Sociology* (1962), pp. 427–42.

Shaw, Marvin E. *Group Dynamics.* New York: McGraw-Hill, 1971.

Smith, Peter B. *Groups within Organizations.* New York: Harper & Row, 1973.

Tosi, Henry L., and Hamner, W. Clay. *Organizational Behavior and Management: A Contingency Approach.* Chicago: St. Clair Press, 1974, pt. 4.

Zander, Alvin. *Groups at Work.* San Francisco: Jossey-Bass, 1977.

_____. *Motives and Goals in Groups.* New York: Academic Press, 1971.

The total organization

4

LEARNING OBJECTIVES

After reading and thinking through the material in this chapter, you should be able to:

1. Discuss the major forms of organization (types of organizational structure).
2. Explain the concept of line versus staff authority.
3. Understand the difference between the functional and project forms of organization.
4. Identify the kinds of tasks best suited for the functional and project forms of organization.
5. Draw your own diagram of a matrix organization and label the most important features.
6. Describe the essential features of a bureaucracy, including some of its potential problems.

An organization is a collection of many things: people, groups, machines, buildings, money, information flow, tradition, and attitudes. To understand your work environment you have to understand the basics of how organizations operate and how they are designed. Today a whole body of knowledge, called organizational theory, has emerged that tries and makes sense of those entities called organizations. Just as psychology emphasizes the understanding of people, organizational theory attempts to explain the nature of organizations.

In this chapter we explain some basic concepts about organizational theory, but that does not imply that the other 18 chapters in this book won't help you understand the nature of organizations. As a case in point, our next chapter deals with office politics. Supervisors would have a difficult time surviving in most organizations if they ignored political byplay.

THE FORMAL AND INFORMAL ORGANIZATIONS

In the preceding chapter we discussed the difference between formal and informal groups. They represent major components of the formal and informal organizations, respectively. In general, the formal organization is anything written down that describes how the organization is supposed to operate. A job description is part of the formal organization. So is the organization chart, the safety manual, regulations about overtime pay, and rules about accepting gifts from vendors. Some large organizations have elaborate manuals that basically represent the formal organizational structure. Among the items you would probably find in a typical manual of this nature would be organizational objectives, organizational policies and procedures, organization charts, job descriptions for key executives, and guidelines for executive titles.[1]

As you might have inferred from our description so far, a formal organization is "that which is legally constituted or decreed by those in authority."[2] It represents how the organization is supposed to function. In practice, the formal organization is supplemented by a looser unwritten arrangement. After the formal organization is laid down, the informal one springs up according to need. It is akin to custom and takes a long time to evolve.

Suppose you are a supervisor in a plastics company. One of your best workers is granted a maternity leave of absence. She tells you she will be back in four months. You need a competent employee to take her place during her absence. Using the formal organization you would put a request in writing to the personnel department. They, in turn, would process your request and interview applicants for this temporary job. You would get your replacement, but it might take a long time.

Instead you use the informal organization. You ask Sue if she has a friend who might want to take over her job during her absence. Sue gleefully tells you the next morning that a good friend of hers (whom she knows to be a very reliable person) would love to take over her job. You arrange for her friend to be

---

[1] William F. Glueck, *Management* (Hinsdale, Ill.: The Dryden Press, 1977), p. 447.

[2] Howard M. Carlisle, *Management: Concepts and Situations* (Chicago: Science Research Associates, 1976), p. 332.

interviewed by the personnel department. Your recommendation carries a lot of weight, and the replacement is hired. You have just made good use of the informal organization.

Meshing of the formal and informal organizations.   As in the case of the pregnant plastic worker, the formal and informal organizations often work in the service of each other. When this occurs, the organizational theorist says there is an integration of the formal and informal structures. One successful meshing of the formal and informal structures took place in a medium-size company:[3]

> A snow shovel manufacturer suddenly found itself faced with an unprecedented backlog of orders one severe winter. Reliance on the formal structure alone would have made it very difficult to meet such a demand. A company policy states: "We shall not incur additional manufacturing costs due to shipping charges levied by suppliers. Suppliers are therefore not authorized to charge us shipping costs for any method of special delivery."
>
> Literal application of this rule would have made it impossible to receive a rush shipment of plastic needed for shovel blades. The head of manufacturing therefore sought an ethical and constructive way around this policy. His decision was to rent a truck for purposes of picking up 1,000 pounds of plastic at their usual supplier. The truck rental fee was then allocated to "business travel." By this informal bending of the formal structure, an emergency situation was solved without violating a company rule. This judicious use of the informal organization was possible because the head of manufacturing had not used up his business travel for the quarter.

LINE AND STAFF AUTHORITY

Jack, a painter used to work in a staff department. Wanting more power, Jack found himself a job in a line department, yet he is still a painter. Jack made the switch from staff to line by resigning from his job in the maintenance department of a large company. He then joined his brother-in-law's construction firm. Jack is still a painter, but he has more power.

Jack's situation illustrates the basic distinction between line and staff. Line activities or units are associated with the primary

---

[3] Andrew J. DuBrin, *Fundamentals of Organizational Behavior: An Applied Perspective,* 2d ed. (Elmsford, N.Y.: Pergamon, 1978), p. 420. Reprinted with permission.

purpose of an organization. If you work for a hospital and you are involved in patient care, you are a line worker or supervisor. If you are an accountant working for an accounting firm, you are a line worker. But an accountant in a hospital is considered staff. (The description of a supervisor's job in Chapter 1 made some of these distinctions.) A staff activity is an advisory or support function. The contribution made by staff personnel is thus indirect. A data processing department in a food service company is a staff department. A food service department (the cafeteria) in a computer company is a staff or support function.

Blurring of line and staff. In practice, the distinction between line and staff is not always so clear-cut. Some modern writers about management have even abandoned the terms *line* and *staff*. (The replacement concepts include terms such as *production subsystems* and *maintenance subsystems*, which essentially translate back to line and staff.)[4] Generally, line departments have line authority. They have the power to make crucial decisions about the primary activities of the organization. Staff groups have staff authority in relation to other departments. They have line authority within their own departments. In today's complex legal environment, staff departments are acquiring more and more authority.

The finance department is one example of a blurring between line and staff. Finance is generally considered a staff function in a manufacturing or sales organization. Yet if the financial analysts say a particular product could not be made or sold at a profit, their recommendation will be treated as if it were an order.

ORGANIZATION BY FUNCTION OR DEPARTMENT

Anybody who has ever worked for a company, attended school, or gone shopping has already been exposed to the functional or departmental form of organization. Even the neighborhood lemonade stand that springs up in hot weather is a mini-example of the functional organization. One seven-year-old prepares the lemonade (the manufacturing or production department). A partner sells the finished product (the sales or mar-

---

[4] Henry L. Tosi and Stephen J. Carroll, *Management: Contingencies, Structure, and Process* (Chicago: St. Clair Press, 1976), pp. 180–88.

FIGURE 4–1
Typical functional organization

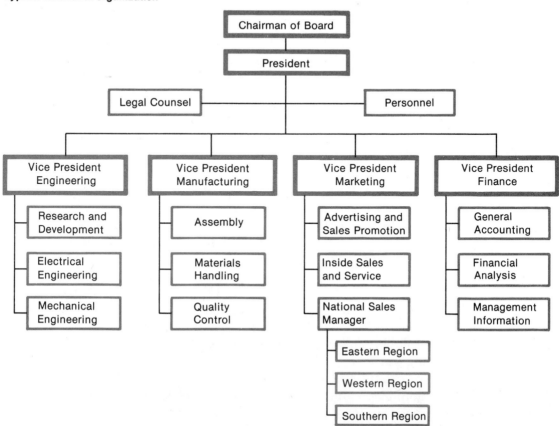

keting department). Inevitably, the first customer is more of a taster and judge (quality control department) than a customer.

Functional organization is the traditional or classical arrangement of large- and small-scale effort. In a functional organization, departments are arranged according to the activity or process they perform such as accounting or purchasing. The Industrial Revolution was based on functional organization, particularly with respect to large-scale specialization of effort. When different departments perform different functions, we have the conventional organizational arrangement. A typical functional organization is illustrated in Figure 4–1. Sole reliance upon a functional organizational structure is becoming infrequent in large companies, yet the functional organization still offers several important advantages.

Functional organizations allow for the benefit of specialization. A medium-sized organization might be able to afford one small operations research department, but could not have one operations research specialist assigned full time to each department. Functional organizations also allow for the *retention* of staff specialists, because career paths are provided for these people. Staff specialists who identify with their profession or occupation rather than their organization often prefer the functional-type arrangement. Said one computer specialist, "After all, it gets pretty lonely out in a decentralized location with no other software people to talk with." Scientists typically prefer to work in centralized laboratories (functional organizations) because of the physical resources and intellectual stimulation offered by such arrangements.

Staff specialists are able to give particular attention to important activities outside of their own small departments, an arrangement known as *functional authority.* Thus, the staff vice president of management development keeps a watchful eye on the developmental activities of both centralized and decentralized units, and this combination of the audit function and professional expertise should benefit the organization.

Functional organizations are particularly well suited to carrying out large-scale repetitive processes. Hershey chocolate bars, for example, lend themselves quite well to functional organization, as do Gideon Bibles and Gillette stainless steel blades. All these are mass produced, well-accepted products with relatively predictable demand.

Disadvantages of functional organizations have been even more closely observed than their advantages. Several of the disadvantages to be discussed below, however, may well be the combined influence between the functional arrangement and organizational size. Complexity and bigness of an organization alone may create morale and identity problems for many people.

"Tunnel vision" and *self-centeredness* are encouraged by functional organization arrangements.[5] Psychological barriers ultimately accompany the physical barriers that are erected between departments or divisions. Oft repeated is the plant man-

---

[5] Walter R. Mahler, "Structuring the Organization," in *Handbook of Business Administration,* ed. H. B. Maynard (New York: McGraw-Hill, 1967), p. 22, sect. 2.

ager's lament: "If I could only get my supervisors to take an overall company point of view." Underlying this narrowness of viewpoint may be the pressures created by having departments competing for the same resources.

Overspecialization can lead to low morale at all levels in the organization. Many, if not the majority, of people find tasks lacking in challenge and excitement once they are mastered. This is true of the well-motivated test-tube technician or the financial analyst with an MBA from the Wharton School. Studies conducted by Worthy at Sears, Roebuck and Company in the early 1950s reached a conclusion that holds true today: Over-functionalization destroys the meaning of the job for the employee.[6]

Delays in accomplishing important tasks are characteristic of functional organizations. Reasons underlying these delays include the poor coordination of effort typical of the functional organization. No one individual in the functional organization besides the company or division head has complete responsibility for costs and profits.

Functional organizations are often ill suited to performing complex tasks, particularly those that differ markedly from the on-going activities of the organization. Project-type organizations have spawned from functional organizations for precisely this reason—the necessity of accomplishing a complex or special purpose mission.

THE PROJECT WAY OF ACCOMPLISHING TASKS

Project management in practice is a term that refers to several related forms of organizational groupings, among them task force, product management, and program management. Despite the various terms, project management invariably involves a temporary group of specialists from diverse disciplines working under a single manager to accomplish a fixed objective or purpose. Project management has achieved its highest popularity in the military, aerospace, and construction industries. Project

---

[6] James C. Worthy, "Organizational Structure and Employee Morale," *American Sociological Review*, April 1950, pp. 169–79.

management as practiced in the United States and Canada has four general characteristics.[7]

1. Project managers operate independently of the normal chain of command and usually report directly to a member of top management.

2. Project managers negotiate directly for their human, financial, and material resources with the heads of line and staff departments whose personnel perform the task assignments for a given project.

3. Project managers serve primarily as coordinators of the organizational forces necessary to complete the project's goals. They are thus accountable for the project's ultimate success or failure, but not always accountable for the performance of the people assigned to the project tasks.

4. The organizational life of a project ends when its objectives are accomplished. (Functional organizations, in contrast, are usually considered to be permanent.)

Project organizations in this chapter are becoming the predominant form of organizational life. Probably no complex organization exists today without some variety of project management contained within its structure. A supervisor is often given the opportunity to work on a project at sometime during a career. It can be a refreshing change from working in a line department. Two types of project organizations worth noting here are individual and staff projects.[8]

Individual project. This type of project management is generally established to coordinate a relatively small task requiring a minimum of human and material resources. Managing a zero-defect or safety campaign are two examples of individual project organization. All work for the project is done within the functional departments (for instance, manufacturing or quality control), and only clerical personnel report directly to the project head. The project manager lacks any direct authority over the functional personnel who perform different project tasks. Indi-

---

[7] Per Jonason, "Project Management, Swedish Style," *Harvard Business Review,* November–December 1971, p. 106.

[8] John P. Cicero and David L. Wilemon, "Project Authority—A Multidimensional View," *IEEE Transactions on Engineering Management,* May 1970, pp. 53–56.

vidual project managers must rely on interpersonal influence (charm) and technical competence to accomplish their mission.

Staff project. The staff project organization is slightly larger in scope than the individual project organization. Projects taken on by the staff organization can be substantial. Conducting an automotive recall program (repairing automobiles already in the hands of customers) is an example of the staff project organization. In aerospace the project manager and subordinates may have responsibility for directing and controlling such functions as project planning, financial planning and control, contract administration, test reliability, and quality assurance. Staff personnel and clerical support report directly to the project manager. Identical to the individual project organization, all functional work for the project is done in the original functional areas of the organization. For instance, this form of project organization would not have its own engineering or manufacturing department.

Staff project managers vary considerably in the amount of formal authority they exert over operating personnel. At one extreme, the staff organization may operate basically as a coordinating body for the functional areas. In this situation, formal authority can only be exerted over staff personnel directly under the project manager's control. At the other extreme, staff project managers may enjoy the luxury of having several individuals for each project area directly under their control. In general, the larger scale the project, the more formal authority given the project manager to accomplish the project's mission.

Classical Principles of Organization

> General guidelines for designing and running organizations were developed during the first 45 or so years of this century. These classical principles still have value to the modern organization, providing they are followed in light of particular circumstances. Twelve of the more widely accepted principles are presented below. They reflect the thinking of contributors to management thought such as Frederick W. Taylor, Henri Fayol, Henry L. Gantt, Lyndall F. Urwick, and Chester Barnard.*
>
> **Specialization of labor.** Work should be divided up among people in such a manner as to produce more and better work with the same effort. Also referred to as the division of work principles.

Classical Principles of Organization (*continued*)

Departmentalization. Work should be organized into logical departments. Among the ways in which departments are assigned include the process performed, the product made, customers served, and geographic region.

Span of control. When the work of subordinates interlocks with one another, no manager should supervise more than five or six subordinates directly. More generally, there is a limit to the number of subordinates a manager can manage effectively.

Unity of command. No subordinate should report to more than one superior at any one time. Doing otherwise leads to the problem of conflict in instructions.

The scalar principle. The line of authority begins at the top of the organization and moves on down to the bottom of the organization. The more clear this line of authority, the more effective will be decision making and communication within the organization.

Delegation. Authority delegated to an individual manager should be sufficient to assure that this manager has the ability to accomplish the desired results.

Responsibility. Superiors must accept responsibility for the work activities of their subordinates. The subordinate has absolute authority responsibility for authority received by way of delegation.

Parity of authority and responsibility. Whenever authority is exercised, responsibility arises. In order to accomplish a delegated task effectively, your authority should match your responsibility.

Authority-level principle. If you have the proper authority to make a decision, you should make that decision and not refer it upward in the organization.

Principle of balance. The application of principles or techniques must be balanced in light of the total organizational requirements for achieving goals.

Principle of flexibility. If management has to deal with a changing environment, it is important to build flexibility into the organization structure.

Subordination of individual interest to general interest. The interests of one employee or group of employees (including managers) should not take priority over the interest of the total organization.

---

* Classical principles of organization are summarized concisely (along with appropriate references) in these two sources: Robert L. Trewatha and M. Gene Newport, *Management: Functions and Behavior,* rev. ed. (Dallas: Business Publications, Inc., 1979), pp. 560–62; and Harold Koontz and Cyril O'Donnell, *Principles of Management: An Analysis of Managerial Functions,* 4th ed. (New York: McGraw-Hill, 1968), pp. 423–29.

Advantages of project organizations

In general, project organizations overcome most of the disadvantages of functional organizations. Project organizations help overcome tunnel vision and organizational egocentricity, allow greater opportunity for achieving broad experience, and in many instances overcome the problems of specialization. Three specific advantages of the project organization not already mentioned are mentioned here.

First, project management encourages identification with the project or product. Overt enthusiasm and "dedication to the cause," to cite one illustration, were rampant among personnel working on the Apollo (moon landing) project. In place of "we in manufacturing" versus "them in quality control," it was "us going to the moon."

Second, project management is well suited for dealing with the unpredictable situation or series of situations. Project organization is inherently flexible because so few employees are permanently attached to its structure. Quick rearrangements of personnel can be made to respond to shifts in consumer demand. Illustrative is the mercurial phase-out of project teams established to bid on large government contracts once the company is out of the running for the contract award.

Third, project management is ideally suited for such special assignments as developing a new product, building a new factory, and investigating departures from the traditional mission of an organization.[9] It is more economical for organizations to work with a new venture on a project basis than to commit vast resources before the profitability of the new venture is reliably determined. Corporate embarrassment can be avoided, for example, if an entire new division is not erected to support a product that may meet with limited consumer demands.

Disadvantages of project organizations

Despite the array of advantages to project forms of organization, it is not without some serious limitations. Three are particularly noteworthy.

---

[9] C. J. Middleton, "How to Set up a Project Organization," *Harvard Business Review*, March–April 1967, p. 74.

First, project organizations create many human problems. Insecurity about possible unemployment, career retardation, and personal development is felt by subordinates in project organizations to be significantly more of a problem than by subordinates in functional organizations.[10] Once a given project is completed, the manager or professional frequently must go through the agonizing process of finding new employment within or outside the firm. One project manager commented: "Regardless of whether the project has a six-month or a six-year life, eventually it will end and the project people know this. They feel the phasing out of a project as a dramatic threat to their security, and the nearer they get to the end the more their anxieties build up."

Second, project managers, to a higher degree than functional managers, feel they are subject to an overdose of make-work assignments. Underlying this problem is a basic explanation. Once a project begins to phase out, the better people are retained rather than laid off. Keeping them busy involves putting them on available work which is "legitimate" but less professionally demanding than their assignments at the height of the project's activity.

Third, complicated authority problems are created by project forms of organization. The project manager typically has to rely more upon personal influence than formal authority in accomplishing the project mission. Strain is thus created upon project managers lacking in strong personal leadership characteristics.

MATRIX ORGANIZATION

A matrix organization is a combination of the functional organization with the project organization. Matrix management attempts to capitalize upon the benefits of specialization (functional organization) and teamwork (project organization). Matrix management is often called *program* management. Similar to project management, the term *matrix management* has different meanings in different organizations. Within the aerospace industry the term *matrix* refers to an organization in which the project

---

[10] Clayton Reeser, "Some Potential Human Problems of the Project Form of Organization," *Academy of Management Journal,* December 1969, p. 467.

FIGURE 4–2.
A matrix type of organization*

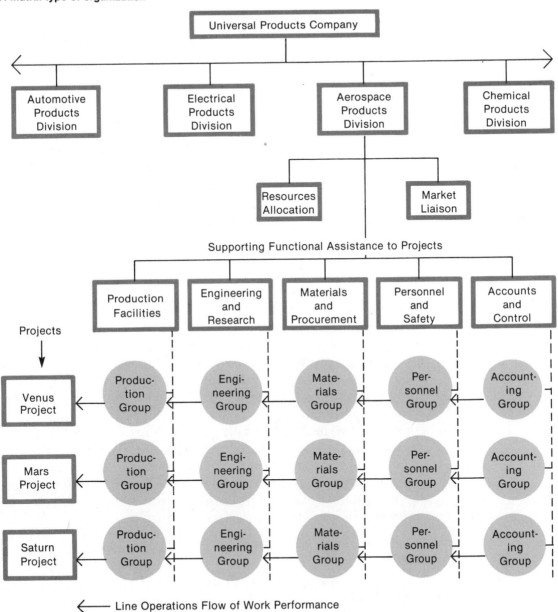

← —— Line Operations Flow of Work Performance

* Project managers borrow personnel for their project teams. Employees return to their functional units (departments) for reassignment at termination of project.)

Source: John F. Mee, "Matrix Management," *Business Horizons,* Summer 1964, p. 71. Copyright 1964 by the Foundation for the School of Business at Indiana University. Reprinted by permission.

manager must borrow the bulk of needed resources from functional organizations or departments.

Program refers to an organization in which a substantial proportion of the human and physical resources are under the direct control of the project manager. Today's large organizations retain some allegiance to functional departments but also utilize project, product, or program managers for specific purposes. Matrix management is thus widespread, even though it is found under different labels. For purposes of simplicity, a matrix organization can be visualized as the superimposition of any form of project or product management upon an already established functional organization.

A conception of the matrix organization is presented in Figure 4-2. The key portion of this figure is found under the Aerospace Products Division. Note that project managers (for example, the person in charge of the Venus Project) borrow talent from such functional groups as Production Facilities or Materials & Procurement. Note also both the economy and the complexity of this arrangement. Venus, Mars, and Saturn project managers all borrow personnel and physical resources from the same functional group. After completion of their project assignment, employees report back to their departments and regular superiors.

The primary advantage of matrix organization is that it combines the advantages of functional and project groupings. Similarly, matrix management is also beset with the disadvantages of project and functional organizations. Although the presence of project or product managers facilitates control and coordination, squabbling over power and uncertain authority can be rampant. Another unfortunate disadvantage of matrix organization is that its sheer complexity, in many instances, has a depressing effect upon morale. When organizations become highly complex, a decrease in job satisfaction is often the result.

THE BUREAUCRATIC ORGANIZATION

"Aggravation, aggravation," said Pedro. "You would think our $20 million company was General Motors. All I want is some simple information about how many parts my customer in Toledo received. Instead of facts, I get some apologies about the company shifting from one system of accounting to another.

Nobody can give me a direct answer on whether or not my customer's order has been filled. I ask myself, 'What are we in business for?'"[11]

Pedro is not alone in his lament. As organizations grow in size, they develop elaborate sets of rules and regulations for conducting their affairs in an efficient manner. Often the move toward this highly efficient, bureaucratic form of organization backfires. What the frustrated individual calls "red tape," the policy maker calls "formal policies and procedures"—elements necessary to keep an organization running smoothly. In the past bureaucracies were exclusively function or departmental organizations. (The term *bureau* is a french word for office or department.) Today large bureaucracies such as General Electric or American Motors are a combination of functional, project, and matrix organizations.

Bureaucracies have seven important characteristics in common.[12] If all of these characteristics worked as designed, a bureaucracy would indeed be a highly efficient form or organization. IBM is one example of a highly efficient bureaucracy. So are McDonald's and the Dallas Cowboys.

A multitude of rules and regulations. In a perfect bureaucracy a supervisor would have little judgment to exercise. Whenever a problem arose, or a decision had to be made, the supervisor would refer to the company manual for the correct answer. An employee might ask a supervisor, "My daughter is the first American Indian to become an astronaut. She is being honored today by the president of the United States. May I have the afternoon off to attend?" In a perfect bureaucracy the supervisor would reply, "I'll have the answer for you in a minute. Let me check the organization manual under 'Special events justifying an afternoon off with pay.' The manual covers every possible contingency."

Impersonality. When rules and regulations exist for the conduct of personnel administration, favoritism is minimized and in

---

[11] Andrew J. DuBrin, *Survival in the Office* (New York: Van Nostrand Reinhold, 1977), p. 47.

[12] This list of seven characteristics was synthesized by Don Hellriegel and John W. Slocum, Jr., *Management: Contingency Approaches*, 2d ed. (Reading, Mass.: Addison-Wesley, 1978), pp. 62–68.

many cases eliminated. *Impersonal* means that everybody is treated the same without playing favorites. At its best it means that no one employee will be given special consideration over others. If a janitor is not allowed to smoke a cigar in the employee lounge, neither is the company president. Even if you smile at the civil servant in the motor vehicle bureau, you will not get a better price on your license plates than would a grouch.

Specialization. In a perfect bureaucracy there would be no overlap among jobs. Every individual would perform a task that she or he knew best. In many instances more than one person would be performing the same job, but it would be by design, not happenstance. Most of the jobs would be broken down into smaller units. The training time to learn new jobs would thus be at a minimum. If a finished parts supervisor retired, that supervisor could readily be replaced by a subordinate. The advantage of task specialization to the organization is that individual workers become more efficient. At the same time, the organization has less reliance on the skills of any one individual.

Overspecialization can reach a point of diminishing returns. When workers are bored by their jobs and rebel against the monotony, the advantages of specialization are lost. As will be discussed in Chapter 8, proper design of jobs can sometimes alleviate the problems of overspecialization. By using methods such as job enrichment, productivity is increased because people become more interested in their jobs.

Multilayered structure. Most large organizations are shaped like pyramids or hierarchies. At the highest level, the job holders have the most power. At each successive level, the job holders have less power than the people above. In some organizations, the first-level manager is 12 rungs below the president. The only people with less power than the supervisor are individual performers such as clerks and production workers. Although bureaucracies are designed to distribute power and influence equally at each organizational level, it rarely works that way in practice. Some functions have more power than others. For instance, marketing usually carries more weight (has more power) than personnel or purchasing.

Fair promotions.   In a bureaucracy people are supposed to be promoted strictly on the basis of job competence. Those promoted to higher positions should have more skills and ability than the people they supervise. The federal Civil Service attempts to make promotions equitable by basing them on competitive examinations and seniority. Under ideal circumstances, playing office politics will not get you promoted in a bureaucracy.

Rational authority.   A bureaucracy is very specific about who has how much authority. You obey orders according to the rank (organizational level) of an individual. If your boss tells you to paint a machine green, you paint it green. If your boss's boss says she hates green and prefers blue, you change the color to blue. If her boss says change the machine back to green, you repaint.

Another implication of rational authority is that workers should not be influenced by the charm or personal appeal of their leaders. A leader's place on the organization chart should determine how much influence that individual has with subordinates. A dynamic, intelligent, and witty first-level supervisor should exert less pull in the organization than a nondynamic, not very bright, and unfunny vice president. (Of course, in a perfect bureaucracy the latter individual might not have become a vice president.)

Logical goals.   A bureaucracy is a logical, rational organization. Every action that is carried out is directed toward achieving an organizational goal. Under ideal circumstances every action taken by an employee at the bottom of the organization contributes to an overall goal at the top. A file clerk working in the Pentagon might file an article about a hand weapon developed in Soviet Russia. This action will contribute in some small way to the Pentagon's overall mission of protecting the United States from potential enemies.

PROBLEMS CREATED BY A BUREAUCRACY

The characteristics of a bureaucracy just described are also the potential advantages of such an organization structure. In practice, a bureaucracy is often an inefficient, cumbersome, and frustrating place to work. Managers in bureaucracies are often aware of these problems but feel helpless to overcome them. An author wrote to a large publisher, inquiring whether they would be interested in examining a just completed manuscript. Three months later an editor wrote the author stating that the publisher would be interested in reviewing the manuscript. The editor commented, "I'm sorry it took me three months to answer your letter, but it got chewed up in our corporate machinery." In the interim the author signed a contract for the book with a small publisher.

Among the many unfortunate side effects of a bureaucracy are rigid rules and slow decision making.[13] These two side effects are worth examining because they contribute to a variety of other problems. Much of the frustration and dissatisfaction that takes place in a bureaucracy stems from these two factors.

Rigid rules are characteristic of most bureaucracies. People who work in a bureaucracy sometimes rigidly enforce rules to avoid risk taking. A credit manager in a store refused to grant credit to a company president because this executive had worked for the same employer less than a year. Prior to the present position, the executive had been vice president for five years with another company. The president was infuriated with the ruling and vowed never to make a purchase at that particular store. In addition the executive demanded an interview with the store manager (who then reversed the credit manager's decision). When asked why an exception wasn't made to the one-year rule for the executive, the credit manager replied: "I didn't want to stick my neck out. Sure, I realized this individual would be a good credit risk. Maybe there was one chance in 100 that the person would prove to be a deadbeat. But if that one chance in 100 came through, I could be nailed for having violated the rule about not giving credit to people who have worked for their present employer less than one year.

Delay of decision making is characteristic of many bureaucracies. Most of them move painfully slow on complex decisions. The delay comes about because a large number of people have to concur before a final decision is made about issues of importance. One frustrated building owner complained that it took four months for the city to issue him a Certificate of Occupancy

---

[13] Ibid., pp. 69–70.

(a certification that the building adheres to the city building code, allowing a transfer of title) after the building had passed inspection. During the delay the prospective buyer backed out of the contract. One of the explanations given the landlord for the length of time required for the issuing of the certificate was that six separate signatures are required.

SUMMARY OF KEY POINTS

- ☐ A formal organization is a written or graphic description of how the organization is supposed to operate. The informal organization is an unwritten and sometimes unspoken arrangement of work activities that supplement the formal organization. Under ideal circumstances the formal and informal organizations work together to help the total organization.
- ☐ A common way of assigning authority is between staff and line departments. Line departments conduct work directly associated with the primary purpose of an organization. Staff departments serve in an advisory or supporting capacity. The distinction between line and staff is sometimes blurred.
- ☐ A functional organization arranges its departments by the activity or process they perform. This traditional type of organization is well suited to accomplishing specific repetitive tasks such as manufacturing automobile tires. Intergroup conflict is common in functional organizations.
- ☐ A project organization is a grouping of people and other resources according to purpose such as launching a new product or landing on Mars. Projects may be small teams or large-scale efforts. Project organizations are well suited for special assignments. Among their disadvantages is the problem of placing people in jobs after a project is terminated.
- ☐ A matrix organization is a combination of the functional and project organizations. Matrix management thus attempts to capitalize on the benefits of specialization (functional organization) and teamwork (project organization).
- ☐ Bureaucracy is a form of organization designed for maximum efficiency. It is characterized by many rules and regulations, a high degree of specialization, a multilayered shape, and rational authority. In practice, bureaucracies often become inefficient as rules and regulations are followed rigidly and decision making is slowed down.

GUIDELINES FOR SUPERVISORY PRACTICE

1. To be an effective supervisor, you must understand the workings of both the formal and informal organization. Learning how the informal organization operates will take longer.

2. All things being equal, you will have more power and authority if you work in a line rather than a staff department. If you belong to a staff group you will have to rely heavily on personal influence in getting things accomplished through other departments.

3. If you work in a functional department, check from time-to-time to see that you and your employees are not becoming too narrow in your viewpoint about your department's importance in relation to others.

4. Similar to working for a staff group, you may have uncertain authority as a member of a project team. You should ask for clarification about the extent of your authority.

5. Being assigned to a project, particularly a successful one, can represent a real boost to your career. As a project member, you are often noticed by influential people in the company.

6. Don't be needlessly frustrated because you work in a bureaucracy. Proper use of its carefully drawn rules and regulations can help you deal effectively with employee requests and complaints.

QUESTIONS FOR DISCUSSION AND REVIEW

1. Give two examples of how the informal organization operates in the place where you work (or most recently worked).

2. What is the formal organization governing the course for which you are reading this book?

3. Line supervisors often feel less powerful than staff specialists. How can this be true considering that line personnel are supposed to be more powerful than staff personnel?

4. Do you think you are better suited by temperament to work in a line or staff department? Why?

5. Is a supermarket a functional or project organization? Explain.

6. Are movies produced by functional or project organizations, or a combination of both? Explain.

7. Organizations are said to use different organization structures at different stages in their history. Explain why this is true.

8. Why does morale tend to be higher in project than functional organizations?

9. Compare the popular meaning of the term *bureaucracy* with the meaning presented in this chapter.

10. What is a *bureaucrat*? Why is the term almost always used in an uncomplimentary manner?

A supervisory problem: The department handyman

Alstair Wentworth, vice president of manufacturing, was visiting the British Vancouver plant of his company. While touring the plant floor he noticed a young man busily engaged in building shelves. The tools he used included a Black and Decker home power saw. Wentworth asked the shelf builder for the name of his supervisor. Wentworth then called for a private meeting with Keefe, the man's supervisor.

Wentworth: Keefe, are you aware of the irregularity taking place on the shop floor. You have a handyman out there building shelves with his own equipment on company time. Have you turned over your department into a hobby shop? I don't like what I see.

Keefe: Mr. Wentworth, no disrespect sir. But the young man you refer to is building shelves for our store room. Yes, he's using his own equipment. He claims his handsaw is better than anything we have in the shop. The wood he's using is mostly scraps we've scrounged around for.

Wentworth: I still don't like the idea. You're going around company rules and probably committing about five safety violations in the process. Stop this activity at once. If you want new shelves for the store room, call the maintenance department.

Keefe: But don't you see Mr. Wentworth, if we go through proper channels for a job like this it won't get done for a year. Somebody higher up will tell us to wait until the next fiscal year. I've gone round and round on that problem before. But if I don't get some new shelves in our store room, the place will be so messy that I will be reprimanded for sloppy housekeeping.

Wentworth: Keefe, I'm telling you to stop breaking company rules.

1. *What does this incident illustrate about a bureaucracy?*
2. *How might Keefe use the Framework for Accomplishing Results, presented in Chapter 1, to solve his problem?*
3. *Do you think it's right for Wentworth to speak directly to Keefe? Or should he speak first to the plant manager? Or somebody else in Keefe's chain of command?*

SOME SUGGESTED READING

Dalton, Gene W., Barnes, Louis B., and Zaleznik, Abraham. *The Distribution of Authority in Formal Organizations.* Cambridge, Mass.: The MIT Press, 1973.

Donavid, J. D. "The Bureaucracy Lives." *Dun's Review,* April 1972, pp. 93–96.

Drucker, Peter F. *Management: Tasks, Responsibilities, and Practices.* New York: Harper & Row, 1974.

————. *The Concept of the Corporation.* New York: John Day, 1946.

French, Wendell L.; Bell, Cecil H., Jr.; and Zawacki, Robert A., eds. *Organization Development: Theory, Practice, and Research.* Dallas; Business Publications, Inc., 1978.

Jackson, John H., and Morgan, Cyril P. *Organization Theory: A Macro Perspective for Management.* Englewood Cliffs, N.J.: Prentice-Hall, 1978.

Hanan, Mack. "Reorganizing Your Company around Its Markets." *Harvard Business Review,* November–December 1974, pp. 63–74.

Hummel, Ralph P. *The Bureaucratic Experience.* New York: St. Martin's, 1977.

Katz, Daniel, and Kahn, Robert L. *The Social Psychology of Organizations.* 2d ed. New York: Wiley, 1978.

Leavitt, Harold J. *Managerial Psychology.* 4th ed. Chicago: University of Chicago Press, 1978, chaps. 24–30.

Miner, John B. *The Management Process: Theory, Research and Practice.* 2d ed. New York: The Macmillan Co., 1978, chaps. 14–17.

Stewart, John M. "Making Project Management Work." *Business Horizons,* Fall 1965, pp. 54–68.

Wileman, David L., and Cicero, John P. "The Project Manager—Anomalies and Ambiguities." *Academy of Management Journal,* September 1970, pp. 269–82.

Office politics

LEARNING OBJECTIVES

After reading and thinking through the material in this chapter, you should be able to:

1. Explain the meaning of the term *office politics*.
2. Give several reasons why office politics is so widespread.
3. Identify and explain several techniques people use to impress their boss.
4. Identify and explain several techniques people use to gain or maintain power.
5. Draw a distinction between honest and devious techniques of office politics.
6. Recognize how office politics might help you.
7. Discuss several strategies for controlling office politics.

At a retirement lunch given him by his co-workers, a 65-year-old office messenger claimed with pride, "I've never played office politics a day in my life." Perhaps this messenger is deservedly proud of a record of nonpolitical behavior, but most people reading this book would not be proud of such modest career progress. Without an understanding of office politics, a person has a limited chance for success in almost any plant, office, or laboratory. Equally significant, if you do not understand office politics you will not be able to understand the nature of a work environment. Political considerations enter into almost every decision made at work about people, machines, and money.

Asked by the instructor for a definition of office politics, a student in a human relations course replied, "How to get ahead without having to work hard." Although the class laughed, this definition was partially correct. Office politics, in the context used here, refers to a variety of techniques and maneuvers for gaining favor, advancing your career, or gaining power in addition to merit or good performance. In other words, to play office politics is to use methods in addition to (or sometimes other than) good performance to gain favor, advance your career, or increase your power. Office politics also refers more to self-interest than to interest in the welfare of others or the company.

When you use office politics in such a way that harm is brought to other employees or the total organization, you are engaging in unethical behavior. Toward the end of this chapter we discuss political strategies that are clearly unethical in almost every application. However, any strategy of office politics can be used in an unethical manner if carried to extreme. In this chapter we will concentrate on political strategies designed to gain favor or power. Chapter 19, about managing yourself, will examine a variety of career advancement techniques. It is logical to consider such techniques as being very political in nature. However, most career advancement strategies include more than performing well in your job.

WHY WE HAVE OFFICE POLITICS

Politicking is all around us. People jockey for positions and try a variety of subtle maneuvers to impress their boss in almost every place of work. To understand the nature of office or job politics, it is important to understand why such actions on the part of rational people are ever present.[1]

Competition for power. The very shape of large organizations is the most fundamental reason people engage in office politics. Only so much power is available to distribute among the many people who would like more of it. It is important to differentiate between power and authority. Power is the ability to control the actions of others, while authority is the right to

[1] The analysis presented here of why we have office politics follows closely and paraphrases that presented in Andrew J. DuBrin, *Fundamentals of Organizational Behavior: An Applied Perspective,* 2d ed. (Elmsford, N.Y.: Pergamon, 1978), chap. 5; and Andrew J. DuBrin, *Human Relations: A Job Approach* (Reston, Va.: Reston, 1978), chap. 6.

control them. A supervisor who was the majority shareholder in a small company would have considerable power among peers although as a supervisor any formal authority would be limited. A vice president in the same company, who is retiring within one year might have much formal authority but limited power. People might not pay much attention to this person's ideas knowing that retirement is eminent and a change of authority will ensue.

As you move down the organization chart, each successive layer of people has less power than the layer above. At the bottom of the organization, people have virtually no power.

Abraham Zaleznik, an organizational psychologist and psychoanalyst, makes this analysis of the inevitability of power:

> Whatever else organizations may be . . . they are political structures. This means that organizations operate by distributing authority and setting a stage for exercise of power. It is no wonder, therefore, that individuals who are highly motivated to secure and use power find a familiar and hospitable environment in business.[2]

Lack of objective standards of performance. Assume that you are a commercial artist. Your firm informs you that in order to become a supervisor you must first complete 500 assignments acceptable to clients. Your path to a promotion would be so clear-cut that you would not need to use political maneuvers to attain a supervisory position. Few organizations have such clear-cut measures of performance or well-defined steps for promotion. Because of this fact, people rsort to job politics in an attempt to move ahead or gain advantage.

People resort to company politics because they do not believe that the organization has an objective (fair) way of judging their suitability for promotion.[3] Conversely, when management has no objective way of differentiating effective from less effective people, they will resort to favoritism in promotion and dispensing choice work assignments. The adage, "It's not what you know but who you know," does apply to organizations that lack clear-cut work objectives.

---

[2] Abraham Zaleznik, "Power and Politics in Organizational Life," *Harvard Business Review*, May–June 1970, p. 52.

[3] Joseph K. Batten and James L. Swab, "How to Crack Down on Company Politics," *Personnel*, January–February 1965, pp. 8–20.

Arnie, a supervisor working for an electronics company, was also a Little League coach. One of the three pitchers on his team, Heather, had much less accuracy than the other two pitchers. Nevertheless, Arnie persisted in appointing Heather as the starting pitcher. Puzzled and mildly irritated, his assistant coach, John, asked Arnie why he relied so heavily on the erratic arm of Heather. He explained, "John, how can you be so naive? I know Heather isn't as good as my other two pitchers. But her father happens to be the plant superintendent in my company. Almost everytime he sees me in the plant he gives me a big smile and tells me how great I am not to be prejudiced against female athletes. I'm sure it's going to lead to a promotion for me."

"But what about your record at the company? Isn't that more important?" asked John. Arnie noted, "What record? One supervisor is the same as another. We rotate from department to department, and nobody has an accurate record of who accomplished what or what we are really supposed to do. Using Heather as my starting pitcher is a good way of getting noticed by the right person."

Emotional insecurity. Some people resort to political maneuvers to ingratiate themselves to superiors because they lack confidence in their talents and skills. As an extreme example, a Nobel-price-winning scientist does not have to curry favor with the administration of the university. The distinguished scientist's work speaks for itself. Winning a Nobel prize has given this scientist additional self-confidence; that individual is therefore emotionally secure.

A person's choice of political strategy may indicate emotional insecurity.

Olaf, a laboratory technician, used body language to express approval of statements made by his boss or other managers in the company. In a group meeting, Olaf could be seen nodding with a yes motion and smiling whenever his boss spoke. His peers joked that Olaf nodded more vigorously and smiled wider, the higher the rank of people talking. In contrast, he was almost expressionless when a peer or hourly worker spoke.

Eventually, his boss became annoyed with Olaf's insincere head gestures. He asked Olaf why he found it necessary to nod approval at almost everything a manager had to say. Changing from a smile to a worried look, Olaf replied, "I don't care what my co-workers think of me. But I want the people who make decisions around here to like me. I thought a worker was supposed to please his boss."

Shift to a democratic management style. A gradual shift in the most frequently used form of leadership style has taken place over the last several decades. Modern management thinking places a premium upon being democratic rather than autocratic. Managers especially in large organizations, are no longer supposed to play the role of the boss whose authority is not to be questioned. Rather, they are supposed to be team players with a democratic approach to subordinates. Many supervisors and higher-level managers find the shift from an autocratic to a democratic style uncomfortable. Their response is to appear democratic. One common tactic is to use committees, conferences, and informal groups as arenas for playing politics and other forms of manipulating.[4]

An excessive use of meetings can also contribute to politics being played from below. A department meeting presents a good opportunity for the office politician to try to impress the boss. During one such meeting a tool and die maker stated, "As for me, I don't mind having to speed up production so much. It's the other people I'm concerned about. They may begin to complain if management doesn't wise up soon and reduce some of the pressure. But I'm certainly not one to complain."

Avoidance of hard work. While conducting research about office politics in not-for-profit organizations, I came upon another purpose behind office politics. In any department where few people are ambitious, or where many are waiting for retirement, office politics is often used to *avoid* work. The rationale for this behavior is that "if you get in good with the boss, you won't have to work so hard." One man regularly complimented his boss on her appearance. She reciprocated by not giving him difficult or unpleasant assignments. It is not unreasonable to assume that office politics is sometimes used to avoid work in business as well as not-for-profit organizations. It is a ploy of the poorly work-motivated individual with a low need for power.

HOW PEOPLE TRY TO IMPRESS THE BOSS[5]

Much of office politics is aimed at developing an improved relationship with the boss. Impressing your boss is a starting

[4] Eugene E. Jennings, "You Can Spot Office Politicians," *Nation's Business*, December 1959, pp. 42–57.

[5] This section is essentially excerpted from Andrew J. DuBrin, *Winning at Office Politics* (New York: Van Nostrand Reinhold, 1978), chap. 4.

point in getting ahead in most organizations. An astute supervisor remains alert to the many techniques subordinates use to curry favor with him or her. Recognizing these maneuvers helps a boss from being unduly impressed by politics rather than performance. Eleven of the most frequently used techniques will be summarized here. Some are more political (less performance related) than others. Most of these strategies are used at all organizational levels, even if they are modified somewhat from the factory floor to the executive suite.

Help your boss succeed. The primary purpose most people are hired in the first place is to help the boss and company succeed. Employees sometimes lose sight of this basic fact of organizational life. Most job activities of an employee should be directed at helping the boss succeed. At its best, it is sensible career advancement strategy. The manner in which this strategy works is illustrated by the case history of one chief manufacturing engineer.

> George learned through the grapevine that a representative from company headquarters would be visiting his plant where he worked as the chief manufacturing engineer. George had also learned from casual conversations with his boss, Gus, that the home office was concerned about the physical appearance of some of the company plants. A few stockholders had complained that the company image was suffering because of the filthy conditions at some of its mills and plants.
>
> George swung into action without first conferring with his boss. He organized a clean-up committee to remove trash and repaint badly smudged doors and walls. The entire clean-up operation took four days—precisely the four days that Gus was out of town on a business trip. When Gus returned he was pleasantly surprised to see the good housekeeping that had taken place in his absence. When the inspection team visited the plant shortly thereafter, Gus was praised for keeping up the company image.
>
> Gus then asked his secretary who had initiated the clean-up campaign. Learning that George deserved the credit, Gus said to his secretary, "Write me a note of commendation to place in George's personnel file. After I sign it, we'll send one copy to George and place it in his personnel file. We need more company-minded people around here."

Display loyalty. A basic way of an employee impressing the boss is to be loyal. Loyalty can be expressed to the supervisor, the department, the division, or the entire organization. A subordinate can express loyalty in many ways other than by being a sycophant (a servile admirer). One characteristic of a loyal subordinate is defending the boss when the latter is under attack by people from other departments.

Defending your boss under such circumstances does not necessarily mean that you think your boss is entirely correct. You can defend the merit in what your boss says without agreeing with the former's entire position. Assume your boss was under attack from another department for being late with the processing of materials needed by them. Your boss contends that delays in shipments by vendors have created the problem. You realize that inefficiencies in the department are also a contributing factor. You might publicly agree with your boss that vendor delays have created problems. In private, you might make suggestions to your boss for improving department efficiency.

Avoid disloyalty. Disloyalty takes many forms, many of which are simply the opposite of being loyal. Attacking your boss publicly, going out of your way to admit that your department's position is wrong, or emphasizing the virtues of a competitor's products are common forms of disloyalty. Disloyalty may not get an employee fired, but one sign of overt disloyalty to a superior and that person might never again be concerned about boosting the employee's career. Seemingly trivial situations are often tip-offs about an employee's loyalty to a boss. Sam, an underwriting clerk in an insurance company made it a personal policy to never attend company or department functions. For instance, he declined invitations to join the division softball team, although a good pitcher, and was never seen at parties given by the boss. At performance appraisal time, his boss gave him a low rating on "loyalty." When the clerk asked his boss for an explanation of this low rating, the latter explained, "You have shown absolutely no interest in this company. To you it's just a place to earn a living. You have no company spirit."

Document your boss's accomplishments. Although less frequently used than many other methods mentioned here, a potentially valuable method of cultivating your boss is to keep a written record of his or her accomplishments. As will be discussed in the final chapter, documenting your own accomplishments is an important strategy of career advancement.

However, documenting a superior's contributions to the organization can help the both of you. Your boss can use the documentation at performance review time or when the department is seeking its share of the budget for the forthcoming year. Your efforts on behalf of the boss and the department will probably be given special notice. A woman working for a safety engineering manager used this technique to advantage.

> Laura was the secretary to Max, the manager of safety engineering. Max and his staff were responsible for preventing accidents in both the factory and office. People assumed Max was doing a good job, but didn't give much thought to the matter. His colorful safety posters were the primary reminder that a safety department existed.
>
> Laura recognized that her boss's contribution to the corporate welfare was difficult for others to gauge. Without asking for her boss's concurrence, Laura kept a daily log of what the department was accomplishing. Many of the items were mundane listings of department activities. Some of the entries in the log were of greater significance. Quarterly, Laura would compare accident frequency information before and after certain programs were initiated. One entry read: "In the year before we placed nonskid pads around the food and beverage vending machine, there were five reported cases of lost-time accidents due to people slipping over spilled coffee, soda, or soup. After the nonskid pads, no such accidents were reported."
>
> Laura's most impressive documentation dealt with the decrease in parking lot collisions since one-way traffic lanes were installed. Fender bumping accidents were reduced from 35 to 4 in a 12-month period. Laura bought her dossier of good deeds to Max just prior to budget preparation time.
>
> Max was highly impressed: "Laura, this is wonderful. The four of us in this department have been working away, doing our jobs and often going unappreciated. Now we can tell the rest of the world what we've really accomplished. It also tells me that you have really caught on to the safety concept. This department might soon have room for an administrative assistant; you would be the logical choice."

Praise your superior to top management. An advanced political maneuver is to inform the highest levels of management about the accomplishments of your boss. The logic behind this tactic is your boss may hear of your kind deed and reciprocate directly by elevating his or her evaluation of you. An indirect result is that if your boss's career is boosted because of the praise, you too may prosper. This assumes that you and your superior have a good working relationship and that you are a candidate for more responsibility. An extreme form of praising the boss to top management took place in a hospital. Sean, a hospital administrator, was asked by the hospital board of directors how he liked working at the hospital. The setting for the conversation was a hospital board meeting.

> Sean replied: "Things are going rather well for me at Hillside. Hospital administration is my career so it's important for me to work for a real pro. So often the chief executive officer at a hospital is a physician who has little regard for the administrative process. Administrators often run the ship as if they are royalty. Not Dr. Jacobs. The man knows how to manage. He keeps a careful eye on what you might call productivity in a hospital. He is very concerned that we keep the hospital beds filled and that we stay within budget. He prefers good patient care to philosophizing. But at the same time Jacobs has concern for the feelings of people. I have seen him personally intervene in a situation where it appeared that a Mexican orderly was the victim of an ethnic slur. The person Dr. Jacobs unbraided was a resident from Harvard Medical School."
>
> One week later Dr. Jacobs commented casually to Sean: "It's good to know that my top administrator and I have compatible management styles. Let me know if at anytime I'm doing anything that interferes with you performing your job the way you want to."

Discover your superior's objectives. A sensible strategy for impressing a superior is to help that individual reach department objectives. Department objectives are not always as explicit as they should be. A politically astute subordinate should therefore ask the department manager what are the department's true objectives. One production scheduler was surprised upon learning of the boss's true objectives. The scheduler believed that the company was trying to produce as many goods as possible. The boss told him, "So long as you asked me, I would say cut down on the production schedules. My boss is beginning to worry that we'll soon be producing goods for inventory. If we slow down production maybe we can cut down the reject rate."

Uncomplicate your superior's life. A potent way of developing a good relationship with a boss is to take problems away from him or her, rather than adding to an administrative burden. The payoff to the practitioner of this strategy is that the boss may develop more confidence in that person. One way to uncomplicate your boss's life is to bring forth solutions to problems instead of always informing your boss of the existence of problems (and not recommending a solution).

Become a crucial subordinate. Several of the strategies for cultivating your boss discussed so far point to the importance of performing well for your boss on crucial tasks—make or break factors in the manager's job.[6] Discovering your manager's objectives is a step toward becoming a crucial subordinate.

L. T., a production assistant in a furniture company became a crucial subordinate to his factory superintendent boss, Ron. In doing so, L. T. set the stage for advancement within his firm.

> The company in question was faced with a serious problem. Small bubbles were surfacing on the finish of tables and desks when they were exposed to temperatures above 80 degrees. Customers by the dozens were demanding refunds or refinishes on desks and tables manufactured by the company. Furniture retail stores, in turn, were demanding credit from the company and threatening to discontinue as customers unless there were guarantees that the bubbling problem was conquered. Managers and specialists alike devoted as much time as they could spare to this mysterious problem with potentially disastrous consequences to the company.
>
> After four days of frantic searching for causes and projecting blame onto others, no logical reasons for the bubbling had been isolated. L. T. swung into action. He telephoned all his acquaintances and former classmates who worked for furniture makers. He asked each of them if they ever had a seemingly unresolvable technical problem at the factory and what they did about it. One acquaintance of L. T.'s said his factory experienced a similar baffling problem of laminate that became unglued. They hired a chemical engineering consultant from Atlanta who solved the problem in three days.
>
> L. T. told his boss about the consultant, the consultant was hired, and the cause of the bubbling was discovered. Apparently one large batch of solvent was contaminated by using the wrong acid in its preparation. L. T.'s boss was enthusiastic about the consultant's efforts and equally enthusiastic about L. T.'s judgment in recommending him.

Listen to your superior. A simple strategy of cultivating a superior is to be a patient listener. Active listening to your boss can take a number of forms: listening to personal problems; asking for suggestions and then following them; nodding with enthusiasm and smiling when the boss speaks; or taking notes during a staff meeting.

---

[6] The concept of crucial subordinate is credited to Eugene E. Jennings, *The Mobile Manager: A Study of the New Generation of Top Executives* (New York: McGraw-Hill, 1971).

Tim, a mechanical engineer, facilitated a good relationships with his boss by demonstrating through his actions that he listened carefully to his boss's suggestions. On one occasion his boss Alex made a comment when he stopped by Tim's cubicle: "Say, that looks like an interesting way to reinforce a valve. Where did you learn about that?"

Tim replied, "Alex, the credit must go indirectly to you. One day over coffee we were talking about the strength of valves. You mentioned that a researcher named Schwartz had written the most comprehensive paper on valves. I sent for a reprint and found the exact information I needed. Did I forget to thank you for that suggestion?"

Maintain maximum boss contact. A popular technique of cultivating or impressing a boss is to maintain frequent contact with that individual. Many office politicians develop a reason for seeing their boss, even if a legitimate reason does not exist. Among their tactics include bringing in telephone messages to the boss, getting a reaction to a routine memo, or asking for clarification on a problem. A risk exists of being seen as a pest or an indecisive person if you overdo the principle of maintaining maximum boss contact.

Be the department watchdog. An almost devious approach to impressing the boss is to keep that individual informed of squabbles and miscellaneous problems within the department. A person who occupies the watchdog role must be careful to pass along only valid information.

An insurance company manager explains why he was forced to recommend that a "watchdog" in his department be transferred to another department:

> At first I trusted Ted. He was a valuable ally. He would tell me if two of my department heads were in too much conflict. I would poke into the matter and try to get things straightened out. Once he told me that one of my managers was saying nasty things about me to the personnel department. I confronted the man without identifying the source. The accusations to the personnel department stopped.
>
> One day Ted told me that Alice, my claims manager, was mailing out her résumé to about half the insurance companies in the business. I asked her if she were discontent with the company since she was exploring the job market. Alice told me she hadn't looked for a job in years. Furthermore she invited me to contact any insurance company I wished to see if she had written to them. She also invited me to search her desk, if I wished.

My conclusion was that Ted was using desperate tactics to either get rid of Alice or impress me that he was highly loyal to me. Whatever the real reason, I recommended he be transferred to another department.

HOW PEOPLE TRY TO GAIN POWER[7]

In recent years researchers and scholars have paid an increasing amount of attention to the study of power in organizations. Power has been likened to money. Not everybody is obsessed with power or money, but few people would refuse more of either if it were offered to them. Supervisors, other managers, and individual performers all have an interest in increasing the amount of organizational power they possess. Without attaining power a person runs the risk of early dismissal in times of a business recession or when political infighting becomes intensified. It is not uncommon for a person in a high position (formal power) to make an early exit from the organization because of the inability to acquire a solid power base. People at lower levels in the organization need at least a modicum of power in order to quality for more responsibility or their fair share of the budget.

Techniques and strategies for gaining and keeping power can be roughly divided into those used at lower levels versus those used at the top of organizations. The first eight strategies discussed in this section are generally used at lower organizational levels. The last two strategies presented illustrate the kind of power plays that take place at the highest organizational levels.

Be distinctive and formidable. A first step in acquiring power is to stand out from the crowd in a favorable way. If you have charisma, grace, or charm, it helps you to exert influence over other people. *Personal power* is the technical term given to this idea. Although it is difficult to mold a bland personality into one of distinction and uniqueness, sometimes an ordinary characteristic suddenly becomes unique. Having a German accent will not add to your uniqueness in Germany, but it can be impressive in the United States. One of the world's best-known management consultants speaks with a German accent al-

---

[7] The information in this section is essentially excerpted from DuBrin, *Office Politics*, chaps. 10 and 11.

though he has been bilingual since early childhood and has lived in the United States for over 40 years.

Seek line responsibility. In almost every organization those people whose work is tied in directly with the mission of the organization (line personnel) have more power than service groups and advisors (staff personnel). A vice president of personnel or the chief company lawyer usually has considerable power but not as much power as their counterparts in line units (such as sales or manufacturing). If you spend your entire career in staff jobs, you may never have as much power or make as much money as people in line positions. An executive secretary who works for the head of manufacturing (a line function) is usually paid more than the executive secretary who reports to the head of maintenance (a staff function).

The nature of the work you are performing is not the crucial factor in determining whether or not you are line or staff. What is significant is how vital that function is to your employer. A photographer is a staff person when working in the photo department of U.S. Steel. When that photographer works for a photo studio the job being performed is a line function.

Play camel's head in the tent. Just as the camel works slowly into the tent inch by inch (beginning with the nose), you might grab power in a step-by-step manner until you acquire the amount of power and responsibility you are seeking at the time. Camel's head has become a widely practiced technique at the middle levels of large organizations where many department heads are trying to enlarge their empires. In many instances this technique is unethical because it does not serve the good of the organization.

One bank supervisor successfully used this technique to double her responsibility. Her official job title was Head Teller. In addition to supervising the tellers, this woman began to personally take care of more and more of the special problems faced by major customers of this small bank. Eventually she was given the joint title of Head Teller and Manager of Customer Service. Shortly thereafter she was authorized to hire two assistants. It is important to recognize that this woman was performing a legitimate function for the bank.

Create your own job. Quite similar to the example just cited, another ethical method of power acquisition is to do something so important for the organization that it is justifiable to expand your activities into a department. Many a company division or government department began with a project handled by one individual. As that project gained in importance and value, it necessitated the employment of an increasing number of people.

> Marsha was a sales representative for a supplier of typewriter and office equipment. She waited on customers who entered the store and made periodic visits to local businesses to stimulate sales. Marsha noticed that an opportunity existed to sell office desks, chairs, and file cabinets to some of her customers. At first she did this on an informal basis by ordering merchandise from a wholesaler when a customer requested a specific item.
>
> Marsha then convinced the store manager to stock a small selection of low-priced office furniture. Business grew at a steady clip and the profit margin on this line of merchandise was better than for office equipment. The store owners then agreed to expand the store in order to create an office furniture department headed by Marsha. At last report, sales of office furniture accounted for about 25 percent of the store's business, and Marsha was negotiating with the owners about becoming a partner in the business.

Control access to key people. A standard approach to garnering power is to occupy a position whereby people have to go through you in order to conduct business with a key person.[8] People tend to be nice to you, including granting you favors, when you control their access to powerful figures. In order to see the chief executive, quite often the appointment has to be cleared through an administrative assistant. Unless that administrative assistant thinks that you have an important reason for seeing the chief, or likes you personally, your request may be rejected without even checking with the chief. Susan Clough, President Jimmy Carter's personal secretary, acquired considerable power through her ability to control whose request went through to the president.

Control the future. Rightly or wrongly, many people believe that personnel specialists have a great deal of influence over who

---

[8] Henry L. Tosi and Stephen J. Carroll, *Management: Contingencies, Structure and Process* (Chicago: St. Clair Press, 1976), pp. 214–17.

gets which future assignments.[9] Because of this belief, some people go along with the requests of personnel staffers in order to stay on their good side. Many supervisors looking for a transfer to a choice department have gone out of their way to curry favor with a personnel manager. Other people attempt to cultivate managers who are known to be influential in making recommendations for transfers and promotions.

Collect and use IOUs. Properly handled, IOUs can be used to bargain for favors, favorable assignments, and even raises and promotion.[10] After you have done somebody of higher rank than yourself an important favor, the former then owes you a favor—the equivalent of gaining some power for yourself.

> Barney worked as a dispatcher in a national moving and storage company. After spending most of his life in Minneapolis, Barney and his wife longed for the chance to live in a southern climate. One day a unique opportunity presented itself, and Barney had enough foresight to recognize its value. An executive in Barney's company wanted a friend's personal belongings shipped in a hurry. A telephone call to Barney (whom the executive knew only slightly) was all the executive needed to make the necessary arrangements for his friend. Thanking Barney for his quick action, the executive stated, "Let me know if I can ever help you out of a jam."
>
> Six months later, Barney telephoned the executive with a request. "Mr. Higgins, do you remember me? I'm Barney Wetherbee, the dispatcher in charge of routing the moving vans. My wife and I have a little problem that requires your help. Her arteries are beginning to harden a little, making cold weather in Minneapolis insufferable to her. We're wondering if I could be given favorable consideration for a transfer to our Miami or Tampa office. We both would be grateful to you for the rest of our lives if the transfer did come through." The executive replied, "I'll see what I can do." Within one year Barney, who had extended himself for the executive (slightly bending company regulations in the process), was transferred to a comparable position in Tampa. His IOU had been reimbursed.

Acquire seniority. The most low-key method of gaining power is to acquire seniority.[11] In our society, longevity in a work organization still comands respect and privilege. Labor unions

---

[9] Ibid.

[10] The basic concept of collecting and using IOUs is credited to Alan S. Schoonmaker, *Executive Career Strategy* (New York: American Management Association, 1971), p. 115.

[11] Ibid., p. 102.

have long emphasized the rights of seniority. Although seniority alone will not prevent you from being ousted from your company or guarantee you more power, it helps. The compulsive job hopper is forever working against the implicit threat of "last in, first out" in both managerial and individual performer jobs. Acquiring seniority in *one particular job* can be as important as acquiring seniority in one particular organization. If you transfer to a new department you may lose your seniority power.

Work on key problems.   In large companies, the people who occupy the most powerful positions are often those who have been identified with the solution to pressing business problems. Similarly, those people who were associated with breakthrough developments in the company tend to become the most powerful executives. This method of power acquisition is the most apparent in the automotive industry where individuals can be associated with particular car models of legendary success, such as the Ford Mustang or the Pontiac Firebird. A supervisor can sometimes benefit from the key problem power play, although it is a high-level maneuver. Supervisors who work on key company projects (such as the Ford Fairmont or the Cadillac Seville) tend to have more power than those supervisors assigned to departments working on less glamorous projects.

Be feared rather than loved.   Around 1515, Niccolo Machiavelli suggested that a prince is better off being feared rather than loved. His reasoning was that it is worthwhile to be both feared and loved, but it is easier to maintain control when you are feared.[12] It is easier to implement a strategy of being feared than loved because it is easier to make people fear you than love you. (The reader will recognize that a strategy of ruling by fear is incompatible with modern approaches to supervision which emphasize an understanding of the problems of subordinates and mutual respect.) One technique frequently used by supervisors who rule by fear is to tell people how dispensable they are. As one foremen told his group, "If any of you guys don't

---

[12] Niccolo Machiavelli, *The Prince* (New York: The Modern Library, 1940), p. 61 (originally published around 1515).

want to do this work properly, we can find a dozen replacements who want to do an honest day's work."

DISHONEST AND DEVIOUS TACTICS

A discussion of office politics would be both incomplete and naive without at least passing mention of dishonest and devious tactics. A recent report on this topic describes 39 different devious political tactics used in places of work.[13] A sampling of four of these techniques will be described here. The reader should keep in mind the fact that such techniques are precisely what we are not recommending and should not be used to win favor, advance your career, or gain power.

Divide and rule. The age-old strategy of encouraging your subordinates to scrap among themselves so they will not form alliances against you is still practiced in business, government, and education. Divide and rule is more frequently practiced by executives than supervisors, although supervisors are not exempt from using this technique. This technique, as with any other devious political strategy, can backfire, as illustrated by the following case history.

> Ned, a division manager, felt that his acceptance was on the decline. His solution was to try to get his three key department heads feuding among themselves. Ned told each department head that his department would be given top priority for moving into a new building currently under construction. Predictably, the three department heads did bicker about who would be relocating. What Ned did not realize is that the department heads also discussed how they knew they would be relocating. When the truth was uncovered, the three men pressed Ned to explain the misunderstanding. Ned blamed the error on a question of misinterpretation. He told the department heads he meant to communicate the fact that their needs for additional space was a top priority for all three departments. The amount of respect Ned commanded eroded further after this incident.

Discredit your rival. A transparent, but still widely used, tactic is to discredit your rival by direct accusation or innuendo. Only a naive boss will accept a damaging statement made by one peer about another without additional confirmation of the ad-

---

[13] DuBrin, Office Politics, chap. 14. The four strategies presented in this section are exerpted from this source.

verse information. Discrediting statements made by a few people desperate to gain advantage are presented for illustrative purposes:

> Plumber talking to supervisor about another plumber: "I wonder if on my next assignment I could work with somebody other than Jack. I've tried working with him but he just doesn't seem to be any good with his hands."

> Employee talking to supervisor about fellow worker: "I think we're really going to miss Vince. I saw him filling out an application to join the CIA."

> Supervisor talking to department head about ambitious employee: "When he's around, Marty is a terrific worker. But he's hard to find. I guess he's usually in some other office, politicking to find a good job for himself."

Cover up the truth. Lying might be the most frequently practiced devious tactic people at all organizational levels use to look good. "Bury the truth" is the gambit of the dishonest office and public politician. "Your check is in the mail" and "your order has already been shipped" are such common lies in business that few people become upset when the mails, rails, airplanes, or trucks are mysteriously a few days late. Dishonesty is so widely practiced that an employee who develops the reputation of being honest is at an advantage.

Take undue credit. A devious political tactic and a devastatingly poor management practice is to take credit for work performed by others.[14] A manager who uses this tactic often takes full credit for the successes of subordinates, but disclaims any responsibility for their failures. The same technique can be used with peers, as practiced by Sam who worked in a computer printing department:[15]

> For each job that was processed, the operator had to log the start and stop time of the job. This list was used to check for responsibility of printing quality and to some extent as a measure of job performance. As each job was set up, Sam would log his operator number even if the job was not processed by him. However, when he observed that the print

---

[14] The basic idea of taking undue credit is credited to Vance Packard, *The Pyramid Climbers* (New York: McGraw-Hill, 1962), pp. 201–2.

[15] This example was researched by Gerard A. Santelli.

quality did not measure up to his standards, he would change the operator log number to that used by one of his co-workers. He did not, however, adjust the printers to produce the proper print quality.

HOW OFFICE POLITICS CAN HELP YOU

People who do not achieve their personal objectives on the job frequently attribute their lack of success to office politics.[16] They feel that favoritism has worked against them—that a less-deserving person has been promoted to a key job. Such contentions are not necessarily the product of paranoid thinking. If you are politically naive you probably will not achieve the success you desire. The antidote from this author's standpoint is for you to practice ethical and sensible politics. One such strategy would be for you to become recognized by upper management for your willingness to volunteer for assignments and your participation in company social functions. Under such circumstances, politics might work in your favor.

HOW TO CONTROL OFFICE POLITICS

Carried to excess, office politics can hurt an organization and its members. Too much politicking can result in wasted time and effort, therefore lowering productivity. Human consequences can also be substantial, including lowered morale and the turnover of people who intensely dislike playing office politics. Four particularly helpful approaches to combatting office politics are recommended here.[17]

Treat excessive politics as another job problem to be solved.   When an overuse of office politics disrupts productivity or morale, the supervisor should regard this situation as another work problem requiring resolution. A systematic approach to the problem, such as the Framework for Accomplishing Results presented in Chapter 1, should be used. Among the critical elements would be to confront office politicians with their counterproductive behavior. For instance, the offender might be told,

---

[16] DuBrin, *Human Relations*, p. 125.
[17] The last three suggestions are excerpted from ibid., pp. 121–23.

"I get the impression you sometimes tell me what you think I want to hear rather than giving me an accurate picture of a problem." The person in question might then be encouraged to be less political and more factual in presenting information about problems to the superior. Review sessions should be scheduled and positive reinforcement given (such as praise) when progress is made toward the goal of becoming less political.

Provide objective measures of performance. As suggested earlier in this chapter, a primary reason we have so much politicking in some organizations is that those organizations do not provide objective measures of measuring performance. When a person knows exactly what is expected in order to qualify for promotion or a salary increase, there is less need for political maneuvering. Even more fundamental, you tend to curry favor with a superior when there seems to be no other way to determine if you are competent in your job.

Provide an atmosphere of trust. Several management observers have noted that this is the best overall antidote to excessive playing of politics. If people trust each other in a company, they are less likely to use devious tactics (or even slightly devious tactics) against each other. People often resort to cover-up behavior because they fear the consequences of telling the truth about themselves. During the last two decades, methods of organizational development have been developed to help bring about openness and trust in organizations. One such technique is to hold leveling sessions among supervisors and managers in which they practice being candid with each other. Evidence has accumulated that in some instances organizational development programs have helped a company or other type of work organization achieve an atmosphere of trust.[18]

Set good examples at the top. When people in key positions are highly political, they set the tone for job politicking at lower levels. When people at the top of the organization are nonpolitical (straightforward) in their actions, they demnonstrate in a subtle way that political behavior is not desired.

A new vice president squelched job politicking in a hurry through an unusual confrontation:

---

[18] One excellent overview of organization development is Michael Beer, *Organization Development* (Pacific Palisades, Calif.: Goodyear, 1978).

Brad called his first official staff meeting as vice president of finance. After a few brief comments about his pleasure in joining the company, he said bluntly: "I've been here only two weeks, yet I've noticed some strange actions that I want stopped right now. I know it's part of the American culture to please the boss, but don't be so naive about it. I'm not pointing the finger at any one person in particular, but you people have been milling around my office like birds waiting for crumbs. If you have some official business and you want to make an appointment with my secretary, that's fine. But if you don't have a legitimate business purpose in seeing me, don't drop by my office. We've got too many things to accomplish to spend time in coffee klatches."

BUSINESS ETHICS AND OFFICE POLITICS

The topic of office politics raises some important ethical issues. An obvious issue is that most people would consider it highly unethical to engage in those political strategies classified as devious and dishonest. Lying, cheating, and stealing to gain advantage are clearly unethical strategies.

Another ethical issue is how much competition the organization (and the supervisor) should encourage among employees. A main contributor to office politics is the fact that people are competing to get ahead. The right amount of competition helps an organization—it keeps people on their toes. But too much competition leads to undesirable consequences such as distortion of information, hiding of failures, falsification of figures, empire building, and mutual distrust among managers and supervisors.

John D. Minch suggests that group incentives can sometimes get people cooperating instead of engaging in unhealthy competition.[19] Management that encourages too much individual competition may find itself faced with an undesirable amount of office politics, plus many of the negative consequences of intense competition.

SUMMARY OF KEY POINTS

- ☐ Office politics refers to a variety of techniques and maneuvers for gaining favor, advancing your career, or gaining power in addition to merit or good performance.

---

[19] John D. Minch in a personal communication with the author, January 8, 1979.

☐ Five major reasons office politics is so widespread are: (1) The competition for power inevitable in a pyramid-shaped organization; (2) The lack of objective standards of performance in many organizations; (3) People's emotional inseucrity; (4) The shift to a democratic management style; and (5) Some people's desire to avoid hard work.

☐ A major set of political behaviors relate to techniques of impressing the boss. Eleven such techniques described in this chapter are: Help your boss succeed; Display loyalty; Avoid disloyalty; Document your boss's accomplishments; Praise your boss to top management; Discover your boss's objectives; Uncomplicate your boss's life; Become a crucial subordinate; Listen to the boss; Maintain maximum boss contact; Be the department watchdog.

☐ Another major set of political behaviors relate to techniques, methods, and approaches of acquiring power. The ten such political tactics described in this chapter are: Be distinctive and formidable; Seek line responsibility; Play camel's head in the tent; Create your own job; Control access to key people; Control the future; Collect and use IOUs; Acquire seniority; Work on key problems; Be feared rather than loved.

☐ Devious and dishonest tactics of office politics are not recommended here as a way of gaining advantage in organizations. However, the sensible use of honest tactics may help an individual achieve personal objectives.

☐ Excessive use of office politics can hamper an organization's effectiveness. Four suggested approaches for its control are: (1) Treat excessive job politics as another job problem to be solved; (2) Provide objective measures of job performance; (3) Provide an atmosphere of trust and openness; and (4) Set good examples at the top of the organization.

☐ Office politics should be used in such a way that ethical standards of conduct are not violated.

GUIDELINES FOR SUPERVISORY PRACTICE

1. Although you may want to get ahead strictly on merit, you cannot ignore the politics being played around you. Understanding what political techniques others are using is an important defensive strategy.

2. A good starting point for the sensible use of office politics is to create a favorable impression on your boss. One recommended strategy to achieve this end is to help your boss succeed.

3. The quest for power is a basic fact of organizational life, although it is not formally acknowledged by most organizations. A sincere way of gaining power is to be distinctive and formidable.

4. If you want to control office politics in your department, you might try three strategies: regard the overuse of job politics as antother personnel problem to be solved; provide objective measures of performance; provide an atmosphere of trust.

5. Political tactics that bring harm to others or the total organization should be avoided because they represent unethical behavior. Office politics should be used to advance your cause but not at the expense of others.

QUESTIONS FOR DISCUSSION AND REVIEW

1. Are "bootlicking" and "apple polishing" forms of office politics? Explain.
2. Is the president of the United States or the prime minister of Canada a good office politician? Explain.
3. Is this chapter a guide to success in business? Why or why not?
4. Define the term office politics using (a) the words used in the text, and (b) your own words.
5. Why do we have so much office politics in general?
6. Describe the reasons office politics existed in your current (or most recent) place of work.
7. Why do self-confident people have less need to play office politics?
8. Which technique of impressing the boss described in this chapter are you the most likely to use? Why?
9. Which technique of impressing the boss described in this chapter are you the least likely to use? Why?
10. How might office politics be used to improve your grade in this course?
11. What would happen if everybody in an organization followed all the strategies of impressing the boss and gaining power described in this chapter? (Exlude the devious and dishonest tactics.)
12. What is a department watchdog? What do you think of the ethics of being a department watchdog?
13. Which of the techniques of gaining power are you the most likely to use? Why?
14. Which of the techniques of gaining power are you the least likely to use? Why?
15. Give an example, not provided in this chapter, of a person who has control over the future.
16. How might a person identify which problems are the "key" ones in order to use the strategy to work on key problems.
17. Which dishonest or devious tactics are frequently used by candidates for political office?
18. Can a person avoid playing office politics? Explain?

FIGURE 5–1

Political orientation questionnaire

	Mostly agree	Mostly disagree
1. Only a fool would correct a boss's mistakes.	———	———
2. If you have certain confidential information, release it to your advantage.	———	———
3. I would be careful not to hire a subordinate with more formal education than myself.	———	———
4. If you do somebody a favor, remember to cash in on it.	———	———
5. Given the opportunity, I would cultivate friendships with powerful people.	———	———
6. I like the idea of saying nice things about a rival in order to get that person transferred from my department.	———	———
7. Why not take credit for someone else's work? They would do the same to you.	———	———
8. Given the chance, I would offer to help my boss build some shelves for his or her den.	———	———
9. I laugh heartily at my boss's jokes, even when they are not funny.	———	———
10. I would be sure to attend a company picnic even if I had the chance to do something I enjoyed more that day.	———	———
11. If I knew an executive in my company was stealing money, I would use that against the person in asking for favors.	———	———

19. What are three suggested ways of controlling office politics?
20. After taking the Political Orientation Scale (Figure 5–1), explain why you think your score is accurate or inaccurate.

A supervisory self-insight exercise: The office politics questionnaire

To gain some tentative insight into your tendencies toward playing office politics and your desire for power, answer the following questionnaire.

Directions: Answer each question "mostly agree" or "mostly disagree," even if it is difficult for you to decide which alternative best describes your opinion.

FIGURE 5–1 *(continued)*

	Mostly agree	Mostly disagree
12. I would first find out my boss's political preferences before discussing politics.	_____	_____
13. I think using memos to zap somebody for mistakes is a good idea (especially when you want to show that person up).	_____	_____
14. If I wanted something done by a co-worker, I would be willing to say, "If you don't get this done, our boss might be very unhappy."	_____	_____
15. I would invite my boss to a party at my house, even if I didn't like the person.	_____	_____
16. When I'm in a position to, I would have lunch with the "right people" at least twice a week.	_____	_____
17. I think it is a good policy to avoid ever telling your boss he or she is wrong.	_____	_____
18. Power for its own sake is one of life's most precious commodities.	_____	_____
19. Having a high school named after you would be an incredible thrill.	_____	_____
20. Reading about job politics is as much fun as reading an adventure story.	_____	_____

Source: Andrew J. DuBrin, *Human Relations: A Job Oriented Approach* (Reston, Va.: Reston, 1978), pp. 123–24.

Interpretation of scores. Each statement you check "mostly agree" is worth 1 point toward your political orientation score. If you score 16 or over, it suggests that you have a strong inclination toward playing politics. A high score of this nature would also suggest that you have strong needs for power. Scores of 5 or less would suggest that you are not inclined toward political maneuvering and that you are not strongly power driven.

A caution is again in order. This questionnaire is designed primarily to encourage you to introspect about the topic under study. The political orientation questionnaire lacks the scientific properties of a legitimate personality test.

SOME SUGGESTED READING

Burger, Chester. *Survival in the Executive Jungle.* New York: The Macmillan Co., 1964.

Donnelly, Caroline. "Warding Off the Office Politician." *Money,* December 1976, pp. 70–74.

DuBrin, Andrew J. *Winning at Office Politics.* New York: Van Nostrand Reinhold, 1978.

_____. *Survival in the Office.* New York: Van Nostrand Reinhold, 1977.

Farnsworth, Terry. *On the Way Up—The Executive's Guide to Company Politics.* New York: McGraw-Hill (UK) Limited, 1976.

Hegarty, Edward J. *How to Succeed in Company Politics.* 2d ed. New York: McGraw-Hill, 1976.

"How to Survive in the Corporate Jungle." *Industry Week,* November 15, 1971, pp. 29–33.

Kanter, Rosabeth Moss. *Men and Women of the Corporation.* New York: Basic Books, 1977.

Korda, Michael. *Power! How to Get It, How to Use It.* New York: Random House, 1975.

McClelland, David C. *Power: The Inner Experience.* New York: Irvington (division of John Wiley), 1976.

McMurry, Robert N. "Power and the Ambitious Executive." *Harvard Business Review,* November–December 1973, pp. 140–45.

Newman, William H. *Administrative Action.* 2d ed. Englewood Cliffs, N.J.: Prentice-Hall, 1963, pp. 86–98.

Pascarella, Perry. "How Can I Keep the Boss Happy?" *Industry Week,* October 13, 1975, pp. 38–43.

"Playing Office Politics, or the Grab for Glory." *Industry Week,* March 23, 1970, pp. 25–30.

Rosemen, Ed. "How to Play Clean Office Politics." *Product Management,* May 1976, pp. 32–36.

Stern, Walter. *The Game of Office Politics.* Chicago: Henry Regnery, 1976.

part
three

Basic supervisory functions

Establishing goals and plans

6

LEARNING OBJECTIVES

After reading and thinking through the material in this chapter, you should be able to:

1. Understand how planning and goal setting contribute to good performance.
2. Describe the basic phases in the planning process.
3. Identify several key characteristics of an effective objective.
4. Explain the essentials of MBO.
5. Establish effective work objectives for yourself and others.

"Man, this job is killing me!" Tom said to himself as he sank into his chair with a heavy sigh. He looked around at the stacks of paperwork demanding his attention: Three of them were "red tag" items, screaming for action to avoid slips in plant production. A half-dozen phone messages were waiting to be answered. And he knew his scheduled one-hour conference with a new employee would be interrupted by more phone calls and a number of casual visitors poking their heads in. He was beginning to get that desperate feeling again, like a rat that finds itself trapped in a maze.[1]

Tom is not alone. Many supervisors are victims of poor planning on the part of themselves, their departments, or their places of work. Without careful goal setting and planning, a supervisor forever works in a "fire department" or "crunch mode." Careful attention to setting goals or objectives and figuring out what

---

[1] Quote from Karl Albrecht, "Are You Running a 'Fire Department'?" *Supervisory Management,* June 1977, pp. 2–3.

steps are necessary to reach those goals helps a supervisor stay on top of the job.

Not all supervisors have considerable latitutde in goal setting and planning. Sometimes higher-ups simply impose goals and plans on the managers below them. Often a supervisor is placed in a job where handling emergencies is a way of life. Nevertheless, almost every supervisor can improve performance (and feel more in control of a job) by incorporating some goal setting and planning into the job.

EVERY ACTION SHOULD HAVE A GOAL

If an organization followed planning to the ultimate degree, every action taken by every worker would be designed to achieve an important goal or objective. Everybody from the proverbial floor sweeper to the chief executive officer would perform every work activity with an organizational goal clearly in mind.

David Hampton refers to this phenomenon as the *network of objectives*.[2] A goal or objective is set at the top of the organization, and everybody else in the organization establishes a set of objectives to help reach the major objective (usually referred to as a goal). The best way to reach an objective is for every action to contribute toward that objective (or goal). Figure 6–1 illustrates both the network of objectives and how small specific actions are carried out with the objective in mind.

A plan-conscious supervisor examines all actions performed and asks, "How does what I am doing right now contribute to a goal I am trying to reach?" One particular activity may contribute to reaching an important objective at one time. At another time the same activity may be a waste of time. One day office supervisor Janet spends five minutes chatting with another supervisor in the parking lot. Janet is basically enjoying the sunshine and passing the time of day. The next day Janet spends five minutes chatting with another supervisor in the parking lot. However, this time she is performing an important work function. She is trying to build a good relationship with a supervisor from another department. In order to do her job properly, Janet

---

[2] David R. Hampton, *Contemporary Management* (New York: McGraw-Hill, 1977), p. 130.

FIGURE 6–1
How individual supervisory actions fit into the network of objectives

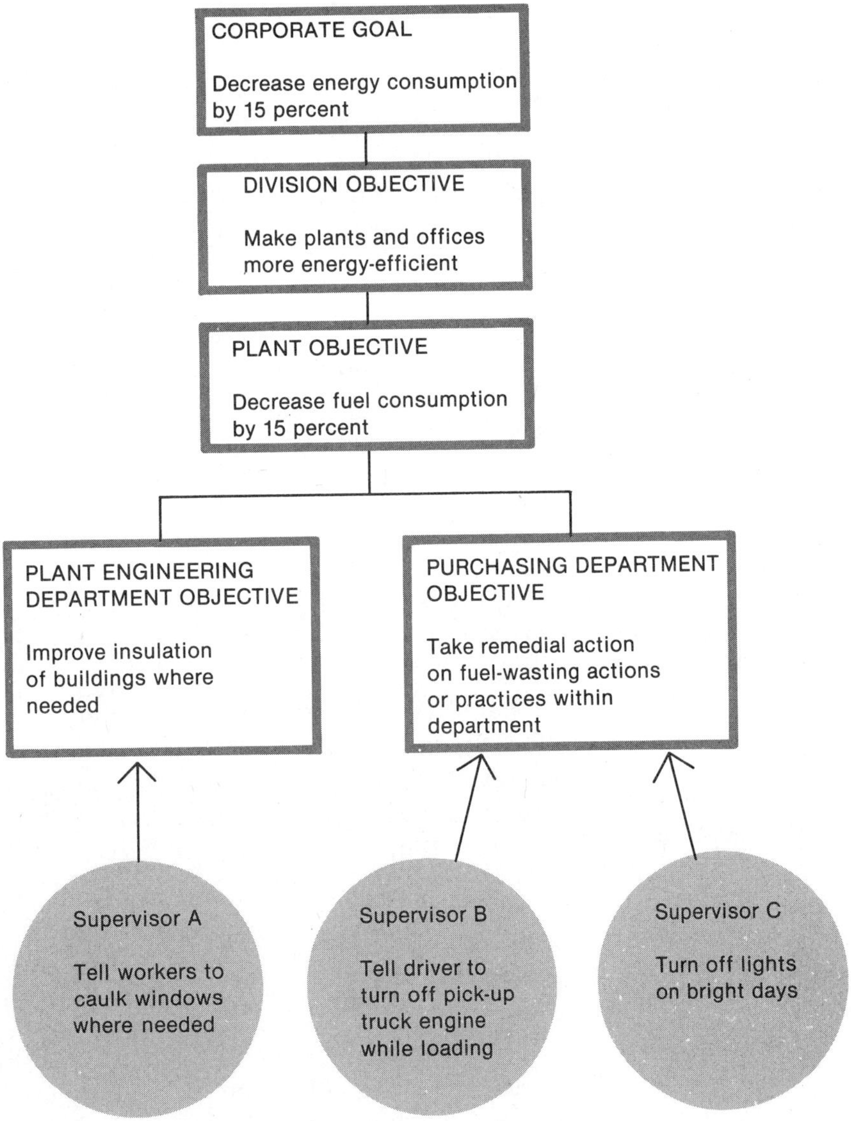

CORPORATE GOAL

Decrease energy consumption by 15 percent

DIVISION OBJECTIVE

Make plants and offices more energy-efficient

PLANT OBJECTIVE

Decrease fuel consumption by 15 percent

PLANT ENGINEERING DEPARTMENT OBJECTIVE

Improve insulation of buildings where needed

PURCHASING DEPARTMENT OBJECTIVE

Take remedial action on fuel-wasting actions or practices within department

Supervisor A

Tell workers to caulk windows where needed

Supervisor B

Tell driver to turn off pick-up truck engine while loading

Supervisor C

Turn off lights on bright days

depends on this other supervisor. Recognizing her objective of having good working relationships with other supervisors, Janet wisely *invests* five minutes on a parking lot conversation.

HOW PLANNING HELPS

Planning is such a broad concept that it carries a number of slightly different definitions. A useful commonsense definition is to describe planning as "advance thinking as the basis for doing."[3] When you plan you set goals (or objectives) and determine what steps will be necessary to achieve those goals. One management consultant has defined a plan as a "set of expected actions to be taken in conjunction with a predicted course of events."[4] Planning involves both setting goals or objectives and establishing plans to reach them.

Planning is considered the primary function of management. Few people have to be convinced of the advantages of planning, yet an analysis of some of its advantages leads toward a more complete understanding of the nature of planning. Effective planning leads to many positive outcomes. Poor planning, or no planning at all, often leads to poor results.

Increased productivity. A primary argument for planning is that organizations, departments, and supervisors who plan achieve better results than their counterparts who do not plan. Think of the difference between a planned and an unplanned vacation. Spontaneity is fun, but have you ever arrived in a strange town hungry and tired, only to find that all hotels, motels, and camp grounds have no vacancies? Did your car ever break down on vacation because your planning did not include preventive car maintenance before the trip?

A number of research studies support the proposition that careful attention to planning by companies leads to improved financial results. One carefully conducted study looked at the results of long-range planning over a seven-year cycle. The researchers matched 18 sets of companies for size, type of indus-

---

[3] James H. Donnelly, Jr., James L. Gibson, and John M. Ivancevich, *Fundamentals of Management: Functions, Behavior, Models*, 3d ed. (Dallas: Business Publications, 1978), p. 62. © 1978 by Business Publications, Inc.

[4] Albrecht, *Supervisory Management*, p. 6.

try, and other key characteristics. In each pair of companies neither one engaged in formal planning at the outset. The one firm in each set began to plan. The differences in results were dramatic:[5]

> The companies that planned outperformed their own past performance and the performance of the nonplanning companies on *every* measure of success, including return on equity, growth in earnings per share, return on investment and many others.

Increased satisfaction and morale. A major psychological benefit of planning is that it creates conditions for high levels of job satisfaction and morale. An essential ingredient for individual satisfaction is to achieve personal goals. Assume you currently read 400 words per minute. If you set a goal of reading 650 words per minute and then reach that speed, you will achieve a sense of inner satisfaction. Setting and attaining work goals (the essence of planning) has a similar effect.

William Glueck observes that without planning, employees do their work without seeing the results.[6] Knowing what the enterprise is trying to achieve helps employees relate what they are doing to the purposes of the department or total organization. A contribution of this nature often leads to increased personal satisfaction and group morale. The employee alluded to in Figure 6–1 who caulks an energy leak will experience some satisfaction in knowing that this is a contribution to the corporate goal of decreasing energy consumption.

One way a supervisor can contribute to employee satisfaction is to help them understand how achieving their daily work goals contribute to reaching department and company objectives. Not every employee cares about contributing to the total effort, but this approach works well for conscientious individuals.

Overcoming the fire-fighting mode. Tom, the manager described at the outset of this chapter, felt trapped because his department was perpetually fighting fires. The most logical es-

---

[5] The study in question is Stanley Thune and Robert House, "Where Long Range Planning Pays Off," *Business Horizons*, August 1970, pp. 81–87. The summary of major findings is quoted from William F. Glueck, *Management* (Hinsdale, Ill.: The Dryden Press, 1977), p. 318.

[6] Ibid., p. 320.

cape from a fire-fighting mode is to engage in more planning. One supervisor of a machine maintenance department in a newspaper complained to me that his entire job was one of fire fighting. He insisted that his job prevented him from devoting time to planning. All of his work was of an emergency nature. Furthermore, he had to answer all the emergency requests from other departments because people wanted to speak only to him.

The supervisor in question refused to accept the potential benefits of better planning. Part of his planning should include training a backup person who could respond to emergencies while he attended to paperwork and planning. Albrecht contends that typical "fire-department" managers are in the crunch mode because of a lack of objectives and a plan for coming to terms with the problems of the department. Also, they lack control over their own time. Managers who fail to plan generally face a career of fire fighting. Their departments can be characterized in this manner:[7]

> The symptoms of the fire department are fairly easy to spot. The most common is that the head man is harried, overworked, and overstressed. Another is the prevalence of "surprises"—unanticipated catastrophes that demand immediate attention—in department operations. Other symptoms include unseasonal peaks in work loads, general increases in internal pressure to meet frantic schedules and unrealistic deadlines, and continuing demands for superhuman efforts. In other words, fear, panic, and terror are the characteristics of the work day.

Contribution to mental health. Effective planning is an important way of preventing potentially harmful stress. When people feel that the job controls them rather than they controlling the job, a feeling of panic results. The panic sensation is usually accompanied by tension and anxiety. Planning helps give people the feeling that they can conquer the demands of their job. Assume that as the manager of a data processing department, a subordinate of yours tells you, "The situation is hopeless. We are so far behind schedule that we will never catch up. Besides, we are making major errors because of it."

You then counter that individual's sense of helplessness with some solid planning: "Okay, the situation looks bleak. But we

---

[7] Albrecht, *Supervisory Management*, p. 3.

can do something about it. I have the authorization to subcontract some of our more routine work to an outside data processing firm. We can also hire three office temporaries for up to a month. I think that should help." Your subordinate will now probably feel an immediate reduction in stress. Over the long range such an approach to stress reduction makes a positive contribution to mental health.

Better techniques of control. One important supervisory function not specifically described in Chapter 1 is controlling. Controlling involves holding people accountable for their results and measuring whether or not these results have been achieved. If you want to practice supervision, you have to control. In order to control you have to explain to people what it is they are expected to achieve and what steps are necessary for the achievement to take place. Sometimes employees help set their own goals and methods. In either case, specifying goals and how to attain them means that planning has taken place. Control is thus only possible as a follow-up to planning. No planning, no control.

One employee cogently illustrated the relationship between planning and control. She noted during a job attitude interview: "My boss complains that I'm not doing my job. But so far he hasn't told me what my job is supposed to be."

PHASES IN THE PLANNING PROCESS

The planning process is composed of a number of overlapping phases. Unlike a technical process, such as manufacturing paint, the phases of planning are somewhat arbitrary. Many different approaches to analyzing the planning process have been advanced. W. Jack Duncan has developed a framework of the planning process that has relevance for supervisory management.[8] As shown in Figure 6–2, planning can be divided into (a) goal formation, (b) forecasting future events and change, (c) developing strategies for implementing plans, and (d) implementation of plans. Phase c overlaps into the organizing function. Phase d can be regarded as organizing as well as part of planning.

---

[8] W. Jack Duncan, *Essentials of Management,* 2d ed. (Hinsdale, Ill.: The Dryden Press, 1978), pp. 285–86.

FIGURE 6–2
Phases in planning and its relationship to organizing and controlling

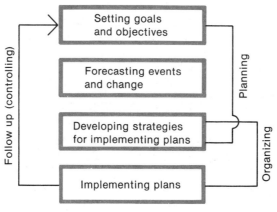

The type of planning you are doing depends to a large extent upon your type of management position. If you are the president of the Checker Motor Corporation, you might be involved in long-range planning that takes into consideration the most likely future of the automobile industry. If you are the supervisor of the bumper assembly department at Checker, your forecasting would probably take into account whether or not the shipment of bumpers will arrive on time.

Supervisors sometimes contend that textbook discussions of planning are irrelevant to them because planning is mostly the function of a specialist or a high-level manager. Bittel, a noted authority on supervisory management, counters with this argument: "Regardless of how much planning help a supervisor may get from his company's centralized scheduling department, the supervisor just won't be able to turn out the work without detailed planning on his own part."[9]

Phase I: Setting of goals and objectives. Here the supervisor participates in setting goals that contribute to higher-level goals.

---

[9] Lester R. Bittel, *What Every Supervisor Should Know*, 3d ed. (New York: McGraw-Hill, 1974), p. 439.

Judd, a hypothetical supervisor of the bumper department at Checker, might examine forecasts from the sales department and conclude that his department will have to install 300 bumpers next month. Production supervisors often establish such clear-cut goals.

Phase II: Forecasting events and changes.   Planning involves making predictions about events and changes that are likely to influence reaching objectives. Judd might contribute to planning here by making inputs such as these:

> I think we can anticipate a rise in absenteeism during the first three days of the deer hunting season.
>
> What would happen if we ran short on those heavy duty nuts and bolts we use to fasten on the bumpers? One year we had that problem.
>
> To assemble that many bumpers, all our equipment would have to be running perfectly. We could afford very little down time on the machines.

Phase III: Developing strategies for implementing plans. Once forecasts of anticipated changes and events are made, specific courses of action are drawn for implementing plans. Judd might formulate some plans (for approval from higher management) such as these:

> I'll give a department pep talk about the importance of good attendance for the heavy production period.
>
> I'll coordinate with the maintenance department to make sure that our machinery is in fine working order.
>
> I'll tell the personnel department about our possible need for temporary help during that period.

Phase IV: Implementation of plans.   Implementation is the actual carrying out of the plans. Judd will have to supervise his workers when they fasten 300 bumpers onto Checker taxicabs and Marathons next month. Implementing is doing. Implementation phases into the control function. Judd will have to keep a watchful eye on daily and weekly production figures to see if the 300-bumper quota can be reached. If figures begin to slide downward, Judd will have to take corrective action. A machine may have to be repaired or replaced; an employee may have to be coached or replaced.

GUIDES TO ESTABLISHING GOALS AND OBJECTIVES[10]

A primary reason many programs of goal setting and planning fail to bring about improvement is that the goals themselves are deficient. Without carefully reasoned goals and objectives, planning can become a meaningless exercise. Effective goals and objectives have certain characteristics in common. They should be kept in mind under whatever system of planning or goal setting you might be working.[11]

Clear, concise, and unambiguous.   Such an objective might be "reduce scrap rate on bumpers 25 percent by June 30 of this year."

Accurate in terms of the true end state or condition sought.   A weak objective for a keypunch operator would be to "become a better keypunch operator." You have to specify what it is that the other person should actually accomplish. A more effective objective would be to "increase current speed to 30 pages of data conversion per hour," or "increase the average daily amount of input transposed." The term *better keypunch operator* needs to be pinned down as tightly as possible.

Consistent with organizational policies and procedures.   A goal or objective that violates company policy only leads its originator into trouble. One caseworker established the objective of making night calls to agency clients in order to improve communications with them. This individual was later chastised by higher management for violating an agency restriction about after-hours work.

Interesting and challenging whenever possible.   An objective is motivational when it stretches your competence—providing it is not so difficult to achieve that it leads to frustration. Psychologists call such objectives *realistic*. In management by objectives programs (to be described later in this chapter), people set a number of routine objectives along with one or two that represent a major challenge (and are therefore motivational). A quality assurance technician might find challenging an objective

---

[10] The discussion in this section is based on Andrew J. DuBrin, *Fundamentals of Organizational Behavior,* 2d ed. (Elmsford, N.Y.: Pergamon, 1978), pp. 284–86.

[11] The first five characteristics are based on Stephen J. Carroll, Jr., and Henry L. Tosi, Jr., *Management by Objectives: Applications and Research* (New York: Macmillan, 1973), p. 72.

which states, "successfully devise a sampling procedure for inspecting our new cold tablets by September 15th of this year."

Jointly set by superior and subordinate. Many programs of goal setting were originally designed to give people an active role in setting their own goals. In practice many goal-setting programs are conducted in such a manner that the superior assigns the goals and objectives to subordinates. One review of MBO programs showed that in 28 percent of the cases, the subordinate is given a set of objectives as prepared by the superior.[12] So long as the subordinate feels committed to, or simply accepts, the imposed objective, it will probably work.

Established in a stable work environment. Short- and long-range objectives are the most meaningful when you are not yanked around from one job or assignment to another. One reason is simply that it is difficult to review the performance of subordinates who have been working for you only a short period of time. Another problem with a quickly changing organization is that it requires a frequent changing of objectives—often midway or sooner in the planned review cycle. As one office supervisor said, "Why set objectives when they will be meaningless two months from now?"

Specifies what is going to be accomplished, who is going to accomplish it, and when it is going to be accomplished. Answering the "who," "what," and "when" questions reduces the chances for misinterpretation. Here is an objective meeting these requirements: "The bumper department supervisor will increase the number of bumpers assembled per month to 300 by March 31st of this year. Bumper assemblies that do not pass inspection will be subtracted from the total."

THE TIME ELEMENT IN GOAL SETTING

Ideally, each goal and objective should be accompanied by a specific date for its accomplishment. The logical approach is to give first attention to those goals or objectives due to be achieved in the short range. Yet this distinction is not absolutely true. Some long-range goals—such as improving the image of your

---

[12] Robert N. Hollman, "Applying MBO Research in Practice," *Human Resources Management,* Winter 1976, pp. 28–36.

department—have to be acted on daily in order to be realized in the long range.

Objectives set in an MBO program usually include a completion date, as mentioned in the previous section. Figure 6–3 illustrates the time element in goal setting. In this example, an office supervisor has established goals over a 4½-month period. The "note" column is a convenient way of recording any problems that arise in achieving the goal or objective. Information of this type can be used the next time the supervisor engages in planning and goal setting.

FIGURE 6–3
The time element in goal setting

Goal or objective	Due date	Date completed	Note
1. Review performance of subordinates	1/15/80	2/12/80	Hit busy period
2. Get leaky pipe repaired	12/16/79	12/16/79	All OK
3. Add two new typists to department	1/31/80		
4. Have duplicating machine overhauled	4/30/80		

Source: Personal communication from John D. Minch, January 8, 1979.

ORGANIZING TO ACHIEVE GOALS

When you organize an activity to achieve goals, you are essentially determining who should do what. An important consideration is to choose the best type of organization design. A supervisor sometimes has considerable authority in organizing the work effort of employees. More often, the supervisor has to work within an existing structure and with existing personnel.

Assume the president of your company has appointed you as president of a newly formed jogging club. You regard the assignment as an honor. Automatically you have accepted the broad goal of forming such a club. Four key principles of organizing to achieve goals should be kept in mind: Select the right organization design; Place competent people in key spots; Delegate where feasible; Use a manageable span of control.

Select the right organization design. Chapter 4 describes in detail the problem of choosing the right shape of organization to accomplish a given purpose. Most likely you would choose a task force structure for your club. Officers of the club would contribute their time in addition to their regular company duties. Perhaps a few meetings could take place on company time, but most of the work would be done after hours. Very little chance exists that you could form a permanent department called the Jogging Club—a traditional functional organization.

Put competent people in key spots. Staffing is a necessary part of organizing. The Jogging Club will consume too much of your time if you do not find competent officers. You would want at least one jogging expert as a club officer. You might want to place a friendly, extraverted, well-liked individual in charge of the membership committee. Effort invested in finding the right club officers will pay handsome dividends in terms of reaching your goal of having a successful club. Almost no organization can function without competent people in key spots. Once systems and procedures are well established, less competent people can be slotted into non-key assignments.

Delegate when feasible. Successful managers at every level delegate work to subordinates. The alternative to delegation is to do everything yourself. Managers who delegate virtually all of their responsibilities are also in error. Managers should usually retain some important work for themselves. If not, your president may ask, "As president of the Jogging Club, what do you actually do?" It is important to exercise some control (follow-up) on work that is delegated. It is also important to delegate interesting assignments of substantial size. For instance, you might delegate the task of investigating other company jogging clubs to your officer in charge of new membership. This individual would then have the chance to visit several other companies at your own company's expense.

Use a realistic span of control. A span of control refers to the number of people a manager supervises directly. If ten people report to you without going through another manager, your span of control is ten. The more similar the work of subordinates, the larger can be your span of control. The more assistance needed by your subordinates, the shorter should be your span of control.

Similarly, the greater the coordination required the shorter the span of control for effective management.

As president of the Jogging Club, it would probably be feasible for every club officer to report directly to you. Only two levels of management would seem to be in order. You might only need about four or five officers to accomplish all the necessary work of the Jogging Club.

WORKING UNDER AN MBO SYSTEM

Management by objectives (MBO) has increasingly become a way of life in both profit and not-for-profit organizations. One survey of 500 leading industrial firms concluded that about one half of them have an MBO, or similar type of management by results program.[13] Community agencies that are fully or partially funded by federal government money almost inevitably use MBO. Supervisors in such organizations generally participate in the MBO program in terms of their own objectives. Technical and professional personnel reporting to supervisors usually participate in MBO. Clerical and production workers may have quotas, but they are infrequently involved directly in the MBO process.

The comments in the preceding section about characteristics of an effective objective are germane here. In addition, a supervisor who wants to work effectively under MBO should be aware of the nature of such a program and some of its more common problems.

Common elements in an MBO program

MBO is fundamentally a systematic application of goal setting and planning to help individuals and organizations be more productive. Since the application of MBO is so widespread, it lacks a format that is uniformly applied in every organization. Certain key elements, however, can be found in most programs. An MBO program typically involves people setting many objec-

---

[13] Fred E. Schuster and Alva F. Kindall, "Management by Objectives: Where We Stand—A Survey of the Fortune 500," *Human Resource Management,* Spring 1974, pp. 8–11.

tives for themselves. However, management frequently imposes key organizational objectives upon people. The top management of an aerospace manufacturer might impose the following objective on everybody involved with the flight-connected aspects of its aircraft: "All flight-related components of our planes must achieve zero defect status." Five steps are usually followed in sequence in an MBO program.[14]

Establishing organizational goals. Top levels of management set organizational goals to begin the entire MBO process. These goals are usually quite broad and sometimes even philosophical. A group of hospital administrators, for example, might decide upon the general goal of improving health-care service to poor people in the community. After these broad goals are agreed upon, a determination is then made of what must be accomplished by divisions or units in order to meet the organizational goals.

Establishing unit objectives. Unit heads then establish objectives for their units (typically departments or divisions). A cascading of objectives takes place as the process proceeds on down the line. Objectives set at lower levels of the organization must be designed to meet general goals established by top management. (Figure 6–1, shown earlier, illustrates this process.)

Lower-level managers and individual contributors have an input into the process because a general goal usually gives considerable latitude for setting individual objectives to meet that goal. The head of the inpatient admissions department might decide that working more closely with the county welfare department must be accomplished if the health-care goal cited above is to be met.

Subordinate proposals. At this point subordinates make proposals about how they will contribute to unit objectives. The assistant to the manager of inpatient admissions might agree to set up a task force to work with the welfare department. Each subordinate is also given the opportunity to set some objectives

---

[14] The steps presented here are a synthesis of information found in Felix M. Lopez, Jr., *Evaluating Employee Performance* (Chicago: Public Personnel Administration, 1968), pp. 227–29; and Ross A. Webber, *Management: Basic Elements of Managing Organizations* (Homewood, Il.: Richard D. Irwin, 1975), pp. 347–50. © 1975 by Richard D. Irwin, Inc. An excellent overview of the MBO process is also found in Duncan, *Essentials of Management,* pp. 315–33.

in addition to those that meet the major organizational goals. Many MBO programs suggest that each participant establish some personal and professional objectives in addition to the standard work objectives. Figure 6–4 shows the work objectives jointly set by one person and his boss.

FIGURE 6–4
Type of memo form used for statement of objectives

Job title and brief job description
Supervisor, Bumper Assembly
  Department:
  Responsible for supervising operations of bumper assembly department. Duties include the training and disciplining of employees. The supervisor must maintain high standards of safety and morale.

Objectives for Judd Mayberry
1. Achieve production quota of 300 sets of bumpers installed per day by July 31 of this year.
2. By November 15 of this year, submit accurate information for preparing next year's budget.
3. Train ten new installation technicians by December 31 of this year. Training must result in technicians who can work up to standard.
4. Visit vendor for bumpers once this year to discuss any quality problems that may exist at the time.
5. Take advanced course in supervision or human relations at local college. Achieve a grade of B or better.

Joint negotiation or agreement. Superiors and subordinates confer together at this stage to either agree on the objectives set by the subordinate or to negotiate further. In the hospital illustration being used here, one department head might state that she wants to reserve ten beds on the ward for the exclusive use of indigent people. Her supervisor might welcome her suggestion but point out that only five beds could be allocated for such a purpose. They might settle for seven beds to be set aside for the needy poor.

Reviewing performance. After an agreed-upon review cycle (typically once quarterly or semiannually), a performance review is held. Persons receive good performance reviews to the extent that they attain most of their major objectives. When objectives are not attained, the manager and subordinate mutually analyze what went wrong. Equally important, they discuss possible corrective actions. Perhaps the individual needs more help from management, such as more clerical support, to reach the objectives.

New objectives are then set for the next review period. To illustrate, one hospital manager agreed to establish a task force to investigate the feasibility of establishing satellite health-care facilities in poor sections of town. MBO is a life-long, continuing process, assuming it is working correctly.

Potential problems with MBO

Despite the frequent favorable mention of MBO, this system of planning and goal setting encounters numerous problems in practice. Many companies have discarded their MBO program after an initial burst of enthusiasm. A general problem is that considerable training is required for people to implement such a program effectively. Most managers and individual contributors need training in setting effective objectives. If objectives are set too loosely, they offer small improvement over a job description. If they are defined too precisely, they may serve as a straitjacket. Three of the more common problems with MBO are discussed next.[15]

MBO is a very time-consuming process. For MBO to work well, substantial amounts of time must be devoted to its planning and implementation. Training programs must be scheduled, elaborate forms must be developed, and countless hours have to be spent in superior-subordinate discussions about objective settings and performance reviews. The paperwork requirements along to MBO seem excessive to many supervisors who are already burdened with paperwork. At least 80 percent of MBO programs require written documentation.

If you view a manager's job as primarily one of implementing an MBO system, the time is not excessive. An authoritarian organization in which superiors simply tell subordinates what has to be done and how to do it is a less time-consuming system of management than MBO.

---

[15] A thorough discussion of problems with MBO is found in Webber, *Management,* pp. 351–55. An analysis of the effective application of MBO is Hollman, "Applying MBO Research," pp. 28–36.

Objectives can become obsessions. Under an MBO system, people realize that their job performance will be rated high to the extent that they reach all their objectives. People thus have a tendency to invest most of their energies in reaching these objectives even if more important problems occur. One sales order specialist set the objective of having a better organized, neater workplace. So much effort was put into attaining this objective that any work that would create a disorganized condition in the work area was resisted. Unfortunately this meant discouraging out-of-the-ordinary inquiries—those that would require foraging through the files.

People resist being measured. Many people resist being measured for various reasons. An underlying fear some supervisors and other employees have is that MBO is really a "shape up or ship out program." These people feel that management wants MBO to prove to people that they are deficient in their performance. Others feel that MBO is beneath their dignity. One tool and die maker stated, "Who needs a form from the personnel department to tell me how to do my job. The day I don't know what I should be doing on the job is the day I'll quit."

A related line of reasoning is that the work of many managers and staff personnel is difficult to measure precisely. Thus many people believe that only people working in jobs where output can be precisely measured (such as a furniture maker) should be subject to MBO.

MBO requires some selling to subordinates. The problems of MBO should be regarded as potential problems. Intelligent application of MBO gives an organization a chance of having people working together in a systematic, organized manner. At its best, MBO capitalizes upon the advantages of goal setting.

Participants in an MBO program need a careful explanation of how it can be beneficial to themselves as well as the total organization. Quite often the problems encountered with MBO systems stem from a lack of thorough training in its techniques and an explanation of its underlying philosophy. One supervisor, a conscientious long-term employee, complained about working under a system that kept score of all activities. The supervisor's manager patiently explained that MBO gives top performers an opportunity to receive credit for outstanding contribution. After the "sales pitch," the supervisor in question realized that MBO documents good as well as poor performance. MBO is a method of getting credit for your contribution.

SUMMARY OF KEY POINTS

☐ Almost every supervisor can improve job performance by incorporating some degree of goal setting and planning into the job.

☐ Every action taken by a manager or individual contributor should have a purpose in mind—it should be related to the attainment of a goal or objective.

☐ Planning has a number of potential advantages to the individual and the organization. Among them are increased productivity, increased satisfaction and morale, overcoming the fire-fighting mode, improved mental health, and better techniques of control.

☐ Planning can arbitrarily be divided into the phases of (a) goal formation, (b) forecasting future events and changes, (c) developing strategies for implementing plans, and (d) implementation of plans. Phase c overlaps into the organizing function; phase d can be regarded as organizing as well as part of planning.

☐ Effective goals and objectives have some or all of these seven characteristics: clear, concise, and unambiguous; accurate in terms of the true end state or condition sought; consistent with organizational policies and procedures; interesting and challenging whenever possible; jointly set by superior and subordinate; established in a stable work environment; specifies what is to be accomplished, who is to accomplish it, and when it is to be accomplished.

☐ Four key considerations in organizing to achieve goals are select the right organization design, put competent people in key spots, delegate where feasible, and use an appropriate span of control.

☐ MBO is the most widely used formal system of goal setting and planning. In general, it has these elements in common: establishing organizational goals, establishing unit objectives, obtaining proposals from subordinates about their objectives, joint negotiation or agreement concerning the proposals, and reviewing performance.

☐ In practice, MBO encounters many problems. Among them are: (1) It can be a very time consuming process. (2) Objectives can become obsessions. (3) Many people resist being measured. As an antidote for these potential problems, the possible benefits of MBO must be effectively communicated to subordinates.

GUIDELINES FOR SUPERVISORY PRACTICE

1. As a supervisor, one of your most important functions is to give your subordinates a clear understanding as to what it is they are expected to accomplish. In other words, you should provide them, with clear-cut objectives or help them establish them.

2. To as full an extent as possible, relate all of your work activities to work goals or objectives. The opposite of goal-related activity is busywork!

3. If you work under any system of goal setting and planning, devote considerable attention to setting effective objectives. (See the suggestions presented earlier in this chapter.) Goal setting and planning will be much more beneficial if the objectives used are of high quality.

QUESTIONS FOR DISCUSSION AND REVIEW

1. What similarities and differences do you see between production standards set for manufacturing employees and objectives or goals set for supervisors?

2. What similarity do you see between learning objectives (as used in this book) and work objectives?

3. In what way do professional athletic teams work under a system of goal setting and planning?

4. If planning is supposed to be so valuable, why do you think so many companies neglect a formal approach to planning?

5. Have you done any goal setting or planning in your personal life? In what way was it helpful or harmful?

6. In some organizations, separate planning departments do most of the planning. The planners then pass along these plans to managers in other departments. What do you think are the advantages and disadvantages of such a system?

7. Planning tends to have higher status than other managerial activities such as disciplining employees. What do you think has led to such high status to planning?

8. To what extent is planning simply common sense?

9. What will happen to your planning if your forecasts are inaccurate?

10. Make up a set of objectives for the president of the United States or the prime minister of Canada.

11. What do you think is the relationship between a person's job description and the objectives established in an MBO program?

12. Under what conditions do you think a person would feel committed to an objective?

A supervisory problem: The reluctant oldtimer

You have been working for six months in the body stamping department of the Checker Motor Corporation. A companywide MBO program is then instituted. After two months of training designed to properly implement the program, you begin to negotiate objectives with the higher level workers in your department. After several successful negotiating sessions, you meet with Frank Harrison, senior tool and die maker in your department. After a brief exchange of pleasantries, he confronts you with this statement:

"It's nice to know that Checker now has a newfangled program. But don't forget we've been a very successful company for over 40 years without such a program. Furthermore, I know my work as well as anybody in this company. I don't need a young upstart supervisor to help me along in figuring out what my job is supposed to be. I wish you would keep in mind that I also earn a good deal more money than you. I wouldn't be paid so much if I needed a supervisor to watch over me. Maybe you should use this MBO program on some of the younger fellows and gals in the department."

1. *How should you react to Frank Harrison's statements?*
2. *What seems to be Frank's underlying problem?*
3. *Should you immediately take this problem up with your boss or the personnel department?*

SOME SUGGESTED READING

Albrecht, Karl. "Are You Running a 'Fire Department'?" *Supervisory Management*, June 1977, pp. 2–8.

Carlisle, Howard M. *Management: Concepts and Situations.* Chicago: Science Research Associates, 1976, chap. 22.

Carroll, Archie B., and Anthony, Ted F. "An Overview of the Supervisor's Job." *Personnel Journal,* May 1976, pp. 228–31, 249.

Dale, Ernest. *Management: Theory and Practice.* 4th ed. New York: McGraw-Hill, 1978.

DeFee, Dallas T. "Management by Objectives: When and How Does It Work?" *Personnel Journal,* January 1977, pp. 37–39, 42.

Dillon, C. R. "MBO, Part 1: Setting Objectives." *Supervisory Management,* April 1976, pp. 18–22.

Drucker, Peter F. *The Practice of Management.* New York: Harper & Row, 1954.

Hampton, David R. *Contemporary Management.* New York: McGraw-Hill, 1977, chaps. 5 and 6.

Humble, John W. *How to Manage by Objectives.* New York: AMACOM, 1973.

Latham, Gary P., and Kinne, Sydney B., III. "Improving Job Performance through Training in Goal Setting." *Journal of Applied Psychology,* April 1974, pp. 187–91.

Latham, Gary P., and Yukl, Gary A. "A Review of Research on the Application of Goal Setting in Organizations." *Academy of Management Journal,* December 1975, pp. 824–45.

McConkey, Dale D. *MBO for Nonprofit Organizations.* New York: AMACOM, 1975.

Mintzberg, Henry. "The Manager's Job: Folklore and Fact." *Harvard Business Review,* July–August 1975, pp. 49–61.

Murray, Richard K. "Behavioral Management Objectives." *Personnel Journal,* April 1973, pp. 304–6.

Oldham, Greg R. "The Impact of Supervisory Characteristics on Goal Acceptance." *Academy of Management Journal,* September 1975, pp. 461–75.

Decision making and creativity

LEARNING OBJECTIVES

After reading and thinking through the material in this chapter, you should be able to:

1. Improve your method for making important decisions.
2. Outline the basic elements in the decision-making process.
3. Understand why feedback is an important part of the decision-making process.
4. Select a method for improving your job-related creativity.
5. Understand how you can bring creative ideas to the job without being a highly creative person yourself.

The supervisor as a decision maker

Maggie Walworth, a mailroom supervisor in a large company, has a headache. She wishes today would be relatively peaceful. But by 9:45 A.M. she is faced with three out-of-the ordinary requests:

> Rolf, one of her mail sorters, wants to know if he can take off next Friday in order to attend his sister's wedding in Toronto. Part of his reasoning: "My sister means more to me than my job."
>
> Kelly, a typist in the department, wants to know if she should stop typing until her typewriter is repaired or replaced. She contends, "My typewriter smells funny. Like something is burning or smoking, but I can't find anything wrong in particular."
>
> Len, her boss, telephones her with an unusual request: "Maggie, could you help us out on a delicate problem? A mentally retarded young man has applied for a job with our company. Do you think you could create a job for him? The company wants to hire some mentally handicapped people, but we don't know where to put people like that."

159

Despite Maggie's hope for a peaceful day, she is now forced to exercise a supervisor's most basic function—that of decision making. Everytime a supervisor makes a choice among alternatives, a decision is being made. If company rules and regulations clearly covered every possible contingency that would arise, decision making would be easy. Maggie could point to the rule book and say, for example, "Kelly, keep typing. At our company a strange odor emanating from a typewriter is not justification for stopping work." Since not every possible contingency is covered by rules and regulations, supervisory decision making requires skill and judgment.

The Framework for Accomplishing Results presented in Chapter 1 is essentially a method for approaching the kinds of decisions faced by supervisors. In this chapter we will probe more deeply into the process and also examine the role of creativity in making decisions.

STEPS IN MAKING A DECISION

A number of similar approaches to managerial decision making have been proposed.[1] All of them center around a systematic and logical, step-by-step approach. Here we will emphasize the approach for making effective decisions formulated by Peter Drucker, a noted management consultant and writer about management topics.[2] Drucker's framework is compatible with the Framework for Accomplishing Results emphasized in this book.

Referring back to Maggie and her pending decision about placing the mentally retarded employee in her department: Her decision making will follow these six steps outlined by Drucker: (1) classification of the problem; (2) definition of the problem; (3) conditions to be satisfied; (4) looking for rightness; (5) action to be taken; and (6) feedback.

---

[1] One such framework, along with a review of several others, is found in Andrew J. DuBrin, *Fundamentals of Organizational Behavior: An Applied Perspective,* 2d ed. (Elmsford, N.Y.: Pergamon, 1978), chap. 3.

[2] Peter F. Drucker, "The Effective Decision," *Harvard Business Review,* January–February 1967, pp. 92–98. See also Drucker's book, *The Effective Executive* (New York: Harper & Row, 1967). Our discussion closely follows Drucker's discussion, but some of his terms have been modified for the purposes of this book.

Classification of the problem. One way of classifying each decision situation is to classify it as routine or unique. (Drucker uses the term *generic* to imply routine.) If the decision is routine, it means that the alternatives have already been specified by company policy or precedent. If an employee asks, "What shall I do, my machine broke down?" the supervisor faces a routine decision. In such cases, the machine maintenance department is contacted immediately.

The decision facing Maggie about the mentally retarded employee is more of a unique event. No particular precedent exists (at least in Maggie's department). Maggie now recognizes that the decision facing her requires a novel solution.

Definition of the problem. According to Drucker, once a problem has been classified as routine or unique, it is usually relatively easy to define. Questions such as these might be asked: "What is this all about?" "What is pertinent here?" "What is the key to this situation?" In Maggie's situation, she would probably be safe to conclude that the problem she faces is one of placing an employee of limited ability in her department.

Truly effective decision makers are aware that a danger in defining a problem is to arrive at a plausible but incomplete definition. Drucker advises: "There is only one safeguard against becoming the prisoner of an incomplete definition: check it again and again against *all* the observable facts, and throw out a definition the moment it fails to encompass any of them."[3] The scientific method is based on testing definitions against all observable facts.

As Maggie ponders about the problem facing her, she may recognize that placing a retarded person in her department has many implications. "How much supervision will this individual require?" "What should the expected level of productivity be?" "Do I or somebody else in the department have the necessary skills to provide this individual with the type of care and attention necessary and desirable?"

Conditions to be satisfied. The next major element or step in the decision-making process is defining clear specifications

---

[3] Drucker, "Effective Decision," p. 94.

about what the decision has to accomplish. Here the supervisor, or any other decision maker, must ask questions such as: "What objectives must be reached?" "What conditions must be satisfied?" "What minimum goals must be attained?"

Maggie might say, "Yes, I'll find a spot in my department for this new job applicant" and still make an ineffective decision. Unless Maggie decides on a course of action that will benefit the job applicant and the mailroom, her decision will not be totally satisfactory. If the retarded person is asked to sort mail and makes drastic mistakes in the process, Maggie will be blamed for mismanagement. An important part of her decision will be finding the right slot for the applicant.

Looking for rightness. At this stage the decision maker looks for the right decision rather than one that is an acceptable compromise. Often what appears to be an acceptable compromise winds up satisfying nobody. Maggie might fall into this trap if she made this decision: "What I propose to do is to hire your applicant for a two-month period. By that time you should be able to find permanent employment somewhere else in the company." It would probably be best for a mentally slow person not to be given a temporary assignment. A person with limited intelligence needs to be brought along slowly with a minimum of change in instructions and routines.

Action. Converting the decision to action is the fifth major step or element in the decision-making process. Unless a decision is implemented, it is really no decision at all. If you decide that "this is the year I will definitely begin to set long-range goals for myself," it is not really a decision until you actually start to set some goals. Drucker observes from his consulting experience that "The flaw in so many policy statements, especially those of business, is that they contain no action commitment—to carry them out is no one's specific work and responsibility."[4]

Maggie then decides to make a concrete decision along with an accompanying plan of action. She will offer the handicapped

---

[4] Drucker, Ibid., p. 96.

applicant a job as a mail deliverer in the company. Duties of the job are to push a mail cart from office to office, picking up letters and packages for delivery to the mailroom. It will involve a one-week training program, including "tagging along" with an experienced mail deliverer. The person presently in the job will be upgraded to a position working with a mail sorting machine.

Feedback. A decision is not complete until you get a firsthand look at the results of your decision. If you decide to accept a position with U.S. Civil Service, you will not know whether or not that is a good decision until you have been on the job awhile. Maggie will have several inputs informing her about the adequacy of her decision. If the company is satisfied with her efforts, she will have some positive evidence. If the handicapped person performs well in the job and is satisfied, she will have additional evidence.

Feedback helps a supervisor with decision making in another important way. What you learn from feedback helps modify your decision. You might decide that your decision to join the U.S. Civil Service was sound, but the job you accepted was not for you. Perhaps you request a job transfer that will improve upon your decision. On the basis of her favorable experience with this one retarded individual, Maggie might, in the future, volunteer to place a similarly handicapped person in the mailroom.

CREATIVITY ON THE JOB

Part of making good decisions is finding creative solutions to problems facing you at work. Contrary to a popular stereotype, the ability to think creatively is not found exclusively among a handful of inventors, scientists, artists, and writers. In truth, creativity is like height, intelligence, and strength. People vary considerably in these dimensions, but everybody has *some* height, *some* intelligence, and *some* strength. Expressing creativity on the job sometimes improves company operations and helps individuals advance their careers:[5]

---

[5] William D. Ellis, "Creativity: A Path to Profit," *Nation's Business*, March 1973, pp. 70–71. Reprinted by permission from *Nation's Business*. Copyright 1973 by *Nation's Business*, Chamber of Commerce of the United States.

A mechanic for a large manufacturing company knew the firm was planning to buy some very expensive machinery to speed up the manufacturing of automotive engine bearings. Eating his lunch under a tree one day, he suddenly envisioned a mechanical device that, installed on the present machines, would streamline the production as effectively as the new equipment. He flattened his brown-paper lunch bag, diagrammed the idea on it and dropped it into the company suggestion box.

The company's engineers took the idea from the brown bag to blueprint form, then made a small model of the device. It worked. Under a company formula, the mechanic was rewarded with a bonus of $35,000 (expressed in 1980 U.S. dollars).

Characteristics of a creative person. A workable definition of creativity is "the processing of information in such a way that the result is new, original, and meaningful."[6] As a supervisor you might think of a complicated mechanical-chemical device which would trap and kill moths in a painless manner. Your production would be novel, but relatively useless from the standpoint of your company.

A creative decision maker lets his or her imagination wander. In addition, that person makes deliberate jumps in thinking and welcomes chance ideas whenever they come along. The decision maker in question ventures beyond the constraints that limit most people. In contrast, the conformist or less creative person "proceeds in an orderly way from point to point. Each step is supported by the preceding step, as if a computer program were being written, a mathematical proof were being derived."[7]

Figure 7–1 summarizes the personality characteristics and traits of people who tend to find creative solutions to many of the problems they face.[8]

Figure 7–1 also summarizes the characteristics of organizations that encourage creativity from employees at all levels. A person with the potential to think of creative alternatives to

---

[6] *Understanding Psychology* (Del Mar, Calif.: CRM Books, 1974), p. 71.

[7] "Jumping to Solutions," *Psychology Today*, December 1977, p. 75. Based on information in Eugene Raudsepp (with George P. Hough, Jr.), *Creative Growth Games* (New York: Harcourt Brace Jovanovich, 1977).

[8] Figure 7–1 is based on information in Andrew J. DuBrin, *Human Relations: A Job Oriented Approach* (Reston, Va.: Reston, 1978), pp. 53–54. The underlying references are Donald W. MacKinnon, "The Nature and Nurture of Creative Talent," in *Readings in Managerial Psychology* (Chicago: University of Chicago Press, 1964), pp. 90–109; and Gary A. Steiner, ed., *The Creative Organization* (Chicago: University of Chicago Press, 1965), pp. 22–23.

FIGURE 7–1
Characteristics of creative people and creative organizations

Creative people
1. Creative people tend to be bright rather than brilliant. Extraordinarily high intelligence is not required to be creative, but creative people are good at generating many different ideas in a short period of time.
2. Creative people tend to have a positive self-image; they feel good about themselves.
3. Creative people are emotionally expressive and sensitive to the world around them and the feelings of others.
4. Creative people, almost by definition, are original in their thinking.
5. Creative people tend to be interested in the nature of the problem itself; they are stimulated (motivated) by challenging problems.
6. Creative people usually suspend judgment until they have collected ample facts about a problem. Thus they are more reflective than impulsive.
7. Creative people are frequently nonconformists. They value their independence and do not have strong needs to gain approval from the group.
8. Creative people lead a rich, almost bizarre, fantasy life. They are just "crazy" enough to serve their creative ends.
9. Creative people tend to be flexible and not authoritarian. Faced with a problem, they reject black and white (categorical) thinking and look for nuances.
10. Creative people are more concerned with meanings and implications than with the small details.

Creative organizations
1. A trustful management that does not overcontrol people.
2. Open channels of communication among members of the organization; a minimum of secrecy.
3. Considerable contact and communication with outsiders to the organization.
4. Large variety of personality types.
5. Willing to accept change, but not enamored with change for its own sake.
6. Enjoyment in experimenting with new ideas.
7. Little fear of the consequences of making a mistake.
8. Selects people and promotes them primarily on the basis of merit.
9. Uses techniques for encouraging ideas, such as suggestion systems and brainstorming.
10. Sufficient financial, managerial, human, and time resources to accomplish its goals.

Source: From Andrew J. DuBrin, *Human Relations: A Job Oriented Approach* (Reston, Va.: Reston, 1978), pp. 53–54.

problems usually needs some encouragement from the organization. An environment that places a premium on risk taking and innovation is one that encourages creativity. An organization that stifles initiative and penalizes people for making any mistakes will tend to discourage persons from displaying their creativity. In general it is easier to discourage than encourage creative response from employees.

As you read the characteristics of creative individuals and organizations listed in Figure 7–1, you will notice some similarities. For example, creative organizations and individuals both show an overall tendency toward being flexible.

Improving your creativity[9]

As a supervisor or potential supervisor, it could be to your career advantage to become a more creative person. If you are already somewhat creative, making a conscious effort to enhance your creativity is likely to be a profitable investment in time. It is usually easier to build on strengths than overcome weaknesses. Here we will suggest four do-it-yourself techniques for improving your creativity. If you want to pursue creativity improvement further, you might refer to appropriate references at the end of this chapter. Also, training programs such as group brainstorming or synectics should also be investigated.

Be curious. Curiosity frequently underlies creative ideas. The person who routinely questions why things work or why they don't work is on the way toward developing a creative suggestion to improve upon what already exists. Many new ideas and products stem from the curious attitude of their developer. An office supervisor in a plumbing supply company encouraged the company to develop a new mechanism that would help stop leaking water closets. This suggestion stemmed from a curiosity as to why so many places had troubles with leaking toilets. The resultant product is built upon a new principle: It uses water pressure to replace the troublesome floating bulb arrangement found in most water closets.

---

[9] The suggestions for improving creativity described in this section are excerpted from Andrew J. DuBrin, *Survival in the Office* (New York: Van Nostrand Reinhold, 1977), chap. 12.

Discipline yourself to think creatively. No matter how much time and money you invest in courses of study or training programs to enhance your creativity, you will not become more creative unless you practice habits of creativity. People labeled as creative discover many of their best ideas in everyday settings. While walking the streets, taking out your garbage, getting your hair cut or coiffed, cleaning your garage, or waiting in line at the bank, look for ideas that could be put to use on your job.

Self-discipline is the underlying method that enables you to cull useful ideas from everyday happenings. You have to discipline yourself to stay alert to useful ideas or combinations of ideas. Once you have developed the mental set of looking for creative ideas, a few ideas may begin to emerge.

> *A traveler cashes in on an idea.* Many years ago, a storekeeper named Jacob Ritty was on a transatlantic voyage. He was fascinated by the device that recorded the propeller revolutions of the ship. Ritty reasoned that the same principle could be applied to keeping track of money received by a retail store. The eventual result was a machine that came to be called a cash register.

Conduct private brainstorming sessions. Brainstorming, as originally developed by Alex Osburn in the latter 1930s, is a technique for group members spewing forth multiple solutions to a problem. Thus a group of six people sit around a table generating new names for a dog food. Anything goes, however bizarre it sounds at the time. A few examples are "Bow Wow Chow," "Pet Steak," "Canine-Fine," and "Boxer Bagels." Later the group refines some of the more promising ideas.

Repeated experiments have demonstrated that good ideas do come out of groups—but good ideas also emerge from private brainstorming sessions. The two previous methods of creativity improvement already described will help you develop the mental flexibility so necessary for brainstorming. After you have loosened up your mental processes, you will be ready to tackle your most vexing job-related problem.

An important requirement of private brainstorming is that you set aside a regular time (and perhaps place) for generating ideas. (Count the ideas discovered in the process of routine activities as bonus time.) Even five minutes per day is much more time than most people are accustomed to thinking creatively about job problems. Give yourself a quota with a time deadline.

> *Creativity in a hardware store.*   Hal was a part owner of a hardware store. He had agreed to take on the assignment of thinking of an effective way of raising some quick cash for his store. Hal allowed himself six days to find a solution to this problem. His proposed solutions were: (1) pawn some expensive merchandise, (2) borrow money from a bank or loan company, (3) establish a fix-it service for minor household repairs, and (4) hold a garage sale for damaged or slow-moving merchandise.
>
> The garage sale idea proved to be a winner. Hal and his co-owner were able to raise several thousand dollars in needed cash and simultaneously clear some of the clutter from their store. As a result, Hal increased his confidence in his ability to think creatively about job problems. (Hal's idea is now widely used in his region by other hardware and home improvement stores.)

Use the personal analogy method.   Synectics, developed by William J. J. Gordon has proved to be an effective method of improving creativity.[10] Among its many components is the personal analogy method. According to this novel method, members of the creativity training group imagine themselves as one of the problem objects. For instance, "If you were a pool outside a motel-restaurant, how would you prevent drunks from jumping into you at night?" Personal analogies can also be done individually.

> *Creativity in the maintenance department.*   Maintenance supervisor Ted was called into his boss's office for a serious conference: "Ted, we've gotten a number of complaints from building tenants that our carpeting looks shabby in a few key places. What the people are complaining about deals mostly with a few high traffic pattern areas. They say our carpeting is shabby, but what they really mean is that the carpeting is worn out near the water coolers, receptionist desk, and elevators. Figure out an inexpensive way to take care of this problem."
>
> Having been through a company-sponsored creativity training program, Ted decided to put the suggestions to work. He thought to himself, "If I were the carpeting on the floor, I wouldn't want to be replaced entirely every time I became a little shabby. I'd want to stay put, the best I could. I wouldn't mind if I were improved a little, but I wouldn't want to be replaced entirely."

---

[10] William J. J. Gordon, *Synectics* (New York: Harper & Row, 1961). See also Gordon, "Operational Approach to Creativity," *Harvard Business Review,* November–December 1956, pp. 41–51.

Ted arrived at an obvious solution. He suggested to his boss that the company purchase carpeting squares—similar to tiles—for the high traffic areas. As the carpet became worn, new squares could be put into place with a minimum of expense. When the building needed carpeting throughout, the square concept could be used on a larger scale. In this way when heavy furniture was moved, the damaged carpeting immediately under it could be replaced with a brand new piece of carpeting.

Where to borrow creative ideas

An established management text lists duplication—copying the success of others—as a type of creativity. "Although not creative in the innovative sense, duplication is certainly creative from the point of view of any organization into which it is brought, for it provides something new for that organization."[11] If supervisors accept the fact that duplication is an important process, they must then search for ideas to duplicate.

One source of good ideas is conversations with people from other departments and specialities. Supervisors who maintain contacts with supervisors or staff specialists from their company, or other companies, have a pipeline to potentially useful ideas. Specialists such as industrial engineers typically gather useful ideas from supervisors. Reversing the process can help bring about reciprocity in the relationships between supervisors and industrial engineers.

Reading also serves as a useful source of creative ideas. Figure 7–2 lists 22 magazines and journals that frequently contain novel ideas about improving job and supervisory effectiveness. Supervisors who peruse magazines or journals of most interest to them would probably uncover a few workable ideas. One supervisor sold a company on the benefits of two people sharing one full-time job after reading an article about job sharing in a personnel magazine.

Books, including text and trade (nontechnical) books, are another natural source of ideas to borrow. Company libraries, general libraries, college libraries, and large bookstores usually have a business section containing many books of potential use to supervisors.

---

[11] Herbert G. Hicks and C. Ray Gullett, *The Management of Organizations*, 3d ed. (New York: McGraw-Hill, 1976), p. 210.

FIGURE 7–2
Examples of magazines and journals useful for borrowing creative ideas

Advertising Age	*Modern Hospital*
American Machinist	*Nation's Business*
Business Week	*Office Management*
Chemical Engineering	*Personnel Journal*
Dun's Review	*Personnel Management*
Electrical World	*Product Engineering*
Electronics	*Product Management*
Factory	*Production Management*
Harvard Business Review	*Purchasing Week*
Industrial Distribution	*Supervisory Management*
Industrial Engineering	*The Wall Street Journal*
Industry Week	

RELATING YOUR DECISION TO COMPANY POLICY

No matter how logically sound your decision might be in a given situation, it must relate back to company policy. Assume Maggie, our mailroom supervisor, became aware that morale in the mailroom was declining. As an antidote, she held a discussion with mailroom employees about the problem. Maggie learns that the group dislikes their drab work environment. She then decides to paint and wallpaper the department using her own funds. Morale might temporarily increase, but Maggie might find herself in trouble with higher management. In her company, supervisors might not have the authority to decorate their own departments.

A sound approach is to hold back on making a final decision about anything until you are sure you have the authority to make such a decision. Sometimes organizational policy manuals, supervisory manuals, or the like will describe the parameters of your decision-making authority. At other times it may be necessary to confer with your own superior before implementing a nonroutine decision. Another value of conferring with a superior about a nonroutine decision is that you might be given clearance to temporarily stretch policy.

QUANTITATIVE TOOLS FOR DECISION MAKING

To aid in the decision-making process, most large organizations make some use of quantitative tools. The widespread use of computers has given impetus to quantitative decision making. Data are easier to obtain and calculations are easier to make through the use of computers. Much of the input for computers comes from the basic forms completed by first-level supervisors. For example, a supervisor's mark senses a form which records how much of raw material A is being used in the manufacture of product B. In this way, the supervisor is a link in the chain of communication by providing key figures to the computer.

In this section we present a brief description of three quantitative tools used in decision making and planning: break-even analysis, decision trees, and PERT charts.

Break-even analysis.[12] Managers at all levels in an organization must be profit and cost conscious. Before adding a new product, equipment, or personnel, it should be clear that the added product, equipment, or personnel will make a financial contribution. Break-even analysis tells us at what point it is profitable to go ahead with a new venture. Several basic terms need to be understood to perform a break-even analysis:

BE = Break-even point, a situation that exists when total revenues equal fixed costs plus variable costs.

P = Selling price per unit, or the revenue generated by the equipment, product, or new employee (such as a sales representative).

VC = Variable cost per unit—costs that vary with the amount produced. Examples include the costs of material and direct labor.

TFC = Total fixed costs—a cost that remains constant no matter how many units are produced. Examples in-

---

[12] Our description of break-even analysis follows closely that presented in James H. Donnelly, Jr., James L. Gibson, and John M. Ivancevich, *Fundamentals of Management: Functions, Behavior, Models*, 3d ed. (Dallas: Business Publications, 1978), pp. 385–92. © 1978 by Business Publications, Inc.

clude rent, utilities, real estate taxes, property insurance, and some administrative salaries.

Q = Number of units.

Using accounting terms, the break-even point occurs when the quantity sold produces a margin above variable costs that equals the amount required for fixed costs. Or simply, where total cost equals total revenue. In algebraic terms,

$$BE = \frac{TFC}{P - VC}$$

Assume you are a manufacturing supervisor for a small automotive supplier. You are trying to decide if it would be worthwhile to fill an order for 11,000 cans of crank case additive. P would be $10 per can; VC would be $6 per unit; and TFC would be $40,000. Using the break-even formula,

$$BE = \frac{\$40,000}{\$10 - \$6}$$

$$= 10,000 \text{ cans of additive}$$

Your firm would earn a profit on the last 1,000 cans of crank case additive. Few small businesses would turn down this business under these terms.

Decision trees. Break-even analysis is used to make determinations about the outcome of basically one decision. Decision trees are used to assess (or speculate about) the outcome of a series of decisions. As the sequences of the major decision are chained out, it soon resembles a tree with branches. Our purposes will be served by taking a decision tree out only two branches.[13]

Assume you are the manager of a motel in northern Michigan. You want to know the advisability of enlarging the motel for next year. The probability of having a good season is 0.6. Correspondingly, the probability of having a poor season is 0.4. (Any mathematical decision-making technique is only as good as the accuracy of these hunches.)

---

[13] Our description of the decision tree follows the logic presented in Fremont E. Kast and James E. Rosenzweig, *Organization and Management: A Systems and Contingency Approach*, 3d ed. (New York: McGraw-Hill, 1979), pp. 382–85.

Your accountant tells you that the payout, or net cash flow, from having a good season with the enlarged motel is $180,000. If you had a poor season, you would have a negative payout of $40,000. With the same (unenlarged) motel, your payout from a good season would be $160,000. But the payout from a poor season would be a loss of $20,000 (See Figure 7–3.)

FIGURE 7–3
One-year decision tree for motel owner

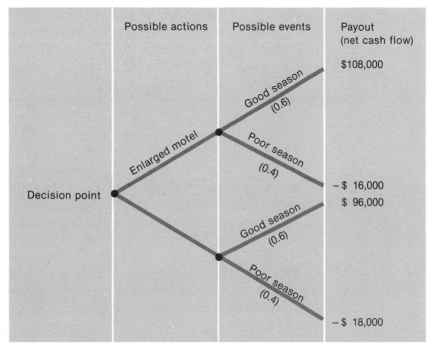

Next, you compute the expected values (*EV*) and add them for the enlarged motel and same motel, separately:

EV enlarged motel: 0.6 × $180,000 = $108,000
                      0.4 × −$ 40,000 = −   16,000
                                                ─────────
                                                $ 92,000
EV same motel: 0.6 × $160,000 =   96,000
                      0.4 × −$ 20,000 = −   8,000
                                                ─────────
                                                $ 88,000

Your decision tree suggests that you are most likely to show a profit of $92,000 if you enlarge your motel. If you do not enlarge, you are most likely to earn a profit of $88,000. After a one-year period you are thus $4,000 better off by investing in an enlarged motel. To derive more information from the tree, it could be extended out a few years. Among the other variables you might plug in would be expected increases in properly value during the next decade, and the future effects of the energy shortage on traffic in northern Michigan.

Program evaluation and review technique (PERT). Quantitative tools are also available to help in the planning of complex projects. PERT, the best known of these tools, is designed for planning the activities required to complete a large-scale, non-repetitive project. It was originally designed by the United States Navy to construct the Polaris missile. Proper application of PERT helps assure that the goals and objectives of the organization will be met.

Two concepts are crucial in understanding the basics of PERT. An *event* is a point of decision or accomplishment of a task. If you were planning for the development and distribution of a nationwide mail order catalog, important events would include the catalog being printed and addresses being affixed to the cover. Events are also called milestones. *Activities* are the physical and mental efforts required to complete an event, such as photographing merchandise which will appear in the catalogue.

The bare essentials of preparing a PERT chart are these:

1. Prepare a list of all the activities necessary to complete the project. This would include purchasing supplies to make the catalog and hiring personnel.
2. Design the actual PERT network, relating all the activities to each other in the proper sequence (see Figure 7–4). Considerable skill and judgment are required at this stage.
3. Estimate the time between events. For instance, how much time will be needed to prepare a mailing list so that it can be linked with shipping the finished catalogs? The estimated times are arrived at by using the pooled judgment of several people. Each person makes three estimates:
   a. Optimistic time (O)—The shortest time it would take if everything went well.

b. Pessimistic time (P)—The amount of time it will take if everything goes wrong, as it often does with complicated projects.

c. The most probable time (M).

4. Compute the expected times for each activity and place them in the appropriate place on the PERT network. Use this formula:

$$\text{Expected time} = \frac{O + 4M + P}{6}$$

5. Calculate the *critical path,* the sequence of events and activities that are followed in order to implement the project. The length of the entire project is determined by the path with the longest elasped time. It is called the critical path because it determines the shortest possible completion time. The critical path in Figure 7–4 requires a total elapsed time of 26 weeks. It is calculated by adding the number of weeks scheduled to complete the activities between events A and B, B and C, C and D.

6. As a control measure, the project supervisor must pay special attention to seeing that all critical events are completed on time. When key activities are falling behind schedule, corrective action must be taken.

In practice, PERT charts often specify hundreds of events and

FIGURE 7–4
A simplified PERT chart

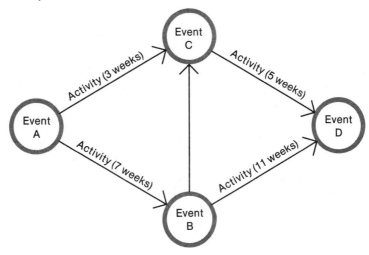

activities. Each small event can have its own PERT plan, similar to each department in an organization having its own organization chart.

SUMMARY OF KEY POINTS

☐ Anytime a supervisor chooses among alternative courses of action, a decision is being made.

☐ According to a conception developed by Drucker, the basic elements in making a decision are: (1) classification of the problem as routine or unique; (2) definition of the problem—arriving at a clarification of its true nature; (3) conditions to be specified—defining clear specifications about what the decision has to accomplish; (4) looking for rightness—essentially looking for the soundest decision rather than a weak compromise; (5) action—converting the decision into action; (6) feedback—gathering information to check on the adequacy of the decision.

☐ Creativity is the processing of information in such a way that the result is new, original, and meaningful. People show individual differences in creativity, similar to the distribution of most human abilities.

☐ Creative persons show flexibility in their thinking and emotional looseness. Creative organizations are those that encourage creativity from their members. They show some similarities to creative personalities, particularly in a willingness to be flexible and take chances.

☐ Among the ways of improving your creativity are being curious, disciplining yourself to think creatively, conducting private brainstorming sessions, and using the personal analogy method.

☐ One way of behaving creatively on the job is to duplicate or borrow the ideas of other people. Sources of creative ideas include conversations with knowledgeable people and reading books and magazines.

☐ All nonroutine decisions should be related back to organizational policy.

☐ Most large organization use some type of quantitative tools to aid in decision making and planning. Three such tools are break-even analysis, decision trees, and PERT charts (or plans). Break-even analysis tells us at what point it is profitable to go ahead with a new venture. The break-even point occurs where total costs equal total revenue. Algebraically, *BE* equals total fixed costs divided by the difference between the price per unit and the variable cost per unit. Decision trees are used to assess the outcome of a series of decisions. The process involves estimating the probability of certain outcomes and computing expected values. PERT charts are used to help plan complex, nonrepetitive projects. PERT uses probabilities in estimating activity time and eventual project completion.

GUIDELINES FOR SUPERVISORY PRACTICE

Claude S. George, Jr., has provided some practical tips on making decisions that are germane here (in addition to the suggestions for decision making already presented in this chapter):[14]

1. *Decide whether the decision is a big or small one.* A small decision does not warrant going through an elaborate framework for decision making. Major decisions (such as whether or not to recommend that a particular individual be fired) can have a big impact on the functioning of your department and on your career.

2. *Rely on established company policy and practices when such precedent exists.* If all thievery should be reported to the security department, you have no leeway in making such a decision about a subordinate.

3. *Seek help from other managers and specialists if in doubt about a decision.* As George suggests, "For example, don't try to solve a safety problem involving electricity. Instead, call the plant electrician or an electrical engineer to give you help.'

4. *Avoid crisis decisions.* Generally you have more time than you realize to make a sound decision. Three minutes of careful reflection can have an overwhelming impact on the quality of a decision. With careful planning, fewer and fewer decisions have to be made on a crisis basis.

5. *Once you have taken action do not ruminate about the decision.* Few people make optimum decisions most of the time. Get feedback about the adequacy of your decision, but do not engage in nonproductive worry about having made a poor decision. Suppose you choose one supplier who proves to be late with the promised supplies. You have no way of knowing if another supplier might have been still later with the merchandise. It is also possible that if you had chosen the other supplier, the material you ordered would have proved defective in the long run.

---

[14] Claude S. George, Jr., *Supervision in Action: The Art of Managing Others* (Reston, Va.: Reston, 1977), pp. 80–81. The italicized suggestions follow closely the points made by George. The quote in suggestion 3 appears on page 80 of *Supervision in Action.*

QUESTIONS FOR DISCUSSION AND REVIEW

1. Give two examples of decisions facing a supervisor important enough to warrant using the decision-making method presented in this chapter.

2. In what way might your personality traits influence your decision making?

3. Illustrate how the decision-making steps described in this chapter could be applied to the situation of a supervisor who decides to request overtime work for a department.

4. Give an example of a "decision" you have reached that has not yet been backed up by action.

5. Give examples of two specific problems likely to be faced by a supervisor that require creative solutions.

6. How might being creative help you in your career?

7. How might you use the suggestion box in your organization as a method of improving your own creativity?

8. Where might a supervisor be able to borrow creative ideas in addition to the two major sources described in this chapter?

9. To your knowledge, is supervision usually considered a creative field? Why or why not?

10. Which characteristics of a creative person (as summarized in Figure 7–1) do you currently possess? Which characteristics that you do not already possess do you think you could develop?

11. Does the place you currently work (or most recently worked) seem to have a "creative climate"? Why or why not?

12. How many customers will be needed, on an average night, for a theatre owner to break even under the following conditions? Total fixed costs for showing the film in question is $1,500. The variable cost per customer is $0.5; the admission price is $5.00.

13. The optimistic time for building an addition to a hospital is 17 months, the pessimistic time is 29 months, and the most probable time is 20 months. What is the expected time?

A supervisory self-insight exercise: The creative personality test

The following test will help you determine if certain aspects of your personality are similar to those of a creative individual. Since our test is for illustrative and research purposes, proceed with caution in mind. This is not a standardized psychological instrument. Such tests are not reprinted in general books.

		Mostly true	Mostly false
1.	Novels are a waste of time. If you want to read, read nonfiction books.	_____	_____
2.	You have to admit, some crooks are very clever.	_____	_____
3.	People consider me to be a fastidious dresser. I despise looking shabby.	_____	_____
4.	I am a person of very strong convictions. What's right is right; what's wrong is wrong.	_____	_____
5.	It doesn't bother me when my boss hands me vague instructions.	_____	_____
6.	Business before pleasure is a hard and fast rule in my life.	_____	_____
7.	Taking a different route to work is fun, even if it takes longer.	_____	_____
8.	Rules and regulations should not be taken too seriously. Most rules can be broken under unusual circumstances.	_____	_____
9.	Playing with a new idea is fun even if it doesn't benefit me in the end.	_____	_____
10.	So long as people are nice to me, I don't care why they are being nice.	_____	_____
11.	Writing should try to avoid the use of unusual words and word combinations.	_____	_____
12.	Detective work would have some appeal to me.	_____	_____
13.	Crazy people have no good ideas.	_____	_____
14.	Why write letters to friends when there are so many clever greeting cards available in the stores today?	_____	_____
15.	Pleasing myself means more to me than pleasing others.	_____	_____
16.	If you dig long enough, you will find the true answer to most questions.	_____	_____

Scoring the test. The answer in the *creative direction* for each question is as follows:

1. Mostly false
2. Mostly true
3. Mostly false
4. Mostly false
5. Mostly true
6. Mostly false
7. Mostly true
8. Mostly true
9. Mostly true
10. Mostly true
11. Mostly false
12. Mostly true
13. Mostly false
14. Mostly false
15. Mostly true
16. Mostly false

Give yourself a plus one for each answer you gave in agreement with the keyed answers.

How do you interpret your score?   As cautioned earlier, this is an exploratory test. Extremely high or low scores are probably the most meaningful. A score of 12 or more suggests that your personality and attitudes are similar to that of a creative person. A score of 5 or less suggests that your personality is dissimilar to that of a creative person. You are probably more of a conformist (and somewhat categorical) in your thinking, at least at this point in your life. Don't be discouraged. Most people can develop in the direction of becoming a more creative individual.

1. *How does your score on this test compare to your own evaluation of your creativity?*
2. *Describe a person whom you think would probably score 15 or 16 on this test. Identify him or her.*
3. *Do the same for a person whom you think would score 0 or 1 on this test.*

SOME SUGGESTED READING

Campbell, David. *Take the Road to Creativity and Get Off Your Dead End.* Niles, Ill.: Argus Communication, 1977.

Getzels, Jacob W., and Csikzentmihalyi, Mihalyi. *The Creative Vision: A Longitudinal Study of Problem Finding in Art.* New York: Wiley-Interscience, 1976.

Harrison, Frank E. *The Managerial Decision Making Process.* Houghton Mifflin, 1975.

Janis, Irving. *Victims of Groupthink.* Houghton Mifflin, 1972.

Joffe, Gerardo. *Make at Least $1 Million (but Probably Much More) in the Mail-Order Business.* San Francisco: Advance Books, 1978.

Kepner, Charles H., and Tregoe, Benjamin B. *The Rational Manager: A Systematic Approach to Problem Solving and Decision Making.* New York: McGraw-Hill, 1965.

Maccrimmon, Kenneth R., and Taylor, Ronald N. "Decision Making and Problem Solving." In *Handbook of Industrial and Organizational Psychology,* edited by Marvin, R. Dunnette., pp. 1397–1453. Chicago: Rand McNally, 1976.

Maier, Norman R. F. *Problem Solving and Creativity in Individuals and Groups.* Monterey, Calif.: Brooks/Cole, 1970.

Mintzberg, Henry. "The Manager's Job: Folklore and Fact." *Harvard Business Review,* July–August 1975, pp. 49–61.

Pounds, William F. "The Process of Problem Finding." *Industrial Management Review,* Fall 1969, pp. 1–19.

Raudsepp, Eugene (with George P. Hough, Jr.). *Creative Growth Games.* New York: A Harvest Book/Harcourt Brace Jovanovich, 1977.

Shull, Fremont A., Jr.; Delbecq, Andrew L.; and Cummings, Larry L. *Organizational Decision Making.* New York: McGraw-Hill, 1970.

Worthy, Morgan. *Aha! A Puzzle Approach to Creative Thinking.* Chicago: Nelson-Hall, 1975.

Motivating people to work

8

LEARNING OBJECTIVES

After reading and thinking through the material in this chapter, you should be able to:

1. Explain the meaning of the term *work motivation.*
2. Understand how and why a supervisor's expectations can influence a subordinate's performance.
3. Explain why positive reinforcement can lead to increased motivation and productivity.
4. Summarize the nine rules for using positive reinforcement.
5. Explain the relationship between job design and work motivation.
6. Define and give an example of job enrichment.
7. Explain why an increase in motivation does not always lead to an increase in performance.

In Chapter 2 we explored how the job behavior of people is influenced by their needs and motives. An understanding of the psychology of motivation alone will not enable supervisors to motivate their subordinates toward accomplishing good work results. This underlying knowledge must be translated into techniques for motivating people. Two widely used techniques for improving or sustaining job motivation, positive reinforcement (PR) and job design, will be featured in this chapter.

In the context used here, work motivation refers to a person expending effort toward the accomplishment of a goal considered worthwhile by the organization. A tool and die maker who studies shop math on personal time in order to improve job skills is well motivated toward work. Another tool and die maker might spend much of the day thinking about boating and much of any leisure time using and maintaining a boat. The latter has low job motivation but high leisure motivation. Most people are motivated to do something (even fishing or drinking beer). Your job as a supervisor is to help increase employee motivation toward work.

SUPERVISORY EXPECTATIONS AND EMPLOYEE PRODUCTIVITY

Before using a specific motivational technique with an employee, it is vitally important to recognize that your expectations of a subordinate can influence the person's productivity. The phenomenon works in a subtle, almost unconscious way. When you believe that a particular employee will succeed, you automatically communicate this belief to the employee without realizing you are transmitting this perception. Conversely, when you expect an employee to fail, that person will usually not dissappoint you. Your expectation of failure has become a self-fulfilling prophecy. Because you believed something to be true, you contributed to its taking place.

This mysterious phenomenon of a superior's expectations influencing employee productivity (and therefore motivation) has been labeled "Pygmalion in the Plant."[1] According to Greek mythology, Pygmalion was a sculptor and king of Cyprus who carved an ivory statue of a maiden and fell in love with it. The statue was brought to life in response to his prayer. Later George Bernard Shaw converted the myth into comedy. Still later, the whole myth was developed into a popular musical called *My Fair Lady*. The point is that you may be able to convert an undermotivated employee into a high producer by the simple expedient of believing that he or she can improve.

POSITIVE REINFORCEMENT AND EMPLOYEE MOTIVATION

In recent years supervisors and other managers have been making increasing use of positive reinforcement in motivating employees. Underlying the use of positive reinforcement on the job is a principle of learning formulated at the turn of the cen-

---

[1] John P. McSweeney, "Pygmalion in the Plant," *Personnel Journal,* August 1977, pp. 380–81. Reprinted with permission, *Personnel Journal,* copyright August 1977.

tury, the Law of Effect: Behavior which appears to lead to a positive consequence for the individual tends to be repeated, while behavior which appears to lead to a negative consequence tends not to be repeated. Suppose you are a programming supervisor. A woman working for you says, "I had to stay late to get it done, but I finally debugged that spare parts inventory program you gave me." If you respond, "Teriffic Sandy, that's the kind of help we need around here," she is likely to work extra hard to debug a program in the future. Assume you instead responded, "Be careful not to stay late when you are not authorized overtime pay. Besides, you could have debugged that program during normal working hours." The probability is that Sandy would not have worked hard (or been strongly motivated) to debug the next snarled program.

To effectively use reinforcement theory, the supervisor must follow certain procedures or rules. Although using positive and negative motivators to influence people would seem to follow the logic of commonsense, it is still a specialized procedure requiring a systematic approach. Most supervisors with a genuine interest in the welfare of people can learn to make productive use of PR on the job. Nine important rules for the proper use of reinforcement theory are presented next.[2]

Rule 1: Choose an appropriate reward or punishment. Most motivational theories point to the idea that the way to motivate people is to use a reward that is meaningful to each particular person. A status-hungry production control technician might work hard just for the opportunity to have a parking space adjacent to the plant superintendent's parking space. A medical technician might boost output if given the chance to do a laboratory workup on an occasional rare disease.

Each reward listed in Figure 8–1 can be related back to the categories of needs mentioned in Chapter 2. Most of these rewards relate to higher-level needs. People display individual differences with respect to which reward will satisfy a certain need.

---

[2] Rules 1, 3, and 4 are credited to Andrew J. DuBrin, *Human Relations: A Job Oriented Approach* (Reston, Va.: Reston, 1978), pp. 32–35. Rules 2, 5, 6, 7, 8, and 9 are credited to W. Clay Hamner, "Reinforcement Theory and Contingency Management in Organizational Settings," in Henry L. Tosi and W. Clay Hamner, *Organizational Behavior and Management: A Contingency Approach* (Chicago: St. Clair Press, 1974), pp. 96–98.

FIGURE 8–1
A checklist of rewards and punishments of potential use in a job setting

Rewards	Punishments
Feedback on desired behavior	Feedback on undesired behavior
Praise, encouragement, and related rewards	Criticism
	Withdrawal of privileges
Approval	Probation
Recognition	Suspension
Comradeship	Fining
Job security	Undesirable assignment
Money	Demotion
Favorable performance appraisal	Withholding of any of the rewards
Privy to confidential information	listed to the left
Challenging work assignments	
Promotion	
Improved working conditions	
Capable and congenial co-workers	
Status symbols	
Desired behavior itself	

For instance, one culturally deprived person might feel virtually self-fulfilled by achieving the status symbol of membership in the company country club. Many people could only achieve self-fulfillment through a highly challenging work assignment. Despite these individual differences, a couple of illustrative generalizations are in order. The need for self-fulfillment or self-actualization might be met partially with rewards such as praise, recognition, favorable performance, receiving a favorable performance appraisal, challenging work assignments, or a promotion. Needs for belonging and affiliation might be met with approval, comradeship, or good co-workers.

When holding out positive rewards does not work, it is sometimes necessary to use mild forms of punishment (negative motivators) to motivate employees. For instance, criticizing a salesperson for attending baseball games during working days may be enough to make that person stop. Motivation enters the picture because it is hoped that more time will now be spent calling on accounts rather than wasting company time.

Figure 8–1 lists a group of rewards and punishments that are feasible in a job environment. Without a knowledge of potential rewards and punishments, it is difficult to make effective use of reinforcement theory. The last item listed under rewards, "desired behavior itself," requires careful attention. Critics of reinforcement theory (or its more technical term, *behavior modification*) contend that it is a system of manipulating defenseless people by dangling carrots in front of them (or sticks in back of them). When reinforcement theory is truly effective, good work itself becomes its own reward.

Assume that early in your working career you detest preparing your income tax form. Yet the threat of punishment (fine, imprisonment, or both) motivated you to do an honest and accurate job of completing the required tax form. As the years passed, you may gradually take pride in preparing your own tax return and perhaps delight in finding all your rightful deductions. What you originally did only at the threat of punishment (preparing your tax returns) ultimately becomes challenging work that is self-rewarding.

Rule 2: Don't reward all people the same. Supervisors who do this are encouraging average performance. If one person made substantial progress in reducing the production of defective parts, that individual should receive more recognition (or other reward) than somebody who made only token progress.

Rule 3: Find some constructive behavior to reinforce. To help another person learn a new behavior, or to keep on repeating an already learned behavior, you have to begin somewhere. Assume that Ken, an individual working for you, keeps a desk so messy that he loses important files. Although you are not obssessed with orderliness, you recognize that Ken's sloppy work habits are interfering with productivity. Following the precepts of reinforcement theory, when Ken makes any progress toward keeping his desk in order, reinforce that behavior. For instance, if you notice that he no longer has old coffee cups on his desk, you might comment to Ken, "I can already see the improvement in your work area. Keep up the progress." Although this process sounds elementary, *shaping* of behavior toward a planned-for objective increases the probability that larger-scale changes will be forthcoming.

Rule 4: Schedule rewards intermittently. Rewarding an employee for constructive work involves the dual consideration of how frequently to give a positive reinforcement and how close in time rewards should follow the constructive behavior. Reinforcement theory often fails as an approach to motivating people because these considerations are neglected.

Years of experimentation with reinforcement theory indicates that people should be rewarded often but not always. If you worked as a shoe store manager, it might be rewarding to you if on an occasional visit to your store your boss told you, "Everything looks just fine around here. The customers seem pleased. Your volume is up and the store looks first class. Keep this up and you'll notice a difference in your salary." However, if your boss gave you the same pep talk every week, the reward would lose its impact.

For maximum effectiveness, rewards (or punishments) should follow close in time to the motivated behavior. Assuming that money motivated you (a safe assumption for about 80 percent of the people studying supervision), you would be more likely to sustain your drive level if hard work led to quick cash. If you were selling life insurance, you would tend to keep on prospecting much more readily if you received your commission in one month rather than six.

Rule 5: Failure to respond has reinforcing consequences. If a supervisor ignores any changes in behavior a subordinate has made as a result of a safety training program, the subordinate will probably no longer repeat the new learning. Similarly, if exceptionally good performance goes unnoticed, an employee may lose any previous enthusiasm for performing in an exceptional manner. As one disgruntled secretary said, "Nobody cares if I get out the department reports on time, so why should I?" Another way of stating this rule is that for reinforcement theory to work, the person being motivated needs frequent, accurate feedback.

Rule 6: Be sure to tell people what they can do to get reinforced. The employee who has a standard against which to measure job performance will have a built-in feedback system. That employee automatically will know how he or she is doing. A supervisor might tell an employee, "I'll recommend that you be promoted to a senior lab technician providing you run an average of 150 tests per month with less than 1 percent ruined specimens." One of the many reasons a sport like basketball is so motivational is that the path to a reward is so clear cut. A player can readily see that by putting the ball through the hoop, a reward will be forthcoming (one or two points). Feedback is immediate under these circumstances.

Rule 7: Be sure to tell people what they are doing wrong. By patiently explaining to subordinates what they are doing wrong, the subordinates will then know what needs to be done to get rewarded. A clerk may be filing too many documents under the "miscellaneous file." That clerk should be told specifically what is wrong with this technique. The supervisor might say, "It is time consuming to look in the miscellaneous file for most pieces of information. Your system needs to be more efficient. The purpose of a filing system is to be able to find information when you need it."

Rule 8: Don't punish in front of others. The punishment (for example, reprimand) should be enough to eliminate the undesired actions. By administering the punishment in front of the work group, the worker may feel ridiculed or humiliated. In response, the person becomes defensive and counterhostile. Many a supervisor has lost the respect of employees by dressing down a group member in front of others.

Rule 9: Make the consequences equal to the behavior. Fair rewards and punishments are best. "Punishment should fit the crime," and rewards should fit the good deed. A person who learns to behave assertively with customers should be rewarded with encouragement of a reasonable sort. Perhaps telling the person, "I think you've become the greatest salesperson in the region" would be overdoing the praise. It would lose its effectiveness because the praise would seem ungenuine.

MOTIVATING PEOPLE THROUGH JOB DESIGN

A number of industrial psychologists, other management advisors, and experienced supervisors contend that if you make jobs interesting enough, there may be less need for dangling incentives in front of people. In other words, productivity can be increased by making jobs more interesting, exciting, and challenging. Productivity can also be increased, according to the job design (or redesign) strategy, by making some jobs less dull. Four different strategies for redesigning jobs to increase motivation and productivity have evolved: job rotation, work simplification, job enlargement, and job enrichment.[3] These categories overlap somewhat and more than one of them may be applicable in a particular job design or redesign effort.

Job rotation

A tired old supervisory joke involves Luke, a box-packer in a factory that manufactured hardware supplies. An industrial engineer, concerned that Luke's motivation and satisfaction would suffer if he continued to pack nuts and bolts all day, redesigned his job. Luke would now spend every other day packing nails. Asked how he liked his new job, Luke replied, "It's really worse. I used to have one dirty, boring job packing nuts and bolts. Now I have two dirty, boring jobs. One day I hate packing nuts and bolts, and the next day I hate packing nails."

Switching assignments thus does not always cure a motivational problem, but many people do enjoy the chance to have more variety in their work lives. Job rotation consists of rotating a worker through a variety of jobs in an area, department, or office. The actual contents and methods of the jobs are unchanged—only the job holder is varied. A person whose job is rotated gets a chance to perform different functions and to work with different people—and this frequently leads to improved motivation and satisfaction. An accounts receivable clerk was given the chance to work every other month in the accounts payable department. The clerk found the experience beneficial in providing a broader outlook on how the company operated. The increased knowledge helped this clerk achieve a promotion to a supervisor in the company.

As in the example just cited, job rotation serves as an excellent training device. A worker who learns to perform more operations becomes a more valuable employee to the company. Richard W. Woodman and John J. Sherwood report some observa-

---

[3] Our discussion of job design and motivation follows closely the ideas presented in Richard W. Woodman and John J. Sherwood, "A Comprehensive Look at Job Design," *Personnel Journal,* August 1977, pp. 384–90, 418. All quotations in this section are direct quotes from Woodman and Sherwood. Many of their ideas are paraphrased in this section of the chapter.

tions made in the Shell United Kingdom participative management programs:

> . . . jobs in the microwax department at Shell's Stanlow Refinery were redesigned so that an operator had a complete unit to control rather than operating only parts of one or more units or processes. Besides being psychologically more satisfying in the sense of doing a complete task, the job redesign made it possible to rotate operators from unit to unit. The direct result of this job rotation was increased operator competency which met both organizational and individual needs in that the operators were better qualified for promotion and the work team had greater flexibility in scheduling.[4]

Work simplification

A long-standing technique of industrial engineering, work simplification, attempts to combine or eliminate those portions of a job which are the least demanding of human abilities. Automation is a widely used technique of work simplification. Many of the onerous clerical tasks at one time performed by people in insurance companies are now performed by computers. By using an existing computer program, a clerk can quickly obtain information that might have taken hours of tedious computation in the past.

As with job rotation, work simplification is generally used in conjunction with other job design methods. Cummins Engine Company is a case in point. At this aircraft engine company, work simplification included the participation of workers and managers in the development of improved work methods. One result was dramatic:[5] "A team consisting of five workers and a foreman first-level supervisor was able to reduce the fabrication cost of an item from $6.00 to $1.88 with no design changes just by recognizing work stations, paying close attention to detailed work movements and the number of times parts were transferred."

[4] Derek W. E. Burden, "Participative Management as a Basis for Improved Quality of Jobs: The Case of Microwax Department," Shell U.K., Ltd.; in *The Quality of Working in Life,* vol. 2, eds. Louis E. Davis and Albert B. Cherns (New York: The Free Press, 1975); cited in Woodman and Sherwood, "Job Design," p. 386.

[5] E. James Bryan, "Work Improvement and Job Enrichment: The Case of Cummins Engine Company," in *Quality of Working Life,* ed., Davis and Cherns; cited in Woodman and Sherwood, "Job Design," p. 386.

Job enlargement

A supervisor can sometimes increase the motivation and satisfaction of an employee by expanding the number of tasks for which the worker is responsible. As the job is enlarged, the worker has to utilize more skills. If the worker is favorably disposed toward a more complicated job, performance may be increased as a result of improved work motivation. Job enlargement has been popular since the 1940s and is widely practiced by supervisors on an informal basis when the supervisor has such discretionary power. In many settings, neither higher management nor the labor union grants supervisors the leeway to enlarge the jobs of subordinates. Woodward and Sherwood provide a capsule description of a historically significant job enlargement program at IBM:[6]

> One of the organization's first attempts occurred at their Endicott plant where jobs were highly specialized. At this plant a total machining operation consisted of four distinct jobs: the machine itself, setups, tool sharpening, and inspection. The work was redesigned using a job enlargement approach combining the four previously specialized jobs into one enlarged job. Thus, the machine operator now sharpened his or her own tools, set up his or her machine, performed the machine operation, and inspected the finished product of his or her own work. The reported results were that increased costs due to higher wages (the new job deserved greater rewards) and additional inspection equipment were more than compensated for by improved quality and worker satisfaction.

Job enrichment

The most advanced technique of modifying job design to increase worker motivation is job enrichment. A job is enriched by building into it more decision making, planning, and controlling functions. A supervisor who provides input into upper management staff meetings has an enriched job. A job is considered enriched to the extent that it demands more of an individual's talents and capabilities, or if the person thinks it is enriched. As the job becomes more meaningful to the person, the worker becomes better motivated and hopefully more productive. Unless a person *wants* an enriched job, these positive results may not be

---

[6] Peter P. Schoderbek and William E. Reif, *Job Enlargement: Key to Improved Performance* (Ann Arbor, Mich.: University of Michigan, 1969); cited in Woodman and Sherwood, "Job Design," p. 386.

forthcoming. One angry worker had this comment to make about a job enrichment program: "My job is more exciting, but it's also more taxing. I'm doing more things now which means I have to learn more skills. I'm more tired at the end of the day. What really gripes me though is that my paycheck hasn't gotten any bigger. If management enriches the job, let them also enrich the paycheck. I don't want to be taken advantage of."

A popular form of job enrichment is to make jobs more exciting by organizing workers into small teams who have total responsibility for the production of an item. The team approach stands in contrast to the high specialization of an assembly line. In many instances, job enrichment through organizing workers into production teams has paid dividends to workers and management. One well-publicized example took place in the Gaines Pet Food Plant in Topeka, Kansas.[7] The objectives in designing this plant were to increase productivity and employee job satisfaction by doing away with the traditional ladder of job classifications and a lock-step assembly line. Also, all personnel were to have an effective voice in running the plant.

In what way was the work unique? Production is built around teams consisting of 7 to 14 members. Three teams are used per shift: processing, packaging, and shipping and office duties. Each team is responsible for dividing its own work among team members, interviewing and hiring job applicants, establishing internal policies and decisionmaking within their area of responsibility. All teams are responsible for their own quality control and such diverse functions as industrial engineering, maintenance, and housekeeping. Workers are encouraged to learn and perform as many jobs on the team as they are capable of doing. When workers do learn more skills, they are compensated accordingly.

In what way is the work environment unique? No time clocks are present. Management has no special privileges such as reserved parking places or separate restrooms. Everybody enters work and leaves work by the same door. Personnel at every level are allowed to use the conference room. When a worker wants to see a manager, it does not require going through channels. There

---

[7] General Foods has a public relations release about the Gaines Pet Food experience. Another source is Richard E. Walton, "How to Conquer Alienation in the Plant," *Harvard Business Review*, November–December 1972, pp. 70–81; cited in Woodman and Sherwood, "Job Design," p. 388.

is a common decor throughout the plant and office: "The worker's locker room has the same carpeting as the plant manager's office."

What about the results? A promising picture for job enrichment through team efforts has emerged, but the results are not all glowing. On the positive side, about 70 people are operating a plant originally estimated by industrial engineers to require 110 people to operate effectively. After the first 18 months of operation, overhead was 30 percent lower than in corresponding conventionally operated plants in the same division of the pet food corporation. Turnover and absenteeism were much lower than industry norms. Preliminary figures indicate an estimated annual cost savings of $600,000. The Gaines experiment in Topeka has more than met the objectives of its designers in terms of productivity and job satisfaction. Despite these optimistic results, Woodman and Sherwood advance a few words of caution:[8]

> Yet problems exist. There is apparently some concern about the pay scales and there are also problems in the interface with the rest of the corporation. The existence of a dramatically different production system within the same organization seems to be the cause of some tension and ambivalent feelings. Even though the Topeka plant is successful in terms of the objectives set for it, its long-run viability is still questionable.

PAY PLANS AND EMPLOYEE MOTIVATION

Under the best of conditions the money employees receive for working can be used to encourage or sustain good performance. Here we will examine some of the conditions under which money *does in fact* act as a motivator. We will also discuss the relationship between four different types of pay plans and employee motivation. As a supervisor, you may not be in a position to establish compensation policy, but you can make recommendations for improving present conditions.

Money as a motivator

Money is likely to be an effective motivator when certain conditions exist or are met. To the extent that these conditions apply to employees, they will probably be motivated by money.

---

[8] Woodman and Sherwood, "Job Design," p. 388.

Money is a potent motivator *when your demand for money is still relatively strong.* When people need money to pay for what they consider important, money is still motivational. When employees live comfortably within their budgets, money tends to lose much of its motivational appeal.

> A supervisor was busily signing up people to work overtime hours for the holiday season. Jenny, a 23-year-old woman, said to not include her on the list. In disbelief, the supervisor said to Jenny: "How can anybody turn down overtime work during the holidays?" Jenny replied, "Money is no big hassle for me. I lead a simple life. I make all my friends and relatives presents. I'd rather spend holiday time with my loved ones than working overtime in a factory, hustling a few extra dollars."

A financial incentive tends to be an effective motivator *when it can change an individual's lifestyle.* Many people will work hard to earn enough money to change the way they live, whether that change involves the purchase of a yacht or a used car. An electronic technician worked about 60 hours per month at night, driving a taxi. His typical gross income for the moonlighting efforts was less than $200. Asked why he was willing to work so hard for close to a minimum wage (as a taxi driver), he answered: "The take-home pay from my night job means the difference between my living at home versus having my own place. If it weren't for my moonlighting, I wouldn't be leading the kind of life I want."

Money is motivational *when it is related to job performance.* One problem with owning a business is that the more hours you work, the more money you are likely to earn. You become addicted to receiving rewards. If, for example, you keep your store open a few more hours per week, you will probably increase your income proportionately. (Your break-even analysis tells you this is true!) Piecework incentive systems, to be described below, follow the same principle of tying pay to performance.

Money tends to be a valuable reinforcer *if a person is tense and anxious about lack of money.* Many worries and concerns are financially based. If you have specific worries about current bills or past debts, it is relaxing (anxiety reducing) to receive money which can be used to take care of those obligations. Maybe you can recall your sigh of relief the last time you received a meaningful sum of money.

Piecework systems.[9]   A pure piecework system can be highly motivational. It follows a formula almost everybody understands: N (number of units) $\times U$ (unit rate) $= W$ (wages). A piecework form of compensation works best under straightforward jobs, where an employee's contribution can be measured directly. Fruit and vegetable pickers (and insurance sales representatives) usually work under a straight piecework pay plan. But since so many jobs require coordinated effort, the use of piecework plans has declined. The system also tends to stimulate envy and greed.

Production bonus systems.   When a bonus system is utilized, incentive payments are supplementary to the basic wage. An employee thus has the security of a steady salary plus an incentive to perform better. Under a bonus system an employee might be working for a basic $6 per hour rate. In addition the worker would receive a 15-cent bonus for each unit produced. Wages would be computed in this manner:

$$(\text{Hours} \times \text{Rate per hour}) + (\text{Number of units} \times \text{Unit rate}) = \text{Pay}$$
$$(\ \ \ 40\ \ \ \times\ \ \ \ \ \$6.00\ \ \ \ ) + (\ \ \ \ \ \ 100\ \ \ \ \ \ \times\ \ \ 15¢\ \ ) = \$255$$

The bonus tends to be motivational when employees believe that the effort required to obtain the bonus is realistic. Also, they must perceive the bonus compensation as worthwhile. In the above situation, would a $15 per week bonus make you contribute extra effort?

Group incentive plans.   Under this system, employees receive bonus compensation when the group (department, division, or the entire company) performs beyond a certain standard. Group incentives work best when individual contributions are difficult to measure, and when coordinated effort is required. Assembling complicated furniture or equipment is one such task requiring coordination.

Employee profit-sharing plans are essentially large-scale production bonus systems. Under profit sharing it is typical for employees to pull together to reach production quotas. In addi-

---

[9] This and the following two discussions of incentive plans follow that presented in Herbert J. Chruden and Arthur W. Sherman, Jr., *Personnel Management*, 5th ed. (Cincinnati: South-Western, 1976), pp. 473–76.

tion, they frown upon employees who shirk responsibility. Group incentives, in general, do spur people toward high performance. At a minimum, companywide bonuses have value in maintaining morale and upholding quality standards of production.

Secrecy versus disclosure. Another important issue in using compensation to motivate employees is whether pay plans should be secret or open. In many civil service jobs and union jobs, pay rates are public information. In the military, the lowest ranking enlisted person has access to the rate of pay of the highest ranking officer. In some businesses, few top executives know even what their co-workers are paid.

There seems to be some motivational value when employees know what rate of pay they can aspire toward in particular jobs. A solution to the secrecy versus disclosure issue would be to publish pay ranges for different jobs. Employees would then have a general idea of what other people are earning. However, their specific pay would still be confidential. Evidence suggests that the majority of employees still prefer to keep their pay confidential.

COPING WITH A LOW WORK ETHIC

At the outset of this book it was mentioned that part of the new supervisory challenge is dealing with employees with a weak work ethic—those people who do not regard hard work as a worthwhile activity in itself. In practice, this means that a supervisor is faced with the task of supervising newcomers to the work force, some of whom have very little interest in their jobs. The supervisor cannot easily adopt the strategy of "shape up or ship out" because the fired employee's replacement may also be disinclined toward hard work. The supervisor is thus left to do the best possible job in motivating people to work who seem to have a minimum natural interest in work.

Our discussion about coping with a weak work ethic in newcomers to the work force does not imply that no newcomers to the work force have a strong work ethic. We are simply stating, that a low work ethic is a challenge to supervisors when it is encountered. A general approach to dealing with a weak work ethic would be to use positive reinforcement or job design as motivational strategies. An approach will be described here that incorporates some of the basic ideas included in reinforcement theory and job design. Our method of coping with the work ethic problem is included in a supervisory training program dealing with this problem.

A three-part strategy. A meaningful way of understanding the work ethic problem is to perceive it as a clash in values. The reason a conflict of wills exists is that a supervisor with a strong work ethic tries to motivate a person with a low work ethic. When a chronologically older supervisor deals with a chronologically younger employee, the situation involves an even stronger clash of values. A three-step procedure is recommended to help deal with this problem:

1. The supervisor is urged to examine any personal prejudices, stereotypes, attitudes, and assumptions about the individual or group with a low work ethic. Self-examination is important to begin the process of coping effectively with a value system in opposition to oneself.

2. Once these self-attitudes are examined, the supervisor is in a position to try to *empathize* with the other individual. Empathy means that a person sees the situation as the other person sees it. It is a question of understanding another's perception. You might be able to empathize with a car thief not wanting to go to prison, but you might not sympathize with that person's plight.

3. After self-examination and empathy have taken place, the supervisor is in a position to develop a strategy for dealing with that individual based upon an understanding of that person's point of view.

A specific example. A production supervisor sometimes encounters the work ethic problem when assigned young (age 21 or less) recruits to the department. As one supervisor said, "What am I supposed to do with a character who says he doesn't care if he's fired? He tells me that if he were fired he could collect unemployment checks or welfare." The three-part approach for dealing with this problem follows this sequence:

1. Look at some of the stereotypes, assumptions, and attitudes you might hold toward young people. Perhaps these perceptions include statements such as these.

    a.   Young people have it made in comparison to my struggle.

    b.   Young males are irresponsible; they are primarily interested in fun and games and in enjoying life.

    c.   Young people want to start at the top. They want a good job right away without really deserving a promotion to a higher rated job.

    d.   Young people are basically unpatriotic and disloyal.

    e.   Young people have a very casual attitude toward work. They show little concern about money or job security.

    f.   Young people like to criticize supervisors and the company.

2. From their point of view, young people may see these issues in another manner.

    a.   Why should we be so hung up about hard work? Being so enthusiastic about work has not done that much for our parents or our country. It only led to more war, more ulcers, more heart attacks, more divorce, and more crime.

    b.   Jobs should provide self-fulfillment and kicks, not simply a way to make a living.

    c.   Work should be socially relevant. It should have a meaning and contribute to the good of society.

    d.   Work should be assigned on the basis of talent, not seniority. If you can do a higher-rated job right away, you should be given that job. It works that way in sports.

    e.   Openness and honesty is very important on the job. If you have a criticism to make, it will do more good when expressed than when hidden.

3. Self-examination and empathy should lead to the formulation of strategies geared to dealing constructively with these beliefs and attitudes. The motivational strategies recommended for dealing with young people are these (in addition to general motivational strategies):

    a.   Conduct discussions about the relevance of your department's work. When people understand how your product helps society and where it fits into the company, it may spur them to higher performance. Suppose your department produced gaskets that were ultimately placed in surgical equipment. If this fact were explained to employees, they might develop a better appreciation of the importance of gaskets.

b. Solicit ideas on some of your projects and activities. If you are able to use ideas submitted by young people, it might have a motivational impact on them. People who appear uninterested in work sometimes show a spark of enthusiasm when their ideas are solicited and/or used.

c. When possible make assignments on total tasks rather than on subparts of a task. Enlarging or enriching a job in this way may sometimes create enthusiasm for work in an individual who appears to have a very weak work ethic.

d. Look for an element of truth in each complaint or criticism advanced by young workers in your department. People sometimes exaggerate their complaints and criticisms in order to gain attention. Criticism that seems uncalled for is sometimes, in reality, a form of exaggerated constructive criticism.

HARD WORK AND JOB PERFORMANCE

Motivation—the expenditure of effort toward achieving an objective the organization wants accomplished—is an important concept about people. Yet it does not fully explain why some people accomplish a lot of work while others are not nearly as productive. Clyde is a highly motivated writer, yet he is a complete flop as an author. He has written six short stories and one novel in the past three years, all of them unpublished. Clyde tries hard, but he does not succeed. Every year countless thousands of people try hard (are motivated) to bowl 300 in one game, but the reasons for their failure lie outside of motivation.

Performance is of much more importance to management than is motivation. The former refers to some outcome that can be used by others, such as units of production or service. Performance can only happen when someone works either mentally or physically. Performance is the result of the application of effort. Technically, performance refers to the multiplication of effort and ability $(P = E \times A)$.

Nonmotivational characteristics. Many well-motivated, hardworking individuals fail to achieve work objectives because they are deficient in such characteristics as problem-solving ability, job-related skills, and appropriate training.[10] To perform a task well, you need to be bright enough to do the task and have the appropriate underlying skills. Such skills are usually acquired through training or direct job experience. Oscar's demise as a staff assistant is a case in point.

> Shortly after graduating from high school, Oscar secured a job as an office boy in a bank. His diligence, good work performance, and business-like appearance quickly won the attention of his supervisors. Within one year Oscar was promoted to a clerical position. Oscar continued to perform well, and gradually developed the idea that he would like to become a bank officer someday.
>
> Two years later Oscar received a promotion to the position of staff assistant. Now he was part of the exempt payroll the equivalent of a professional position in bank. Part of Oscar's responsibilities in his new position was to prepare written reports about the bank's consumer loan program. Oscar's reports were roundly criticized by his immediate superior. As hard as Oscar tried, his reports were still deficient. Finally, Oscar was transferred to a clerical position in another department because, in his supervisor's judgment, he was not properly trained for the position.
>
> Oscar failed in his first try as staff assistant, but his drive level prevented him from permanently failing. Through self-study combined with appropriate night courses, Oscar eventually developed the skills and abilities required of a staff assistant.

Group factors.   Another reason well-motivated people sometimes are not high producers is that the work group may influence them to hold back on their performance. Group norms may discourage some people from being superior performers even if they are well motivated. In such situations, the group acts as a constraining influence on the person (providing the individual is concerned about group acceptance).

> Frank was hired as a laboratory technician in a medical laboratory that ran diagnostic tests for individual physicians, group medical practices, and clinics. Wanting to elevate himself to a supervisory position, Frank worked up to nearly his capacity. Within one month, he was approached by Al, the informal group leader in the lab. Al admonished Frank, "Cut

---

[10] Our discussion of these factors borrows heavily from two sources: Henry L. Tosi and Stephen J. Carroll, *Management: Contingencies, Structure, and Process* (Chicago: St. Clair Press, 1976), pp. 127–36; and Edgar F. Huse and James L. Bowditch, *Behavior in Organizations: A Systems Approach to Managing* (Reading, Mass.: Addison-Wesley, 1973), pp. 52–55.

out the showboating. You're running more urine analyses than two of us combined. If you want to be one of us, cool off on that mass production mentality of yours."

Frank gradually reduced his output about one third, reasoning (or rationalizing) that the work pace he originally set for himself could lead to diagnostic errors.

Technological factors. The old adage, "You need the right tools to accomplish the job," sheds light on the relationship between motivation and performance. Unless people have the appropriate tools, machines, facilities, and equipment to accomplish their job, desire alone will not get the job done. Thus management, through its control of resources, creates the conditions whereby well-motivated people can accomplish work objectives.

> A plant manager showed a 10 percent decrease in salvage rate and a 40 percent decrease in delayed orders in comparison to the previous year. A personnel specialist from the home office visited the plant to talk about the significant improvements. "You must be taking those management development programs very seriously. It appears you're now doing a better job of motivating your staff."
>
> "Not particularly," replied the plant manager. "I finally got authorization to put in some of the equipment we've needed for years. Now a person can put in a decent day's work without having to worry about machine breakdown."

SUMMARY OF KEY POINTS

☐ Enough reliable information is known about human motivation to translate this knowledge into techniques for motivating people on the job.

☐ Work motivation refers to expending effort toward the accomplishment of an organizational goal.

☐ Your expectations of a subordinate's performance can influence that employee's actual job performance. There is a tendency for employees to live up to (or down to) a supervisor's expectations of them.

☐ Underlying the use of reinforcement theory on the job is the principle that if an employee's behavior is rewarded it will tend to be repeated. Also, if behavior is not rewarded or punished it will tend to decrease in frequency.

☐ Nine rules have been formulated for the use of positive reinforcement (PR) on the job. Among the most important considerations are: choosing an appropriate reward or punishment, scheduling rewards intermittently, and telling the person what behavior will lead to a reward or punishment.

☐ Another major motivational strategy is to increase motivation through improved job design. By making a job more appealing (or less appealing), increases in motivation and satisfaction may result. The four major strategies of motivation through job design are job rotation, work simplification, job enlargement, and job enrichment—enriching the content of the job in order to appeal to an employee's higher level needs such as recognition and self-fulfillment.

☐ Money will be influential in motivating employees under certain conditions: (1) The person to be motivated has a strong need for money; (2) The amount involved can change the person's lifestyle; (3) The money earned is related to job performance; (4) The employee is tense and anxious about a lack of money.

☐ Compensation plans that are designed to motivate employees include piecework systems, production bonus systems, and group incentive systems. Group incentive systems tend to be motivational and create fewer management problems. A modified form of a secret pay plan seems to be slightly preferable to a completely open plan.

☐ A suggested strategy for coping with the work ethic problem with some employees consists of three parts: (1) Examine your own prejudices and biases, attitudes, and assumptions about the person(s) you are trying to motivate; (2) Empathize with the individual(s); (3) Develop a strategy based on your understanding of the person's point of view.

☐ Hard work or increased motivation does not always lead to increases in performance or productivity for three reasons: (1) Nonmotivational characteristics such as problem-solving ability, skills, and appropriate training may also influence performance; (2) The group may discourage the person from being a high producer; (3) Unless people have the appropriate tools, machines, facilities, and equipment to accomplish their job, desire alone will not get the job done.

**GUIDELINES FOR
SUPERVISORY
PRACTICE**

1. Raise your expectations of your employees' performance, and their performance may rise to meet your expectations.

2. A practical way of increasing productivity is to use positive reinforcement (PR) on the job. In general, reward constructive behavior and ignore or punish nonconstructive behavior. However, to use PR effectively you must carefully follow the rules suggested in this chapter.

3. Jobs can be designed or redesigned to increase motivation. Generally speaking, a supervisor should follow company guidelines when using this motivational strategy. Assuming you have the authority (and a given employee wants more challenge), you might try rotating assignments, broadening the scope of jobs, or adding more exciting and challenging elements to the employee's job. A related strategy is work simplification—combining or eliminating those portions of a job least demanding of human abilities.

4. If you are trying to motivate employees who have a low work ethic, use the following three-part approach: Examine your own prejudices; Empathize with the person; Develop a strategy based on your understanding of that person.

5. Increasing employee motivation alone will not increase productivity. People also need the proper ability plus the appropriate technical and organizational resources. Finally, the group must be on your side.

**QUESTIONS FOR
DISCUSSION AND
REVIEW**

1. Why are some people so hard working while others seem to be lazy?

2. What is the difference between motivation and performance?

3. In what way can a supervisor's expectations influence the performance of subordinates?

4. Give an example of how high expectations of a person might actually lower that individual's performance?

5. Define the Law of Effect and explain how it can be used to motivate employees.

6. Does the use of positive reinforcement by a supervisor manipulate employees against their will? Explain.

7. What would be an appropriate reward to increase your level of work output?

8. What would be an appropriate punishment or threat of punishment to keep your performance level high in a job you disliked?

9. Why is feedback on performance necessary in motivating people on the job?

10. How does the use of reinforcement theory fit into the Framework for Accomplishing Results presented in Chapter 1?

11. Why isn't it a good idea to reward people every time they do something right?

12. What is the difference between job enlargement and job enrichment?

13. What are some ways in which the job of a supervisor in a commercial laundry could be enriched?

14. How might the "job" of a student be enriched?

15. What is your reaction to the statement, "You can accomplish anything if you want it badly enough?" What bearing does the information presented in this chapter have on this statement?

A supervisory problem: The valuable plumber

You are the project supervisor for the construction of a small professional building in a suburban location in the southeastern United States. Your basic responsibility is to make sure that the building is constructed on time, according to plan, and within budget. You notice that the plumbing work has fallen about one month behind schedule. The delayed plumbing installation is creating problems for the other trades people. For instance, the mason cannot install the tile until the piping and plumbing fixtures are fitted into place.

You confront Gabe, the head plumber, about this problem. He says, "I don't enjoy being rushed. I like to take my time and do things right. Deadlines are made to be broken in the construction business." Angered, you call your boss and suggest that Gabe be replaced by a more time-conscious head plumber.

Your boss replies, "Are you kidding? Because of the construction boom in this town it would take at least six months to get another plumber to replace Gabe. Don't replace him, motivate him. Be careful not to squeeze him too hard. I don't want him quitting on us. Then we would be in big trouble."

1. *What, if anything, should you do about your boss's position on the problem?*
2. *What should be your approach to motivating Gabe?*
3. *How might you prevent Gabe's attitude from spreading to other trades people on the job?*

SOME SUGGESTED READING

DuBrin, Andrew J. *Managerial Deviance: How to Handle Problem People in Key Jobs.* New York: Van Nostrand Reinhold, 1976.

Ford, Robert. "Job Enrichment Lessons for AT&T." *Harvard Business Review,* January–February 1973, pp. 96–106.

Herzberg, Frederick. *Work and the Nature of Man.* Cleveland: World Book Company, 1966.

Hinrichs, John R. *The Motivation Crisis.* New York: AMACOM, 1974.

Kirby, Peter G. "Productivity Increases through Feedback Systems." *Personnel Journal,* October 1977, pp. 512–15.

McGregor, Douglas. *The Human Side of Enterprise.* New York: McGraw-Hill, 1960.

McSweeney, John P. "Pygmalion in the Plant." *Personnel Journal,* August 1977, pp. 380–81.

Moore, Lewis B. "Motivation through Positive Reinforcement." *Supervisory Management,* October 1976, pp. 2–9.

Rotondl, Thomas, Jr. "Behavior Modification on the Job." *Supervisory Management,* February 1976, pp. 22–27.

Rush, Harold M. F. *Job Design for Motivation.* The Conference Board, 1971.

Sorcher, Melvin, and Goldstein, Arnold P. *Changing Supervisor Behavior.* Elmsford, N.Y.: Pergamon, 1974.

Terkel, Studs. *Working.* New York: Pantheon, 1972.

Wallin, Jerry A., and Johnson, Ronald D. "The Positive Reinforcement Approach to Controlling Employee Absenteeism." *Personnel Journal,* August 1976, pp. 390–92.

Woodman, Richard W., and Sherwood, John J. "A Comprehensive Look at Job Design." *Personnel Journal,* August 1977, pp. 384–90, 418.

Zenger, John. "Increasing Productivity: How Behavioral Scientists Can Help." *Personnel Journal,* October 1976, pp. 513–15, 525.

Communicating with people

9

LEARNING OBJECTIVES

After reading and working through the material in this chapter, you should be able to:

1. Explain the basic steps or elements in the communication process.
2. Explain why so many communication problems exist in organizations.
3. Be aware of strategies to circumvent most of these barriers to communication.
4. Realize the importance of improving your communication skills.
5. Develop a plan for improving your communication skills.
6. Deal with rumors effectively.
7. Appreciate the challenges of communicating to higher management and adjust your strategy accordingly.

At 8:30 A.M. Brent, a production supervisor, picked up a cloth that had been dropped on the production floor. That's about the only job-related action taken by Brent all day that did not involve communicating with another person. Communication is the basic process by which managers get things accomplished. Without communicating with people you cannot carry out such supervisory functions as motivating, leading, administering discipline, or resolving conflict. Communication, obviously, is not exclusively a supervisory process. It is also the basic process by which everything between people happens in an organization.

Communication in the context used here refers to the transmission of information between and among people in organizations. Our particular concern is face-to-face communication. Without placing limits on the topic of communication, this chapter would include such far-reaching topics as public speaking, preparation of annual reports, and the uses and abuses of CB radios.

STEPS IN THE COMMUNICATION PROCESS

A generally accepted way of understanding how communication works is to break the process down into separate steps. In order for one person to get a message across to another, certain events have to take place. These events can also be considered

FIGURE 9–1
Steps in the communication process

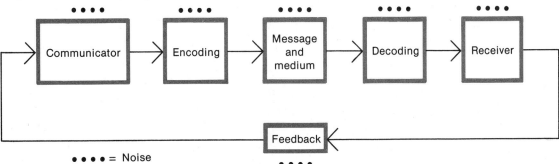

• • • • = Noise

Source: James L. Gibson, John M. Ivancevich, and James H. Donnelly, Jr., *Organizations: Behavior, Structure, Processes,* 3d ed. (Dallas: Business Publications, 1979), p. 410. © 1979 by Business Publications, Inc.

steps or elements, as shown in Figure 9–1. They include a communicator, an encoder, a message, a medium, a decoder, a receiver, feedback, and noise or interference.[1] Each element in the model can be examined in the context of a supervisor communicating with employees.

---

[1] This model of the communication process was synthesized by James L. Gibson, John M. Ivancevich, and James H. Donnelly, Jr., *Organizations: Behavior, Structure, Processes,* rev. ed. (Dallas: Business Publications, 1976), p. 319–21. © 1976 by Business Publications, Inc. Their model is based on two original sources: Claude Shannon and Warren Weaver, *The Mathematical Theory of Communication* (Urbana: University of Illinois Press, 1948); and Wilbur Schramm, "How Communication Works," in *Process and Effects of Mass Communication,* ed. Wilbur Schramm (Urbana: University of Illinois Press, 1953), pp. 3–26.

Communicator. In this situation the communicator is one particular supervisor, Michelle. The communicator in a work context is an employee with ideas, intentions, information, and a purpose for communicating. If the employee has good communication skills, communication will proceed more smoothly.

Encoding. Something must take place within the communicator's brain to translate the communicator's ideas into a form usable by other people—a language expressing the communicator's purpose. Among humans, the primary form of encoding is language. The purpose of encoding is to provide a vehicle for translating ideas and purposes into a message.

Message. The encoding process results in a message. In this instance Michelle wants to communicate to her employees the message that the company has placed a temporary ban on overtime work. Such a message will be communicated verbally. Messages are sometimes communicated nonverbally. An angry employee might communicate his or her anger by glaring at the supervisor or another employee.

As noted by Gibson, Ivancevich, and Donnelly, "Managers have numerous purposes for communicating (sending messages) such as to have others understand their ideas, to understand the ideas of others, to gain acceptance of themselves or their ideas, or to produce action."[2] In this instance Michelle hopes to get across the information about the ban on overtime without adversely affecting morale. The nature of your message exerts an influence on the medium you choose. As an extreme example, a supervisor would not ordinarily write a letter to an employee's spouse informing the latter that the former lost a finger in a work accident.

Medium. The medium carries the message. Organizations provide information to members in a variety of ways including face-to-face conversations, written memos, telephone calls, bulletin board announcements, company newspapers, and even *pink slips* (notices of dismissal). Information is sometimes communicated by not sending a message. If you requested a transfer and receive no response, after awhile you will probably assume that your request has been denied.

Body language, or nonverbal communication, is another me-

---

[2] Gibson, Ivancevich, and Donnelly, *Organizations,* p. 320.

dium often used in organizations. One supervisor commented during a training conference on human relations, "I have one guy in my department who tells me loud and clear when he's going to have a bad day. And he doesn't say anything. I just look at his face when he enters the office in the morning." If Michelle looks discouraged and sullen when she makes a no-overtime announcement, it will tell her employees that she sympathizes with them. Should Michelle snicker, or look enthusiastic, most employees will receive a message such as "It makes me happy to know that some of you will be disappointed."

Decoding.   Once the message is sent it is detected by the sense organs of the receiver. Those employees who can hear receive air vibrations that enter into the complicated mechanisms of the inner ear and travel to the brain. Deaf employees can sometimes read lips. Sighted employees will observe some of the body language communicated by the sender. Decoding basically refers to the thought processes of the receiver.

In order to decode a message, the receiver must make an interpretation of the information. How we interpret a message depends to a large extent upon our past experience with similar messages, or our *frame of reference.* If Jim, an employee in Michelle's department, was laid off three weeks after the last overtime ban, his reaction to Michelle's message will be negative. More will be said about the interpretation of messages later in our discussion of barriers to communication.

Receiver.   The receiver is the person for whom the message is intended. As just noted, the receiver decodes the message. One of the biggest problems in sending messages is that it is difficult to predict how the receiver will interpret the message. A receiver-oriented communicator gives careful thought to the person receiving the message. In order to understand the receiver you have to know something about human perception in general and that person in particular.

Feedback.   Feedback tells us whether or not the message was received, and the manner in which it was received. In order to receive feedback, the sender must engage in a two-way communication with the receiver. Michelle should ask her employees for their comments and questions about the overtime ban. A one-way communicator receives no feedback. This person just dumps the message and then leaves the scene. A postal carrier engages in one-way communication by design. The carrier delivers the mail but does not solicit a reaction from the receiver. One of the reasons is that two-way communication is time consuming.[3]

Feedback may be *direct* or *indirect.* Michelle might receive direct feedback by discussing the overtime ban with her employees after making the announcement. She might find, for example, that her people have some additional questions such as "How long is temporary?" Indirect feedback may be provided by the behavior of people in response to the message. If two employees in the department resign, or if accidents suddenly increase, it can be inferred that the message was unpopular.

Noise. The series of four small dots scattered throughout Figure 9–1 signify that noise or distortion takes place at every stage in communications. Communication problems are so widespread in organizations one might conclude it is difficult to send an undistorted message. Often the distortion is unintended. An older executive at a company picnic told a clerk that he looked "gay." The clerk, who prided himself on being heterosexual, took offense. The executive was using the term *gay* in its older connotation—that of joviality, without any implication about sexual preference.

COPING WITH COMMUNICATION PROBLEMS

Our discussion of steps or elements in the communication process has already hinted at some of the many reasons so many problems exist in face-to-face communication. Problems of this nature are so common in organizations that it is worth further examining their source. Seven primary reasons seem to underly distortions in face-to-face communication.[4] They will be discussed next along with possible antidotes.

Inadequate listening. It is difficult to get your message across to a subordinate or superior who is doing a poor job of listening.

[3] An excellent discussion of one-way versus two-way communication is found in Harold J. Leavitt, *Managerial Psychology,* 4th ed. (Chicago: University of Chicago Press, 1978), chap. 10.

[4] All but the first reason follow closely information presented in Andrew J. DuBrin, *Fundamentals of Organizational Behavior: An Applied Perspective,* 2d ed. (Elmsford, N.Y.: Pergamon, 1978), pp. 319–25.

People have impoverished listening skills for many reasons. When the subject is controversial, people often wait to jump in and defend themselves rather than attend carefully to what the sender is saying.[5] At other times people are distracted because they are preoccupied with problems of their own. A store supervisor had to leave early one night. She therefore requested that one of the sales clerks lock the door at closing time. Overnight, the store was vandalized. When confronted about the problem in the morning, the clerk said in his own defense, "I guess I didn't hear you tell me to lock the door. I just broke up with my girlfriend, so I can't concentrate on what people are telling me."

One approach to overcoming the problem of inadequate listening is to elicit feedback from the intended receiver of your message. The store supervisor might have asked the clerk (right after the discussion about locking the door): "Okay, what have we agreed on? It's very important that there is no slipup on this security measure."

A still more basic approach to overcoming the problem of poor listening is to hold off communicating your message until the it looks like the receiver is listening. For instance, until people have finished their conversation with others, they will rarely attend to another message.

Preconceived ideas.   "People hear what they want to hear" is a widely used cliche that tells us something important about a major barrier to communication. People frequently have their mind made up on an issue and are not willing to accept new evidence. A trucker might believe that obeying the 55 m.p.h. speed limit will result in poor gasoline mileage. A message sent by a supervisor that driving at that speed yields optimum gasoline economy will probably not change the trucker's opinion.

One strategy a supervisor might use to get a message across to a closed mind is to confront that person about the situation. One successful life insurance agent routinely uses this pitch: "I know you're a busy person. I'm busy too. Do you already have your mind made up about life insurance or are you willing to listen."

---

[5] A primary source about the importance of listening is Carl Rogers and Richard E. Farson, "Active Listening," reprinted in Carl Anderson and Martin J. Gannon, *Readings in Management* (Boston: Little, Brown, and Company, 1977), pp. 284–303.

Such an appeal has a slight shock value that *sometimes* facilitates getting new information across to others.

Denial of contrary information.   A variation of the barrier of preconceived ideas is the human tendency to deny contrary information. People deny information they don't want to hear as part of defensive communication—the tendency to receive messages in such a way that our self-concept is protected. Suppose a supervisor has worked his way up from the shop floor without the benefit of a degree beyond high school. As part of his self-concept, he considers himself to be a promotable person. He will therefore not hear (deny) a comment from the personnel manager that "only first level managers with formal education beyond high school will be considered for further promotion."

The phenomenon of distorting facts to fit our already existing beliefs (that are important to the preservation of the self-concept) is also called *cognitive dissonance.* We try to eliminate those facts (cognitions) that do not fit (are dissonant) with what we want to believe.

> A radio manufacturer had a number of returns from dealers on one particular model. The dealers had returned these models because of customer complaints. A factory official noted that most of these returns were traceable to one inspector. (The company used a label system that identified each inspector.) When confronted with the problem, the inspector offered this explanation: "I still say it's not my fault. I do not remember inspecting those radios. I don't care if they are my inspection tags. Maybe some other inspector has been using my tags."

It is no easy task overcoming barriers to communications that are the product of defensive communication. One positive strategy is to communicate sympathy and understanding in order to lower the other person's defensiveness. If an employee of yours were having problems concentrating on work, presumably because of financial problems, you might approach him in this manner: "Tim, nobody in this department escapes problems once in awhile. I notice that you're not your old self lately. Is there anything we can discuss to help you?"

In contrast, an approach most likely to enhance his defensive communication would be: "Tim, tell me the truth. Are your financial problems making a poor employee out of you?" As aptly described by Robert F. DeGise, an internal consultant at Caterpillar Tractor Company:

> Clearly, a supportive climate permits the most effective communication. The more supportive the climate, the less likely we are to distort our communicating with personal feelings, interests, and values. Similarly, we perceive more accurately as we become less defensive. And as the element of threat diminishes, so does the need to defend ourselves. Finally, as defensiveness subsides, we can better focus on what is being said and what the intended meaning of the message is. In a nondefensive mode we are not compelled to attack or counterattack, so we can develop a supportive relationship with others.[6]

Personalized meanings.   Words have different meanings to different people. An entire field of study, semantics, has been built around this widely accepted aspect of communication. Semantics is the study or science of meaning. In this book we use the term *supervisor* to indicate a person who occupies a first-level management position. In a hospital, or federal civil service, the term *supervisor* refers to a number of different levels of management. A case history from a manufacturing company, illustrates the barriers to communication created by personalized meanings:

> The president of a large manufacturing company was quoted in the local newspaper as saying: "Technical competence is not dead in our society and this will be shown in our company. I see an increasing emphasis for us upon technical competence." During the next several weeks, small group discussions were held in individual departments to discuss the implications of this statement. A perceptive personnel manager recorded some of the different *meanings* attached to the phrase "technical competence."
>
> Engineers, in general, were encouraged because they interpreted "technical" to refer to engineering as opposed to administration, manufacturing, or marketing. One engineer stated, "At last, the importance of our efforts to the company is being recognized."
>
> According to a manufacturing manager, some production workers were upset by the president's statement. They interpreted it to mean that higher productivity levels would be needed to obtain the same wage rates. (This was a nonunion shop.)
>
> Two members of the management training program felt the statement

---

[6] Reprinted, by permission of the publisher from "Recognizing—and Overcoming Defensive Communication," by Robert F. DeGise, *Supervisory Management*, March 1977, © 1977 by AMACOM, a division of American Management Associations, p. 38. All rights reserved.

implied that younger administrative employees might be cut, because the company was shifting away from administrative work and toward technical work.

The industrial nurse (who overhears many concerns of employees when they visit the company medical facility) commented that the public statement was interpreted as an early warning of an impending layoff. According to this interpretation, poor performers—those considered by the company to be technically incompetent—were in jeopardy of losing their jobs.[7]

To overcome the problem of semantics, supervisors should be sensitive to key words that might have different meanings to them than to subordinates, superiors, or co-workers. A supervisor in Los Angeles might warn subordinates not to arrive at work under the influence of alcohol. A problem in semantics might be encountered if the supervisor said, "Remember, nobody should come to work high." *High*, especially in California, usually refers to a state of intoxication induced by illegal drugs or chemicals. In other parts of the country, high also refers to alcoholic intoxication.

A related aspect of semantics is knowing which key words are in good favor with others. Thus a supervisor who wants to gain favor with superiors might incorporate into everyday conversation such terms as *cost effective, accountable for results,* or *bottom-line results.*

Low motivation or interest of receiver.   A close relationship exists between communication and motivation. People tend to listen with attention and interest to those messages that promise to satisfy an active need of theirs.[8] If your message does not relate to an active need, it may receive only partial attention or be ignored. Successful advertising appeals usually center around what a product or service can do for you. For instance, "You can be a 'Pepper' too, if you drink Dr. Pepper."

Assume that a supervisor, while browsing through a bookstore, noticed this text. On the cover of the book was this statement: "If you buy this book, it helps the publisher to stay in business. Besides the author can then buy a car for his oldest

---

[7] DuBrin, *Organizational Behavior*, p. 322.

[8] Herbert J. Chruden and Arthur W. Sherman, Jr., *Personnel Management*, 5th ed. (Cincinnati: South-Western, 1976), p. 290.

son." Few supervisors would be motivated to accept such an appeal. They would rather read a message such as "this book will give you timely tips to help make you a more successful supervisor."

To overcome the barrier erected by potentially low interest or motivation on the part of the receiver, try to make important messages appeal to human motivation. Suppose a construction supervisor has an unpleasant overtime assignment to offer a few employees—that of removing a septic tank from an abandoned property. One appeal might be, "Who would like to earn enough money this weekend to buy a TV set for your family?"

Poor reputation of sender. Messages are sometimes not received at all because the sender of the message is not trusted. A person who has communicated misinformation in the past runs the risk of not being taken seriously the next time an attempt is made to communicate. One dietician resigned from a position in a high school. The supervisor, upset over the resignation, demanded an explanation. The dietician replied, "I needed more money, so I took a job in a company where the pay is higher." The supervisor retorted, "But I told you that you would be receiving a 9 percent salary increase next month." To which the dietician replied, "Yes, but you've said the same thing several times before and nothing happened."

The obvious antidote to this communication barrier is to communicate honestly. A reputation for honest communication takes a long time to build, but it is well worth the time in terms of being a credible person. A specific method of developing the reputation of a sincere person is to *reinforce words with action.* Stated in another way, keep your promises and you will eliminate one more barrier to communication. If you say to a subordinate, "I'll review your performance next week," be sure you conduct that performance review next week.

Poor communication skills. A key barrier to communication is underdeveloped communication skills on the part of the sender. To be an effective communicator you need to develop spoken, written, and nonverbal methods of expression. A major reason many people do not advance in their careers is that they lack polished communication skills—particularly in face-to-face speaking and writing. Most readers of this book are aware of what needs to be done to become a more effective communicator. Reviewing and putting into action what you learned in your last course about communication skills should begin the process of improvement. The following section of this chapter is designed to serve as a brief refresher.

IMPROVING YOUR COMMUNICATION SKILLS[9]

Face-to-face speaking. Most employees at all levels could use improvement in public speaking, but only top executives and some training or public relations specialists are required to give speeches. What most people do need is improved ability to express their ideas in face-to-face meetings, such as conferences and two-way discussions. Any course in conference leadership would help you achieve this end. Four experience-based suggestions, if carried out, should help the reader improve face-to-face speaking skills.

1. Take the opportunity to speak in a meeting whenever the occasion arises. Volunteer comments in class and committee meetings, and capitalize on any chance to be a spokesperson for a group.

2. Obtain feedback by listening to tape recordings or dictating equipment renditions of your voice. Attempt to eliminate vocalized pauses and repetitions of phrases (such as "OK" or "you know") that detract from your communication effectiveness. Ask a knowledgeable friend for an opinion on your voice and speech.

3. Use appropriate models to help you develop your speech. A television talk-show host or commercial announcer may have the type of voice and speech behavior that fits your personality. The goal is not to imitate but to use that person as an approximate guide to generally acceptable speech.

4. Practice interviewing and being interviewed. Take turns with a friend conducting a simulated job interview. Interview each other about a controversial topic or each other's hobby.

[9] Portions of this section of the chapter are excerpted from Andrew J. DuBrin, *Human Relations: A Job Oriented Approach* (Reston, Va.: Reston, 1978), pp. 188–91.

Writing. Few supervisors devote a substantial amount of their workday to report writing. However, a substantial number of supervisors have to write an occasional memo or business letter. Substandard ability on such tasks can be a source of embarrassment to the writer of the memo or letter. The following five suggestions should serve as a reminder about how to improve your business writing skills.

1. Read a book about effective business report writing and attempt to implement the suggestion it offers.

2. Read material regularly that is written in the style and format that would be useful to you in your work. *The Wall Street Journal* and *Industry Week* are useful models for most forms of job-related writing. Another useful model for improving your writing is the business section of your local newspaper.

3. Practice writing at every opportunity. As a starting point you might want to write memos to the file (perhaps without actually filing them) and letters to friends and relatives. People who seem to have natural talent in writing are often those individuals who discipline themselves to practice their skill. People who are successful in getting an article published have often experienced many rejections of their articles in the past.

4. Get feedback on your writing. Ask a co-worker to critique a rough draft of your reports and memos. Offer to reciprocate. Editing other people's writing is a valuable way of improving your own. Feedback from a person with more writing experience and knowledge than you is particularly valuable. For instance, comments from an instructor about a submitted paper would be highly valued. So would comments from a public relations or communications specialist about a company memo.

5. Before proceeding ahead with the actual writing of a report or memo, prepare a brief outline.[10] The outline serves as a framework or skeleton of any carefully composed written document. At a minimum, the outline should consist of a list of the key points you want to cover. Beneath each key point you might add a comment or two about the information each key

---

[10] A useful exposition of this topic is Allen Weiss, "Outlining: An Indispensable Tool for the Business Writer," *Supervisory Management*, July 1977, pp. 18–25. See also Allen Weiss, *Write What You Mean: A Handbook of Business Communication* (New York: AMACOM, 1978).

point is to convey. Outlining saves time and usually results in an improved written document.

Nonverbal communication. Body language and other forms of nonverbal communication can also be improved. Published information related directly to this topic is difficult to find. Here are four suggestions to tentatively consider.

Obtain feedback on your body language by asking others to comment upon the gestures and facial expressions that you use in conversations. Have a videotape prepared of you conferring with another individual. After studying your body language, attempt to eliminate those mannerisms and gestures that you think detract from your effectiveness (such as moving your knee from side to side when being interviewed).

Learn to relax when communicating with others. Take a deep breath and consciously allow your body muscles to loosen. The tension-reducing techniques to be discussed in Chapter 19 should be helpful here. A relaxed person makes it easier for other people to relax. Thus you are able elicit more useful information from other people when you are relaxed.

Use facial, hand, and bodily gestures to supplement your speech. (But do not overdo it.) A good starting point is to use hand gestures to express enthusiasm. You can increase the potency of enthusiastic comments by shaking the other person's hand, nodding approval, smiling, or patting him or her on the shoulder.

Avoid using the same nonverbal gestures indiscriminately. To illustrate, if you want to use nodding to convey approval, do not nod with approval even when you dislike what somebody else is saying. Also, do not pat everybody on the back. Nonverbal gestures used indiscriminately lose their communications effectiveness.

HOLDING EFFECTIVE MEETINGS WITH EMPLOYEES

Despite the many criticisms made of meetings, they are an inevitable part of work in any modern organization. At one time or another a boss finds it advisable to communicate information to or receive information from a group of people. Meetings are well suited to such a purpose because they allow for the benefits of two-way communication. Instead of belaboring what is potentially wrong with meetings, it is more profitable to examine ways in which meetings can be effective. A supervisor who wants to conduct productive meetings with employees might give serious consideration to the following ten points.[11]

Have a specific agenda. Effective meetings are characterized by an agenda prepared in advance; this agenda should be communicated to participants several days to a week before the meeting. Participants can then pull together any necessary information they wish to bring to the meeting. Assume that Max, a stock supervisor in a furniture retail outlet, wants to call a safety meeting. He should telephone or write each person in advance, telling them about the safety meeting.

Stick to the agenda. An agenda is sometimes easier to prepare than adhere to. During the meeting Max must keep people focused on the safety topic. If not, the department employees might use the opportunity to express gripes about wages, the poor quality of shipping containers, and so forth. Such topics are worthy of discussion, but should be discussed at a later meeting.

Prepare in advance. The meeting leader (in this case Max) should collect all necessary facts, figures, and charts prior to the meeting. Inexperienced conference leaders often neglect this basic fact. Max might want to bring in a letter of complaint from the company personnel director about the high accident frequency in this particular store. Absenteeism figures due to work accidents in the inventory department would also be germane to the meeting.

Encourage a balanced contribution. An essential skill of the person who leads a meeting is to encourage widespread participation. Shy or fearful employees will need encouragement. A comment useful in bringing forth commentary for a quiet member is "Mary, what has been your observation about this point?" Mary will usually say something. Max, should then offer Mary some positive reinforcement such as "Thank you, Mary, that gives us something to think about."

Curtail dominating members. Most meetings are attended

---

[11] Our list of suggestions is based in part on two sources: Gary Dessler, *Personnel Management: Modern Concepts and Techniques* (Reston, Va.: Reston, 1978), pp. 146–47; and George Strauss and Leonard Sayles, *Personnel: The Human Problems of Management,* 2d ed. (Englewood Cliffs, N.J.: Prentice-Hall, 1967), pp. 269–81.

by one or two members with a compulsive desire to control the meeting with their thoughts and feelings. To keep this from happening, the leader must firmly control the verbal behavior of the domineering member. Here are three comments by the leader useful in this regard:

> John, I get your point. Who else would have a comment on this point?
>
> John, I'm looking for some other opinions now. We'll get back to you later.
>
> Enough is enough. We want to get opinions from everybody in this meeting.

If the meeting is one of a series of meetings, the domineering person can be confronted individually shortly after the first meeting. Since Max is both the meeting leader and the superior of each member, he should have enough power to have his request granted.

Provide summaries for each point. An effective conference leader provides summaries of each major point after they are made. Doing so provides an all-important structure to the meeting and gives members the feeling that something specific is being accomplished. Max might make a point such as this: "It seems that we've all agreed we are getting too many cut fingers in removing furniture from their shipping crates. Maybe we should enforce a rule about using work gloves while unpacking furniture."

Contribute ideas. Meeting leaders should play more than the administrative function of coordinating the ideas of others. They should contribute an occasional idea related to the problem under study. *When* to contribute such ideas is an important consideration. If supervisors contribute ideas too soon, the employees might think that they are looking for concurrence. New ideas and thoughts, therefore, are thought to be not welcome. After others have contributed their ideas, the supervisor might then step back from the leader role and contribute a suggestion.

A helpful statement prior to contributing an idea is "Let me act as a group member for a moment. Here is an idea I would like to contribute. One technique for avoiding collisions between the fork lift truck and the furniture racks is. . . ."

Encourage group interaction. A meeting loses its advantage of two-way communication when all communication pathways are among the leader and members. It is better for the members to react to each other's comments. At times, mild challenges are in order. In the safety discussion somebody might offer the suggestion, "I think we should process only one order at a time. When one is done, we go on to another. That would keep the aisles clear." Another participant might retort, "If we do that we'll be out of business. Most of our business occurs in a couple of peak hours per day. Since the customers carry away their own furniture, they wouldn't want to stand around for two hours while we process one order at a time."

Discourage lengthy discussion about irrelevant issues. A well-deserved criticism of many business meetings is that they allow for lengthy discussion about trivial matters. Those members not involved in the issue quickly become bored and restless. If Max found that his employees were discussing at length the type of vehicles customers use for hauling furniture, he would be well advised to halt the discussion. A simple declarative statement usually works well in this type of situation. An example: "We just don't have time to deal with that topic now."

Arrive early and stay late. Many people who conduct meetings use the "breathless boss" technique whereby they come rushing into the meeting, late, after everybody else has arrived.[12] It seems more advisable for the boss to arrive a few minutes early and get prepared in terms of laying out any charts or papers. Staying a few minutes after the meeting is also a useful technique. One or two individuals might have comments that they prefer to make to the supervisor in private. For instance, "Yeah, Bill talks a good game about safety. But he's the worst violator in the department. He turns corners with his fork lift like he were driving in a demolition derby." Participants might also have questions related to the meeting that they prefer to ask in private. For instance, "You mean it's all right for me to say what I really think in a meeting?"

DEALING WITH RUMORS

"Did you hear about the new retirement plan? If your age plus your number of years of service with the company adds up to 60,

---

[12] Richard J. Dunsing, "You and I Have Simply Got to Stop Meeting This Way—Part 5: Changes Leaders Can Make," *Supervisory Management,* January 1977, p. 22.

you'll be asked to retire at half pay. Suppose you are 50 years old, you have ten years seniority, and your annual salary is $15,000. You can take a vacation at $7,500 per year for the rest of your life. The statisticians in the personnel department figure the plan will actually save the company money in the long run.''

Within a few days after this rumor started, hundreds of company employees were busy making plans for their new life style. One 40-year-old who began work at the company at age 20 had already ordered a set of plans to build an A-frame house in the woods!

A supervisor should be prepared to face the nagging problems of dealing with rumors—those messages that get transmitted through the organization even though they are not based on any official word.

What causes rumors?   Rumors are based on the worries, concerns, fears, anxieties, and wishful dreams of people. People start rumors about topics of importance to them. The retirement rumor just described (which occurred in a company in the communications business) took place during a budget crunch. The company was looking for innovative ways of saving money.

Another cause or rumors is maliciousness. One supervisor was passed over for promotion. In retailiation, the individual initiated a rumor that a new product was experiencing extensive quality problems in the field. Many employees were upset by this rumor because the company was counting heavily on this new product.

How can rumors hurt an organization!   The biggest problem with rumors is that they are capable of disrupting work and lowering morale. Employees who are ruminating over a rumor will divert some of their efforts away from their jobs. As the rumor travels along the grapevine—the informal communication channel—it will cause some people to do foolish things. Layoff rumors are a good example. Hearing a rumor about a layoff, some high-performing employees will quickly find new employment. They fear looking for a new job while out of work. Unfortunately for the company, the best employees usually are the ones who find new employment the most quickly.

What can a supervisor do to control rumors?   A full disclosure of the facts is the best antidote to a true or false rumor. Suppose a rumor is circulating that the organization will soon have a new chief executive officer. If the rumor is true, the supervisor might call a department meeting (after obtaining clearance from above) and make an announcement of this type: "What you've been hearing is true. Mr. Watkins will be accepting early retirement at the end of this year. A committee has already been appointed to find a suitable replacement. They are looking inside and outside the organization for the right person. Everything is proceeding according to plan."

If the rumor is false, the supervisor should nip it in the bud. One supervisor artfully stopped the early retirement rumor, described earlier, in this way: "I'm 55 years old, and I joined the company five years ago. If that pipe dream about the 60-and-out plan were true, I'd already be packing my bags for Florida. The retirement plan listed in the Employee Handbook is still the official word on retirement. The 60-and-out plan never existed."

COMMUNICATING WITH HIGHER MANAGEMENT

Much of what we have said so far in this chapter applies to communication upwards as well as sideways or downward. Nevertheless, communicating with your boss, and sometimes with managers higher in the organization, has its unique challenges. A cardinal rule in communicating upwards is that the higher the rank of your receiver, the more concise you have to be in your presentation. By virtue of their positions and their personalities, executives tend to be impatient people. One vice president of a large company uses this stock phrase when visited by a member of lower management: "OK, you have five minutes. What is it?" A rambling, poorly organized spoken presentation usually creates a poor impression on higher management.

Lester R. Bittel offers some advice about what types of information should be communicated to upper management—even when a specific request for information has not been made. Upper management usually is receptive to information that relates to areas in which they are held responsible, controversial matters, or attitudes and morale.[13]

---

[13] Lester R. Bittel, *What Every Supervisor Should Know*, 3d ed. (New York: McGraw-Hill, 1974), pp. 74–75.

Matters for which your superior is held accountable. Your boss is usually eager to obtain information that relates directly to the attainment of management's objectives. Such matters would include quality, quantity, delivery dates, or accidents. A sound political strategy is to bring your boss as much good news as possible. At other times it may be necessary to bring forth the bad news rather than trying to conceal the truth.

If your boss is unavailable, critical information should be brought forth to your boss's superior. One assembly supervisor told the plant superintendent, "I know my boss is going to be very unhappy. But we cannot get those motors assembled by the promised date. We've had too much absenteeism of experienced workers." Instead of being punished by the absent boss when the latter returned to work the next day, the supervisor was praised. By bringing the late assembly problem to management early enough, the customer purchasing the motors was able to make appropriate adjustments in the delivery date.

Matters which may cause controversy. Suppose as a kitchen supervisor you had to break up a fight between two kitchen help. In the process you threw one of the combatants to the ground and he turned his ankle. Such a squabble will cause controversy. You are best advised to get to your boss with the facts as soon as possible.

Matters relating to attitude and morale. Upper management is usually isolated from people involved in direct clerical or production work. Yet, they have a strong interest in keeping informed about the "pulse" of the organization. An important vehicle for such upward communication is the first-level supervisor. Your impressions of job attitudes and morale can provide valuable input. Bittle advises, however, "Tell him (your boss) about good reactions as well as bad. But never, never play the role of a stool pigeon or go to him with information gained in confidence."[14]

---

[14] Ibid., p. 75.

SUMMARY OF KEY POINTS

☐ The communication process can be broken down into the following elements or steps: It begins with a *communicator* who *encodes* the thought to be sent into language. The resulting *message* can be communicated verbally or nonverbally over a medium such as speaking or a written memo. Once the message is sent it is *decoded* by the receiver. *Feedback* is essential for the sender to know if the message has been correctly received.

☐ Communication problems in organizations exist for a number of primary reasons: inadequate listening, preconceived ideas, denial of contrary information, personalized meanings, low motivation and interest on the part of the receiver, poor reputation of the sender, and poor communication skills.

☐ A strategy can be developed to cope with most of these potential barriers to communication. Above all, it is essential to recognize that these barriers exist and to take corrective remedial action.

☐ Improving your communications skills can contribute to your effectiveness as a supervisor and as a career person. Three modes of communication can stand improvement for most senders of messages: face-to-face speaking, writing, and nonverbal or body language.

☐ An important part of the supervisory job is to hold an occasional meeting with employees. Ten suggestions are made to improve the effectiveness of such meetings: have a specific agenda, stick to the agenda, prepare in advance, encourage a balanced contribution from people at the meeting, curtail domineering members, provide summaries for each point, contribute ideas yourself, encourage group interaction, discourage lengthy discussion about minor issues, and arrive early and stay late.

☐ A rumor is a message that is transmitted through the organization although it is not based on any official word. Rumors reflect the concerns of people and are sometimes based on maliciousness. The best way to deal with a rumor is to confront employees with the truth. Also, try to nip rumors in the bud.

☐ Communications with higher management should be concise and strictly limited in time. Higher management should be kept informed of matters for which they are held accountable, matters which may cause controversy, and matters relating to the attitudes and morale of employees.

GUIDELINES FOR SUPERVISORY PRACTICE[15]

1. In communicating with others, it is important to recognize that your message frequently will not be received as you intend. It is therefore important to be aware of potential barriers to communication and to adjust for them. As a basic example, if your employees are waiting to go to lunch, they may not listen carefully to your message.

2. Practice two-way rather than one-way communication if you are concerned about getting your message across.

3. An important general suggestion for improving your communications with others is to understand their frames of reference (points of view) before composing or delivering your message.

4. While delivering your message, ask for verbal feedback and be sensitive to nonverbal cues (such as yawning or squirming) about how your message is getting across.

5. An important determinant of the effectiveness of your communications is your credibility. You will be perceived as credible to the extent that your behavior reinforces your words.

6. Effective speaking, writing, and listening skills are a valuable asset to supervisors in most organizations.

QUESTIONS FOR DISCUSSION AND REVIEW

1. What is the biggest communication problem at the place where you work or attend school? What evidence do you have that this problem exists?

2. Which element or step in the communication process do you think is liable to the most "noise"? Explain.

3. Do you think a deaf person could do an effective job of leading a group of people with normal hearing? Why or why not?

4. What are some limitations of a speech as a communications device?

5. Speakers continue to be in demand at colleges, trade associations, and various clubs. Why do you think people believe in this mode of communication?

6. Give examples from your own life of the communication barrier, "denial of contrary information."

7. What are the various personalized meanings people attach to the words *boy* and *girl*—particularly in a job environment?

8. In what way are effective communication skills useful in playing office politics?

---

[15] These suggestions follow closely those presented in Andrew J. DuBrin, *Fundamentals of Organizational Behavior: An Applied Perspective* (Elmsford, N.Y.: Pergamon, 1974), p. 297.

9. Give some examples of how nonverbal communication is used during a basketball or football game by players and fans alike. Do not simply discuss hand signals used by officials or players such as the one for "time out."

10. Which of the 11 rules for conducting an effective meeting presented in this chapter is the most frequently violated in meetings you have attended?

11. What suggestions for communicating to higher management can you add to those described in this chapter?

12. Have you heard a good rumor lately? How did it start? How was it transmitted?

A supervisory problem: Why didn't you tell me sooner?

Jennie, a seamstress at Jo-Jo Fashions, rapped on the glass partition separating her boss, Biff, from the production floor. With an air of impatience, Biff said, "Come in, come in, what do you want now?"

Jennie: Biff, I'm sorry to bother you. But I won't be able to get anymore work done today.

Biff: What's the matter? You don't look sick to me.

Jennie: Biff, I'm not sick. But my machine is drenched with water and there's wet plaster all over my bolts of cloth. Part of the ceiling above my work area just caved in!

Biff: Good Lord, let me take a look. (Jennie and Biff walked quickly down to her work station.) What a mess. This is the dumbest thing I've ever seen happen. Didn't you have any warning that the ceiling was going to collapse? Why didn't you tell me about it sooner?

Jennie: Biff, we've had that leak from the restroom upstairs for weeks. I wanted to tell you about it, but you know you're not the easiest person to talk to about a problem.

Biff: What are you talking about? Anybody can see me about a problem anytime. Now the company is out maybe thousands of dollars.

1. *What barriers to communication seem to be illustrated by this problem?*
2. *Who seems to be more at blame? Biff or Jennie? Why?*
3. *What constructive actions might Biff take to insure that a problem of this nature does not occur again?*

SOME SUGGESTED READING

Banville, Thomas G. *How to Listen—How to Be Heard*. Chicago: Nelson-Hall, 1977.

DeGise, Robert F. "Recognizing—and Overcoming—Defensive Communication." *Supervisory Management,* March 1977, pp. 31–38.

Dunsing, Richard J. "You and I Have Simply Got to Stop Meeting This Way—Part 5: Changes Leaders Can Make." *Supervisory Management,* January 1977, pp. 18–29.

———. "You and I Have Simply Got to Stop Meeting This Way—Part 1: What's Wrong with Meetings." *Supervisory Management,* September 1976, pp. 2–13.

Estrada, Ric (illustrator). *Conference Leadership*. New York: AMACOM, 1977.

Ewing, David W. *Writing for Results in Business, Government, and the Professions*. New York: Wiley, 1974.

Haney, William V. *Communication and Organizational Behavior*. rev. ed. Homewood, Ill.: Richard D. Irwin, Inc., 1973.

Max, Robert R. "What's Your Communications 'I.Q.'?" *Supervisory Management,* April 1977, pp. 13–15.

O'Leary, Lawrence R. *Interviewing for the Decisionmaker*. Chicago: Nelson-Hall, 1975.

Rogers, Everett M., and Rogers, Rekha Agarwala. *Communication in Organizations*. New York: The Free Press, 1976.

Roseman, Ed. "How to Sell Your Ideas." *Product Management,* November 1975, pp. 43–46.

Stevens, Betsy. "You Were Saying . . . Improving Communication with Clerical Workers: The Non-Sexist Directive." *Personnel Journal,* April 1977, pp. 170–72.

Vinci, Vincent. "How to Be a Better Speaker." *Nation's Business,* August 1975, pp. 59–62.

Weiss, Allen. "Outlining: An Indispensable Tool for the Business Writer." *Supervisory Management,* July 1977, pp. 18–25.

———. *Write What You Mean: A Handbook of Business Communication*. New York: AMACOM, 1978.

Leadership of employees

10

LEARNING OBJECTIVES

After reading and working through the material in this chapter, you should be able to:

1. Understand the meaning of leadership.
2. Describe seven leadership styles.
3. Illustrate how the situation can influence which leadership style will probably bring the best results.
4. Be aware of adapting your leadership style to fit the situation.
5. Identify some specific behaviors involved in practicing participative management.
6. Understand the complexities of delegation.
7. Give directions and orders in a sensible manner.
8. Recognize the supervisor's role in maintaining morale.
9. Identify several specific behaviors associated with effective supervisory leadership.

THE SUPERVISOR AS A LEADER

Ram, an Asiatic Indian, was hired by his company as a laboratory technician. Although educated for such work, and apparently intelligent, Ram performed way below standard in his position. After several attempts at coaching Ram, his supervisor informed his boss and the personnel department of problems with the young technician. Ram was then purposely transferred into a department supervised by an Indian. Within one month Ram's performance exceeded standard. The new supervisor explained that she was able to establish rapport with him. Apparently Ram felt more comfortable being supervised by a person with a cultural background similar to his own.

229

The first supervisor in this situation was unable to exercise leadership. In contrast, the second supervisor was able to lead Ram. This anecdote illustrates the nature of leadership—directing people by exerting personal influence. A review of 20 years of research on the topic offers this definition of leadership: "An attempt at interpersonal influence, directed through the communication process, toward the attainment of some goal or goals."[1]

Leadership is such a comprehensive activity that we examine it last in our discussion of supervisory functions. As mentioned in Chapter 1, leadership is part of directing. However, it refers specifically to directing people by exerting personal influence of a *legitimate and nonviolent nature*. We add this qualifier because without it leadership would also include such devious maneuvers as blackmail, imposing drugs on people, and holding them at knife or gun point!

Anytime a supervisor influences a person to do something that is not simply a requirement of the job, that person is exerting leadership. You are functioning as a leader if you raise morale, encourage high levels of performance, help an employee with poor attendance to improve the problem, or gently coerce a problem employee to bathe regularly. You are not exerting leadership when a productive employee in your department continues to perform in such a manner or when a rational employee agrees to wear safety goggles. When people behave in their usual manner or simply comply with regulations, leadership has not been exercised. Since the world is not overpopulated with ideal employees, the supervisor often has to act as a leader. Even high performing employees who fit the solid-citizen designation sometimes need constructive leadership.

SUPERVISORY STYLES

Informal descriptions of supervisors have long been used to describe the characteristic way a particular supervisor goes about leading subordinates. Included here are terms such as *bull of the woods, pussycat, iron fisted, red neck, good ole boy, good ole*

[1] Edwin A. Fleishman, "Twenty Years of Consideration and Structure," in *Current Developments in the Study of Leadership*, ed. Edwin A. Fleishman and James G. Hunt (Carbondale: Southern Illinois University Press, 1973), p. 3.

gal, tyrant, and *social worker.* Leadership researchers have contributed dozens of ways of characterizing leadership styles. Perhaps over 1,000 studies have been conducted that bear directly on the problem of understanding the actual job behavior of leaders.[2] Many of these studies also attempt to investigate which leadership style works best in which situation. To simplify our study of supervisory styles we will examine seven styles that are usually incorporated directly or indirectly into most discussion of methods of classifying leadership styles.

Authoritarian style[3]

An authoritarian supervisor attempts to retain most of the authority within the group. Many companies encourage authoritarian behavior on the part of their supervisors. Authoritarian types make all the decisions and assume subordinates will comply without question. Drill sergeants and professional football coaches are usually authoritarians. The authoritarian supervisor generally gives minimum consideration to what subordinates are likely to think about an order or decision. An autocrat (a synonym for the term *authoritarian*) is sometimes seen as rigid and demanding by subordinates.

Many well-known, highly successful leaders are authoritarian in style. Charles Revson, the founder of Revlon, managed his empire in a strongly autocratic manner. Former U.S. President Lyndon B. Johnson was known to be highly autocratic in his dealings with subordinates. The McDonald restaurant chain is managed autocratically.

In some situations, a supervisor is best advised to use an authoritarian leadership style. One example would be a high-accident-risk work area where the employees were not particularly knowledgeable about the potential risks. The supervisor would have to be autocratic in making pronouncements such as

---

[2] Two key reference works here are Ralph M. Stogdill, *Handbook of Leadership* (New York: The Free Press, 1974); and Paul Hersey and Kenneth M. Blanchard, *Management of Organizational Behavior: Utilizing Human Resources*, 3d ed. (Englewood Cliffs, N.J.: Prentice-Hall, 1977).

[3] A classic article about the first three styles described here is Robert Tannenbaum and Warren H. Schmidt, "How to Choose a Leadership Pattern," *Harvard Business Review*, March–April 1958, pp. 95–101. Our discussion is also influenced by a modern analysis of the same topic: Jack Halloran, *Applied Human Relations: An Organizational Approach* (Englewood Cliffs, N.J.: Prentice-Hall, 1978), pp. 308–15.

"don't smoke near those chemical drums" or "wear acid-proof
gloves whenever you enter the work area marked off by red
lines."

Participative style

A participative leader shares decision-making authority with
members of the group. Participative leaders consult with group
members on most decisions of consequence. They rarely make
arbitrary or unilateral decisions. Instead, they would engage in
such practices as: present the idea and invite questions; present
a tentative decision subject to change; present the problem, get
suggestions, and make the decision.[4] (More will be said about
this topic later in the chapter.)

There are basically two types of participative leaders—
democrative and consultative. Democratic leaders confer final
authority to the group. They are essentially collectors of group
opinion. Democratic leaders help the group accomplish what it
wants to accomplish and abide by the group decision. Democratic leadership thus has more relevance for community leadership situations than for most work settings. Consultative leaders require a high degree of involvement from subordinates. But
they make it clear that they alone have authority to make final
decisions.

The participative style is suited to leading competent and
well-motivated people who want to get involved in making decisions and giving feedback to the boss. A participative style is also
useful when the supervisor wants employees to feel committed
to a particular decision or course of action. A supervisor might
ask the group, "What should we do with people in the department who leave debris behind after using the lunch area?" If the
group agreed on a fitting punishment, they would tend to accept
the punishment if it were administered.

A participative supervisory style generally works best with
highly skilled or professional employees. If there is no room left
for decision making (if approaches have already been agreed
upon by management), participative management has limited
usefulness. In highly repetitive, machine-paced operations, little
room is left for employee problem solving. In such situations, a

---

[4] Tannenbaum and Schmitt, "Leadership Pattern," p. 96.

supervisor who wants to use a participative style must look for aspects of the job that are not already programmed. Soliciting suggestions on safety or general working conditions might be helpful in this regard.

Free-rein style

A free-rein supervisor is a very casual leader. This person issues general goals and guidelines to the group and then does not get involved again unless requested. The only limits directly imposed on the group are those specified by the leader's boss: "So long as it doesn't violate company policy, do what you want." Such an extreme degree of employee freedom is rarely encountered in a work setting. One exception might be a pure research laboratory where scientists and engineers are granted freedom to tackle whatever problems they find interesting.

A supervisor will rarely meet with effectiveness when using free-rein leadership. One problem is that a free-rein leader is often perceived as lazy or indifferent. In a rare situation where a group of skilled workers need no help or encouragement from management, the free-rein style might be effective. The hypothetical pure research laboratory alluded to above is one setting in which free-rein leadership might be appropriate. In this current era of accountability, a free-rein supervisor would probably fall into disfavor with higher management.

High-task and low-relationship style[5]

A fruitful way of classifying leader or supervisory styles is to take into consideration two aspects of behavior at the same time. Two critical aspects of leader behavior relate to emphasis on getting work accomplished and to emphasis on relating to employees. Paul Hersey and Kenneth Blanchard provide these key definitions:[6]

---

[5] This and the next three leadership styles are based on a synthesis of earlier leadership studies presented in Hersey and Blanchard, *Human Resources,* pp. 103–4 and chap. 7.

[6] Ibid., p. 104. Their definition is based on a series of classical studies conducted at Ohio State University. The original source is Ralph M. Stogdill and Alvin E. Coons, eds., *Leader Behavior: Its Description and Measurement,* research monograph no. 88 (Columbus, Ohio: Bureau of Business Research, Ohio State University, 1957), pp. 42–43.

234

Task behavior—The extent to which leaders are likely to organize and define the roles of the members of their group (followers); to explain what activities each is to do and when, where, and how tasks are to be accomplished; characterized by endeavoring to establish well-defined patterns of organization, channels of communication, and ways of getting jobs accomplished.

Relationship behavior—The extent to which leaders are likely to maintain personal relationships between themselves and members of their group (followers) by opening up channels of communication, providing socioemotional support, "psychological strokes," and facilitating behaviors.

If you classify leaders as being high or low on both dimensions of behavior, four different combinations are possible, as depicted in Figure 10–1. In our brief descriptions of these four styles, we

FIGURE 10–1
Four key leader or supervisory styles of behavior

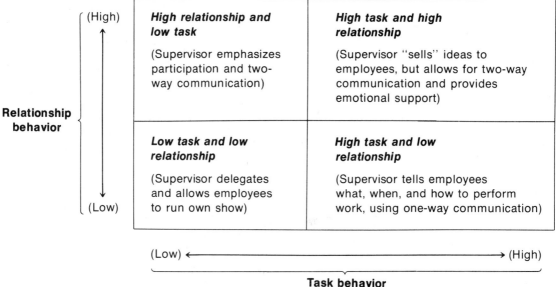

also take into account the dimension of effectiveness. As with the three previous styles, each style is likely to be effective in *some* situations.

A high-task and low-relationship supervisor emphasizes showing employees how to get the tasks accomplished and spends a minimum of time giving them emotional support or reassurance. Given a situation where the employees are inexperienced with the work to be performed, this style may prove effective. The high-task and low-relationship style may be well suited to many situations where seasonal help are involved. Seasonal employees may be unfamiliar with the task and thus require direct guidance on performing the work properly. A high-task and low-relationship leader is not necessarily rude or discourteous. The leader simply takes the expedient route of focusing on work rather than people.

High task and high relationship

The high task and high leader relationship spends considerable time showing people how to get the work accomplished and providing them emotional support. The high-task and high-relationship style is often considered the most generally useful because it results in high productivity and personal satisfaction. A more critical look at this style would suggest that it works best in situations where people need an active and involved supervisor. When employees are lacking in self-confidence and technical skill, the high-task and high-relationship style is particularly useful. If you were supervising a group of young men and women who had just completed a job-training program for hard-core unemployed people, a high-task and high-relationship approach would have the highest probability of success. Individuals of such limited work experience and formal education generally need all the help they can get from their supervisors.

High relationship and low task

A supervisor using the high-relationship and low-task style gives employees much encouragement and support but a minimum of guidance about performing the actual work. In some situations employees do not need technical instruction but they do need to "lean on" their supervisor. A supervisor was in charge of a repetitive production operation in a room where the temperature was consistently over 100 degrees Fahrenheit. This leader was able to reduce turnover in the department by conveying sympathy to employees about their working conditions and also allowing ample time for griping.

A beauty salon operator might also profitably use the high-relationship and low-task leadership style. Hair stylists are usually technically competent people who resent work instructions but do welcome pampering by the boss.

Low relationship and low task

A supervisor using this style is essentially a free-rein leader. Subordinates are given considerable latitude in performing their work. Also, they are given very little emotional support, encouragement, and praise. Supervisors who use this style are thus free to perform their own administrative and technical tasks.

The low-relationship and low-task supervisor allows followers to run their own show. When subordinates are highly skilled and psychologically mature, this style can be effective. A chief of medicine might run a department in this manner. So might the supervisor of a group of master mechanics or experienced tool and die makers.

Theory X and theory Y

The best-known method of classifying leadership styles is based on differences in assumptions you make about people.[7] Douglas McGregor believed that if managers basically trusted subordinates, they would allow them to participate in decision making (Theory Y). On the other extreme, if managers distrusted subordinates, they would tend to supervise them quite closely. In capsule form, these famous sets of assumptions are as follows:

Theory X assumptions:

1. People dislike work and therefore try to avoid it.
2. People dislike work, so managers are forced to control, direct, coerce, and threaten subordinates to get them to work toward company goals.
3. People prefer to be directed, to avoid responsibility, to seek security. In general, they have little ambition.

---

[7] Douglas McGregor, *The Human Side of Enterprise* (New York: McGraw-Hill, 1960), pp. 33–57.

Theory Y assumptions:

1. Work is a natural part of people's lives; people do not dislike work.
2. People are self-motivated to reach goals to which they feel committed.
3. People are committed to goals providing they attain rewards when they reach their objectives.
4. Under favorable conditions, people will seek and accept responsibility.
5. People have the capacity to be innovative in solving job-related problems.
6. People are basically bright, but in most job settings their potentials are underutilized.

ADAPTING YOUR STYLE TO THE SITUATION

In order to be effective, a supervisor must adapt a leadership style to the situation. Making such an adaptation assumes that you have the skill to diagnose the situation and to change your basic supervisory behavior. With careful reflection and observation, most supervisors can identify which supervisory style should work the best. Two major constraints on choosing your style must be given careful consideration: your personality style and the style of leadership practiced by your management.

Your basic personality traits and characteristics exert a profound influence on how you go about leading others. If you are basically a trusting and friendly person, you would be inclined toward a participative, or low-task supervisory style. If you are basically a demanding and domineering person, your most natural style would be that of an authoritarian or high-task leader. If you were a distrustful person with a pessimistic view of people, you would tend to provide close or tight supervision (the high-task orientation). These are just a few of the ways in which personality influences leadership style.

The leadership style used by your boss and other key managers in your organization exerts an influence on your style of supervision. If your company seems to favor a permissive, lenient approach to managing employees, your inclination would probably be to do the same. On the other hand, assume you observe that the managers in your company with the biggest jobs are highly task oriented, with little regard for the feelings of people. Subtle pressures will then exist for you to adopt a similar leadership style in handling your subordinates.

Important clues in choosing a leadership style

A realistic way of determining which supervisory style is best suited to the situation is to begin by observing both the characteristics of your employees and the environmental pressures and demands. Either or both sets of information may suggest a starting point in choosing the optimum style of supervision for the occasion.

Personal characteristics of your subordinates. In general, competent people—those who are well trained, intelligent, and well motivated—need a minimum of guidance and emotional support from their supervisor. Leaders in such situations are best advised not to interfere with the work activities of their employees. Another characteristic of subordinates that influences the most effective leadership style is their degree of authoritarianism.[8] Authoritarian people (strict and unyielding) have a tendency to prefer task-oriented leaders. Also, they tend to dislike a participative style of leadership. Authoritarian employees prefer to have things spelled out for them in precise detail.

The best supervisory style in a given situation can be influenced by how well the subordinates think that they can perform their work. If employees are confident in what they are doing, they sometimes resent a supervisor giving them careful instructions.

Environmental pressures and demands. Factors related to the job itself and the conditions surrounding the job are a second set of factors influencing the choice of supervisory style.[9] Under conditions of heavy stress, threat, or pressure, most people want a leader to take forceful charge of the situation. In crisis situations, people are pleased to have the leader give specific orders and directives. Firechiefs are expected to be high-task leaders, at least while a fire is being fought.

---

[8] Alan C. Filley, Robert J. House, and Steven Kerr, *Managerial Process and Organizational Behavior*, 2d ed. (Glenview, Ill.: Scott, Foresman, 1976), p. 255.

[9] A technical discussion of this topic is found in Elmer Burack, *Organization Analysis: Theory and Application* (Hinsdale, Ill.: The Dryden Press, 1975), pp. 315–18.

The type of technology is another example of how environmental demands influence which leadership style is the most appropriate. In a craftlike operation, most of the subordinates will be highly skilled and will therefore need a minimum of instruction and guidance. A supervisor in such a situation should therefore emphasize giving the workers autonomy (freedom to make their own decisions).

The other extreme is a mass-production operation where the contribution of one department depends on the contribution of other departments. An appliance assembly plant would be one such operation. The production process cannot tolerate deviations from standard, so the supervisors involved have to ensure that policies and procedures are rigidly enforced. They would utilize a high-task orientation in leading subordinates.

FIGURE 10–2
Twelve different work situations and a recommended supervisory style for dealing with each one

Work situation	Recommended supervisory style
A. Crisis: People in a state of confusion or panic, such as a parts shortage, equipment failure, or natural disaster	High task and low relationship or authoritarian
B. Complex technology, inexperienced employees	High task and low relationship at outset
C. Undesirable, repetitive job, average employees	High relationship and low task
D. Self-sufficient, capable workers performing job they enjoy	Low task and low relationship or participative
E. Employees dislike working; job is undesirable	High relationship and high task
F. Start up of new operation; job descriptions are vague	High relationship and high task
G. Group of people "doing time" until retirement	High relationship and low task
H. Inexperienced but well-meaning employees	High relationship and high task
I. Repetitive work; employees with average motivation	High relationship and low task
J. Employees are performing interdependent tasks requiring coordination by supervisor	High task; emphasis on relationship depends on emotional maturity of employees
K. Emotionally immature employees; average skill level	High task and low relationship
L. Employees are childlike or "prima donnas" but talented	High relationship and low task

Matching the supervisory style to the situation. Classifying situations can become complex when you take into account the almost endless combinations of different types of people and environmental pressures and demands. The approach recommended here is to first specify 12 different work situations that probably account for the bulk of work settings. These are listed in Figure 10–2. Adjacent to each of these 12 work situations is a recommended supervisory style to match that situation. To illustrate, work situation E is one in which "employees dislike working and the job is undesirable." The supervisory style most likely to be effective in this situation is high relationship and high task. Employees of this nature need a substantial amount of help from their supervisor. The supervisor will have to coach them, encourage them, and provide them detailed job instructions.

Using Figure 10–2 is much like using the Framework for Accomplishing Results presented in Chapter 1. You diagnose the situation and then choose a course of action that has a high probability of achieving good results. If the style recommended in the table does not work, you modify your style until you find a style that does produce the results you want.

HOW TO PRACTICE PARTICIPATIVE MANAGEMENT

Participative management appears to be the leadership style with the fastest growing rate of acceptance. So far European countries are far ahead of the United States and Canada in their use of participative management.[10] In Europe it is common to see worker involvement in plant management. It is possible that by the mid 1980s, U.S. law will demand some form of participative management in plants and offices. The proposed human resources development act provides a framework for federally financed experiments in labor-management cooperation. Its purpose is to give workers a greater voice in conducting and preserving their jobs.

Upper management has a major role in establishing participative management, particularly at a policymaking level. First-

[10] Robert H. Keppler, "What the Supervisor Should Know About . . . Participative Management," *Supervisory Management*, May 1978, p. 34–36.

level supervisors have to deal with participative management on a daily basis. For instance, top management may establish a work standards committee and invite two production workers and one file clerk to serve on the committee. First-level supervisors, however, would be responsible for using participative management on a day-by-day basis. They would have to engage in specific supervisory practices that encourage participation. The scope of the task is suggested by a modern definition of participative management: "A process by which workers and managers get together to make decisions that directly affect job performance."[11]

A supervisor who practices participative leadership must engage in certain activities that are seen as participative by employees and members of upper management. In other words, participative management is an abstract idea that must be translated into specific actions in order to be workable. Fortunately some hard data exist about what a supervisor has to do to actually practice participative management.[12] A researcher at Harvard Business School asked 318 high-level managers their opin-

FIGURE 10-3
The 10 highest participation characteristics

	Rank
Gives subordinates a share in decision making.	1
Keeps subordinates informed of the true situation, good or bad, under all circumstances.	2
Stays aware of the state of the organization's morale and does everything possible to make it high.	3
Is easily approachable.	4
Counsels, trains, and develops subordinates.	5
Communicates effectively with subordinates.	6
Shows thoughtfulness and consideration of others.	7
Is willing to make changes in ways of doing things.	8
Is willing to support subordinates even when they make mistakes.	9
Expresses appreciation when a subordinate does a good job.	10

Source: Larry E. Greiner, "What Managers Think of Participative Leadership," *Harvard Business Review*, March–April 1973, p. 114. Copyright © 1973 by the President and Fellows of Harvard College; all rights reserved.

---

[11] Ibid., p. 35.

[12] Larry E. Greiner, "What Managers Think of Participative Leadership," *Harvard Business Review*, March–April 1973, pp. 117–27. Copyright © 1973 by the President and Fellows of Harvard College; all rights reserved.

ion about the nature of participative management. In general a participative leader was seen as an extroverted, sensitive person who openly shares decisions and authority with subordinates. Surprisingly high agreement was found on what practices by a leader are participative in nature.

The ten leadership practices most frequently cited as indicating a participative leadership style are presented in Figure 10–3. The rank to the left of each practice indicates the relative importance attached to each practice by the executives giving their opinion. The higher the rank, the more the practice indicates participative leadership. As commonsense would suggest, the leadership practice most clearly reflecting a participative style is "Gives subordinates a share in decision making."

THE ART OF DELEGATION

Participative leadership is essentially a form of delegation in which responsibility for decision making is delegated to subordinates. Participative management is thus not possible without some degree of delegation. Delegation is also the lifeblood of collective effort. The organizing function of management is only possible through the delegation of responsibility from higher to lower levels in the organization.

Delegation is the managerial act of "letting go"—passing authority down to subordinates. As a supervisor you might delegate to an employee the authority to represent your department in an important meeting. By delegating such authority, you do not escape accountability for the manner in which the task is performed. If the person you send to the meeting makes no contribution, you have done a poor job (as well as your designate). Thomas J. Atchison and Winston W. Hill report that there are a number of reasons why some managers may not want to let go and why some employees may resist accepting the delegated authority.[13]

"I can handle it better than you." Supervisors often believe that they can perform the delegated assignment better than the employee. As a result of this attitude, they do not project confidence in the employee's ability to perform the delegated task.

---

[13] Thomas J. Atchison and Winston W. Hill, *Management Today: Managing Work in Organizations* (New York: Harcourt Brace Jovanovich, 1978), pp. 102–24.

Poor skill in delegation. Some managers have not developed the proper skills for delegation. In order to delegate, a manager must be able to plan, organize, and communicate effectively to employees. Delegation is not simply dropping an assignment on somebody else's lap.

Poor control systems. Delegation does not work effectively unless a good system of control and feedback has been established. When you delegate, you need to establish a formal or informal system of monitoring progress on the delegated assignment. You have to know how things are progressing, and employees must have accurate feedback on their own performance.

Delegation can consume too much time. If you delegate a complicated assignment to an employee, that employee might need substantial information to properly discharge the newly acquired authority. So much information might need to be transmitted, that delegation hardly seems worth the effort.

Employee resistance. Some employees are fearful of accepting authority owing to a basic lack of self-confidence. Or they may believe they will be criticized if things go wrong. Still others may not have the right training to handle the delegated task. Occasionally an employee will simply prefer to shirk new responsibility: some people are poorly motivated toward achieving work goals.

Assign duties to the right people. An important first step in insuring that delegation proceeds smoothly is to delegate tasks to the right people. Assignments should be made on the basis of capability. As one supervisor told the boss, "Sure, I should delegate more. But in order to delegate, you need somebody to delegate to. That's where my delegation falls down." The person to whom you delegate a task should have the proper motivation and skill to carry out the job. A counterbalancing principle is that if a supervisor does not delegate, you will not build a department of competent employees. A good practice in this regard is to start small with an inexperienced employee. Delegate noncomplex tasks to that person at first, and gradually increase the complexity of your assignments.

Grant people enough authority to accomplish delegated tasks. As is widely known, but not so widely practiced, employees at all levels need enough authority—and the right kind—to get their work accomplished. The problem is particularly acute with delegated tasks. Often an employee is assigned a task but doesn't have enough formal authority to gain the cooperation of others in carrying out the task. A staff specialist in a bank was assigned the project of studying the work habits of tellers and other bank employees. In order to carry out the delegated task, it was necessary for employees to fill out a complicated time diary. In the process of trying to collect information, the comments received were: "Come back later when I'm not so busy," or "I'm just not interested in that type of survey from the main office." Although responsible for collecting the information, the staff specialist lacked the authority to gain the compliance of others.

Keep some important tasks for yourself. An important principle of delegation is to use discretion when delegating important work assignments. For example, a supervisor should not delegate a task that involves confidential information.[14] If an employee in your department were undergoing treatment for an alcohol abuse problem, you should not delegate to another subordinate the task of checking on the progress of the troubled employee. Matters involving budgets or personnel problems should ordinarily not be delegated. Problems calling for the unique technical expertise of the supervisor should also be handled by the supervisor.

Despite the principle just mentioned, it is crucial that a supervisor delegate some challenging and interesting tasks along with the more routine. To do otherwise, you run the risk of being accused of only delegating "dirty work." A good way of increasing morale is to occasionally delegate a choice assignment such as sending a subordinate on a field trip to visit a customer installation.

If possible, it is best to avoid "yo-yo" delegation. One manager assigned a supervisor the task of looking for energy leaks in the plant. Later the same manager discovered that the company president was quite interested in energy conservation. Quickly, the manager took back the assignment of looking for energy

---

[14] Opinion expressed by Lester R. Bittel, *What Every Supervisor Should Know*, 3d ed. (New York: McGraw-Hill, 1974), p. 134.

leaks. The manager decided to personally conduct the search because of its political importance. The supervisor became disgruntled about the incident.

GIVING DIRECTIONS AND ORDERS

An inescapable part of any leader's job is to give directions and orders to followers. Similarly a supervisor must occasionally give orders to employees however well informed they might be about their job responsibilities. Employees differ widely in their reactions to orders. At one extreme are those who almost automatically accept authority. At the other extreme are those who are supersensitive about being ordered to do anything. The proper way of giving any directions or orders depends on the particular circumstance, including the employee involved and the nature of the direction or order.[15] Nevertheless, four general principles should be kept in mind when making commands or requests to subordinates.

Follow the law of the situation. Orders, directions, commands, and requests that appear logically based on the requirements of the moment generally meet with a minimum of resistance.[16] If your department is suddenly flooded by a broken pipe, most of your employees will be glad to help rescue valuable papers from potential water damage. Orders that flow naturally from the situation are also depersonalized. In the burst-pipe incident just cited, nobody is likely to feel picked upon to help in the rescue operation.

Often a supervisor must interpret the situation to employees. A printing supervisor was reprimanded by the boss because of a customer complaint that books were falling apart in the hands of book readers. The boss addressed the problem in this manner with good results:

> We're under a lot of pressure. One of our biggest customers, _____ Publishers, says they are getting a lot of returns on this book (holding it

---

[15] A thorough discussion of giving orders by supervisors is found in Theo Haimann and Raymond L. Hilgert, *Supervision: Concepts and Practices of Management,* 2d ed. (Cincinnati: South-Western, 1977), pp. 246–50.

[16] The concept of the law of the situation can be traced to Mary Parker Follett. See H. C. Metcalf and Lyndall F. Urwick, eds., *Dynamic Administration: The Collected Papers of Mary Parker Follett* (New York: Harper & Row, 1941).

for his employees to see). The darn thing is falling apart in the hands of students. They are demanding refunds from the bookstore. The bookstore is demanding credit from the publisher. The publisher is demanding rework from us. And my boss is demanding an explanation from me. From now on, I want everybody here to do a better job of checking bindings before they leave this shop.

Speak with confidence but not hostility.   Effective order givers act as if they expect compliance. Apologies are rarely called for in issuing directions and orders. On the other extreme, orders that are issued in a hostile manner will either be resisted or create morale problems. Assume it is 9 A.M. and that an accounting supervisor needs a particular set of figures by noon. Following is how the same order might be given in three different modes: confident, apologetic, and hostile:

Confident: Meg, I'll need the figures on the Pinnacle Company by noon. Please let me have them by then.

Apologetic: Meg, I hate to bother you. I know you have enough work to do to keep two bookkeepers busy. But is there any way you might be able to get the figures on the Pinnacle Company to me before lunch? I hope I'm not being unreasonable.

Hostile: Meg, listen carefully to me. Drop whatever else you might be doing now. Get me those Pinnacle figures by noon, sharp. And I don't want to hear any explanations about some trivial problem that's holding you back.

Follow the doctrine of reasonableness.   A reasonable order, directive, or direction is one that is legitimate as seen by the employee. Legitimate in this sense refers to power that seems to fit within the sphere of what an employee is willing to do for money. In today's world it is illegitimate to expect a subordinate to wash your car, mow your lawn, or iron your clothing. Nor does a union electrician consider it reasonable or part of the job to repair a wooden door or install a mechanical part. Some orders require more pause for reflection before reaching a judgment about their reasonableness. Is it reasonable to expect a secretary to type a letter 15 minutes before quitting time the day before a major religious holiday? Is it reasonable to order a postal worker to deliver mail by foot when the wind chill factor is minus 40 degrees Fahrenheit?

Orders must be explicit and intelligible. An effective order is understandable and relatively unambiguous. (The comments made about effective objectives in Chapter 6 are generally applicable to effective orders. See also the discussion of overcoming barriers to communication in the previous chapter.) If an order is complicated, it is of vital importance to ask for the employee's interpretation of the order. It is important to obtain feedback on your effectiveness in communicating the order.

MAINTAINING MORALE

One of a supervisor's major responsibilities is to maintain a reasonable level of morale within a department. A major problem in controlling morale is that almost anything that happens to an employee while at work can influence morale. Thus a supervisor has limited ability to influence that vague state of mind called morale.

Morale can be defined as "a composite of feelings, attitudes, and sentiments that contribute to a general feeling of satisfaction."[17] To say "my morale is high" is tantamount to saying "I feel good." Morale sometimes refers to individuals and sometimes to groups. The term *esprit de corps* or team spirit basically refers to group morale.

Since morale deals with a person or group's overall level of satisfaction , it is potentially influenced by a wide range of supervisory actions. Every chapter in this book has implications for morale. To cite just two examples: If supervisors help decrease accident frequency, they are warding off potential morale problems. When supervisors carry out the leadership function of motivating people, they may be simultaneously elevating morale.

Why is morale important? Extremes in morale are of enormous significance to an organization. High morale often (but not always) leads to improved productivity, decreased turnover, improved attendance, and decreased sabotage along with a decrease in other forms of conflict. Morale also has an important humanitarian consideration: Low morale over a prolonged basis contributes to poor mental health. People unhappy at work often become unhappy off the job.

---

[17] Halloran, *Applied Human Relations*, p. 129.

248

Although most of the suggestions in this book have implications for morale, there are five leadership practices that have direct bearing on individual and group morale. All of them are also mentioned directly or indirectly in this chapter and at other places in this book. Each of these practices will therefore be described briefly.

Be considerate. Substantial documentation exists that the considerate or high relations leadership style contributes to employee morale.[18] People feel better and often work better when they receive reassurance and support from their supervisor. Considerate leaders don't necessarily neglect production. Instead, they place equal emphasis on concern for people and concern for production. A widely accepted leadership training program, the managerial grid, coaches managers on how to go about getting maximum production from highly satisfied subordinates.[19]

Maintain open lines of communication. Bonnie, a records clerk, had what she considered an embarrassing problem. She developed a cyst on the lower end of her spine which required minor surgery. Bonnie was eager to return to work after a one-day absence, but she realized it would be uncomfortable for her to sit down for prolonged periods of time. At the start of her workday she went directly to George her supervisor and said, "George, I don't want to be a pest, but I would prefer if I could do my job standing up for the next day or two." George replied, "Bonnie, so long as you get your job done, I don't care if you work in a hammock." Bonnie left George's office with a smile and made this parting comment, "Thanks for being so easy to talk to. I feel great."

The incident about Bonnie and George illustrates the relationship between supervisors and employees that can occur by maintaining open lines of communication and thereby improving morale. People feel better (have higher morale) when they can approach a boss about a variety of work and work-related problems. Supervisors who shut off communication channels between themselves and subordinates are inviting morale problems.

---

[18] Information about considerate behavior and morale is summarized in Gary Dessler, *Personnel Management: Modern Concepts and Techniques* (Reston, Va.: Reston, 1978), p. 282.

[19] See Robert R. Blake and Jane S. Mouton, *The New Managerial Grid* (Houston, Tex.: Gulf, 1978).

Allow for participative management. Participative management sometimes raises productivity and usually raises morale. Thus a supervisor who includes employees in the decision-making process (and carries out some of the other practices listed in Figure 10–3) is creating conditions favorable to high morale. The underlying psychology is that most people are flattered when their opinion is sought on an important issue. As one assembler expressed his or her (the questionnaire was anonymous) opinion in an attitude survey: "My boss makes me feel like somebody important. If we get a customer complaint about something, he asks my opinion about what the company is doing wrong. I may not be a college graduate but I have a lot of wisdom stored up in my head."

Practice good management. Over the years hundreds of guidelines have developed for practicing good management. Almost any book about management, human relations, supervision, or business psychology contains many direct or indirect tips for carrying out effective management practices. If a supervisor held to many of these practices, the net effect would undoubtedly be increased morale among subordinates. To cite one of hundreds of possible examples, most human relations books admonish the boss to criticize privately, not publically. Yet many supervisors persist in "chewing out" employees in front of their co-workers. A supervisor who refrains from such public criticism would ward off some serious morale problems. In a sense, morale would be elevated because it would not be lowered.

Create a good physical environment.[20] The physical environment often influences morale. Morale tends to be higher when people work in a safe, comfortable, and esthetic physical setting. Factors such as dirty washrooms and shower facilities and inadequate eating areas and parking facilities tend to lower morale. A first-level manager rarely has the authority to revamp the physical environment. Yet that manager, however, can take steps to insure that the immediate department is clean and neat. A supervisor can also make recommendations to higher management about improving the physical environment. It is generally considered within reason for a first-level manager to rec-

---

[20] A concise discussion of this topic is found in Halloran, *Applied Human Relations,* pp. 153–56.

ommend a repainting of the department or to request that a broken vending machine be repaired or replaced.

THE JOB BEHAVIOR OF EFFECTIVE SUPERVISORS

Hundreds of studies have investigated the issue of which specific actions make for effective supervisory leadership. The conclusions they reach about leadership effectiveness, however, must be interpreted with caution. Leadership depends to a large extent upon the specific situation, as described earlier. With this caution in mind, below are 11 generalizations about the leadership practices of effective supervisors—those who maintain high productivity and morale.

Effective supervisors have influence up the organization. Employees respond positively to supervisors who are able to influence higher-level managers and staff personnel. Supervisors with such influence are able to fight for the demands of their subordinates.

Effective supervisors provide emotional support and consideration to subordinates. Having good human relations skills of this nature is often more important for morale than productivity. An emotionally supportive leader would engage in such activities as listening to subordinates' problems and offering them encouragement.

Effective supervisors differentiate themselves from subordinates. A good leader is not simply another member of the department. This leader plans, regulates, and coordinates the activities of subordinates, but does not become directly involved in performing their work.

Effective supervisory leaders tend to exercise general (loose) rather than close (tight) supervision. With some exceptions, most employees feel better and work better when they have breathing room in carrying out their chores.

Effective supervisors establish realistic objectives. As described in Chapter 6, objectives in each department should fit in with the objectives of the overall organization. They should give people a chance to stretch their capabilities, but should not be unrealistically difficult.

Effective supervisors provide the necessary resources. An important requirement of a leader's job is to insure that people have the proper tools, equipment, and personnel to accomplish their objectives.

Effective leaders make their expectations known. The best-documented fact about leadership is that followers function better when they know what they have to do to achieve work goals. To accomplish this end, the effective leader uses both formal and informal communication.

Effective leaders provide adequate rewards for good performance. Good supervisory leaders are also good motivators of subordinates. They are skillful in using positive reinforcement, as outlined in Chapter 8.

Effective supervisory leaders delegate authority and encourage employee participation where the situation so warrants. Through delegation and participation supervisors can multiply their own capabilities, raise morale, and increase productivity.

An effective leader identifies and removes barriers to effective performance. The supervisor has a responsibility to replace faulty equipment, see to it that unsafe conditions are corrected, and help troublesome employees to be either rehabilitated or replaced.

Effective leaders give frequent feedback on performance. Employees are told how they can improve and given encouragement for the things they are doing right. Ineffective leaders, in contrast, often avoid confrontation and give limited positive feedback.

Many of the points raised in this list are described in more detail in this and other chapters. The above will serve as a brief review and checklist.

SUMMARY OF KEY POINTS

☐ Leadership is an attempt at influencing people directly through the communication process toward the attainment of some goal or goals. The influence exerted is of a legitimate and nonviolent nature.

☐ A supervisory or leadership style is the characteristic way in which a supervisor goes about (behaves in the process of) leading subordinates. A leader with a given style might occasionally use a backup style in another situation.

☐ Eight widely discussed leadership styles form the basis for most methods of categorizing leadership styles. In review, they are:

1. Authoritarian—the leader attempts to retain most of the authority in the group. All the important decisions are made by the leader.
2. Participative—the leader shares decision-making authority with group members. Two subtypes here are democratic and consultative.
3. Free rein (laissez-faire)—the leader gives over virtually all authority to the group.
4. High task and low relationship—an emphasis on getting the job done rather than on working with people.
5. High task and high relationship—emphasis on both strong attention to getting work accomplished and giving emotional support to people.
6. High relationship and low task—strong emphasis on giving support to people and weak emphasis on getting work accomplished.
7. Low relationship and low task—weak emphasis on both working with people and getting work accomplished; essentially the free-rein style of leadership.
8. Theory X versus Theory Y—styles based on opposite assumptions about human nature. If you believe people are basically lazy and dislike work, you tend to prod them and supervise them closely (Theory X). If you believe that people are well motivated and enjoy work, you tend to be participative (Theory Y).

☐ Effective leaders adapt their styles to the situation facing them. To be adaptive you must correctly diagnose the situation facing you. One major clue is the personal characteristics of your subordinates. The more capable and self-sufficient they are the less leadership you have to exert. A second clue is environmental pressures and demands. For instance, in a crisis or emergency situation, a directive, high-task style is best.

☐ A useful approach in choosing the right leadership style is to size up the situation and then adapt your style to one that experience suggests will work well in that situation. Figure 10–1 presents

12 frequent leadership situations and the corresponding recommended leadership style.

☐ Participative management is gaining in popularity. In practice it involves such behavior as giving subordinates a share in decision making, keeping subordinates informed of the true situation, and staying aware of the status of morale and trying to keep it high.

☐ Delegation makes the organizing function possible. Five suggestions for effective delegation are: assign duties to the right people, grant enough authority to allow delegated tasks to be accomplished, keep some important tasks for yourself, delegate some challenging tasks, avoid "yo-yo" delegation.

☐ Giving directions and orders is an important part of a supervisor's job. Four suggestions in this regard are: follow the law of the situation, speak with confidence but not hostility, follow the doctrine of reasonableness, give orders that are explicit and intelligible.

☐ Morale is a compositive of feelings of attitudes and sentiments that contribute to a general feeling of satisfaction. Thus almost any action taken by a supervisor can influence morale. Five general strategies for maintaining high morale are: practice consideration toward employees, maintain open lines of communication, allow for participative management, practice "good management," create a good physical environment.

GUIDELINES FOR SUPERVISORY PRACTICE

1. If you stand back from your group and simply take care of administrative tasks and answer an occasional question, you are not exerting leadership. You have to get directly involved with subordinates (such as coaching them) in order to exert leadership.

2. The best way of being an effective leader is to adapt to the demands of the situation. In order to be adaptive, you may have to compensate for your natural personality traits. For instance, if you are a basically authoritarian personality, it will take extra effort for you to be participative.

3. Leaders are often judged by their ability to maintain high morale. Morale is such a general condition that it can be influenced by almost any action taken or not taken by a supervisor. In general, "good" supervision increases morale and "poor" supervision lowers morale. What constitutes good and poor supervision is essentially the topic of this and other books written about supervision.

QUESTIONS FOR DISCUSSION AND REVIEW

1. Is the job of a supervisor good training for future leadership positions? Why or why not?

2. How does a highly automated production process affect a supervisor's ability to influence employees?

3. What style of leadership do you think is practiced by the current president of the United States or the prime minister of Canada?

4. How would you characterize the leadership style of the best boss for whom you have worked?

5. How would you characterize the leadership style of the worst boss for whom you have worked?

6. What leadership style would you recommend for supervising the work of migrant farm workers? Explain.

7. What do you think is the most frequently practiced leadership style in American and Canadian manufacturing plants?

8. How would most of the students in your class react if the instructor in this course used a free-rein teaching style?

9. What leadership style would you recommend for supervising the work of a group of mentally retarded adults engaged in making simple furniture?

10. What do you see as two or three disadvantages to participative management?

11. Why are so many managers hesitant to delegate work?

12. Under what circumstances do employees tend to accept orders and directions from staff specialists?

13. What actions by a supervisor tend to raise *your* morale?

14. What actions by a supervisor tend to lower *your* morale?

15. How does the discussion in Chapter 1 about effective supervisors relate to the topic of leadership?

A supervisory problem: "There's not much left for me to do"

Chuck, the production superintendent at the *Daily Chronicle,* notices that Barney, one of his pressroom supervisors, seems to be down in the dumps. "I'd better look into this problem soon," Chuck thinks to himself. That afternoon he asked Barney to join him for a cup of coffee.

"Barney, I can't help but notice that you're not your old self lately," commented Chuck. "Anything you'd like to share with me?"

"Thanks for asking," said Barney. "It's nice of you to notice that my morale has been slipping lately, Chuck. I guess automation has kind of gotten to me."

"What do you mean by your comment about automation getting to you?" asked Chuck.

Barney replied, "Quite frankly, sometimes I wonder what I'm supposed to be doing. Most of the people I supervise are technicians who know more about what they are doing than I do. To give you an example, I really don't know if my mark-up man is doing his work right. I'm no expert in mark-up work. It's too technical for me. This new technology has swept past me. Setting a newspaper into type is now just pushing a lot of buttons. I'm beginning to think there's not much left for me to do."

1. *How should Chuck counsel Barney about his feelings that there is not much left for him to do?*
2. *Do you see anything wrong with the way in which Barney perceives the supervisory and leadership role?*
3. *What constructive course of action do you recommend that Barney should take?*

SOME SUGGESTED READING

Blake, Robert R., and Mouton, Jane S. *The New Managerial Grid.* Houston, Tex.: Gulf, 1978.

Donnelly, John F. "Participative Management at Work." *Harvard Business Review,* January–February 1977, pp. 117–27.

Fiedler, Fred E. "The Leadership Game: Matching the Man to the Situation." *Organizational Dynamics,* Winter 1976, pp. 6–16.

Fiore, Michael V., and Strauss, Paul S. *How to Develop Dynamic Leadership: A Short Course for Professionals.* New York: Wiley, 1977.

Frew, David R. "Leadership and Followership." *Personnel Journal,* February 1977, pp. 90–95, 97.

Fulmer, William E. "The Making of a Supervisor 1977." *Personnel Journal,* March 1977, pp. 140–43, 151.

Greiner, Larry E. "What Managers Think of Participative Leadership." *Harvard Business Review,* March–April 1973, pp. 111–17.

Hall, Jay. "What Makes a Manager Good, Bad, or Average?" *Psychology Today,* August 1976, pp. 52–53, 55.

Hersey, Paul, and Blanchard, Kenneth M. *Management of Organizational Behavior: Utilizing Human Resources.* 3d ed. Englewood Cliffs, N.J.: Prentice-Hall, 1977.

Hollander, Edwin P. *Leadership Dynamics: A Practical Guide to Effective Relationships.* New York: The Free Press/Macmillan, 1977.

Keppler, Robert H. "What the Supervisor Should Know About . . . Participative Management." *Supervisory Management,* May 1978, pp. 34–40.

Lassey, William R., and Fernandez, Richard R., eds. *Leadership and Social Change.* 2d ed. La Jolla, Calif.: University Associates, 1976.

Motowidlo, Stephan J., and Borman, Walter C. "Relationships between Military Morale, Motivation, Satisfaction, and Unit Effectiveness." *Journal of Applied Psychology*, February 1978, pp. 47–52.

Sheridan, John H. "Is There Still Room for Bold Managers?" *Industry Week*, December 5, 1977, pp. 52–62.

Tannenbaum, Robert, and Schmidt, Warren H. "How to Choose a Leadership Pattern." *Harvard Business Review*, March–April 1958, pp. 95–101.

Thompson, David W. *Managing People: Influencing Behavior.* St. Louis: Mosby, 1978.

Supervisory skills
and techniques

Resolving conflict

LEARNING OBJECTIVES

After reading and working through the material in this chapter, you should be able to:

1. Be ready to resolve your next conflict in an effective manner.
2. Comprehend why so much conflict exists in organizations.
3. Explain both the beneficial and detrimental aspects of conflict.
4. Be aware of several techniques you might use on your own to resolve job conflict.
5. Recognize that game playing is a form of conflict.
6. Understand some of the measures an organization can take to prevent or reduce conflict.

Rob, a cannery supervisor, was asked by a high school guidance counselor to attend the annual career day. He would be one of many guests from the community representing different occupations. Rob made appropriate arrangements with his boss in order to attend career day. One of the first questions a student asked Rob was, "What do you spend most of your time doing?"

Candidly, Rob replied: "It seems like I spend most of my time settling one kind of a dispute or another. Two of my workers might be having a go-around. Or maybe I have to work out a hassle with one of the gang from industrial engineering. To add to the fun, I might have to do a little alligator wrestling with the union steward. My job's about as peaceful as that of a hockey referee."

Rob may be giving a dramatized version of the life of a produc-

259

tion supervisor in a cannery, but he does point to an important demand placed upon a supervisor. An effective supervisor must be able to resolve conflict. Skill in conflict resolution is also an important requirement for advancing your career. Almost every responsible job contains some element of conflict.

Conflict, in the sense used here, refers to a hostile or antagonistic relationship between two or more people. Rob's relationship with the steward or a representative from the industrial engineering department is sometimes hostile. Conflict also refers to an incompatibility between goals. If you choose one, you cannot have the other. If you attend night school you cannot work the second shift. Thus your job and your school work are in conflict.

In this chapter we examine the major types of conflict facing the supervisor. Of major significance for the practice of supervision, we will also describe useful techniques of resolving conflict.

WHY WE HAVE CONFLICT ON THE JOB

Conflict is an inevitable human condition both on and off the jobs. To develop more effective skills in resolving destructive types of conflict, it is helpful to examine some of the underlying reasons that conflict is so widespread. Seven reasons will be mentioned here that probably account for most of the conflict a supervisor can expect to face at work.

Aggressive nature of people.   If human beings, in general, had friendly, pleasant dispositions we would not have so much homicide, suicide, other forms of physical brutality, war, sabotage, child abuse, or pet abuse. Many people seem to have aggressive (in the hostile sense) urges seeking expression.[1] Since people spend so much time on their job, it is natural that they express some of their aggressiveness on the job. The higher the job level held by an employee, the less likely aggressiveness will be expressed physically. It is not unusual for nonskilled workers to become embroiled in fisticuffs, but executives and professionals usually express their hostility with words alone. Devious meth-

[1] A famous book advancing this idea is Desmond Morris, *The Naked Ape* (New York: Dell, 1969).

ods of office politics such as discrediting others or firing rivals are about the most aggressive methods used at the top of the organization.

Competition for limited resources.   A major reason we have conflict in many areas of life is that too many people want the same prize. Since only so many people can share the same resource, conflict results.[2] Only a handful of people can be promoted to top positions. Only so much money can be allocated to each department for physical improvements such as new machinery or interior decoration. In a job setting, people also strive to gain their share of limited supplies of status, prestige, and interesting assignments. Even the company parking lot has a limited supply of choice parking places—considered a precious resource by some people.

Clashes of values and interests.   Considerable conflict in organizations comes about simply because different departments and different people have dissimilar values and interests. Union and management conflict represents the most familiar example of this almost inevitable form of conflict.

Different departments often enter into conflict because of basic difference in values, interest, or outlook. The familiar conflict between manufacturing and marketing illustrates this principle. Marketing holds strongly that customers are the happiest when they are offered a variety of products and can get these products delivered promptly. Marketing, hoping to please its customers, pushes manufacturing to meet these demands. Manufacturing, in contrast, can perform its function most efficiently when products are standardized, volume is predictable, and variety is limited. Manufacturing thus accuses marketing of submitting to unreasonable customer demands that play havoc with production schedules.

Some jobs breed conflict.   Sometimes the very position you occupy leads you into conflict with other people and groups. By the mere process of trying to do your job, some of your goals

---

[2] A classic article about this topic is Muzafer Sherif, "Superordinate Goals in the Reduction of Intergroup Conflict," *American Journal of Sociology,* December 1958, pp. 349–56.

clash with others. Quality control supervisors may face this problem. They often have to inform other people that the work they are performing is substandard.

A credit supervisor in a credit bureau explains how his position breeds conflict: "Often I think of giving up my job because of all the enemies I make. A big part of my job is to listen to complaints from people who don't agree with our evaluation of their worthiness as a credit risk. They rant and rave and blame us for their own lousy credit history. What they don't seem to realize is that I'm only doing my job. I just collect information and put it together for others. Nobody ever calls us with something nice to say."

Difference in goals and objectives. Another source of conflict is the fact that people at work have different objectives. Some employees, for example, pursue the objective of performing the least amount of work possible for the maximum reward. The company, on the other hand, would like people to perform the maximum amount of work for the minimum amount of wages (within reason).

A company truck driver was held over for three hours, out of town, because of a vendor who did not have a vital part ready for shipment. Upon his return, his supervisor asked the driver what he did with the three hours. He replied, "I had a few cups of coffee and caught up on the newspaper. Then I shot a little pool." The supervisor criticized the driver for not having done something constructive with his downtime, such as polishing the truck. An argument ensued.

Different methods proposed to reach a common goal or objective. Conflict sometimes arises even when two people or groups share the same goal. An antagonistic relationship might develop because the two sides choose different methods to reach the same goal or objective. A retail store was experiencing a much higher than tolerable "inventory shrinkage" (stealing by employees and customers). Top and middle management agreed that something must be done about the problem. One enthusiastic store manager implemented an informant system whereby employees would receive a cash bonus for informing on other employees who were pilfering merchandise. The manager soon found that this was in conflict with top management who felt that such a "spy system" would undermine morale. The manager expressed the opinion that even though the goal of cutting shrinkage was accepted, there was not much chance of doing something really effective about the problem.

Line versus staff prerogatives. Most supervisors inevitably come into conflict with staff departments over a work-related issue.[3] In general, a staff person is supposed to advise a line person. Yet in many instances, staff people do not advise first-level managers—they act with considerable power. Many supervisors feel that staff specialists have thus taken away many of their prerogatives. Few supervisors in business, government, or other places of work have the authority to fire an employee without consulting with the personnel department. Engineering departments virtually dictate work methods to many department supervisors. Conflict ensues when a supervisor expresses reluctance in going along with the staff specialist.

THE GOOD SIDE OF CONFLICT[4]

The message of this chapter is not that all conflict should be reduced or eliminated. Properly managed, moderate doses of conflict can be beneficial. Perhaps you can recall an incident in your life when conflict proved to be beneficial in the long run. Here we will discuss the major potential benefits of conflict in a job environment. These benefits have a higher probability of taking place when conflict is properly managed. The methods of conflict resolution described later in this chapter point to proper ways of managing conflict.

Conflict is the root of change. Without some degree of conflict many worthwhile changes would have never come about. In one company, supervisors were placed on the nonexempt payroll, thus excluding them from most of the privileges shared by

---

[3] A thorough discussion of this topic is presented in Ross A. Webber, *Management: Basic Elements of Managing Organizations* (Homewood, Ill.: Richard D. Irwin, 1975), pp. 390–93. © 1975 by Richard D. Irwin, Inc.

[4] The basic reasoning in this and the following section follows that presented in Andrew J. DuBrin, *Fundamentals of Organizational Behavior: An Applied Perspective*, 2d ed. (Elmsford, N.Y.: Pergamon, 1978), pp. 358–60.

members of management. Supervisors continued to grumble about their plight. At one time they talked openly to management about a search for a supervisor's union to represent them. Finally upper management granted the supervisors exempt status.

People learn and grow as a result of conflict. In a tranquil work situation a danger exists that people will become lethargic. Conflict tends to rev people up, stimulating their curiosity and imagination.[5] If a supervisor is in conflict with a staff specialist over methods of work improvement, both parties may learn two things: How to justify the merit of their own methods of work improvement and how to resolve this type of line-staff conflict.

Conflict sometimes helps to relieve monotony and boredom. Workers sometimes kid with each other in a hostile manner to add enjoyment to their workday. The banter that takes the form of mutual insults about ethnic background and physical appearance falls into this category. Talks about conflicts in the office tend to add sparkle to coffee-break conversations, even if the people discussing the conflict are not personally involved in the dispute.

Conflict can provide diagnostic information about problem areas in a department or a company. In a situation where quality control and manufacturing are in constant conflict, it might indicate that manufacturing was using inferior methods or quality control was being unrealistic. If a supervisor and a worker are in frequent squabbles about a company regulation, it might indicate that the regulation needs clarification.

One company ran into conflict about paying people who arrived at the plant on the day of a major snowstorm when the plant had been officially closed. The people who made it to work through the storm demanded a full day's pay for their effort. The company finally passed a ruling that hourly employees would not be paid if they arrived to work when the plant had been ordered shut because of weather conditions.

As an aftermath of conflict, unity may be reestablished. Two people or two departments who feud and later resolve their dif-

---

[5] W. Clay Hamner and Dennis W. Organ, *Organizational Behavior: An Applied Psychological Approach* (Dallas: Business Publications, Inc., 1978), p. 351. © 1978 by Business Publications, Inc.

ferences may become stronger allies. A young supervisor witnessed two employees engaged in a fistfight in the company parking lot. Both were given two-day work suspensions. Upon their return to work, the supervisor was hesitant to have them work along side of each other. One of the workers informed the boss, "Don't worry about a thing. Now that we've had it out, we're two good drinking buddies."

THE BAD SIDE OF CONFLICT

As is commonly believed, conflict can have many detrimental consequences to individuals and the organization. Uncontrolled conflict can lead to such destructive outcomes as arson and heart attacks. Five of the major detrimental consequences of conflict will be mentioned here.

Prolonged conflict between you and others can be injurious to your physical and mental health. High doses of conflict are a source of stress to many people. One supervisor found herself in *role conflict* for many years. Her immediate boss emphasized quality, while her boss's boss thought quantity was more important. If she pushed quantity, one part of her role (expected behavior) was being carried out correctly. If she pushed for quality, another part of her role would be carried out correctly. Her conflict related to the fact that she could not satisfy both demands at the same time. She developed back and neck pains so severe that she asked to be transferred to a position with less conflict.

Conflict diverts time, energy, and money away from reaching important goals, such as making a profit. A supervisor who spends part of her workday arguing with the people from production engineering is taking precious time away from the more important requirements of her job. Executives, too, sometimes squander resources because of their conflicts. One division general manager was in conflict with his head of manufacturing. As a show of strength, he subcontracted to a job shop the manufacturing on a new product. According to one financial analyst, this show of strength cost the company over $350,000 during the first two years of the product's life.

Conflict often results in self-interest (looking out for number one) at the expense of the larger organization. People embroiled in a conflict typically become quite self-centered.[6] The owner of a plumbing contracting firm argued with a plumbing union official that the official should be a working boss—one who did some of the actual plumbing work instead of only supervising the activities of other plumbers. The union official would not accept this reasoning. In retaliation, he ordered the union plumbers off the job. As a result the company owner hired nonunion workers for the assignment. The self-interest of the union official resulted in a lost contract for his plumbers. (You might argue from another point of view that the self-interest of the owner resulted in inferior (nonunion) plumbers being assigned to the job, thus shortchanging the building owners.)

Intense conflict may result in disastrous financial consequences. Sabotage is usually the by-product of labor and management conflict. Management may retaliate by firing the alleged saboteurs; among them may be innocent people. In the automobile industry, sabotage is most likely to come about when employees think their contract demands will not be met by management. Much of this sabotage, however, is annoying rather than grossly destructive. One assembler placed two loose bolts in the frame of a luxury coupe. Many labor hours were incurred at the dealer before the source of the annoying rattle was found.

When conflict is intense enough, people sometimes lie or distort information. To win a point, a group or person in conflict may present an untrue picture of their position. As described in a book about human relations:[7]

> One group of highly specialized quality-control people were called superfluous by a manufacturing group. The quality-control group enlisted the help of allies in the field to document their value to the company. Such friends were told to submit anecdotes about the worst quality control problems that they had encountered. A convincing, but unrepresentative, presentation was then made of the importance of a supraquality control group for keeping equipment in the field running smoothly.

---

[6] William H. Newman, Charles F. Sumner, and E. Kirby Warren, *The Process of Management: Concepts, Behavior, and Practice,* 3d ed. (Englewood Cliffs, N.J.: Prentice-Hall, 1972), p. 199.

[7] Andrew J. DuBrin, *Human Relations: A Job Oriented Approach* (Reston, Va.: Reston, 1978), pp. 94–95.

RESOLVING CONFLICTS ON YOUR OWN[8]

Supervisors often have to resolve conflicts between themselves and other people or between two or more subordinates. In either situation, the effective supervisor tries to resolve these conflicts before they fester into problems requiring assistance from upper management or staff specialists (such as organization development specialists, psychologists, or personnel workers). When such conflicts cannot be resolved by a supervisor, they should not be hidden, but dealt with at a higher level. In this section we will describe a few methods of conflict resolution a supervisor might use.

Compromise. It is difficult to avoid using compromise to resolve some conflicts. A compromise takes place when one party agrees to do something if the other party agrees to do something else. "I'll stop coming to work a few minutes late if you'll stop keeping me a few minutes late on Fridays." Compromise remains a realistic approach to resolving a wide range of conflicts. Most labor versus management disputes are settled through some type of compromise. For instance, "You can have one more floating holiday per year if you will accept a postponement on the dental benefits package."

Practice gentle confrontation. We highly recommend this method of dealing with conflict between individuals—particularly when the person with whom you are in conflict has a power advantage over you. In using this technique, you make a candid statement of the problem facing you without hinting at any form of violence or retaliation. Here is how it works:

> Pam is hired into a company as a senior programmer with the understanding that after six months of orientation she will be promoted to a systems analyst position. After five months of good service, Pam is ready to claim her system analyst title. At this point, her boss departs from the company, and a new manager, Alex, takes over. Alex issues the edict that, because of a retrenchment in the company, there will be no promotions in his department (where Pam is working) for another six months.
>
> A poor strategy for Pam to use would be to file a complaint with the vice president of personnel or the company president that she has been treated unjustly. Even if she wins her point (and her deserved promotion), she will have alienated herself from her new boss, Alex.

---

[8] Much of this section is excerpted from Andrew J. DuBrin, *Survival in the Office: How to Move Ahead or Hang On* (New York: Van Nostrand Reinhold, 1977), chap. 5.

According to the technique of gentle confrontation, Pam should request a conference with Alex and patiently explain to him that his edict has cancelled out a prior commitment—one that may not have been put in writing. It would seem important for Pam to indicate that she feels victimized by a change in policy and ask if Alex could help her with the situation. Assuming that Alex is a rational person, he may likely bend his new edict. To save face, he will probably agree that his policy was not meant to be retroactive.

Disarm the opposition.   The purpose of this method of resolving conflicts is to lessen conflict by removing a person's armament—usually negative criticism of you. An essential part of this strategy is to place the issues on a problem-solving basis once the opposition has been disarmed. It is almost as if the opposition has some punishment they want to clobber you with. Once you have clobbered yourself by agreeing with the criticism made of you, the opposition is satisfied, and the two of you can get to the serious task of conflict resolution.

Assume you are the manager of the parking lot associated with a baseball park. There is a sudden increase in the number of complaints to the ball park owners about car vandalism and theft. Your boss is upset and demands to see you immediately. He begins to rant and rave about the vandalism problem. Instead of acting defensively, you agree with the critical view. You say something to the effect, "Vandalism has certainly become a major problem in recent months. I'm as concerned as you are. What do you think we can do about the problem?"

Your response has two crucial elements: You agree with the criticism about vandalism, thus making it somewhat unnecessary for your boss to belabor the point; You have enlisted his help in solving this mutual problem.

Exchange viewpoints and images.   A well-accepted method of conflict resolution is for the two antagonists to demonstrate to each other that they understand each other's point of view. "Image exchanging" can be done between groups, between yourself and another person, or with two of your subordinates. The essential ingredient is that both sides clearly state their own position and that of the person with whom they are in conflict. Assume that you are the supervisor of the meat department in a large supermarket. Two of your employees, Gino and Harry are in continual conflict over the issue of housekeeping. Here is the recommended scenario:

You: Harry and Gino, let's get together this afternoon in the back office. I want you two fellows to work out this housekeeping problem.

You: (Later that afternoon.) Harry, you go first. Tell your side of the story. Then tell him what you think his side of the story is.

Harry: I guess anything is worth a try. The way I see it, Gino, you leave your work area in a mess. Even some of the knives are dirty. The blades on some of the cutting machines still have blood on them. Then when I come in to take over, I have to clean up your dirty work. I don't see why a second-shift butcher should have to clean up for the first-shift butcher. You probably think that I'm being too picky. I think I once overheard you say that I thought I was Mr. Clean.

You: Good enough Harry. Now Gino it's your turn. Tell Harry your side of the story. Also tell him what you heard him say.

Gino: Harry, I think you're making too much of a fuss about a few occasions in which everything wasn't cleaned up properly. The way I see it, the first-shift meat cutter has about twice the work of the second-shift butcher. Therefore if I give you a little extra cleaning up to do, I think it's justified. I hear what you are telling me very clearly. You get upset if everything isn't nice and clean when you come to work. You also think I'm being inconsiderate.

After these opening comments, the stage has been set for an ironing out of misunderstandings and misperceptions. For instance, Gino implied that in his perception, the second-shift meat cutter should not be opposed to taking care of some housekeeping for the first-shift supervisor.

Capitalize upon your anger. One of the by-products of conflict is that people get angry, including you. Your anger could lead to your demise if you physically assault your opposition or verbally abuse a superior. In contrast, you can make constructive use of your anger if properly managed. Anger is an energizer, and this increased energy can be used to goad you on toward higher levels of achievement. Anger can also be used for dramatic effect—to illustrate by action that you are a person who does not care to be taken advantage of, or that your point of view should be taken seriously.

Teresa, a manager of training, believed strongly that the company needed a human relations training program for first-level supervisors. During a meeting with her superior and line management to discuss her proposal, she made this pitch: "Gentlemen, we are drowning in grievances and potential grievances. We are on the verge of the biggest labor dispute this company has ever known. And I'm upset. Very upset. I'm livid with anger. You are denying my request for the one thing that can put a halt to these unnecessary grievances—a training program that will help our supervisors deal with human problems before they get out of hand. Why did you hire me if you won't let me take care of important problems?

Three days later, Teresa's human relations training program was approved.

Dissipate the other person's violence. In some instances, your conflict with another person is so intense that the individual is verbally violent, or at least highly emotional. The best conflict resolution technique in such situations is to let the person's anger dissipate before you retort with your side of the story. Until the other party has expressed most of his or her angry feelings, the person won't listen to your side of the story. If you are trying to resolve conflict between two employees, let them dissipate most of their angry feelings toward each other before working out their differences.

A refinement of this technique is to encourage a person who is upset with you to express all angry feelings. After your opponent has finished the opening statement, you add "What else don't you like about me?" By then your opponent is calmed down sufficiently to get matters down to a problem-solving basis.

INTERPRETING THE GAMES EMPLOYEES PLAY

A special conflict resolution technique is based on knowledge gained from *transactional analysis* (TA).[9] One facet of TA relevant here is game playing. A good deal of game playing goes on in organizations. Many of the conflicts you face on the job stem from the fact that somebody is playing games with you whether your adversary realizes it or not. A *game* (in the TA framework) can be described as a human interaction that takes place repeatedly which on the surface seems to be of genuine intent but contains a concealed motivation. The person is really out to "zap you" or deliver a "negative stroke." Games have been given

---

[9] A job-related basic introduction to TA is Muriel James, *The OK Boss* (Reading, Mass.: Addison-Wesley, 1975).

labels such as "Now I've Got You, You SOB." Here is how "SOB" works in practice:[10]

> One afternoon, instead of attending a committee meeting you have been assigned to by your company, you spend two hours at lunch with an old friend. The next day the committee head drops by your desk to comment, "We missed you at the meeting yesterday. How come you weren't there?"
>
> You reply, "I gave priority to some other activity I had planned for yesterday. I'll be able to make the next meeting."
>
> He replies, "Isn't that peculiar? I took a late lunch hour after the meeting broke up. As I was looking for a luncheonette, I saw you coming out of a restaurant with somebody not from our office. Is that your excuse?"

A logical way to squelch this kind of game recurring in other contacts with the committee head is to interpret the game directly: "It's obvious you were trying to trap me into saying a falsehood, which I didn't. If you knew I was at a restaurant during your meeting, why did you ask me where I was?" With a little practice you can be skillful at interpreting much game-playing activity even if the game being played against you has not yet been labeled by TA. The general principle is to look for the hidden motive and interpret that directly to the other individual.

APPEALING TO A THIRD PARTY

At times you may be in a conflict situation that seems unresolvable by the means already discussed. In these situations you may have to enlist the help of a third party with power—more power than you or your adversary have. Hierarchical organizations have a built-in mechanism for dealing with such situations.[11] You make an appeal to positional authority, usually a superior common to both you and your opponent. A boss in this situation will usually settle the dispute. That person will decide who is right and who is wrong and perhaps order a compromise. Common superiors more skillful in techniques of conflict resolution would probably try to get the two of you to work out your

---

[10] DuBrin, *Survival in the Office*, pp. 76–77.

[11] A technical discussion of this approach is found in Webber, *Management*, pp. 606–8.

conflict in their presence. Perhaps the boss would utilize image exchanging.

A variation of this technique is to appeal to a more powerful third party when your opponent has more power than you. Assume that your boss thinks you are unfit for promotion to a higher paying job. You disagree strongly but your boss feels right about the opinion. Your best recourse would be to request a meeting with your boss's boss to have your dispute resolved. As described earlier, it is best to resolve conflicts on your own before bringing them up the line.

Another alternative is to confer with a staff specialist outside your chain of command to help you resolve the conflict. A technical problem might be brought to an engineering manager, while a personnel problem might be brought to a personnel manager.

USING THE ORGANIZATION TO RESOLVE CONFLICT

As organizations have become more aware of the importance of resolving conflict, structures have been adapted to prevent, reduce, or eliminate conflict. Supervisors rarely have the authority to redesign part of an organization, but they should be aware of such methods of conflict resolution. Five of them will be mentioned here.[12]

Teams. Grouping organizational activities into teams rather than functional units or departments helps resolve some types of conflict between groups. People who work for a team tend to cooperate with each other. They recognize how important teamwork is to accomplish the project and often identify with the success of the project. How team arrangements contribute to morale was discussed in Chapter 4.

Liaison groups. A novel way of preventing conflict in organizations is to keep two groups with high potential for conflict away from one another. An intermediary is chosen who communicates information back and forth between the two groups. To illustrate, some large companies use "demand analysts" to translate manufacturing requirements to marketing and marketing requirements to manufacturing. One advantage of inter-

---

[12] See DuBrin, *Organizational Behavior,* pp. 365–67.

mediary persons is that they are perceived as not having a vested interest in either group.

Using a liaison group is similar to one supervisor sending a messenger to talk to another supervisor with whom the former is in conflict. It is far better to face up to the conflict yourself and work toward its resolution.

Exchange of members.   A helpful approach to getting people to understand each other's points of view (and to therefore lessen conflict) is to trade members between groups. As a group becomes more ingrown, the members tend to exaggerate their own worth and undervalue the contribution of the other group. A "good person versus bad person" feeling can develop if groups become too homogeneous. When personnel are exchanged between the two groups, some of the animosity is lessened. Reassigning people in this way can achieve the benefit of introducing different viewpoints in the two groups. As the group members get to know each other better, they tend to reduce some of their distorted perceptions of each other.

Exchanging of members works best when people have the necessary skills to be transferred to the other department. Also, they should welcome such an opportunity as a chance to broaden their experience. As one supervisor said after being transferred into a position in manufacturing engineering, "I was skeptical at first, but then I found out they don't wear horns in engineering."

Committees.   A creative use of committees is to use them as a method of promoting understanding between people, thus reducing or preventing conflict. As people from various groups get to know each other better as a result of their working together on a committee, increased understanding and tolerance is often the result. A specific benefit from committee members is that the parties formerly in conflict with each other come to realize they are pursuing similar overall goals. To achieve such benefits, committee members must be carefully chosen to represent different parts of the organization. To promote understanding about the importance of safety, one company established a safety committee. The members chosen included people from both high- and low- or no-accident frequency areas.

Ombudsman.   A number of organizations have created a new position to help resolve conflict between supervisors and

274

employees.[13] An important criterion for being selected as an ombudsman is the ability to listen. An ombudsman takes the problem of lower-level factory personnel to somebody higher in management. The ombudsman position was created because factory workers often feel they do not have sufficient power to

handle disputes with their immediate superior. When a company has a labor union, employees who believe they have a grievance would speak directly to a union steward. When employees bring their problem to an ombudsman, it is usually because they have been treated unfairly. An ombudsman often listens to complaints about racial discrimination or other forms of unfairness.

SUMMARY OF KEY POINTS

☐ Conflict refers to a hostile or antagonistic relationship between two or more people. The general underlying cause of conflict is

[13] I. Silver, "The Corporate Ombudsman," *Harvard Business Review*, May–June 1967, p. 77.

an incompatibility between goals. The demands of A and B are mutually exclusive.

☐ The major reasons for, or sources of, conflict can be summarized as: the aggressive nature of people, competition for limited resources, clashes of values and interests, differences in goals and objectives, different methods proposed to reach a common goal or objective, some jobs breed conflict—they have "built-in" conflict, disputes over line versus staff prerogatives.

☐ Conflict is not necessarily harmful to individuals or the organization. Among its advantages are: Conflict is the root of change; People learn and grow as a result of conflict; Conflict sometimes help relieve job monotony and boredom; Conflict can provide diagnostic information about problem areas in a departmenr or company; As an aftermath of conflict, unity may be reestablished.

☐ Conflict also has some detrimental aspects: Prolonged conflict between individuals can be injurious to physical and mental health; Conflict can divert time, energy, and money away from reaching important goals; Conflict often results in self-interest at the expense of the larger organization; Intense conflict may have disastrous financial consequences; Under intense conflict, people sometimes lie or distort information.

☐ A number of techniques have been developed that supervisors might use in resolving conflicts on their own. They include: compromise, gentle confrontation—bringing your problem to the attention of the other person in a tactful way, disarming the opposition, exchanging viewpoints and images, capitalizing upon the potential benefit of anger, dissipating the other person's violence.

☐ Another general strategy for resolving conflict on your own is to confront people with the games they might be using against you. You must first recognize the hidden motive and then interpret it to the person playing the game.

☐ A widely used method of resolving conflict is to bring the dispute to the attention of a third party who has the positional (formal) authority to decide who is right.

☐ Organizations sometimes have certain built-in structures which help resolve conflict. Among them are: work assignments by teams, liaison groups, exchange of members between groups in conflict, committees—whereby members learn to appreciate different points of view, the ombudsman position—an individual who listens to disputes and grievances and helps people resolve them at higher organizational levels.

GUIDELINES FOR SUPERVISORY PRACTICE

1. Conflict is an inevitable part of organizational life; it cannot be ignored. Instead, you must learn to cope with or capitalize on conflict.

2. Conflict in moderate amounts can help your department. It may keep people mentally alert and act as a spur to good performance.

3. It is to your advantage as a supervisor to learn effective techniques of resolving conflict. A general principle is that you should first attempt to work out your conflicts with other people by yourself. If that doesn't work, you will then have to go outside your department for help.

4. If two of your subordinates are in conflict, try first to get them to resolve their conflict by themselves. If that doesn't work, you should help them resolve their differences. As a next step, bring their problem to the attention of higher management or a staff specialist.

QUESTIONS FOR DISCUSSION AND REVIEW

1. What is the biggest conflict with another individual that you face these days?

2. Which techniques of conflict resolution described in this chapter are sometimes used by a hockey referee? Explain.

3. Describe some positive consequences that have emerged from conflict in your life.

4. Which method of resolving conflict is the most frequently used in the place where you now work or most recently worked?

5. Several executives have noted that when people are happy with their jobs, they are embroiled in fewer conflicts. What is your reaction to this observation?

6. What role does money play in creating conflict on the job?

7. In your opinion, why do some employees get into so much conflict while others get into so little conflict?

8. Is a prize fight a conflict? Why or why not?

9. Name three jobs not mentioned in this chapter that you think breed considerable conflict. Why do they breed conflict?

10. Suppose the instructor in this course gave you a failing grade because you refused to change a flat tire on his or her car. What method would you use to resolve your conflict with your instructor?

11. How does office politics contribute to conflict?

12. Give an example of how you or somebody else you know successfully applied the technique of gentle confrontation.

13. Do you think that large companies should hire a professional person full time to serve as a conflict resolution specialist? Why or why not?

A supervisory problem: The disappointed new car owners

You are the general manager of an automobile dealership, Deauville Motors. In the last three weeks you have received telephone calls from 12 new car customers complaining that they are disappointed with the service at Deauville. One of their major complaints is that the repair service is not nearly as prompt as they thought it would be. Concerned about the situation, your first step is to discuss the situation with Al, the service manager:

Al states, "Don't blame me for what's happening to our customers. We do the best we can. My mechanical supervisor says he can't push his workers any harder than he is doing now. He's already had two resignations in the past two months. The pace out there is murderous."

You ask, "What seems to be causing the hectic pace? How is your planning and work scheduling?"

"I'm doing a fine job of planning and scheduling," replies Al. "But we can't cope with the preposterous lies the salesmen are telling customers. They tell them any repair will only take about one hour. They even promise customers that they will drive a late model car while theirs is in the shop. They wind up renting a car or being driven by a friend."

You then comment. "Al I'll get back to you later after I speak to Harvey (the new car manager)."

You ask, "Harvey, why are we getting so many complaints from customers about repair service?"

"I thought you knew the reason behind that problem," answers Harvey. "That service department won't move on things. They take a day and a half to repair the simplest thing. One customer who bought a car with a $13,000 sticker price needed a new headlamp. The service department tied up her car for the whole day. She was so ticked off, I think we've lost her as a future customer. "I think you should straighten out that service department."

1. How do you intend to resolve the conflict between the new car manager and the service department?
2. How do you intend to improve customer service?
3. Which department do you think is at fault, the sales or the service department? Why?

SOME SUGGESTED READING

Acuff, Frank, and Villere, Maurice. "Games Negotiators Play." *Business Horizons,* February 1976, pp. 70–76.

Berne, Eric. *Games People Play.* New York: Grove Press, 1964.

Bowen, Donald D., and Nath, Raghu. "Transactions in Management." *California Management Review*, Winter 1975, pp. 73–85.

Butler, Arthur G., Jr. "Project Management: A Study in Organizational Conflict." *Academy of Management Journal*, March 1973, pp. 84–101.

DuBrin, Andrew J. *Survival in the Office: How to Move Ahead or Hang On.* New York: Van Nostrand Reinhold, 1977, chap. 5.

Filley, Alan C. *Interpersonal Conflict Resolution.* Glenview, Ill.: Scott, Foresman, 1975.

Likert, Rensis, and Likert, James Gibson. *New Ways of Managing Conflict.* New York: McGraw-Hill, 1976.

Long, Donald R. "Tearing Down Departmental Walls." *Industry Week*, July 30, 1973, pp. 30–34.

Mealilea, Laird W. "The TA Approach to Employee Development." *Supervisory Management*, August 1977, pp. 11–19.

Schmidt, Warren H., and Tannenbaum, Robert. "Management of Differences." *Harvard Business Review*, November–December 1960, pp. 107–15.

Seiler, John A. "Diagnosing Interdepartmental Conflict." *Harvard Business Review*, September–October 1963, pp. 121–32.

Smith, Manual J. *When I Say No, I Feel Guilty.* New York: Dial Press, 1975. Bantam ed., 1975.

Webber, Ross A. *Management: Basic Elements of Managing Organizations.* Homewood, Ill.: Richard D. Irwin, 1975, chaps. 24, 25, 26.

Coping with change

12

LEARNING OBJECTIVES

After reading and working through the material in this chapter, you should be able to:

1. Understand that change has both positive and negative consequences to individuals and organizations.
2. Summarize the major effects change is likely to have on employees.
3. Explain in your own words why so many people resist change.
4. Describe several strategies for overcoming employee resistance to change.
5. Develop several strategies for coping with change in your work or personal life.

A company listed on the New York Stock Exchange wanted to replace one half of its production work force. The problem they faced was that the company needed workers with electronic skills to replace those with mechanical skills. Top executives at the company were opposed to massive layoffs of employees. A plan was therefore implemented that would result in mass resignations. The company announced plans to relocate their plant 750 miles from its present location. Every employee affected by the move was offered the opportunity to relocate at company expense. As predicted, very few employees below the management level accepted the offer. Almost 75 percent of the technologically obsolete workers resigned. The company replaced those people with new employees who possessed skills now needed by the company.

Although you might describe the above plot as diabolical, it does illustrate an important fact about human nature. People frequently resist change. Rather than experience an upheaval in their lives, three fourths of the work force in this situation refused job transfers. (The incident also illustrates how difficult it is for some people to acquire new technical skills.)

One of the most demanding challenges faced by a supervisor is to learn techniques of effectively managing change. The change to be managed is often change faced by employees. At other times it is change faced by the supervisor. In this chapter we examine how change affects people and how to effectively cope with change.

HOW CHANGE AFFECTS EMPLOYEES

A supervisor is at an advantage in coping with change when that individual is aware of the wide range of reactions people have to change. Change that affects employees are major upheavals at home such as marriage, divorce, and death. On the job, people may have strong reactions to changes in: machinery, tools, and equipment; work procedures and methods; personnel; formal organizational structures; informal organizational structures.[1] As with everything else about human beings, how they react to change varies considerably from individual to individual. Three broad types of reactions will be noted here.

Stress and shock. A junior chemist was discovered by his supervisor sitting at a desk performing no apparent work. Yet the chemist was busily shuffling papers and making nervous movements with his face, body, and hands. The supervisor recommended that the chemist visit the company doctor. A brief interview with the doctor revealed that the young man was suffering a mild shock reaction as a result of having experienced *change overload.* In the previous 30 days the man had gotten married, gone on a honeymoon, bought a new car, rented a new apartment and moved, and started a new job. He had been overwhelmed by change. Too much change in too short a period of time can exert severe stress on the human system.

Alvin Toffler popularized the idea that many people have ad-

---

[1] Jack Halloran, *Applied Human Relations: An Organizational Approach* (Englewood Cliffs, N.J.: Prentice-Hall, 1978), p. 233.

verse reactions to too much change. *Future shock* is the term he uses to indicate how change overwhelms people. It refers to "the dizzying disorientation brought on by the premature arrival of the future."[2] When you are totally unprepared to face the future, you are likely to experience future shock.

Positive reactions to change.   Instead of experiencing shock, some people welcome most changes in their work and personal life.[3] Many employees jump at the chance to be transferred, relocated, or learn a new skill. Some people even enjoy the challenge of major disruptions in their personal life. In general change is welcomed if people think it will provide them personal benefits. Some people have an optimistic outlook on most changes. In the past they have benefited from change, so they are predisposed to accept change in the present and future. A good place to introduce change in a department is with an enthusiastic person who will probably welcome the change.

Resistance.   A safe generalization is that most people tend to resist change. Much of this chapter concerns methods of dealing with this fact. Resistance to change is sometimes open and explicit. A supervisor might announce to an employee that from now on the individual will be taken off salary and placed on piecework. The employee states unceremoniously, "I quit." Other forms of resistance to change are more subtle.

One method of resisting change is passive-aggressive behavior. The person expresses aggressiveness or hostility by being passive. A tenant in a two-family house was displeased to learn that the rent had increased $25 per month. In the past the person had been a cooperative tenant. Two weeks after the increase was in effect, the renter observed that one of the toilets never stopped flushing. As an expression of hostility toward the landlord, the problem was not reported. The landlord inferred a leak was present after receiving a $350 water bill three months later.

The most extreme resistance to change manifested by employees is direct, aggressive behavior. Wildcat strikes and sabo-

[2] Alvin Toffler, *Future Shock* (New York: Random House and Bantam Books, 1970), p. 11.

[3] Andrew J. DuBrin, *Fundamentals of Organizational Behavior: An Applied Perspective*, 2d ed. (Elmsford, N.Y.: Pergamon 1978), p. 415–16. See also Laird Mealiea, "Employee Resistance to Change: A Learned Response Management Can Prevent," *Supervisory Management*, January 1978, pp. 16–22.

tage often come about because employees are violently opposed to a major work change about to be implemented by management. A man who worked for several years on the assembly line of a major automotive plant reports the following example of aggressive reaction to change:

> The company decided to automate the plant for this new automobile to the fullest extent possible. As it worked out, the whole plant looked like some kind of science fiction, so few people were needed to run the line. As you can imagine, the union and the workers didn't go for this maneuver by management. All of a sudden these new (mentions model of compact car) started coming off the line all screwed up. Upholstery was slashed with knives, exterior paint was scratched, bulbs were missing from tail lights, and hinges were missing from some doors. Everybody said management wouldn't get away with automating the hell out of a plant, and workers were proving it.[4]

WHY PEOPLE OFTEN RESIST CHANGE

When people resist change it is usually because they think that the particular change will do them more harm than good. Two industrial psychologists speculate that people go through an almost unconscious calculation about the effects of a particular change.[5] If their subjective probability is high that the particular change will be beneficial, they are enthusiastic about the change. Conversely if they calculate the odds of the change helping them are not in their favor, they resist change. Five more specific factors seem to account for most of the reasons that employees obstruct or resist change: (1) economic reasons, (2) fear of the unknown, (3) disruptions to personal relationships, (4) personal inconveniences, and (5) difficulty in breaking a habit.[6]

Economic reasons. Money enters into the decision-making process of the vast majority of people who work for a living. If the company introduces a change that some employees think

---

[4] DuBrin, *Organizational Behavior*, p. 415.

[5] Joseph Tiffin and Ernest J. McCormick, *Industrial Psychology*, 5th ed. (Englewood Cliffs, N.J.: Prentice-Hall, 1965), p. 425.

[6] This section follows the discussion in three sources: George Strauss and Leonard R. Sayles, *Personnel: The Human Problems of Management*, 3d ed. (Englewood Cliffs, N.J.: Prentice-Hall, 1975), pp. 242–50; DuBrin, *Organizational Behavior*, pp. 416–20; Stan Kossen, *The Human Side of Organizations*, 2d ed. (San Francisco: Canfield Press, 1978), pp. 236–42.

will provide them more money, they will be positively disposed toward that change. If employees think a work-related change will lose them money, they will most probably resist the change. Production workers often fear that a new incentive system will make it more difficult for them to earn the same income. Sales representatives often resist new compensation packages for the same reason: they question whether it will be to their economic advantage.

Fear of the unknown.   An exception to the idea that people accept change they think is potentially beneficial relates to fear of the unknown. People sometimes resist change simply because the outcome of change is not entirely predictable. One supervisor working in Buffalo, New York, developed chronic sinusitis. A physician told the supervisor the only permanent cure would be to live in a warm, dry climate. The supervisor succeeded in obtaining a transfer to a distribution center the company operated in Phoenix, Arizona. At the point of making final arrangements, the supervisor declined the job offer. The explanation to both the company and mate was, "I guess, I'll suffer along with a pain in the head a little longer. At least I know what I'm dealing with here in Buffalo. Who really knows what's going to happen to us in Phoenix?"

Disruptions in personal relationships.   A classic discussion about overcoming resistance to change contends that people rarely resist technical changes.[7] What they do resist is the changes in personal relationships associated with technical changes. These days many companies electronically transfer payroll checks to a bank. By doing so several employees in the payroll department will make fewer trips to the bank. Many will miss their pleasant social contacts with bank tellers and officials. Much of some employees job satisfaction stems from the social life they have associated with their work.

One company came close to going out of business because they overlooked the importance of changes in personal relationships. They decided to hire their own commission sales representatives to replace the manufacturer's representatives they had been using for ten years.[8] Shortly after making these

---

[7] Paul R. Lawrence, "How to Deal with Resistance to Change," *Harvard Business Review*, May–June 1954, p. 54.

[8] Howard Klein, *Stop! You're Killing the Business* (New York: Mason & Lipscomb, 1974), chap. 7.

changes, they found their business suffered a 40 percent decrease in sales. The old customers resented losing their long-established contacts with the manufacturer's representatives.

Instead of continuing to order from the same company, thus dealing with new people, they continued their association with the manufacturer's representatives. The difference was that the reps now represented another company. Most of the customers had formed allegiances to the manufacturer's representatives, not the company.

Personal inconveniences.   A fact about most changes confronting an employee is that they result in personal inconvenience of one sort or another. When a company changes the decimal to the metric system, many employees face inconveniences. Among them are developing a different mental set about quantities, learning the metric system, using new tools, converting old data to the metric system, and even speaking part of a new language. What will be your reaction when a co-worker says to you: "You know that imposing receptionist—the one that's 1.8 meters tall. Did you know that her car gets over 12 kilometers to the litre?"

Difficulty of breaking a habit.   Stan Kossen points out that it is difficult to implement some changes simply because the old way has become a habit.[9] Each major habit is usually associated with a series of minor habits that people also resist breaking. A file clerk in an insurance company said she did not want to transfer to an office 20 blocks from the place she had worked for three years. Her explanation: "All the stores I like are within a few blocks of where I work now. If I transfer, I'll have to find new places to shop."

Employee habits retard change, but most employees eventually do acquire new habits that are important to their work. Habits are learned. When pocket calculators were introduced to industry, some employees resisted using them. Among their complaints were: "Nothing that small could be reliable enough to replace an electronic calculator," and "With the small amount of calculating I have to do, I'll continue to perform my calculations by hand."

---

[9] Kossen, *Organizations,* pp. 239–40.

REDUCING EMPLOYEE RESISTANCE TO CHANGE

Since changes are inevitable and employees resist change, a supervisor often faces the task of overcoming or reducing such resistance. A general strategy a supervisor might use in effectively introducing change is to take into account the reasons people will most probably resist change. For instance, armed with a knowledge of how new habits are formed (Chapter 2) the supervisor should encourage people to develop new habits required by the work change. If employees discard their slide rules and begin using pocket calculators (as required by the work change) they should be complimented.

Seven strategies for reducing change will be described next.[10] As usual, most of these strategies work best when the supervisor is handled in a similar manner by higher management. If you are a supervisor, the management climate above you exerts a strong influence on your behavior in relation to your employees.

Discuss the changes.   A straightforward technique for reducing resistance to changes is to openly discuss the changes with the employees affected. A written document explaining the changes might be a masterpiece of communication. Yet unlike a supervisor, a written document cannot answer questions. Two-way communication helps reduce some of the concerns an employee might have about the pending work changes. In one factory the company decided to install a complete set of modern washroom and shower facilities for employees. An unskilled worker asked his boss if he might ask a question about a very important matter. The important matter proved to be a concern whether or not washup time would now be reduced because the new shower facilities would be more efficient.

Allow for participation.   The best documented way of overcoming resistance to change is to allow people to participate in formulating the changes that will affect them.[11] In some in-

---

[10] Halloran, *Applied Human Relations,* pp. 244–52; Kossen, *Organizations,* pp. 242–45; DuBrin, *Organizational Behavior,* pp. 420–27.

[11] A book-length analysis of this topic is Alfred J. Marrow, David G. Bowers, and Stanley E. Seashore, *Management by Participation* (New York: Harper & Row, 1967). An historically important study here is Lester Coch and John R. French, Jr., "Overcoming Resistance to Change," *Human Relations,* vol. 1, no. 4 (1948); reprinted in Paul Lawrence and John Seiler, *Organizational Behavior and Administration* (Homewood, Ill.: Richard D. Irwin, Inc., 1965), pp. 931–32.

stances the situation will allow for participative leadership of this type. At other times the changes are of such a nature that there is little room for employee input about making the changes. When bus companies in some cities no longer allowed drivers to make change (unintentional pun), the drivers had no say in the matter. Many of them welcomed such a shift in work procedures. Others, however, felt uneasy dealing with hostile passengers who insisted they be allowed to remain on the bus although they did not have the exact change.

The underlying psychology is uncomplicated as to why employee participation helps reduce resistance to change. When an individual or group of individuals contributes ideas to a proposed change, disapproving or resisting that change is tantamount to disagreeing with oneself.[12]

Use a gradual approach. People are less likely to suffer from future shock (or any other stress reaction) when they face gradual rather than sudden change. A supervisor may not have the responsibility to decide whether or not a work change will be made. Yet that supervisor might be able to advise management whether or not the group seems ready to be able to absorb another change.

One office supervisor impressed higher management with her astuteness by warning them of possible change overload in her department. At a staff meeting, she made these comments: "I think I should hold off introducing those cartridge typewriters this month. During the last month we moved from a large bullpen arrangement to office landscaping. Many of the women feel that they have been cut off from contact with each other. Then the company decided to stagger working hours to help with the traffic congestion problem. A few of the clerks had to find new car pools for themselves. How about a moratorium on any other big changes for at least 30 days?"

Avoid threats and coercion. Resistance to change is sometimes overcome by forcing people to accept the changes. The "ramrod" approach has its distinct drawbacks. People who are forced to comply with changes, without even the opportunity to

---

[12] DuBrin, *Organizational Behavior*, p. 426.

discuss the changes, may harbor resentment. Such resentment may later manifest itself in such negative outcomes as work of a lower quality, higher absenteeism, and lowered morale.

Coercive tactics often backfire in the long range. When the job market is tight most employees accept a work change offered to them on a "like it or leave" basis. When the job market loosens up, those employees who were the object of such a threat may take a job elsewhere. A small machine tool company was acquired by a larger company. An immediate change forced upon the company was a time clock system for recording attendance. Several model makers complained that punching a time clock was beneath their dignity. Management's only answer was, "It's a brand new ball game now." Within three months, three out of the six model makers resigned and accepted positions at other companies.

Point out the financial benefits. Since so many people are concerned about the financial implications of work changes, it is helpful to discuss these matters openly. If employees will earn more money as a result of the change, this fact can be used as a selling point. An unwritten rule seems to exist in business, industry, government, and education that a change toward a more hazardous (or more inconvenient) assignment carries along with it a boost in pay. North American employees who relocate to the Mideast are compensated far beyond the difference in cost of living between the two areas. Military personnel who work in submarines receive a monthly premium for hazardous duty. At one community college instructors who teach a course in the nearby state prison receive bonus pay.

A supervisor needs to be informed of the potential financial benefits of a major work change. One company laid off one third of its work force. The remaining employees found their work load increased substantially. Supervisors were told to inform employees that the drastic layoffs would benefit the company financially. Should the company make a profit, it would then be possible to give employees more substantial salary increases.

Avoid social upheavals. It follows from our earlier discussion that one way to reduce resistance to change is to minimize changes in personal relationships stemming from the change. Some types of change, such as relocation, inevitably result in social changes unless an entire organization is relocated. Under those extreme circumstances, there are still major changes in contacts with people outside of work.

It is a difficult task for a supervisor to control most social changes when a major modification takes place such as the formation of work teams. Assume that a company shifts one part of the company from a department structure to a team structure. A supervisor, with approval from higher management, might ask employees to nominate those individuals with whom they would like to work. Where feasible, teams could be formed of people who wanted to work together—thus minimizing social upheavals.

One caution is in order: A construction company who tried the nomination approach discovered that there were a few employees most people wanted to work with, and a few with whom nobody wanted to work. Each of the unpopular (or disliked) employees was assigned to a different team. Dissatisfaction with the teams was minimized, but no team was composed exclusively of people who wanted to work with each other.

Put adaptable people in key spots. An important strategy for the effective introduction of change is to place adaptable or flexible people into jobs most directly associated with the change. When a new machine is introduced into an office or factory, there are usually grumbles to the effect that the new machine is inferior. If an adaptable, flexible, and optimistic person is the key operator of the new machine, this person will help bring about its acceptance.

Who is an adaptable and flexible person? A practical way of identifying such an individual is to review a person's history of adapting to other changes. People who have been cooperative in the past about sudden changes in work assignments, transfers, or who adapted quickly to new work routines are the most likely to be flexible in the future. Past history is often a good indicator of future behavior.

Another approach to selecting flexible people would be through psychological evaluation consisting of tests and interviews. Although the results would not be conclusive, personnel psychologists should be able to identify those people who have a high probability of being flexible in adapting to changes. Such information could serve as a supplement to supervisory judgment about the employees willingness and ability to adapt to change.

COPING WITH CHANGE YOURSELF

So far we have emphasized how the supervisor can help employees cope effectively with change. A related topic is how supervisors might cope with change themselves. Several of the suggestions already described can be related to yourself. What works for subordinates will often work for you. Yet there is merit in examining seven strategies formulated specifically for the career-minded person who wants to cope with change.[13]

Ask "what's in it for me?" Answering this question about change could improve your attitude toward the change you are facing. A fundamental reason many people resist change is that they believe that the outcome of the forthcoming change will be negative for themselves. Few people object to changes that they perceive as unequivocally advantageous. The supervisor with a highly critical boss is usually quite receptive to a new boss taking over the department—a change that is usually perceived with trepidation. If you analyze an impending job-related change, you may be able to ferret out some hidden advantages for yourself.

Accept some anxiety as natural. Anxiety (or tension) is almost universally associated with change or the prospects of change. Both self-confident and unsure people experience internal feelings of uneasiness when a major work or life change is imminent. You'll do a better job of coping with change if you accept these internal feelings as normal. The internal feelings of apprehension you experience in response to change or its prospects are as normal as the similar feelings you would probably experience if you learned that the Internal Revenue Service planned to audit your tax returns.

---

[13] This section is largely excerpted from Andrew J. DuBrin, *Survival in the Office* (New York: Van Nostrand Reinhold, 1977), chap. 9.

Get the facts. Much of the resistance we erect stems from our fear of the unknown. When the facts become known, the impending change often seems a little less ominous. In the absence of facts, people often distort negatively the true picture about the consequences of change. Such was the case of the following individual:

> Clem, a salesman for hospital supply equipment, learned that his company's sales program would be shifted somewhat from direct selling to selling through distributors. Overtly upset, he confided to his wife: "Cancel those plans for the new inground swimming pool and patio. Forget about having our daughter's teeth straightened. The company has just pulled the rug out from under me. We're going to be selling through distributors, and I'll be losing most of my commission business."
>
> The next day Clem stormed into his boss's office with the same lament. Despite discouragement with Clem's immature behavior, his boss confronted Clem with the facts. First, the shift to distributors simply meant that the company would sell the low-volume items through distributors. Second, sales representatives would now be asked to call directly only on accounts with big potential. Third, the net effect of these changes would be to increase the earnings of sales representatives.
>
> Clem had no founded reason to resist change in this instance. Had he collected the relevant facts before emoting, Clem would have created a more favorable impression upon his boss.

Develop flex in your attitudes. An underlying reason many people resist change is that they perceive change as good or bad, right or wrong, workable or unworkable. Rigidity of this type leads you to welcome some changes as all good and others as all bad. Recognition that you are rigid (if you, in fact, are) must precede the development of flexibility. As you develop the ability to examine multiple sides to an issue, you become better able to cope with change.

One company finally decided to place all supervisors on the exempt payroll—an example of a change that has both advantages and disadvantages for supervisors. Yet most supervisors in the company seemed to consider the change as either good or bad. Those in favor of the change focused on the issue that supervisors had finally become part of management. Those opposed to the change focused on the issue that it would no longer be possible to receive pay for overtime work. The supervisor would now be *exempt* from overtime pay.

Avoid change overload. As described at the outset of this chapter, some of the worst cases of future shock come about because an individual is swamped by a series of major changes in a short period of time. Major changes in life are more readily coped with when a number of them do not have to be managed simultaneously. Two changes coming at once can have a more powerful impact upon a person than the combined effect of the same changes happening one at a time.

One supervisor received a promotion to night superintendent. He would now be earning more money and have more responsibility but would also be following a new work and social schedule. Predictably he began to experience tension as a result of this major change in his life. A week later his oldest daughter decided to leave home and share an apartment with a roommate. His wife then requested that owing to his new status in life, they should move to a home in a more expensive neighborhood. He wisely refused, offering this explanation to his wife: "I'd like a new home too. But please let me first absorb these big changes I've just been through."

Avoid the procrastination trap. A generally ineffective, yet widely practiced method of dealing with change thrust upon us, is to procrastinate until the situation worsens. Many people faced with the necessity for making a work-related change delay taking any action. Instead of mobilizing to face the challenges, the change-overwhelmed person freezes. Executives, as well as supervisors, are not immune from procrastination, as illustrated by company-owner Edwin:

> Edwin's company prospered for many years because of its exclusive patent on a small electric motor that was used primarily for windshield washer assemblies. About 75 percent of the firm's business centered around shipments of these useful, reliable motors. A patent for these motors was issued in 1963, granting Edwin's company a 15-year exclusive on their manufacture. After 1978, it would be open season for any company that wanted to compete in the production of this type of small electric motor for windshield washers.
>
> As the years went by, Edwin held casual conferences with his engineering staff about the importance of developing a new high-volume product for the company. However, there was little commitment behind Edwin's utterances. By 1974, Armand, his sales manager, pleaded with Edwin to accelerate a new product development program. Edwin replied,

"Not a bad idea, but we don't want to rush into production with a product of little proved value."

By 1976, Ralph, the manufacturing manager, joined Armand's plea: "Edwin, the day for the end of our exclusive use of the patent is coming pretty close. Even if one of the bright young development engineers came up with a useful product idea tomorrow, it would take about two years to have it ready for shipment to customers."

Edwin replied this time, "What you say is generally true. But we can move faster than that if we have to. Besides, how do we know for sure that other people really want to get into competition with us? We may be battling an illusory enemy."

One year later, the management team had their annual discussion about new product development. The furor over the importance of offering the public a new product intensified. Edwin replied, "As president, I have to be a moderating influence. We're acting as if we might be going out of business tomorrow. You've been telling me this for several years, yet our sales have shown a steady increase." Armand explained, "Edwin, our sales increase is due more to inflation than any marketing breakthroughs on our part. If we don't get off our corporate behinds soon, we'll be liquidating our machines and furniture by 1976."

"Okay, fellows," answered Edwin, "Next year I promise to form a new product development committee that will really grab this problem by the horns. Just tend to the shop in the meantime."

Edwin did form the new product development committee in 1977, but he did not heed the recommendations of the committee. By 1978 orders for the new motors began to dwindle as the company's customers learned that a Japanese distributor was now able to supply the motors at a much lower cost. Other competition also emerged: a Detroit-based job shop that had attracted national attention because it hired only physically handicapped employees began to manufacture and sell a similar line of motors. At that point, three of Edwin's top people left the company in recognition of its forthcoming demise. At the end, Edwin was forced into liquidation. He had no company and no product to sell.

Recognize that change is not irreversible. The mistaken notion that most changes are irreversible is yet another reason why change makes people anxious. If you can emotionally accept the fact that something can be done to reverse change (for instance, it is possible to be employed again by the company you quit), the threat of change seems less ominous. Another example is that many supervisors are reluctant to accept a staff position, fearing that if they fail at or dislike such work, their career has been tarnished. On the contrary, supervisory experience supplemented with experience as an individual contributor will ordinarily enhance a career. A combination of line and staff work makes an individual more valuable to most organizations.

SUMMARY OF KEY POINTS

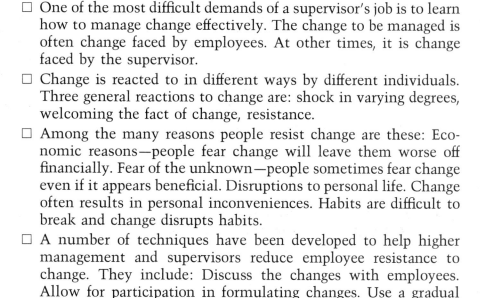

☐ One of the most difficult demands of a supervisor's job is to learn how to manage change effectively. The change to be managed is often change faced by employees. At other times, it is change faced by the supervisor.

☐ Change is reacted to in different ways by different individuals. Three general reactions to change are: shock in varying degrees, welcoming the fact of change, resistance.

☐ Among the many reasons people resist change are these: Economic reasons—people fear change will leave them worse off financially. Fear of the unknown—people sometimes fear change even if it appears beneficial. Disruptions to personal life. Change often results in personal inconveniences. Habits are difficult to break and change disrupts habits.

☐ A number of techniques have been developed to help higher management and supervisors reduce employee resistance to change. They include: Discuss the changes with employees. Allow for participation in formulating changes. Use a gradual approach in implementing change. Avoid threats and coercion. Point out the potential financial benefits of the change. Avoid upheavals in human relationships as a result of the changes. Put adaptable (flexible) people in key spots.

☐ A number of strategies are worth trying in an attempt to cope with change yourself. The strategies described in this chapter are: Figure out how you will benefit from the change. Accept some anxiety about change as natural. Get the facts about the impending changes. Develop flex in your attitudes. Avoid making too many major changes in your life in a close time frame. Avoid procrastination when you face a major change that needs to be undertaken. Recognize that change is not irreversible.

GUIDELINES FOR SUPERVISORY PRACTICE

1. You have no alternative but to learn how to manage or cope with change. Change is inevitable and the rate of change seems to be accelerating. If you do not learn how to manage or cope with change, you will soon become obsolete.

2. Persons complaining vehemently about the amount of change they are exposed to might be suffering a stress reaction to change. Tread lightly in exposing them to any more changes.

3. If a subordinate of yours displays passive-aggressive behavior in response to change, your best antidote is a rap session with that person

about this type of behavior. One good conversation opener is "what about this job makes you unhappy?"

4. Changes often have to be sold to employees in order to bring about a smooth implementation of the change. Few people would resist change if they benefited economically from the change, most of the consequences of the change were spelled out in advance for them, their interpersonal relationships at work were undisturbed, and inconveniences were kept to a minimum.

5. Learning how to adapt to change can help your career in another important way. It will help you develop the reputation of an adaptable and flexible (and therefore promotable) individual.

QUESTIONS FOR DISCUSSION AND REVIEW

1. Based on your observations and reading, what types of change are the most often resisted by employees? What do you think accounts for this resistance?

2. Do you know anyone who suffers from future shock? Describe this person's situation as fully as you can.

3. Give an example or two of a company that was unable to adapt to change. Justify your example.

4. What are some reactions people have to turning 30? Why is this such a significant change for some people?

5. What jobs are you aware of that require considerable adaptation to change?

6. What occupation would you recommend to a friend who claims an inability to tolerate much change?

7. Review the case history in this chapter about Edwin, the procrastinating company owner. What do you think is the underlying reason (or reasons) Edwin procrastinated so much about introducing a new product?

8. Which habits in relation to your work would it be the most difficult for you to break?

9. What change in your work or personal life were associated with threats or coercion? What was your reaction to these tactics?

10. Answer (a) if you are not a native Alaskan; answer (b) if you are a native Alaskan.
    a. What is the minimum salary you would require to accept a five-year assignment in Anchorage, Alaska? The job would be a good one in your field of speciality. Explain.
    b. What is the minimum salary you would require to accept a five-year assignment in Miami Beach, Florida? The job would be a good one in your field of speciality. Explain.

A supervisory problem: They want a paycheck in their hands

Roz, a payroll supervisor, was paid a visit by her boss and company controller, Augie. Before dropping by her office, Augie telephoned to say he had something important to discuss.

Augie: Roz, I notice you have not yet come up with the names of two people in your department who you are able to declare surplus. You've missed your objective. We want to trim down the controller's department by 25 percent. So far no word from you.

Roz: Augie, it's not that I don't want to comply. The fact of the matter is that we're shorthanded in my department. We need to hire another payroll clerk or start authorizing overtime pay.

Augie: But Roz, I thought with the new direct deposit of payroll plan, you would have at least two clerks to spare.

Roz: That's the point. The direct deposit of payroll is sparing me very little work. In fact, I think it's creating more work. Very few employees are willing to have their paychecks deposited in their bank. So far only about 25 percent of employees have signed up for the program. I spend a good deal of my day answering complaints from employees who say they will have nothing to do with the program.

Augie: What seems to be the problem, Roz?

Roz: You should take over my phone one day and find out for yourself. Employees tell me they don't trust the bank. They're afraid the paycheck won't reach the bank on time. Or they are afraid creditors might go right to their bank and withdraw money owed them. Another excuse I get is that working is no fun if you don't get a paycheck. I think the last reason is the most significant. Our employees are accustomed to getting paid in a personal way. They want a paycheck in their hands. I can't spare a payroll clerk until more of our employees go along with the direct deposit plan.

1. *What should Augie do next?*
2. *Do you think Roz is being resistant to change herself?*
3. *What suggestions can you offer that will help the company influence more employees to have their paychecks directly deposited into their banks?*

SOME SUGGESTED READING

DuBrin, Andrew J. *Fundamentals of Organizational Behavior: An Applied Perspective.* Elmsford, N.Y.: Pergamon, 1978, chap. 10.

———. *Survival in the Office*. New York: Van Nostrand Reinhold, 1977, chap. 9.

Halloran, Jack. *Applied Human Relations: An Organizational Approach.* Englewood Cliffs, N.J.: Prentice-Hall, 1978, chap. 8.

Hersey, Paul, and Blanchard, Kenneth H. "The Management of Change: Part Three: Planning and Implementing Change." *Training and Development Journal*, March 1972.

Hollis, Joseph W., and Krause, Frank H. "Effective Development of Change." *Public Personnel Management*, January–February 1973, pp. 60–70.

Kossen, Stan. *The Human Side of Organizations*. 2d ed. San Francisco: Canfield Press, 1978, chap. 10.

Lawrence, Paul R. "How to Deal with Resistance to Change." *Harvard Business Review*, May–June 1954, pp. 49–57.

Lewis, William C. *Why People Change: The Psychology of Influence*. New York: Holt, Rinehart and Winston, 1972.

Marrow, Alfred J.; Bowers, David G.; Seashore, Stanley, E.; (eds). *Management by Participation*. New York: Harper & Row, 1967.

Mealiea, Laird W. "Employee Resistance to Change: A Learned Response Management Can Prevent." *Supervisory Management*, January 1978, pp. 16–22.

Roseman, Ed. "Making Change Work for You." *Product Management* now *Product Marketing*), December 1975, pp. 30–33.

Strauss, George, and Sayles, Leonard R. *Personnel: The Human Problems of Management*. 2d ed. Englewood Cliffs, N.J.: Prentice-Hall, 1967, chap. 13.

Student, Kurt R. "Changing Values and Management Stress." *Personnel*, January–February 1977, pp. 48–55.

Dealing with the problem employee

LEARNING OBJECTIVES

After reading and working through the material in this chapter, you should be able to:

1. Deal more effectively with problem employees.
2. Identify some of the major causes of ineffective performance.
3. Understand how to confront persons with their unacceptable behavior.
4. Explain, in your own words, the control model for dealing with ineffective performance.
5. Use discipline in a more effective manner.
6. Explain the recommended approach for dealing with alcoholic and drug-addicted employees.

Ineffective employees consume a disproportionate share of a supervisor's time. One hostile and uncooperative employee, for example, may require more supervisory time than five friendly and cooperative employees. One woman worked her way into a supervisory position after a ten-year stint as a full-time homemaker. Asked about the comparison between homemaking and working as a supervisor, she commented: "I think I spend more time babysitting now than I did when I was home. You'd never believe some of the squabbles the people in my department expect me to settle. Just yesterday I was asked to do something about a clerk in the office who chews garlic."

This chapter presents an organized approach to dealing with the problem employee. The suggestions for dealing with problem employees incorporate aspects of methods for practicing supervision described at other places in this text. One section deals specifically with the problem of alcoholism and drug addiction because of the special difficulties they present to management.

CAUSES OF SUBSTANDARD PERFORMANCE

A large number of different factors can contribute to substandard job performance at any one time. A person might be predisposed toward becoming a problem employee because of an underlying emotional problem. Persons with low frustration tolerances ("short fuses") may become problem employees because they frequently display adult temper tantrums. Employees who fight with their families every night may experience excessive fatigue on the job. Another employee may be tense and anxious to the point of requiring tranquilizing drugs. Constant use of the drug may create drowsiness which in turn impairs job concentration.

Figure 13–1 summarizes most of the known causes of substandard performance.[1] It is not always necessary for the supervisor to correctly diagnose the underlying reason why a person has become a problem employee. The supervisor's essential task is to identify that a problem exists. One employee may be losing time from work. The underlying reason could be financial problems, family problems, diabetes, back pain, or drug abuse. The supervisor's job is to document the substandard performance and then influence the employee to do something about the problem. Much more will be said about this approach later.

At other times, a diagnosis of the cause of the problem is useful. When the supervisor has the authority and ability to do something about the cause of the problem, a diagnosis may prove useful. If the supervisor believed that a given employee had become an ineffective performer because the person was not receiving enough supervision (7c in Figure 13–1), the remedy would suggest itself: Personally provide that person more super-

---

[1] Figure 13–1 is based on information presented in John B. Miner and Frank J. Brewer, "The Management of Ineffective Performance," in *Handbook of Industrial and Organizational Psychology*, ed. Marvin D. Dunnette (Chicago: Rand McNally, 1976), pp. 997–98.

FIGURE 13–1
List of factors contributing to ineffective performance

1. Intelligence and job knowledge.
    a. Poor communication skills.
    b. Poor problem-solving ability.
    c. Inadequate job training or experience.
    d. Brain damage from injury or toxic substance.
2. Emotional illness and personality disorder.
    a. Neurotic disorders (such as disruptive anxiety, depression, excitement).
    b. Psychotic disorders (bizarre, inappropriate behavior).
    c. Personality disorders (including lying, cheating, stealing, alcoholism, drug addiction).
3. Individual motivation to work.
    a. Low level of effort.
    b. Frustration of motives leading to erratic performance.
    c. Excessively low personal work standards.
4. Physical characteristics and disorders.
    a. Physical illness or handicap.
    b. Inappropriate physical characteristics such as height, weight, strength.
    c. Poor coordination or agility.
5. Family and personal problems.
    a. Family crises, fights.
    b. Divorce, separation, loss of boyfriend or girlfriend.
    c. Misfortune of family member or friend (severe illness, death, disappearance, accident, injury).
6. Work group pressures.
    a. Ostracism from the group.
    b. Group pressures to hold back performance.
7. The work organization.
    a. Improper job placement.
    b. Overpermissive supervision.
    c. Excessive span of control (not enough supervision).
    d. Unrealistic job standards.
8. Cultural and societal problems.
    a. Subculture that discourages effective work performance.
    b. Conflict with law such as financial problems, traffic violations.

Source: The general outline and many of the specific items in this figure are from John B. Miner and J. Frank Brewer, "Management of Ineffective Performance," in *Handbook of Industrial and Organization Psychology,* ed. Marvin D. Dunnette (Chicago: Rand McNally, 1976), pp. 997–98.

vision; or place that person under the wing of an assistant supervisor.

CONFRONTING THE PROBLEM[2]

Confrontation is the bedrock on which a workable system of control of ineffective performance is constructed. Improving upon ineffective performance inevitably involves another person—presumably the poorly performing employee's immediate supervisor—confronting the employee with the specific behavior and its consequences. The supervisor with an ineffective subordinate must communicate clearly to a subordinate what it is about the work behavior that significantly departs from acceptable job performance. Unless this confrontation is conducted effectively, a vital early step in the control of ineffective performance has been mismanaged.

Confrontation suggestions

Despite the importance of confrontation in the control of ineffective performance, it is a skill rarely well developed by managers. Confrontation follows the discovery and detection (diagnosis) of ineffective performance. At this stage many supervisors feel awkward and uncomfortable because they must inform subordinates that they are not performing up to standard. Few supervisors welcome such a meeting. Part of the difficulty is thinking of an opening comment that will set the stage for the conversation to follow. The following suggestions, if practiced, will improve a supervisor's confrontation skill.

As difficult as it may seem, attempt to relax. If you appear overly tense, you might communicate the message in body language that you are not confident of the position you are taking about the person's unacceptable behavior or job performance. Perhaps a role-playing or rehearsal interview with a person from the personnel department (or outside the company) will be helpful in reducing your tension about the interview.

Getting to the central purpose of the meeting almost immedi-

---

[2] This section of the chapter is excerpted in part from Andrew J. DuBrin, *Managerial Deviance: How to Handle Problem People in Key Jobs* (New York: Van Nostrand Reinhold, 1976), chap. 5.

ately is strongly recommended. Discussions about vacations, the company parking lot, professional sports, or business conditions have some small value as warm-up material for *other* kinds of interviews. The gravity of the matter to be discussed should be communicated during the first few minutes of the interview.

Avoid being apologetic or defensive about the need for the meeting. Every organization has a responsibility both to the outsiders it serves and to itself to insist on acceptable job performance. For instance there is no need to say, "Perhaps it's a case of mistaken identity, but word has gotten back to me that you've been napping in the storeroom during working hours." Let the suspected ineffective performer correct you if the situation is a case of mistaken identity.

Confrontations about poor job performance should be conducted in a private, quiet work area or office with no interruptions allowed. Since many supervisors lack such facilities of their own, a conference room or borrowed office may have to be used.

Confrontations about unacceptable performance and behavior should be conducted with feeling (particularly sincerity) but not with hostility. Confrontations do not have to be nasty exchanges. Nonhostile confrontation attempts to place problems of ineffective performance on a problem-solving basis. Hostile confrontation is directed more toward accusation and getting *even* with the confronted person for failure to perform or behave properly. Here are two examples of nonhostile confrontation:

> There's something we must talk about. You give many signs of having a drug problem. Tell me about it.
>
> We have something very serious to talk about in relation to your attendance. My records show that you have been absent six of the last eight Mondays.

Confront job-related behavior, not personality traits. Quite often ineffective performance appears to be traceable to a personality quirk or intellectual deficit of the employee. The essential skill to be acquired in constructive confrontation is to translate such unacceptable behavior into its job-related consequences. If a person is too temperamental and thus gets into frequent arguments with others, the supervisor needs to confront the problem. It is poor practice to tell that employee,

"You're a hothead and you had better shape up." It is better supervisory practice to say, "You argue so frequently with other employees that they are not giving you the cooperation you need to get your work done." Our later discussion of constructive discipline will again touch on this topic.

ESTABLISHING IMPROVEMENT GOALS

Once ineffective performance has been identified and the employee confronted about the problem, the next step is to set goals for improvement. The control model for dealing with ineffective performance, shown in Figure 13–2, summarizes the major

FIGURE 13–2
The control model for dealing with ineffective performance

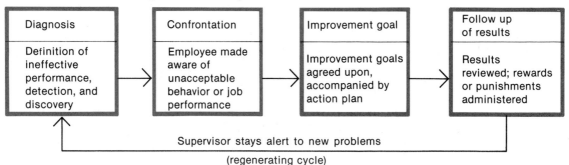

Diagnosis	Confrontation	Improvement goal	Follow up of results
Definition of ineffective performance, detection, and discovery	Employee made aware of unacceptable behavior or job performance	Improvement goals agreed upon, accompanied by action plan	Results reviewed; rewards or punishments administered

Supervisor stays alert to new problems

(regenerating cycle)

steps involved in dealing with problem workers.[3] It follows the same logic and is only a minor variation of the Framework for Accomplishing Results presented in Chapter 1.

An improvement goal for dealing with problem employees should have the same characteristics as improvement goals used in an MBO program. Everything said about the characteristics of an effective objective is also germane here. (See Chapter 6.) It is particularly important to remember that the goals or objectives established be translated into specific actions or behaviors that are to be changed for the good. An objective such as "become less cantankerous by July 4th of this year" is not specific enough with respect to what behavior should be changed. It would be

---

[3] Our control model is based on a model developed by John B. Miner, *Personnel Psychology* (New York: The Macmillan Co., 1969), p. 238.

better to specify something like, "Decrease by one half the number of times you say 'No' when asked to perform a special assignment."

The more severe the problem to be corrected, the shorter the time period should be to reach the objective. If you were dealing with an employee who was playing the numbers on company time (thus interfering with work) you might want to set up an improvement goal with a two-week deadline. In general, short-term objectives are more effective than long-term objectives in trying to bring constructive change with a substandard performer.

A sampling of improvement goals. A few samples of improvement goals for problem employees will help you grasp the concept of a *behavioral objective*. It is difficult to specify every piece of relevant information in an objective. It is crucially important that both supervisor and employee agree as to what the objective means. Six illustrative improvement objectives for problem employees are as follows:[4]

> Phase out wholesale TV and jewelry sales business conducted on company premises within 30 days.
>
> Reduce personal time away from office to two hours per month within 60 days.
>
> Reduce typing errors, including strikeovers, to one per page of finished copy within 45 days.
>
> Mop floors in such a manner that within 30 days we receive no more than one complaint per week from management about the appearance of the floor.
>
> Reduce by 80 percent the average discrepancy between data of shipment and actual shipment. Achieve this increased accuracy within 45 days.
>
> Reduce instances of "bad-mouthing" your colleagues to people outside the department to zero within two weeks.

Establishing the action plan. When an improvement objective is established, the person who is trying to reach the objective sometimes is aware of what specific actions must be taken to reach it. In order to reach the objective of reducing instances of bad-mouthing, the person simply has to learn to keep quiet.

---

[4] These objectives follow those presented in DuBrin, *Managerial Deviance*, p. 114.

More often it is necessary to draw up a specific plan of action to insure that the objective will be reached. If an alcoholic employee agrees to decrease absenteeism to one day per month, more than willpower may be necessary. One action plan in this case might be for the employee to enroll in (and attend) an alcohol abuse clinic.

Suppose a subordinate of yours cannot concentrate on work because of financial problems. The employee might agree to the objective, "Decrease by 80 percent incidents of concentration lapses. Make these improvements within 30 days." An action plan must be established to help in reaching this admirable objective. Perhaps a debt counseling agency could provide assistance. Or it might help to arrange meetings with creditors to work out an equitable arrangement with them. An action plan increases the probability that a behavioral objective will lead to concrete improvements.

FOLLOWING UP ON PROGRESS

After improvement goals and action plans are established, the supervisor must still play an active role. Problem employees need frequent follow-up. The more severe the problem the greater the need for follow-up and review. For example, it might be necessary to check up every other day on an employee with a personal hygiene problem.

The follow-up and review session can be a formal session in which superior and subordinate meet in a conference room or office. Sometimes it is equally effective to hold a three-minute informal discussion at an employee's work station. A simple question such as "what was your salvage rate today?" can serve as an interim review session.

Review sessions, at best, are essentially counseling or coaching sessions. (Coaching, in its larger context, will be discussed in the following chapter.) The supervisor attempting to bring about constructive change must review performance and offer encouragement or sometimes administer discipline. A few basic principles relating to coaching and counseling subordinates deserve mention.[5]

---

[5] These suggestions follow information presented in Andrew J. DuBrin, *Fundamentals of Organizational Behavior: An Applied Perspective*, 2d ed. (Elmsford, N.Y.: Pergamon, 1978), pp. 278–82.

Of prime importance, the manager counseling the subordinate must display a helpful and constructive attitude in the review sessions. An exemplary statement during the first review sessions would be: "How are things going in your attempt to get to work on time (attempts to speed up transactions with customers, cut down on trips to the water fountain, and so forth)?" Without the expression of a helpful and constructive attitude, persons being coached are likely to perceive the review sessions as routine procedures to document their problems.

Listening is fundamental to the review process. Giving the person whose behavior is under review a chance to talk about a problem will sometimes hasten the process of change. While talking about attempts to deal with a problem, the employee might arrive at some new understanding that will hasten change. During a coaching session about his chronic lateness, a technician said: "I guess one of the reasons I've been coming to work lately is that I want to get fired. If I wasn't working, I wouldn't have to pay my ex-wife alimony."

Job problems which might be hampering the problem employee's progress should be solved. The supervisor should routinely inquire, "Is there anything I'm doing (or not doing) that could be interfering with your making the changes we agreed upon?" Several typists said that they could not improve their error rate unless the boss curtailed radio playing in the typing pool. They claimed that some types of music made them lose concentration. (A subsequent ban on radio playing proved that they were right.)

A similar line of questioning about job-related problems can also reveal that the action plan may require recalibration. Modifying an action plan thus becomes an important aspect of the review sessions. Tom, an engineering manager with a penchant for making promises to other managers which he does not keep, told his boss, Arnie: "Okay, I know I've got a problem. We've talked about it. I'm trying to change. But please stop breathing down my neck. I don't mind talking about my following through on promises once and awhile, but every day is too much."

Documentation of both progress and lack of progress toward reaching the improvement goals should be part of the review session. Documentation can lead to meaningful confrontation. A statement such as: "You are still having a problem with staying around the office," is more likely to meet with resistance than the statement: "I needed to consult you about a problem last Thursday. I couldn't locate you, and nobody else seemed to know where you were."

Documentation of progress toward overcoming a problem can serve as a subtle form of positive reinforcement. Thus a worker who has been feuding with people in other departments might be told: "A lot of people have mentioned to me how cooperative you've been lately. What you are doing is certainly improving our relationship with other departments."

Rewarding improvement

An important part of the control model for dealing with ineffective performance is to reward people for improvement. In some instances rewards can be administered directly during the review sessions. For instance, an employee who improves a safety record might be praised during the review session. At other times, the review sessions can be used to promise or plan rewards. An employee might make significant progress in bringing an attendance record up to an acceptable level. The boss might promise the following reward: "Keep up your good attendance one more month, and we will consider you eligible for promotion to the next job level."

The mechanics of dispensing rewards have already been described in Chapter 8. Here it is worth mentioning *why* rewards should be administered during the review session. Of primary importance, rewards will help strengthen the improved behavior. A change in behavior is much more likely to be more than a temporary phenomenon when it leads to a desired reward. Second, rewarding people for overcoming problems is good human relations practice. The morale of an individual will probably be elevated when that person learns firsthand that "in this company, a person is given a second chance."

MAKING CONSTRUCTIVE USE OF DISCIPLINE

Punishment has an important role to play in bringing about changes in employee behavior. From the standpoint of the organization, administering discipline is also necessary to help establish outer limits to employee conduct. An organization that fails to discipline employees when their behavior becomes unacceptable is actually encouraging misconduct. Discipline and punishment have a better chance of bringing about improvements in behavior when certain conditions are met. A guideline of 13 such conditions is presented next.[6] They should be considered an aid to supervisory action in conjunction with the suggestions made about punishment in Chapter 8.

Use an appropriate punishment.   An appropriate punishment has two major characteristics. First, it should be commensurate with the offense. A minor rules infraction should receive a minor punishment. Overly severe punishments encourage counterhostile behavior and usually lead to a formal grievance. Second, an appropriate punishment is one that works for that particular individual. Some employees enjoy receiving a one-day suspension without pay—they welcome a day off from work anytime! For them suspension could almost be classified as a reward. A note of caution. Regulations may not allow different punishments for the same offense.

Make the offense clear.   Effective discipline must answer the employee's question, "What did I do wrong?" Your purpose in administering discipline is changed behavior in the direction of compliance with rules and regulations. To meet this end, the offense must be stated precisely. A specific statement of the infraction is preferable to a generality. The statement "You wore no hat in the 'hard hat' area" is preferable to "You have disregarded safety on this construction site."

Calm down before acting.   A poor time to administer discipline is when you are under the influence of heated emotion. A better time is when you have calmed down enough to view the infraction in proper perspective. One supervisor was later embarrassed because he had to withdraw a punishment he administered while upset over a problem. He told a mechanic who came

---

[6] These suggestions stem from two major sources: Gary Dessler, *Personnel Management: Modern Concepts and Techniques* (Reston, Va.: Reston, 1978), pp. 332–36; and W. Clay Hamner and Dennis W. Organ, *Organizational Behavior: An Applied Psychological Approach* (Dallas: Business Publications, 1978), pp. 77–80. © 1978 by Business Publications, Inc.

to work one hour late, "Pack up and never come into my shop again."

Use progressive discipline. A cardinal rule of making constructive use of discipline is to administer sanctions in order of increasing severity. Most organizations have formal policies to this effect. An example of an appropriate sequence of stages in discipline is furnished by William F. Glueck:[7]

☐ Counsel the employee. "The supervisor determines if in fact a violation took place, explains to the employee why the violation significantly affects productivity, and suggests that it should not happen again."

☐ If a second violation occurs, the supervisor again counsels with the employee, but this time notes that the violation will be entered in the employee's personnel file. If the violation is serious, a warning may be given about the consequences of a future recurrence.

☐ If poor performance is the main issue, the employee may request transfer or be transferred to another job.

☐ "If counseling and warnings do not result in changed behavior, and if a transfer is not appropriate, the next step normally is a disciplinary layoff."[8]

☐ Next comes *dehiring,* a deliberate attempt to get the employee to resign. It is suggested to the employee that he or she has "permission" to begin looking for another job. Dehiring requires considerable documentation by both the supervisor and company.

☐ Firing, or discharge, is the last alternative after all other approaches have been tried. Firing often backfires in a union shop because the fired employee might file a grievance and win. Discharging an employee is a complicated, time-consuming process that should be used only when corrective measures have been tried first. Certain violations such as theft, sabotage, physical violence, and insubordination, however, may be grounds for immediate discharge.

---

[7] William F. Glueck, *Personnel: A Diagnostic Approach,* rev. ed. (Dallas: Business Publications, 1978), pp. 718–19. © 1978 by Business Publications, Inc.

[8] Ibid., p. 718.

Respect the employee's dignity. Humiliating an employee is unlikely to change this person's behavior in a positive direction. The basic human relations principle familiar to most supervisors, "criticize in private," is particularly relevant here. Publically chewing out anybody robs them of dignity. A less obvious principle to practice is "criticize the act, not the person." People get defensive when their personal traits and characteristics are under attack. It is much preferable to attack poor work. It is better to say, "Your production is 50 percent below quota for the third week in a row" than "Your laziness and inefficiency have showed up for the third week in a row."

Dessler suggests that using an otherwise innocent, one-time offender as an example also robs a person of dignity.[9] It is the industrial equivalent of placing an elementary school student on the "dunce stool" or making the student wear a "dunce cap."

Discipline must be depersonalized and consistent. Effective discipline is related to clearly communicated rules, not to the caprice of managers or supervisors. Persons you dislike should only be disciplined when they violate a rule. Similarly persons you like should be disciplined whenever they violate the same rule. One advantage of a bureaucracy is that discipline is depersonalized. Rules and regulations are clearly stated and serve as guides to proper conduct. People therefore know what is expected of them and how to avoid being disciplined.

The supervisor should not say, "You're fired." An attorney suggests that no matter how outrageous the employee's misconduct, the supervisor should check any impulse to say, "You're fired."[10] Almost every suggestion for dismissal is subject to review from at least one higher level of management. A thorough investigation of the offense is usually required before an employee can rightfully be dismissed. At best the first-level supervisor can initiate a dismissal decision for review at higher levels of management. Instead of shouting, "You're fired," the supervisor might shout, "Now you're in trouble."

---

[9] Dessler, *Personnel Management*, p. 334.

[10] Reprinted, by permission of the publisher from "Due Process in Discipline and Dismissal," by Michael J. Shershin, Jr. and W. Randy Boxx, *Supervisory Management*, November 1976, © 1976 by AMACOM, a division of American Management Associations, p. 3. All rights reserved.

How bad is it to fire a deserving employee?

Firing anybody has its unpleasant aspects. Both the employee and the organization must share a sense of failure; the fired individual may undergo financial hardship and mental anguish; a grievance might be filed against the firm. Nevertheless, firing an employee who *should* be fired sometimes has positive consequences for the employee and the organization.*

1. *The shock may be therapeutic.* After being fired the employee may realize that he or she must perform better in order to stay employed. Many alcoholics report that they would have never reformed unless finally fired because of their poor performance stemming from alcohol abuse.

2. *Department morale may show a spurt.* The poor performer's co-workers are often happy to know that one must carry a fair share of the work load to stay employed. Why should any physically fit person be carried along by somebody else?

3. *The fired individual often winds up getting a new job for which the person is better suited.* Soon that individual becomes a solid performer instead of a marginal one.

4. *After being fired, many employees improve their occupational status.* A study conducted by THinc Career Planning Corporation revealed that 60 percent of fired managers wound up finding better jobs. As with situation (3), a better home life is often the result because job pressures are decreased.

5. *Firing a poor performer usually creates a job opening for a more deserving and better qualified employee.* Getting rid of "deadwood" thus creates new opportunities within the department or organization.

6. *Firing a substandard performer can help increase the productivity of the people who are not fired.* Employees learn unequivocally that the organization sets lower limits to acceptable performance—and sees that they are enforced.

7. *After being fired, people often reevaluate their lives and think through their lifestyle.* One man fired as a supervisor in a small firm decided that he would be better off as an individual worker in a large organization. What he really wanted was a predictable and orderly work life. He came to dislike the many hours of uncompensated overtime required by his small employer.

* John D. Minch suggested this discussion and contributed several of the ideas.

Get the facts.   A disciplinary decision should be delayed until adequate facts about the alleged offense have been collected. Documentation is important. Often a couple of people will have to be interviewed to learn more about the circumstances surrounding the rules infraction. Sometimes it is important to determine if the employee or the work equipment is at fault. Here is some legal advice regarding the first action to take in regard to a seemingly serious offense:[11]

> Investigate the circumstances of an alleged offense thoroughly. The employee should be told the nature of the offense and interviewed by his supervisor and, if possible, one other member of management (usually the personnel director). The employee's version of the circumstances surrounding the alleged offense should be obtained, including the reasons for his actions and the names of anyone else the employee feels will support his position. The employee who is sent home should be informed to return not more than 24 to 72 hours later to receive the company's decision concerning discipline. He should be told that if the company finds his position to be valid, he will be put back to work and paid for the time off. He should also be told that if the company disagrees with his actions, appropriate discipline will be imposed.

Discipline and punishment should be applied early.   An important principle of learning and motivation is that the punishment should be applied early in the history of the offense. If employees are discovered using a company photocopying machine to reproduce cub scout or girl scout announcements, they should be criticized quickly. The underlying psychology is that "the longer an undesired response is allowed to occur unpunished, the stronger it becomes, and the more resistant it becomes to any method of behavioral control."[12]

Punishment should quickly follow the offense.   Punishment should quickly follow the undesired behavior in order to strengthen the association between the behavior and its consequences. If an employee is caught making home repairs with company equipment and machinery, a reprimand should follow quickly. "The speedier the punishment, the greater information

---

[11] Ibid., p. 4.

[12] Hamner and Organ, *Organizational Behavior*, p. 78.

value it has to the recipient and the more it seems like a natural and automatic result of the behavior."[13]

Punishment should have information value. Employees who are disciplined or punished should learn something specific from the experience. The employee cited above should learn the general principle that you need special permission to use company resources to work on home (or moonlighting) projects. A punished or disciplined employee should be given a thorough explanation of what actions were considered undesirable and what can be done to correct those actions. If a supervisor follows most of the suggestions in this list, punishment will have an informative value.

Punishment should not be softened by undeserved rewards. It is natural to feel some guilt after administering discipline. To mollify such guilt, a supervisor will sometimes compensate the punished employee with an undeserved treat. For instance a supervisor who suspended an employee for a safety violation might offer to buy lunch that day. Or, as a parent you might buy your child a surprise toy after paddling his or her backside.

Do not back down when you are right. After you have taken all the necessary steps to deal with an employee who has violated a rule, do not give a "suspended sentence." If a rule is worth establishing, it is worth enforcing. Changing your mind on imposing penalties for misconduct or unacceptable job performance promotes an atmosphere of looseness. A firm and consistent supervisor sticks to a rational decision unless circumstances change.

DEALING WITH ALCOHOLIC AND DRUG-ADDICTED EMPLOYEES

Alcoholism and drug abuse among employees constitutes a significant problem facing managers at all levels in the organization. Abundant statistics have been collected about how alcoholism adversely influences job performance.[14] Data collected by

---

[13] Ibid.

[14] These statistics about alcoholism are summarized in Stanley E. Kaden, "Compassion or Cover-Up: The Alcoholic Employee," *Personnel Journal*, July 1977, p. 357. Reprinted with permission of *Personnel Journal*, copyright 1977.

the National Council on Alcoholism estimates that up to 10 percent of employees are alcoholics. These employees are absent approximately three times as often as the nonalcoholic employee. Alcohol abusers are involved in two to four times as many job-related accidents as nonalcoholics. Off-the-job accidents, such as those taking place on the highway, are four to six times as numerous. Sickness and accident benefits paid out for alcoholic employees are three times greater than for employees who are not alcoholic.

Information about the extent and consequences of drug abuse among employees is less clear-cut. In one study, employers in New York State estimated that approximately 12 percent of their employees had smoked marijuana at some time during their lives. About 7 percent had used marijuana in the past six months; 2 percent of them smoked pot on the job. Hard drugs, such as heroin, were used much less frequently.[15] Prescription drugs, such as barbiturates and tranquilizers, can also be used to the point of abuse.

Here is not the place to engage in a wide discussion about the incidence of alcoholism, drug abuse, or other substance abuse. Of immediate significance to the practicing supervisor is that people under the influence of alcohol or other drugs are likely to show serious impairment in job performance. Judgment can be clouded, concentration and coordination may function below average, or the person may suffer dizzy spells. Work under these conditions tends to be performed in spurts and slumps.

Although this fact is difficult to document, the opinion has been expressed by many people that alcoholism and drug addiction (particularly marijuana) account for many of the quality problems found in manufactured goods. Clerical employees, also, may produce many errors stemming from impaired concentration. One study about the effects of marijuana on humans concluded: "As the amount of marijuana increases, there is a shift from tranquility, apathy, and mild euphoria to distortions of perceptions, especially regarding time, and finally, with large amounts to disorientation and hallucinations."[16]

[15] Carl Chambers and Richard Heckman, *Employee Drug Abuse* (Boston: Cahners Books, 1972), cited in Glueck, *Personnel*, pp. 708–9.

[16] B. E. Leonard, "Cannabis: A Short Review of its Effect and the Possible Dangers of its Use," *British Journal of Addiction* 64 (1969): 121–30. See also Robert E. Willette, ed., *Drugs and Driving: National Institute on Drug Abuse*, research monograph II (Washington, D.C.; Department of Health, Education and Welfare, 1977).

What the supervisor should do

Dealing with problems of alcoholism and drug addiction that impair job performance, attendance, punctuality, and so forth follows the control model featured in this chapter. The supervisor detects the existence of a substance abuse problem; confronts that employee; makes an appropriate referral; and then follows up on progress. If the employee is making progress with the treatment, the supervisor dispenses encouragement. If progress is not being made, the supervisor gradually tightens the discipline.

Stanley E. Kaden, a clinical psychologist, describes the essence of an approach to employee alcoholism that has proven effective in a large number of companies. When such a concrete, focused program is used, it is not uncommon for 80 percent of alcoholic employees to be rehabilitated. The same model can be used for other forms of substance abuse. Kaden writes:[17]

> In companies where alcoholic recovery programs work best, regular performance evaluation and merit rating systems have become the diagnostic tool of supervisors. Supervisors are trained to be alert, too, and to document any signs that the employee's job performance is deteriorating . . . (Supervisors) are cautioned not to play "doctor," and not to discuss any suspicions as to drinking being the cause for poor work. What the supervisor should *not* do is as vital a part of the training as is the instruction having to do with careful evaluation and documentation of job performance. Under this sort of training, the supervisor learns to confront the employee whose work effectiveness is slipping, through a series of warnings of increasing severity, to the point of final confrontation. The quality of this confrontation, sometimes referred to as "benevolent coercion" (but which we prefer to call "supportive confrontation") is basically a sophisticated, expanded version of the old "shape up or ship out."
>
> The message, in essence, becomes: "Your job performance is going downhill. Despite a number of warnings, you don't seem to be able to get back on the track and stay there. Unless you can bring your performance back up, you will lose your job. However, we suggest that you get some professional help and we will steer you to someone who can advise you as to what steps to take."
>
> At this time, the employee is reminded of the company policy; he or she is given reassurance that seeking professional help will not jeopardize his or her job, and that his or her confidentiality will be protected.
>
> The employee is then referred to a particular individual within the

---

[17] Kaden, "Compassion or Cover-Up," p. 358.

company who serves as a program coordinator or employee assistance administrator. Regular employees of the company who are recovered alcoholics often fulfill this position. One of the primary functions of that person is to have a wide range of information as to the various professional and paraprofessional agencies and systems in the community to which the employee can be referred for help.

Coordination with the personnel or labor relations department

The supervisor is not alone in dealing with problem employees. When a situation looks particularly troublesome, it is natural to involve the next higher level of management (your boss). In many instances of dealing with problem employees, it is helpful to coordinate your activities with the personnel or labor relations department.[18] It is time to coordinate your efforts with the personnel department once it appears that a reminder or two will not remedy the personnel problem you face.

One reason for conferring with the personnel or labor relations department is to obtain technical or professional expertise. A member of the personnel department might have specialized skill in dealing with problem employees. Or just talking about your strategy for handling the problem with a neutral third party may provide you some valuable insights. One supervisor commented after such a discussion with a personnel specialist, "You mean I should just flat out tell the guy I think he has been lying about his production records?"

Another reason for conferring with the labor relations department is to discuss the legal implications of the problem you are facing. There is a due process in discipline and dismissal both with respect to the law in general and the union contract (assuming your employees are represented by a union).[19] It is important to make sure that your approach to discipline does not violate a civil liberty or the union contract. One female supervisor planned to discipline a subordinate because she wore no bra under her T-shirt. The former claimed the latter was "creating a disturbance." A representative from the personnel department

---

[18] An illuminating discussion of this topic is Susan A. Goodwin, "The Personnel Director as High-Status Friend," *Supervisory Management*, August 1977, pp. 2–10.

[19] See Shershin and Boxx, "Due Process."

dissuaded the supervisor from persisting in her efforts. Her charges about creating a disturbance would be too difficult to prove.

A third reason for conferring with the personnel department about a disciplinary problem is simply one of documentation. Accurate records about behavior and performance are valuable when it comes time to review employees for promotion. At the other extreme, it is easier to dismiss a problem employee when it is documented that four different supervisors have faced similar disciplinary problems with the individual.

SUMMARY OF KEY POINTS

☐ People become problem employees (ineffective performers) for a wide variety of reasons. Among these factors are: unsuitable level of intelligence or job knowledge; emotional illness or personality disorder; low level of work motivation; unsuited physical characteristics or physical disorders; family and personal problems; pressures from the work group to perform poorly; poor handling by the organization; cultural pressures toward poor performance.

☐ Confrontation is the bedrock on which a workable system of controlling ineffective performance is constructed. Suggestions for improving your confrontation skills include: Try to relax; Immediately get to the central purpose of the meeting; Avoid being apologetic or defensive about your purpose; Confront in a private place; Use feeling but not hostility; Confront job-related behavior, not personality traits.

☐ The control model for dealing with ineffective performance presents an overall plan for bringing about constructive changes in employees whose performance is substandard. Its basic elements are: diagnosis of the problem; confrontation about the problem; specifying improvement goals and an action plan; follow-up on results. The cycle is regenerated as the supervisor stays alert to problems.

☐ An improvement goal for dealing with problem employees should have the same characteristics as improvement goals used in an MBO program. It is particularly important that the goals or objectives established be translated into specific actions or behaviors that are to be changed in a positive direction.

☐ An action plan specifies what the employee and others must do to enable employees to attain their improvement goals.

☐ Follow-up and review sessions are an important part of dealing with problem employees. At best, review sessions are essentially counseling or coaching sessions. It is helpful for the superior to listen carefully to the subordinate, help solve job problems interfering with the employee's performance, and document the presence or absence of progress.

☐ Discipline and punishment are likely to contribute to performance, or change behavior in a positive direction, when 13 conditions are met. Translated into suggestions, these conditions are: Use an appropriate punishment. Make the offense clear. Calm down before acting. Use progressive discipline—begin with a gentle warning and work toward threats of dismissal. If necessary, an employee must finally be terminated. Respect the employee's dignity. Depersonalize discipline—discipline should be related closely to violations of specific rules. The supervisor should not say, "You're fired," but should recommend such action to higher management. Get the facts about the ineffective performance or the unacceptable behavior. Discipline and punishment should be applied before the unacceptable behavior has proceeded very far. Punishment should quickly follow the offense. Punishment should have information value. Punishment should not be softened by undeserved rewards. Do not back down when you are right.

☐ The general strategy recommended for dealing with serious offenses such as alcohol and drug abuse problems follows closely the control model. People with these problems should be confronted and encouraged to seek outside help. The supervisor should conduct follow-up sessions to determine if progress is being made and to offer encouragement. Discipline must be administered if progress is not being made concerning the alcohol or drug problem.

GUIDELINES FOR SUPERVISORY PRACTICE

1. Dealing with problem employees ordinarily consumes a disproportionate amount of a supervisor's time. If you implement the control model for dealing with ineffective performance, you may be able to deal more efficiently and effectively with problem employees.

2. The aspect of coping with ineffective employees generally presenting the most problem to supervisors is confrontation. It is therefore helpful

to practice your skills in nonhostile confrontation. Role playing is a helpful technique for improving such skills.

3. Despite your efforts at dealing with ineffective employees, some of them will ultimately have to be terminated. Before recommending to higher management that a subordinate be dismissed, you should document your case and have tried diligently to help that employee improve performance.

QUESTIONS FOR DISCUSSION AND REVIEW

1. Why not just fire problem employees and be done with it?
2. Based on your experience, do most problems with employees arise because of their job skills or personality characteristics? Explain.
3. What do you think are one or two of the underlying reasons that so many supervisors dislike to confront problem employees?
4. Formulate two improvement goals for an employee who spends too much time "hiding out" in the rest room.
5. What actions should supervisors take that will allow them to be alert to performance and behavior problems among subordinates?
6. How many months should you give problem employees to overcome their problems before they are terminated?
7. According to the control model, an ineffective employee should be rewarded once he or she becomes effective. Is it fair to other employees to reward someone else just for doing his or her job?
8. Assume an 18-year-old man steals an $8,000 automobile. He is caught, convicted, and sent to jail for two years. What rules, if any, of constructive discipline seem to be violated by sending him to jail?
9. In one newpaper production department, if an employee is caught spitting on the floor, he or she is fired immediately. What do you think of this rule?
10. Suppose a supervisor discovers that her best technician works four nights a week as an exotic dancer at a local bar. Should the supervisor confront her about her second job? (Incidentally, moonlighting is not prohibited in this company.)
11. Suppose a co-worker of yours has a drinking problem, making it difficult for you to perform certain parts of your job. How should you handle this situation?
12. Suppose you accept the assignment of giving a speech about the management of ineffective performance. What will be your punch line (the last sentence in your talk)?

A supervisory problem: A very personal matter

A group of supervisors were gathered at a company conference. The conversation soon turned to personnel problems. Tyler spoke last:

"Fellows and gals, sorry to upstage you, but I get the prize for the toughest employee problem. It's one so sensitive that I doubt any of you have an instant cure. But if you are willing to listen to me, I'd be grateful for any suggestion you might have.

"Production is king in my division and we need all the able bodies we can find. I've got this 250-pound fellow in my department who carries the obvious nickname "Moose." He's never gotten into an actual physical fight with anybody in the department. But he's kind of hot-tempered and a loner.

"Yet my problem with Moose is not his temper. It's that he's the most unclean person I've ever had working for me. He has a terrible perspiration problem and his clothes are filthy. He swabs himself with handkerchiefs and lays them out on top of his machine to dry.

"At least once a week another employee in the department tells me I should do something about Moose. That he's got to learn to shower every day and wear clean clothes. Sure, I know it's my responsibility to inform my employees of problems. But this one is far too delicate. It would take a lot of finesse to tell a 250-pound, hot-tempered production guy that he smells bad."

1. *What suggestions can you offer Moose's boss?*
2. *What would be a good opening line with which to confront Moose?*
3. *Does Moose's supervisor have the right to insist that he practice better personal hygiene?*

SOME SUGGESTED READING

Armor, David J.; Polich, Michael; and Stambul, Harriet B. *Alcoholism and Treatment.* New York: Wiley-Interscience, 1978.

Chambers, Carl D., and Heckman, Richard. *Employee Drug Abuse.* Boston: Cahners Books, 1972.

DuBrin, Andrew J. *Managerial Deviance: How to Handle Problem People in Key Jobs.* New York: Van Nostrand Reinhold, 1976.

Else, J. David. "Treat or Treatment for Alcoholics?" *Industry Week,* April 26, 1971, pp. 48–50.

Follmann, Joseph F., Jr. *Alcoholics and Business: Problems, Costs, and Solutions.* New York: AMACOM, 1976.

Goodwin, Susan A. "The Personnel Director as High-Status Friend." *Supervisory Management,* August 1977, pp. 2–10.

Jennings, Ken. "The Problem of Employee Drug Use and Remedial Alternatives." *Personnel Journal,* November 1977, pp. 554–60.

Kaden, Stanley E. "Compassion or Cover-Up: The Alcoholic Employee." *Personnel Journal,* July 1977, pp. 356–58.

McCoy, Robert C. "Performance Review: Confronting the Poor Performer." *Supervisory Management,* July 1976, pp. 12–16.

Martin, Richard G. "Five Principles of Corrective Disciplinary Action." *Supervisory Management,* January 1978, pp. 24–28.

Miller, Laurence M. *Behavior Management: The New Science of Managing People at Work.* New York: Wiley-Interscience, 1978.

Miner, John B., and Brewer, J. Frank. "The Management of Ineffective Performance." In *Handbook of Industrial and Organizational Psychology,* edited by Marvin D. Dunnette, pp. 995–1029. Chicago: Rand McNally, 1976.

Rudd, Howard F., Jr. "Supervising the Mentally Handicapped: The Procedures, the Rewards." *Supervisory Management,* pp. 31–34.

Schramm, Carl J.; Mandell, Wallace; and Archer, Janet. *Workers Who Drink: Their Treatment in an Industrial Setting.* Lexington, Mass.: Lexington Books, 1978.

Shershin, Michael J., Jr., and Boxx, W. Randy. "Due Process in Discipline and Dismissal." *Supervisory Management,* November 1976, pp. 2–9.

Walker, Joseph J. "Counseling Sessions That Do Some Good." *Supervisory Management,* November 1976, pp. 10–15.

Walsh, Richard J. "Ten Basic Counseling Skills." *Supervisory Management,* July 1977, pp. 2–9.

Whitehead, Ross. "The Incredible Cost of Booze." *Industry Week,* September 2, 1974, pp. 28–32.

Training and evaluating employees

14

LEARNING OBJECTIVES
After reading and working through the material in this chapter, you should be able to:

1. Appreciate what steps have to be taken to do an effective job of training employees.
2. Understand the supervisor's role in orienting new employees.
3. Discuss the kind of work habits that should be encouraged among new (and old) employees.
4. List about seven important principles of effective on-the-job training.
5. Identify several important training errors.
6. Describe a simplified, but useful, system of evaluating employees.

Training and evaluating employees are yet two more complex sets of skills necessary for success as a supervisor. Staff specialists from the personnel (or human resources) department provide much assistance in training and evaluating employees. Nevertheless, the first-level supervisor cannot avoid direct responsibility for these activities. Once employees have completed a formal company training program, they usually require additional on-the-job training. After elaborate systems of employee appraisal have been developed or selected by the personnel department, it is still the supervisor who actually evaluates employees.

What is the relationship between employee training and evaluation? Training is intended to prepare employees so they will be able to perform their jobs in a satisfactory or better manner.

321

Evaluation is part of the control process. It is used to make a determination as to how well employees *are* performing their jobs.

Employee evaluation, in a sense, also evaluates the supervisor. It partially indicates how effective the supervisor is as a trainer, or how well employees have been trained. As the previous chapter would suggest, however, people become ineffective employees for many reasons in addition to inadequate training.

THE SUPERVISOR AND EMPLOYEE ORIENTATION

New employee training begins with an orientation program. Most medium- and large-sized organizations have elaborate orientation programs conducted by staff specialists. The program may include tours of the facilities, talks by various department heads, filmstrips, movies, videotape presentations, and ample supplies of printed information. Orientation programs are often so complex that the new employee feels overwhelmed and bewildered. When the new employee is finally sent to the assigned department, a new type of orientation begins. As aptly stated by Gray L. Carpenter, the president of a consulting firm:

> Whatever suggestions, guidance, groundwork, and assistance may be provided by personnel specialists, new-employee orientation remains a line management responsibility. Moreover, no other person has so much influence on the attitude, morale, and performance of a new employee as his or her immediate supervisor. Accordingly, no matter what else may be involved, the climax of the orientation program is the meeting between the newcomer and his or her supervisor.[1]

A generally sound procedure is for the supervisor to continue the orientation process in a gradual manner. Information should be transmitted to the employee, based upon that individual's need at the time. The employee can be reminded that most of the important orientation information is contained in the employee orientation booklet. Employees typically forget much of what they learned during the formal orientation program. It will therefore be necessary to rediscuss important matters with new employees. Also it is often advisable to encourage new employ-

---

[1] Gray L. Carpenter, "New-Employee Orientation," in *Handbook of Business Administration* ed.-in-chief, H. B. Maynard (New York: McGraw-Hill, 1967), sec. 11, p. 81.

ees to contact the personnel department for clarification of personnel policies.

The supervisor's orientation checklist

A useful practice is for the supervisor to use a formal checklist as a guide to orienting new employees. Joseph Famularo has prepared one such checklist, as shown in Figure 14–1.[2] It is general enough to be used in most organizations. You will note that many of the items included in the form are probably covered in the formal orientation conducted by the personnel department. Note, for example, item VII, that deals with working conditions. Such crucial issues bear repeating, even for the purpose of determining if the employee comprehends them.

As discussed in Chapter 2, it is convenient for employees to "not hear" information that conflicts with their preferences. One woman who was accustomed to being paid weekly became upset when she was not paid after her first week of work at her new job. She told her supervisor that she needed money for groceries and was completely without funds. Her boss explained that the company policy of paying twice a month was explained to her in orientation. After a series of phone calls, the company finally arranged for the woman to receive a short-term loan from the company credit union.

Making the new employee feel at home.   A new employee at any job level tends to feel somewhat insecure and anxious when starting a new job. The supervisor can help by making that employee feel at home on the job.[3] The encouragement and support an employee receives the first few days can go a long way toward eliminating a new employee's fear that a wrong employment decision has been made.

Related to helping an employee feel comfortable on the new job is the question of alerting the person to other employees with negative attitudes. A sound approach is to make this type of factual presentation to the new employee: "Like any other company, some of our employees are very happy, and a handful are

---

[2] Joseph Famularo, ed.-in-chief, *Handbook of Modern Personnel Management* (New York: McGraw-Hill, 1972), chap. 23, pp. 24–25.

[3] Theo Haimann and Raymond L. Hilgert, *Supervision: Concepts and Practices of Management,* 2d ed. (Cincinnati: South-Western, 1977), p. 218.

FIGURE 14–1
Supervisor's orientation checklist

Employee's name: _____

Discussion completed (please check each individual item)

I.   Word of welcome _____

II. Explain overall departmental organiza-
     tion and its relationship to other
     activities of the company

III. Explain employee's individual contri-
     bution to the objectives of the depart-
     ment and his starting assignment in
     broad terms _____

IV. Discuss job content with employee and
     give him a copy of job description
     (if available) _____

V.   Explain departmental training
     program(s) and salary increase
     practices and procedures _____

VI. Discuss where the employee lives and
     transportation facilities _____

VII. Explain working conditions:
     a. Hours of work, time sheets
     b. Use of employee entrance and
         elevators
     c. Lunch hours
     d. Coffee breaks, rest periods
     e. Personal telephone calls and mail
     f. Overtime policy and requirements
     g. Paydays and procedure for being
         paid
     h. Lockers
     i. Other _____ _____

VIII. Requirements for continuance of em-
      ployment—explain company standards
      as to:
      a. Performance of duties
      b. Attendance and punctuality
      c. Handling confidential information
      d. Behavior
      e. General appearance
      f. Wearing of uniform _____

FIGURE 14–1 (*continued*)

> *Discussion completed (please check each individual item)*
>
> IX.   Introduce new staff member to manager(s) and other supervisors. Special attention should be paid to the person to whom the new employee will be assigned.   _____
>
> X.   Release employee to immediate supervisor who will:
>   *a.* Introduce new staff member to fellow workers
>   *b.* Familiarize the employee with his work place
>   *c.* Begin on-the-job training   _____
>
> If not applicable, insert N/A in space provided.
>
> _____   _____
> Employee's Signature   Supervisor's Signature
>
> _____   _____
> Date   Division
>
> Form examined for filing:
>
>   _____   _____
>   Date   Personnel Department

Source: *Handbook of Modern Personnel Administration* by Joseph Famularo, ed.-in-chief. Chap. 23, pp. 24–25. Copyright © 1972 by McGraw-Hill Inc. Used with permission of McGraw-Hill Book Company.

bitter for one reason or another. But please don't lose your enthusiasm for your new job just because you hear a few bitter comments. Be your own judge."

ENCOURAGING GOOD WORK HABITS

An important part of training new employees is to encourage effective work habits. Independent of the type of skill required in a job, good work habits are helpful to the organization and to the employee's career. Unfortunately many employees (including professionals and managers) have poor work habits. A supervisor who is enthusiastic about good work habits and who *practices* good work habits serves as a positive model for employees. Techniques for developing good work habits yourself will be discussed in the last chapter of this book. Here we will indicate several different sets of work habits that should be strongly encouraged on almost any job. Some may sound moralistic and trite, but they are still of vital importance to productivity.

Good housekeeping. Cleanliness on the job remains an important virtue. Littered, soiled, and malodorous work areas are a source of discontent to many conscientious employees. Poor housekeeping also leads to a wide variety of accidents. Visitors to the work site, such as home office executives, customers, and state inspectors, give a company poor marks for poor housekeeping. A supervisor should make special note of good housekeeping by praise, recognition, and verbal appreciation.

Punctuality and good attendance. New or old employees should be reminded of the importance of adhering to high standards of punctuality and attendance. A supervisor should be alert to openly discussing two popular myths entertained by an unknown number of employees. One is that a certain amount of sick days are "owed" to an employee. Sometimes employees who have not used up their sick days will find reasons to be sick toward the end of the calendar year. Another myth is that "absence is better than lateness." Some employees believe that it is somehow more honorable to be absent because of illness than late because of a reason such as oversleeping. Consequently, the employee who oversleeps calls in sick rather than face the embarrassment of arriving to work late.

Efficiency is important. Efficiency basically refers to the amount of resources that are used to accomplish a given end. If a secretary consumes six sheets of bond paper to produce an acceptable one-page letter, this person is being inefficient. Scrap is the product of inefficiency. As the scrap rate increases, profits decrease. Wasted time is also a form of scrap. The scrap, however, is invisible until it shows up in lowered profits or failure to stay within budget. A caseworker who takes two hours to process a client that other caseworkers could process in 30 minutes is contributing to organizational inefficiency. A supervisor must frequently emphasize the importance of being efficient with both tangible materials and time.

Quality is important. Fostering a positive attitude toward high-quality manufactured goods or services is considered constructive supervisory behavior in most organizations. Quality has relevance even for inexpensive goods. The supervisor may still be obliged to push for quality work on the part of employees, within the limit of the design of the product. For instance, if a company manufactures inexpensive bookcases made of thick cardboard and a thin layer of wood, employees might be urged to do the best quality job they can within the limits of assembling such a bookcase.

Ethics and integrity. The manner in which customers, clients, or the public is treated by employees falls loosely into the category of work habits. Ethics and integrity are best taught by example rather than by lecture. Supervisory attitudes toward the public and co-workers may influence employee attitudes about those two groups. A life insurance supervisor at a large agency in Toronto describes how he encourages ethics and integrity among his employees:

> Ethics boils down to a very simple issue. I tell the fellows and gals working for me that if they would want to be treated the way they treat clients, that's good ethics. If they wouldn't want to be treated the way they are treating the client, then they are being unethical. I try to use the same ethical approach in handling my people. We never hire a life insurance rep just so we can sell policies to his or her family and friends. We want people who will stay with us for the long haul because they are suited to this business.

Steady pace. In most jobs, it pays dividends in efficiency to work at a steady clip. The spurt worker creates many problems for management. Some employees take pride in working rapidly, even when it results in a high error rate. A supervisor should try to counsel such an employee to slow down with the goal of improving productivity.

Cut down on "schmoozing." A poor work habit practiced by millions of employees is schmoozing. A schmoozer engages in such activities as telling jokes, lingering at the water cooler, telephoning a friend on company time, wandering around the plant, office, or lab, or taking a long lunch break. Sociologist Robert Schrank contends that schmoozing relieves worker boredom and monotony and thus is useful.[4] But too much schmooz-

---

[4] Robert Schrank, "How to Relieve Worker Boredom," *Psychology Today,* July 1978, pp. 79–80.

ing is a waste of the precious resource called time. A supervisor should both discourage too much employee schmoozing and personally avoid overdoing this practice.

WHEN IS EMPLOYEE TRAINING NEEDED?

Before embarking upon an employee training program, organizations sometimes conduct a survey to determine if training is needed. If the findings are affirmative, an analysis will be conducted to determine which type of training will do the job. Supervisors provide useful input into the analysis of training needs. Above all, the supervisor can learn much about training needs simply by getting into the work area and making observations. A casual conversation with operators might reveal, for example, that they are having difficulty in implementing OSHA regulations.

Among the more common indicators that training is needed are when absenteeism and turnover increase, quality falls, overtime increases without a corresponding increase in output, production drops, and accidents increase.

An analysis of training needs by the personnel department in conjunction with supervision will sometimes indicate the presence of overtraining. One symptom of overtraining is when people complain about being supervised too closely. In an emphasis to prevent mistakes, supervisors will sometimes give too much guidance to employees. The result can be lowered performance.

PRINCIPLES OF EFFECTIVE ON-THE-JOB TRAINING (OJT)

Training, or the acquisition of skills, is one aspect of learning. All that was said about the nature of human learning in Chapter 2 thus has relevance for training people on the job. Psychologists and other specialists in human behavior have extensively studied the conditions under which training proceeds most effectively. These principles of learning can be translated into ten suggestions that the supervisor can use in training employees on the job:[5]

---

[5] Points 1, 9, and 10 in this list are derived from Delbert W. Fisher, "Educational Psychology Involved in On-the-Job Training," *Personnel Journal,* October 1977, pp.

1.   The supervisor must recognize that OJT is a joint effort. Employees are not trained or taught. They must be active participants in a joint undertaking between themselves and their trainer or boss. The kindergarten teacher who says, "Let's learn to tie our shoes" is using an important training principle.

2.   The trainee learns best by doing. Most job skills are not unlike golf, bowling, or tennis. Verbal instructions provide you helpful guidelines but most of the learning takes place through active practice.

3.   A motivated or interested learner learns more quickly than a less-motivated counterpart. In other words, if trainees want to learn, they will learn more quickly. Part of the problem here is finding people who want to acquire job skills. If an employee can be shown the personal benefits from learning a new skill, that individual's level of motivation will often be increased.

4.   Feedback is essential. The trainee needs frequent knowledge of results. Feedback helps point to what the person is doing both wrong and right. For example, one good way to learn how to sharpen pencils is to observe when the point breaks from over-sharpening. Equally effective is to observe when the pencil is sharpened to a fine but sturdy point.

5.   Learning proceeds best when the learner's correct response is immediately reinforced. Sometimes the correct response is self-reinforcing. If you learn how to program a computer and it produces the desired results, the reinforcement is built-in. In most situations the supervisor who is doing the training must dispense verbal rewards such as: "You've got it right. You're doing fine."

6.   Learning should be meaningful—it should make sense to the trainee. Learning with understanding is more permanent and more transferable to other situations than learning by rote. Explaining the principle behind a particular step in a job can aid understanding. One example: "The reason you put the Teflon coating on at this stage is to reduce the friction on the bearings.

516–19. The other seven points are derived from R. E. Silverman, "Learning Theory Applied to Training," in *The Management of Training,* ed. C. P. Otto and O. Glaser, (Reading, Mass.: Addison-Wesley, 1970), cited in Ernest J. McCormick and Joseph Tiffin, *Industrial Psychology,* 6th ed. (Englewood Cliffs, N.J.: Prentice-Hall, 1974), pp. 239–40.

Friction will wear a bearing down to the point where it no longer does the job."

7. Trainees learn more effectively when they learn at their own pace. Earlier we stated that people should work at a steady pace. These two principles are not incompatible. A steady pace could be slow and steady, or rapid and steady. Above all, it is important to avoid crash training.

8. Guided practice in a variety of settings is helpful. Applying your new skill to several situations is helpful in solidifying the new learning. A new driver who practices that new skill with several automobiles gains in self-confidence. An automotive repair trainee who installed brake linings on several different car models would develop more skill than someone who practiced on only one model.

9. The supervisor must be a good listener. As noted by Fisher, a director of education and training in a veteran's hospital:[6] "Listening involves the supervisor in examining the work situation. It requires that the supervisor accept what is said in a nonjudgmental manner. Active listening on the part of the supervisor encourages the subordinate to speak freely and to explore the problem. This type of listening helps the subordinate accept suggestions for improvement in the work situation."

10. The supervisor must create a climate of trust and acceptance. It is easier to learn when you are trusted and accepted. Perhaps this is an ideal learning condition. Many marine recruits have been successfully trained at Paris Island, where the climate is one of harassment and rejection. However, few people would be willing to repeat the training experience.

Training errors to avoid

A general way to avoid training errors would be to adhere to the ten principles or suggestions just outlined. Claude S. George, Jr., has suggested four commonsense training approaches to avoid errors that are commonly made by well-intended supervisors:[7]

---

[6] Fisher, "Educational Psychology," p. 519.

[7] Claude S. George, Jr., *Supervision in Action: The Art of Managing Others* (Reston, Va.: Reston, 1977), pp. 140, 144.

☐ *Avoid feeding the trainee too much information at one time.* The training pace, as mentioned above, should be geared to the trainee's ability to comprehend the information. Look for signs of confusion on the part of the trainee to indicate when the pace has become too rapid.

☐ *Avoid talking without showing.* Most people learn better by concrete example of how to do something, than by discussion alone. Job skills that involve a good deal of hand movements can best be taught in the same way you would teach somebody a technique in sports. Show a shipping clerk how to wrap a package, don't just demand perfection.

☐ *Avoid impatience.* Impatience can destroy a learning environment. Many parents are unable to teach their children to drive because they intimidate them by a display of impatience. A good coach or trainer displays patience and understanding.

☐ *Avoid making the trainee tense.* Being too impatient, watching too closely, or displaying anger when the employee makes a mistake are some of the common ways in which supervisors breed tension. Too much tension can lead to confusion and irrational mistakes. A learner is usually already tense. It is self-defeating for you to increase his or her tension level.

USING COACHING TO SUPPORT TRAINING

After an employee has been properly trained in the job, the supervisor's responsibility as a trainer does not end. The supervisor should stand ready to coach subordinates on an as-needed, day-by-day basis. As a coach, the supervisor gently confronts employees with their mistakes and makes suggestions for corrective action. The supervisor is also alert to encouraging good performance.

The terms *counseling* and *coaching* are sometimes used interchangeably, but an important distinction can be drawn between the two terms. A counselor listens more than a coach does and is more concerned with feelings than with action. Counseling deals more with the long-term development of an employee; coaching deals more with the here and now. You might coach an employee about how to treat customers better, but counsel the person about career advancement with the company.

The control model for coaching

The control model for dealing with ineffective performance, described in the previous chapter provides a suitable framework for coaching employees.[8] Your general goal in coaching is to sustain high levels of performance and correct behavior that detracts from good performance. In brief review, a supervisor would use this format in coaching a subordinate.

Detection of the need for coaching. Assume that Jack, an orderly, has forgotten some of his training and begins to act in an abrupt and unfriendly manner toward hospital patients. Hanna, his boss, detects this behavior.

Confrontation of problem or mistake. Hanna asks to speak with Jack and begins her coaching session with this comment, "Jack, it looks like you've forgotten some of the human relations training. You seem to be quite abrupt with patients. I heard you snap at an elderly man to wait his turn."

Development of an action plan. Hanna and Jack jointly work out a plan whereby Jack will remember to monitor his own impatience when he is busy. (He notes that he tends to be the most impatient when he is harassed.)

Review of progress. Hanna systematically follows up on Jack's progress in handling hospital patients. She makes some of her own observations and listens carefully for complaints from patients. A month later Hanna and Jack discuss the fact that his progress has been substantial. Hanna reinforces Jack's behavior by complimenting him on his handling of patients during the last month.

EVALUATING EMPLOYEE PERFORMANCE

Performance appraisal is a formal way of recording and documenting the job performance of employees. Few medium- or large-sized work organizations exist today which do not utilize some system of evaluating and recording worker performance. Winston Oberg has summarized the multitude of purposes behind employee evaluation systems:[9]

---

[8] An expanded discussion of this point is found in Andrew J. DuBrin, *Human Relations: A Job Oriented Approach* (Reston, Va.: Reston, 1978), pp. 200–204.

[9] Winston Oberg, "Make Performance Appraisal Relevant," *Harvard Business Review,* January–February 1972, p. 61.

☐ Help or prod supervisors to observe their subordinates more closely and to do a better coaching job.

☐ Motivate employees by providing feedback on how they are doing.

☐ Provide back-up data for management decisions concerning merit increases, transfers, dismissals, and so on.

☐ Improve organization development by identifying people with promotion potential and pinpointing developmental needs.

☐ Establish a research and reference base for personnel decisions.

However laudatory these purposes of performance appraisal, they are not always met. Some people believe that the proper use of an MBO system (as described in Chapter 6) will help an organization achieve these purposes.[10] The approach outlined in the control model for dealing with ineffective performance (Chapter 13) is designed to increase the probability that performance appraisal will bring about improvement in performance. In review, the general approach recommended for evaluating employee performance, *and bringing about any needed changes,* follows this format:

Step one is to confront employees about how well they met job expectations. We assume that each job has definable standards of performance.

Step two is to specify what areas for improvement, if any, exist. For instance, "You are still getting shipments to the door of the customer an average of 40 minutes later than the promised delivery date."

Step three is to follow up on the results of the performance evaluation session. With the late delivery problem, the supervisor might hold a review session one month later to discuss the timeliness of shipments since the last review session.

Objective standards of performance

In recent years, personnel specialists have encouraged organizations to rate employees at every level on the basis of how well they achieved work results. The opposite approach is to rate people on their personal characteristics such as dependability

---

[10] An analysis of the benefits of MBO is Henry L. Tosi and Stephen J. Carroll, *Management: Contingencies, Structure, and Process* (Chicago: St. Clair Press, 1976), chap. 11.

FIGURE 14–2

RAMCO

PERFORMANCE REVIEW REPORT

STEP PROGRESSION

NONEXEMPT SALARIED EMPLOYEES

Name_____   Job title _____

Review date _____   Step no. _____

PLACE A CHECK IN THE BOX WHICH BEST DESCRIBES EACH FACTOR

	MARGINAL	ACCEPTABLE	GOOD	VERY GOOD	SUPERIOR
LEARNING PROGRESSION: How quickly employee is learning the functions of the job	☐	☐	☐	☐	☐
PLANNING: Employee's ability to plan work efficiently	☐	☐	☐	☐	☐
QUALITY: Employee's ability to produce work that is neat and free from errors	☐	☐	☐	☐	☐
QUANTITY: Employee's actual output in relation to that required by the job	☐	☐	☐	☐	☐
COOPERATION: Employee's attitude and relationships with others	☐	☐	☐	☐	☐
PUNCTUALITY: Amount of tardiness when reporting to work or returning from coffee breaks	☐	☐	☐	☐	☐
ATTENDANCE: Extent of employee's absenteeism from job during regular working hours	☐	☐	☐	☐	☐

OVERALL RATING	Marginal performance	Acceptable performance	Good performance	Very good performance	Superior performance
	☐	☐	☐	☐	☐

Recommend for step progression: Yes_____   No_____

Supervisor _____   Date_____

Superior_____   Date_____

Industrial relations _____   Date_____

Employee interviewed (date) _____

Additional comments: _____

_____

and initiative. Assume an employee had a scrap rate of only 1 percent (and the average rate was 8 percent). It would be considered good practice to rate that employee highly because of this fact. It would be considered poor practice to simply state that the employee was "careful." The EEO much prefers that employees be rated on objective standards of performance than on personality traits.

A performance appraisal system based on MBO is thus preferable to a system that rates people based on supervisory impressions of personal characteristics. Unfortunately, most employers still use evaluation forms based mostly on personal traits. The form shown in Figure 14–2 rates people on seven dimensions of work performance. Each supervisor who uses the form has standards posted for each job, to which the company and union agree. Only the dimension of behavior called "cooperation" might be criticized as being based largely on subjective impressions. Yet cooperativeness is a valuable characteristic of any employee at any job level.

An ideal evaluation system would evaluate employee performance only against observable standards of performance. A basketball team's standing in the league would be an example of a rating based on objective standards of performance. The number one team would have the best winning and losing record. Ranking teams on a nationwide, state, or provincial basis, however, gets back to the realm of subjective impressions. Aside from rating people objectively, a good evaluation system gives people a chance to discuss their job and future.

A simplified approach to employee evaluation

Herbert H. Meyer has studied the employee evaluation process for much of his professional lifetime, 20 years of which were spent with the General Electric Company. Meyer has proposed a simplified approach to performance appraisal which he believes (and his research indicates) overcomes a major problem of performance evaluation: Employees become defensive when they are given a "report card" comparing them precisely to other employees.[11] Meyer's research reveals that employees were more likely to react defensively than constructively to suggestions for improving performance. (It is nevertheless important to confront employees about problem areas.)

---

[11] Herbert H. Meyer, "The Annual Performance Review Discussion—Making It Constructive," *Personnel Journal,* October 1977, pp. 508–11.

An outline of Meyer's "better way" is shown in Figure 14–3. The specific steps in the discussion format to performance evaluation proceed in this manner:

FIGURE 14–3
Performance review discussion

Employee's name _____

Date of discussion _____

Introduction
    Put employee at ease.
    Purpose: Mutual discussion of how things are going.

Employee's view
    How does he/she view job and working climate?
    Any problems?
    Suggestions for changes, improvement?

Supervisor's view of employee's performance
    Summary statement only.
    Avoid comparisons to others.

Behaviors desirable to continue
    Mention one or two items only.

Opportunities for improvement
    No more than one or two items.
    Do not present as "shortcomings."
    Keep it work-related.

Performance improvement plans
    Plan should be employee's plan.
    Supervisor merely tries to help and counsel.

Future opportunities
    Advancement possibilities?
    Future pay increase possibilities?
    Warning for poor performer.

Questions
    Any general concerns?
    Close on constructive, encouraging note.

First, the employee is notified that a discussion is scheduled. That individual is told to prepare for the discussion what improvements he or she could make. In preparation for the discussion, employees are told to think about personal improvements, improving their contributions, and plans for the future.

The supervisor might start the discussion by asking, "As you look at it, how are things going on the job?" Such questioning enhances two-way communication. Telling people outright how they are doing encourages only one-way communication. Later in the discussion the supervisor presents the general evaluation.

Second, the supervisor can then introduce the discussion of improvement in job performance or opportunities for advancement. The focus in this part of the discussion "should be on future opportunities and plans rather than on past failures."[12]

Third, a natural closing topic of discussion is usually what the future might hold for the employee. High-performing and ambitious employees might want to discuss growth opportunities. In contrast, more security-conscious employees might simply want reassurance that their jobs are secure. In highly stable organizations, discussions about future opportunities might be perceived by higher management as stirring up discontent.

Whether the employee being evaluated is ambitious or unambitious, a discussion of self-development and self-improvement represents a good upbeat way of closing the interview. For instance, "I think your taking a course in the metric system is a fine idea. It could help you now and in the future."

The critical incident technique. The two methods of employee evaluation described so far include elements of many evaluation methods. Both give the supervisor an opportunity to evaluate employees on the basis of traits and specific actions. Many other methods of employee evaluation are currently available. A unique approach among them is the *critical incident technique.* It is used to evaluate people on the basis of "make or break" elements of their job.

Using this technique, personnel specialists and operating supervisors (and other managers) prepare lists of statements indicating very effective or very ineffective employee actions. These critical incidents are then combined into different categories for different jobs. The performance categories for a receptionist position would, of course, be quite different than those for a fire fighter position.

After the critical incidents and categories have been developed, the evaluator prepares a log for each employee. During the evaluation session, the supervisor can discuss these critical incidents with the employee. Discussing critical incidents helps make the evaluation process more specific and objective. One problem encountered with the critical incident method is that

---

[12] Ibid., p. 510.

the supervisor might not have been around when the employee did something "critically good." (Other evaluation methods are not exempt from this problem.) Following are three critical incidents for evaluating a maintenance technician. The last one relates to "very ineffective" critical behavior.

> Returns injection molding machine to full operation within 60 minutes after breakdown.
>
> Notifies management of potentially hazardous condition with any machine for which he or she is responsible.
>
> Gets into arguments with operating employees over the causes of machine failure.

SUMMARY OF KEY POINTS

☐ The first-level supervisor has direct responsibility for training and evaluating employees. After employees have completed training conducted by staff specialists, they usually require some additional on-the-job training. After a system of employee appraisal has been developed or selected by the personnel department, it is still the supervisor who actually evaluates employees.

☐ Although personnel specialists assist in orienting new employees, the supervisor has considerable responsibility in this area. A checklist is helpful for the supervisor to use in carrying out the orientation process. Making the employee feel at home is part of orientation.

☐ An important part of training new employees is to encourage them to practice good work habits. Among the good habits or practices to encourage are: good housekeeping, punctuality and good attendance, work efficiency, quality, ethics and integrity, working at a steady pace, minimize schmoozing.

☐ Principles of learning provide helpful guidelines for training employees. Some of these principles are: (1) Training is a joint effort between superior and subordinate. (2) The trainee learns best by doing. (3) Feedback is essential. (4) Correct responses should be reinforced immediately. (5) Learning should be meaningful. (6) Trainees should learn at their own pace. (7) Guided practice in a variety of settings is helpful. (8) The trainer must create a climate of trust and acceptance.

☐ Four training errors to avoid are: feeding the trainee too much information at one time; talking without showing; impatience; making the trainee tense.

☐ Coaching by the supervisor is an important supplement to training. As a coach, the supervisor gently confronts employees with their mistakes and makes suggestions for corrective action. In addition, the supervisor encourages good performance.

☐ Performance appraisal is a formal way of recording and documenting job performance of employees. If properly conducted, a performance appraisal can motivate an employee and help that individual develop. A simplified approach to employee development is recommended here. It emphasizes the supervisor and subordinate jointly discuss how the employee is doing and what improvements can be made for the future. A discussion of self-improvement and self-development should be part of the appraisal process.

☐ The critical incident method of employee evaluation is used to evaluate employees on the basis of how well they performed on certain "make or break" factors within their jobs. These factors are derived from a list of very effective and very ineffective behaviors related to that particular job.

GUIDELINES FOR SUPERVISORY PRACTICE

1. Training new employees continues to be an important part of a supervisor's job since turnover and transfer rates are high in many work organizations. Also, when new work methods are introduced, employees will require retraining. It is therefore advisable for you to improve your skills as a trainer.

2. As a supervisor you can make a significant impact on reducing early turnover by properly orienting employees. It is important to teach them new job skills and also to make them feel at home in your department.

3. Properly evaluating your employees can help them improve by identifying their needs for improvement. It can also help the organization by providing accurate information for transferring and promoting employees.

QUESTIONS FOR DISCUSSION AND REVIEW

1. How would modeling or imitation be used in teaching employees job skills?

2. Why not use "sink or swim" as a method of on-the-job training?

3. Think of the last time you were trained by a supervisor. What was right and what was wrong with the training you received?

4. What suggestions would you have for improving employee orientation programs?

5. What items might you add to the supervisor's orientation checklist shown in Figure 14–1?

6. In some college cafeterias students leave dining tables in a littered condition. What kind of student training program would you recommend to help with this problem?

7. What are some of the risks involved for supervisors when they try to encourage high ethics and integrity among their employees?

8. What should supervisors do when they conclude that an employee is not bright enough to learn the skills required for an assigned job?

9. Think of the time you learned to drive a car. Which of the principles of learning described in this chapter were followed? Which were violated?

10. What do you see as the advantages and disadvantages of a performance appraisal system in which *employees* are evaluated by peers?

11. What do you see as the advantages and disadvantages of a performance appraisal system in which *supervisors* are evaluated by peers?

A supervisory problem: "Fair" can be a fighting word

"We've been discussing your performance for 30 minutes now," said Maggie to Brenda, one of the secretaries in the word processing department. "As your supervisor, it's my obligation to make sure that you understand what I am saying. Let me summarize the results of your performance appraisal."

"Fine with me," replied Brenda, "What I've heard so far sounds pretty good."

"Overall, we rate your performance above average," stated Maggie. "You are a good performer and you do high quality work. We certainly are glad to have you here at Plattsburg General Hospital. As agreed, you could put a little more effort into taking courses that would give you some more knowledge of business skills."

"Yes, Maggie, I'll agree to that," answered Brenda. "But what about my chances of getting ahead? You know, becoming a supervisor or an administrative assistant."

"Brenda, I think that's where you fall down a little," Maggie emphasized. "Ms. Smathers, the office manager, and I both agree that your potential is fair, but not outstanding. It seems that you have a long way to go before you are eligible for a promotion. You just don't seem ready for more responsibility at this point in your career."

"Now wait a minute," said Brenda. "You are the boss, and your opinion is important. But I think I'm plenty ready for promotion. Given a chance, I could handle any assignment that would be expected of a supervisor in the word processing section."

Maggie urged soothingly, "Brenda, don't get upset. What I'm referring to is that you need more polish. More finesse. You're still not mature enough in your actions to be a supervisor or administrative assistant. Let's talk about your chances for promotion again in a year or so."

"Sorry Maggie," replied Brenda, "I'm not buying what you're telling me. I want some specifics about why you think my potential for more responsibility is only fair."

1. *How should Maggie handle Brenda's last request?*
2. *What criticisms can you make of the way Maggie has conducted the portion of the performance appraisal session described here?*
3. *What comments might you have about the way in which Brenda has reacted to the appraisal of her potential?*

SOME SUGGESTED READING

Bell, Chip R. "Informal Learning in Organizations." *Personnel Journal*, June 1977, pp. 280–83, 313.

Byham, William C., and Robinson, James. "Building Supervisory Confidence—A Key to Transfer of Training." *Personnel Journal*, May 1977, pp. 248–50.

Fisher, Delbert W. "Educational Psychology Involved in On-the-Job Training." *Personnel Journal*, October 1977, pp. 516–19.

Goldstein, Arnold P., and Sorcher, Melvin. *Changing Supervisor Behavior* Elmsford, N.Y.: Pergamon, 1974.

Kearney, William J. "The Value of Behaviorally Based Performance Appraisals." *Business Horizons*, June 1976, pp. 75–83.

Kellogg, Marion S. *What to Do about Performance Appraisal.* New York: AMACOM, 1975.

McCormick, James H. "An Old Standby that Still Works." *Training and Development Journal*, October 1971, pp. 3–7.

McGregor, Douglas. "An Uneasy Look at Performance Appraisal." *Harvard Business Review*, May–June 1965, pp. 89–94.

Maier, Norman R. F. *The Appraisal Interview: Three Basic Approaches.* La Jolla, Calif.: University Associates, 1976.

Meyer, Herbert H. "The Annual Performance Review Discussion—Making It Constructive." *Personnel Journal*, October 1977, pp. 508–11.

Oberg, Winston. "Making Performance Appraisal Relevant." *Harvard Business Review*, January–February 1972, pp. 61–67.

Smith, Howard P., and Brouwer, Paul. *Performance Appraisal and Human Development*. Reading, Mass.: Addison-Wesley, 1977.

Utgaard, Stuart B., and Davis, Rene V. "The Most Frequently Used Training Techniques." *Training and Development Journal*, February 1970, pp. 40–43.

Zawacki, Robert, and Taylor, Robert. "A View of Performance Appraisal from Organizations Using It." *Personnel Journal*, June 1976, pp. 290–92, 299.

part
five

Special challenges
and demands

Selection of employees and supervisors

LEARNING OBJECTIVES

After reading and thinking through the material in this chapter, you should be able to:

1. Understand the basics of employee and supervisory selection.
2. Discuss briefly at least five different tools used in the selection of employees and supervisors.
3. Have enough information in mind to begin practicing the art of employment interviewing.
4. Know how to conduct yourself when being interviewed for a job.
5. Describe the basic nature of tests of (a) job knowledge, (b) special abilities, (c) mental ability, (d) personality, and (e) vocational interests.

As a potential supervisor you may someday be evaluated for a supervisory position.

As a practicing supervisor, you are (or might be) involved in selecting employees for jobs within your department.

You are planning to climb the organizational ladder. It is therefore foreseeable that in the future you will be evaluated as a candidate for a middle management position.

If any of these three previous statements apply to you, it is to your advantage to know something about the complex process of selecting people for jobs. In this chapter we briefly examine several basic selection tools. If you need or want to know more about personnel selection, consult the references listed under

Some Suggested Reading at the end of the chapter. Our focus is on the selection of employees and supervisors. The same general principles also apply to the selection of people for higher level management positions.

JOB APPLICATION FORMS

Job application forms remain an indispensable part of the selection process. A job candidate's completed form provides basic information about a person's schooling, job experiences, citizenship, special skills, and the like. Because of fair employment legislation, most companies no longer ask questions about a person's age, religion, sex, or race. A job application form used by an internationally prominent company is shown in Figure 15–1.

In addition to providing biographical information used for record keeping, the application blank also provides some information supposed to be related to job success. Some employers arrive at conclusions about your intelligence and ability to organize your thoughts on the basis of how you answer the questions. It is therefore to your advantage to complete job application forms as neatly, accurately, and completely as possible in the time alloted. One young man applied for a job at the service department of a large automobile dealership. His answer to the question, "What type of job do you want?" was "I'm not particular." The office supervisor immediately rejected his application.

Weighted application forms. The questions on some application forms are related to job success on the basis of statistical analysis. In one company, for example, it was found that 85 percent of applicants for production work who dropped out of high school before age 17 proved to be unsatisfactory employees. It should not be concluded, however, that this same fact would be true for all types of beginning jobs in all types of companies.

To be hired, a job applicant must achieve a certain minimum total score on the weighted application form. The total score is a composite of a series of items which are directly related to job success or failure.[1] Some scoring keys are based on negative indi-

---

[1] A concise summary of the use of weighted application forms is presented in Duane P. Schultz, *Psychology and Industry Today,* 2d ed. (New York: The Macmillan Co., 1978), pp. 90–91.

FIGURE 15–1
A sample job application form

APPLICATION FOR EMPLOYMENT

COMPANY   An Equal Opportunity Employer—M/F

PLEASE PRINT CLEARLY

Name (Last)	(First)	(Middle)	Social Security Number	Date of Application

Address (No. and Street)	(City)	(State)	(Zip Code)	Area Code	Tel. No.

If You Have Ever Been Employed or Attended School Under Another Name, Please Provide That Name in This Space.

PERSONAL DATA

Are You at Least 18 Years of Age ?   ☐ Yes ☐ No

Can You Work Any Shift?   ☐ Yes ☐ No

Would You Accept:
☐ Part-time employment
☐ Full-time employment
☐ Temporary employment
☐ Permanent employment

Are You a Citizen of the U.S.?   ☐ Yes ☐ No
If No:
Have You the Legal Right To Remain Permanently in the U.S.?   ☐ Yes ☐ No

What Kind of Work Do You Prefer?
1st Choice   2nd Choice

Have You Ever Worked For __Co?__   Which Plant or Division?   Date From   To

U.S. Military Service   Branch _____   Date From _____ To _____   Was Discharge Dishonorable? ☐ Yes ☐ No

Military Specialty _____

EDUCATION

	School	Name	City, Town And State	Years	Subjects of Specialization	Date Graduated	Degree
	Elementary	(Circle Highest Grade Completed)	3 4 5 6 7 8				
	High School						
	College						
	Business or Trade School						
	Night or Other						

PREVIOUS EMPLOYMENT (Give Full Details)

List All Employers in Order Starting with Present One

Name	Address and Telephone No.	Dates From	To	Kind of Work	Wages	Reason For Leaving

REFERENCES (Other Than Relatives)

Name	Address	Business or Occupation

Any Relatives Working for Company?

Name	Relationship	Plant

FILE

NAME

I hereby authorize _____ to conduct any investigations considered necessary for my employment.

SIGNATURE _____

cators. Three examples: You are a high school drop out; You changed employers more than three times in one year; You have no permanent address.

An important word of caution: Questions on the weighted application and total scores on the application must be related to success on the job, according to the Equal Employment Opportunity Commission (EEOC) guidelines. The same principle holds true for all other selection methods, including tests, interviews, and reference checks. In addition, the content of the questions should be job related. For instance it might be true that people without a permanent address are unstable and therefore poor employees. But to be within the spirit of the Civil Rights Act, that lack of a permanent address must be job related. Such a fact would be difficult to prove unless the employee were required to perform part of the job at home.

JOB INTERVIEWS

Interviews, similar to application forms, are universally used methods of employee selection. Although many scientific studies have shown that the interview is not a very accurate method of predicting actual job behavior, it remains indispensable. The interview allows for a give and take between the two parties, which is possible with no other selection device. Interviews also have a human quality. They avoid the impersonality of an organization hiring an individual without the benefit of a face-to-face meeting.

Screening versus evaluation interviews. Early in the selection process—usually right after the job candidate has completed the application blank—a brief screening interview is conducted. The supervisor or a personnel worker spends 15 minutes asking "knock-out" questions. Answering key questions in a certain way immediately disqualifies the applicant. Three such knock-out questions are these:

Are you willing to work nights? (The job under consideration is a night job.)

Do you wear glasses? (The job under consideration is for a company pilot. Government regulations require that company pilots have 20–20, uncorrected vision.)

Can you type? (The job in question is for a typist.)

An evaluation interview attempts to make a careful assessment of the candidate's qualifications for the job. It usually occurs as a final stage in the selection process. Evaluation interviews usually last from 30 to 90 minutes. The balance of this section of the chapter deals with the evaluation interview.[2]

Content of the employment interview

Most job interviewers ask similar questions. An interviewing expert, Felix M. Lopez, says that the applicant's past history, education, work experience, and personal qualifications form the basic content of the job interview.[3]

Personal qualities. Hundreds of personal traits and characteristics might be gleaned from observing the candidate's actions during an interview. Training and experience in interviewing are important to avoid the trap of reaching unjustified conclusions about a candidate's personal qualities. You should focus on personal qualities required for the position such as physical appearance, grooming, verbal skills, poise, and assertiveness. For instance if an applicant is so shy that he or she won't ask any questions or voice a personal opinion, you might conclude that the applicant is nonassertive.

Achievement in school. By discussing achievement in school, you can sometimes reach conclusions about how diligently the individual works and gain information about natural preferences. If a woman applies for a position as a mechanic's helper and has taken several shop courses, you might conclude that she has a genuine interest in mechanics.

Work experience. Here you might be able to assess such factors as technical skills, progression in responsibility, and reasons for leaving former jobs. Specific questions can help pinpoint whether or not the person has genuine knowledge about a job-related topic. One such probing question might be, "Tell me,

---

[2] Larry A. Pace and Lyle F. Schoenfeldt, "Legal Concerns in the Use of Weighted Applications," *Personnel Psychology,* Summer 1977, pp. 159–66.

[3] Felix M. Lopez, "The Employment Interview," in *Handbook of Modern Personnel Administration,* ed.-in-chief, Joseph J. Famularo (New York: McGraw-Hill, 1972), chap. 13, pp. 4–5.

what is the biggest problem you have encountered in using plastic instead of metal nuts and bolts?"

Skills in dealing with people.   Observations can be made of how well the candidate relates to you. Is the candidate polite, friendly, courteous, resentful, angry, crude, shy, and so forth? Lopez observes that specific questions must be asked about the applicant's "family history, leisure-time activities, hobbies, and community interests to ascertain his or her social adjustment."[4]

Career and work orientation.   For jobs with growth potential, it is helpful to know if the applicant is the kind of person who is looking for growth. Questions here should include those about short- and long-range goals and attitudes toward work. Questions of this nature might help determine whether or not the candidate is "serious" about work.

Suggestions for conducting the interview

A skilled interviewer carefully follows a plan that lists questions to be asked. In addition, interviewers take careful notes during the interview. Interview forms usually include questions about the type of information mentioned in the previous section under content of the interview. Your personnel department will often have such an interview form available. Following is a list of several specific suggestions to keep in mind when conducting an employment interview:

Prepare in advance.   Adequate preparation includes reviewing the completed application form and preparing a few questions based on that information. For instance, "How come you are looking for work as either a file clerk or a sales representative?"

Find a secluded place, free from interruptions.   The ideal, and only truly acceptable, place to conduct a job interview is in the privacy of an office or conference room. A supervisor frequently lacks such a luxury. If you conduct an interview behind an office partition, place an "interview in progress" sign outside your partition. Many supervisors borrow an office for purposes of conducting a selection or employee appraisal interview.

Use a brief warm-up period.   To relax a candidate and estab-

---

[4] Ibid., p. 5.

lish rapport, it is helpful to spend a few minutes talking about nonjob-related topics such as sports, the candidate's trip to the office or plant, or high school attended. After a few minutes of warm-up, move gradually into more job-related questions, such as, "What is your present job?"

Ask open-ended questions. A standard approach of getting the candidate to talk is to ask questions that do not call for one- or two-word answers. Suppose you want a candidate to talk about the reason for leaving a previous job. A recommended question would be, "Why did you leave your last job?" A less-effective question would be, "Did you leave your last job because you were dissatisfied?" It would be easy for the candidate to answer a yes or no to the latter question, thus providing very little information.

Use a few broad, general questions. Another effective way of keeping the interviewee talking (and thus revealing much important information) is to ask general (or vague) questions. Three examples are: "Tell me about your days in high school." "What kinds of jobs have you enjoyed the most?" or "What kind of work makes you happy?" People reveal a lot about themselves when they are faced with ill-defined questions.

Dig for additional details. As a follow-up to asking broad questions, it is often necessary to probe for more specific information on a particular topic. Digging for details in this manner is also called *narrowing.* Here is how it works in practice:[5]

Supervisor: What kind of jobs do you prefer?

Candidate: I like jobs with lots of pressure.

Supervisor: What appeals to you about pressure?

Candidate: Pressure keeps you busy. It's much easier to keep busy when there is a lot to do and you have a deadline to meet.

Supervisor: What do you do when you have to set your own deadlines?

Candidate: I'm only human. I tend to dog it a little bit unless my boss keeps me busy.

Spend most of the time listening. An effective interviewer spends most of the interview time listening to the person being interviewed. It is characteristic of inexperienced interviewers to talk as much or more than the interviewee. When an inevitable

---

[5] This example is based on Andrew J. DuBrin, *The Practice of Managerial Psychology* (Elmsford, N.Y.: Pergamon, 1972), pp. 42–43.

pause takes place in the interview, do not jump in with a comment or question. Let the interviewee be responsible for saying something of importance or asking a question. Silence on the part of the interviewer can be a valuable tool in learning about the candidate.

Provide the candidate information about the organization. At the beginning or end of the interview, give the candidate details about the job, department, and company that might not have been provided by the personnel department. Similarly, it is helpful to answer any questions the candidate might have about the job, department, company, or even *you.* One successful job candidate had the courage to ask a prospective supervisor, "What kind of a boss are you?" (The supervisor replied, "Ornery as a polecat when an employee of mine goofs off.")

Have a wrap up. When the interview is about 85 percent completed with respect to elapsed time, the interviewer begins to bring it to a close.[6] By this time the interviewer has a good overview of the candidate's strengths and weaknesses for the position. The interviewer should summarize with a brief discussion of what has been discussed during the interview. The candidate should also be encouraged to ask questions during the wrap-up.

Since most hiring decisions are group decisions, the supervisor should not give the candidate a yes or no answer. The supervisor should tell the candidate what will happen next: where to go next and when the company will be in touch.

How to handle yourself when being interviewed

At some point in your career, you will probably be on the receiving end of a selection interview. Even if you stay with the same employer for the balance of your working career, you might be interviewed for an internal promotion or transfer. Some of the suggestions made for conducting an interview can simply be turned around. As a case in point, while the interviewer is trying to relax you, find ways of relaxing yourself. You might exhale or make a deliberate effort to loosen your muscles. (See the discussion in Chapter 20 about coping with job-related

---

[6] Lopez, "Employment Interview," p. 7.

tensions.) The following suggestions are designed to get you successfully through the job interview and are particularly important.[7]

1.   Do your homework. Be familiar with pertinent details about your background and work experiences, including the names of references. Knowledge of the major activities or business of your prospective employer is also helpful.

2.   Have reasons to justify your plans. If you are trying to make the jump from individual worker to supervisor, explain why a supervisory job appeals to you. For instance, "I welcome the challenge of teaching employees how to do things right."

3.   Focus on important aspects of the job, not upon its trivial elements. Job candidates unfamiliar with being interviewed often relieve their anxiety by asking questions about noncontroversial topics such as working hours, frequency of getting paid, and cafeteria facilities. All of these considerations may be important to you, but discuss them after the basic issue of the nature of the job has been discussed.

4.   Do not be overly concerned about hidden meanings behind questions. Often the person conducting the interview does not have any particular rationale behind the question asked. Unless your responses to these so-called "trick questions" are way out of line, much of what you say goes unrecorded. One such "off-the-wall" question is, "If you had to choose one, what type of animal would you like to be?"

5.   Be prepared for a frank discussion of your strengths and weaknesses. It is worthwhile to prepare in advance for this almost inevitable question. Contending that you have no weaknesses or areas for improvement would make you appear either defensive or uninsightful.

6.   Allow the interviewer to talk. Do not feel impelled to fill every free second of the interview with your own commentary. Many employment specialists and other interviewers like to make comments during an interview. They also need time to provide you information about the company and job. Exercise your intuition to determine when the interviewer is through talking and wants you to carry the conversation.

---

[7] Several of these suggestions are based on Andrew J. DuBrin, *Survival in the Office* (New York: Van Nostrand Reinhold, 1977), chap. 16.

7. Answer every question in as nondefensive and straight-forward manner as possible. An interview is supposed to sample the kind of behavior you will exhibit on the job. Most employers would prefer to hire an individual who can be placed under mild pressure without becoming defensive or upset.

8. Ask a few intelligent questions. A rule of thumb is to ask only questions of real interest to you (in order to avoid appearing insincere). Following are five questions of the type that will usually meet with good reception in an employment interview. Ask them during pauses or when asked if you have any questions:

> If hired, what would I actually be doing?
>
> What kind of advancement opportunities are there in your company for outstanding performers?
>
> What is the company's attitude toward people who make constructive suggestions?
>
> What do I have to accomplish to be considered a success on this job?
>
> Is there anything I've said so far that requires further explanation?

9. Show how you can help them. A major job-getting strategy is to explain to a propsective employer what you think you can do to help the company. It is a much more effective strategy than trying to sell the prospective employer on your good qualities and characteristics. If you were applying for the job of a supervisor in a department that you knew had a high scrap rate, you might try this thrust: "Here is what I would do to reduce scrap if I were the supervisor: . . . I've used this approach with success in the past."

REFERENCE CHECKING

Any employer skilled in selection techniques uses reference checks to verify basic information on your application blank and obtain opinions on your past work performance.[8] Misrepresenting yourself on the application blank, or in the job interview, usually automatically disqualifies you from the job in question.

---

[8] An excellent discussion of reference checking is found in Clemm C. Kessler, III, and Georgia J. Gibbs, "Getting the Most from Application Blanks and References," *Personnel*, January–February 1975, pp. 53–62.

Today, workers can legally demand to see most personnel records unless they sign a waiver. Past employers are thus hesitant to make any strongly negative or potentially libelous statements about an individual. If you are the person doing the reference checking, it is therefore best to obtain references over the phone. Here are two questions helpful in learning something about the weak points of a job candidate:

Okay, it's good to know that _____ was a fine employee. Please tell me about any problems you had with _____.

Nobody is perfect. How could _____ have been an even better employee?

SELECTION TESTS OF JOB KNOWLEDGE AND SPECIAL ABILITIES

The basic purpose of selection tests is to predict how well a given individual will perform on the job under consideration. Thousands of tests have been developed for this purpose. When a test does its intended job of predicting future behavior, it does so because it is an accurate sample of that behavior. Thus a person who scores high on a test of blueprint reading should in fact be good at reading blueprints.

Specialists in the development of employment tests (generally personnel psychologists) have always contended that only those tests should be used whose merit can be statistically demonstrated. Since 1964, much legislation has passed in support of this idea. A fair test according to the EEOC meets three important standards:[9]

It does not discriminate against individuals because of their race, color, religion, sex, or national origin.

It can be shown statistically that people who score highly on the test perform highly on the job. Also, people who score low on the test, in general, score low on the job.

The test is job-related. For example, if the test measures energy, energy should be a factor in job success.

To begin our sampling of selection tests, we will discuss four types of tests that meet with the least controversy. Few people

---

[9] A current summary of this topic is "Uniform Guidelines on Employee Selection Procedures," *Federal Register*, December 30, 1977, pt. 8.

would deny their relevance to job performance. They include work sample tests, achievement tests, tests of mechanical aptitude, and tests of psychomotor ability.[10]

Work sample tests. As its name implies, a work (or job sample) test requires that the individual perform some of the operations of the job applied for. Usually actual job equipment is used, but if the equipment is particularly expensive or hazardous, simulated equipment might be used. A scoring scheme is worked out which includes minimum passing scores.

Work sample tests have been devised for such operations as driving a truck. Candidates are required to maneuver around a small course without striking rubber markers. The U.S. Army Quartermaster Corps at one time had a similar test for measuring skill in driving a forklift truck. Candidates for welding jobs are sometimes required to weld, and a scoring scheme is applied to the finished product. Typing tests are also considered work sample tests.

Achievement tests. Tests of this nature are similar to classroom tests that measure knowledge of a subject. The tests can be written or oral. To qualify as a selection device, the test must be scientifically developed. Civil service exams that people take to qualify for promotion are usually achievement tests. So are the tests used to qualify a person as a certified public accountant (CPA).

Mechanical aptitude tests. Much machinery used in offices and plants can be operated by simply pushing a button or flipping a switch. Yet hundreds of jobs still call for mechanical know-how. Tests of mechanical aptitude or ability thus continue to play an important part in screening of candidates. Tests of this nature ask questions that cannot be answered by intelligence alone. To score high you need both mechanical know-how and, quite often, mechanical experience. Many people of high general intelligence score poorly on tests of mechanical aptitude. These are the same people who often are unable to change a flat

---

[10] Our discussion is based on Ernest J. McCormick and Joseph Tiffin, *Industrial Psychology*, 6th ed. (Englewood Cliffs, N.J.: Prentice-Hall, 1974), chap. 6.

tire. Here is an example of the type of question you would find on a test of mechanical aptitude:

> In order to get the maximum power from an ordinary hammer, hold the handle:
>   a. Close to the hammer head.
>   b. Right in the middle.
>   c. Down by the bottom.

Psychomotor ability tests.   Eye-hand coordination, dexterity, manipulative ability, and the like are important in a wide variety of jobs. Outstanding baseball, golf, and tennis players often are people who are gifted in eye-hand coordination. So are outstanding tool and die markers and model makers. The components of psychomotor ability include:

Control precision: Tasks requiring finely controlled muscular adjustments, such as moving a gauge to a precise setting.

Manual dexterity: Tasks involving skillful arm and hand movements in manipulating large objects under conditions of speed. Many assembly-line jobs require good manual dexterity.

Reaction time: The ability to respond to a signal. Fast reaction times are required for truck drivers and process control technicians, among many other workers.

Among the tests of psychomotor ability are those that require the individual to insert pegs in holes or pass a rod through a ring without making contact with the ring. (The popular saying about "being a round peg in a square hole" may have stemmed from observations about a psychomotor test.)

Tests of mental ability

Intelligence, or problem-solving ability, is one of the major differences among people that affects job performance. As commonsense would suggest, there is an advantage to being bright in performing a complex job. If a job is unusually simple—such as stuffing envelopes seven hours per day—not being so bright would be an advantage. Intelligence quotient, or IQ, is in reality just one measure of intelligence, just as classifying a person as having superior intelligence is a measure of intelligence.

Intelligence is not a pure characteristic. It includes a variety of specialized aptitudes contributing to problem-solving ability. Among the known components of intelligence are verbal, numerical ability, and inductive reasoning ability. Inductive reasoning would be required when a supervisor has to figure out the solution to a problem for which a prescribed solution does not exist. For instance, figuring out why a particular machine has stopped when nothing is apparently wrong.

A few sample test items. Most readers of this book have taken mental ability tests at various stages of schooling or in the process of applying for a job. For review, below are three sample test items of the type that appear on a standardized mental ability test used by employers. Question *A* measures verbal comprehension; question *B* measures numerical comprehension; question *C* measures inductive reasoning.

A. A cautious person is:
1. Wealthy.
2. Careful.
3. Ignorant.
4. Satisfied. .... ( )

B. In the following series, which two numbers should come next?
16 18 17 20 18 22
1. 19 and 24
2. 23 and 27
3. 19 and 23
4. 25 and 26 .... ( )

C. Read the three statements below:
A is lighter than D.
B is heavier than D.
A weighs more than C.
Who is heaviest? .... ( )

Tests of personality and interest

Personality and interests are more difficult to measure by means of tests than are job skills or mental ability. Yet, they are very important on the job. Most failures on the job are not attributed to a person's amount of intelligence or technical ability— but to personality characteristics or interests. When your job involves dealing with people, your personality and interests play a particularly important role. If a supervisor is overly abrasive (personality) and dislikes people (interest), that supervisor will probably be a poor performer.

Personality tests. Hundreds of tests of many different types are available for measuring personality. In a work organization paper and pencil tests are generally used. In a counseling center you might also see tests such as the Rorschach inkblot method, or those requiring you to write stories about a photograph presented you. Here is one example of a personality test item:

	Mostly agree	*Mostly disagree*
I become impatient when I have to wait on a long line.	_____	_____

A wide variety of personality characteristics could have a bearing on supervisory effectiveness. In Figure 15–2 we present a

FIGURE 15–2
Personality traits and their optimum quantity for supervisory effectiveness

Trait measured by personality test	*Desirable score for most supervisory positions*
Emotional stability	High
Intraversion-extraversion	High extraversion
Energy	High
Initiative	High
Self-confidence	High
Suspiciousness	Low
Poise...............................	High
Dominance	Medium to high
Responsibility	High
Self-control	High
Flexibility	High
Psychological mindedness	Medium
Need for acceptance	Medium

representative list of 13 personality traits, characteristics (or dimensions) that are measured by standardized tests of personality. Adjacent to each personality dimension is a tentative notation of the amount of that trait, characteristic, or dimension desirable in *most supervisory jobs.* To illustrate, in most supervisory jobs it would be important to display initiative. But in some companies, initiative on the part of supervisors is discouraged; they are supposed to follow rules strictly.

Vocational interests tests.   If you are performing work in line with your interests, you are usually more productive and satisfied. Tests that measure a person's interests in comparison to other people performing the same kind of work thus have a place in job selection. The following anecdote illustrates how holding a job not in line with your interests can lead to dissatisfaction:

> An industrial psychologist was providing a tool and die maker an interpretation of the latter's interest test. The tool and die maker had recently taken the test as part of a program in career counseling. The psychologist told him that his test profile reflected very low interest in the mechanical, science, and mathematical scales—a very unusual pattern for a tool and die maker. In contrast, he showed dominant interests in much more socially oriented occupations such as public speaking, social service, and teaching.
>
> With a burst of emotion, the tool and die maker exclaimed, ''That's it. You've hit it. I've hated being a tool and die maker all my life. I'll never forget the first day of my apprenticeship. As my first project, I was forced to file a metal cube. The sound made me sick. It's been a lifetime of agony. I hate coming to work but tool and die making is all I know.''

Interest tests generally require you to indicate the strength of your interests in such things as various jobs, recreational ac-

FIGURE 15–3
Sample interest test item*

1.	Actor	L	I	D
2.	Aviator	L	I	D
3.	Architect	L	I	D
4.	Astronomer	L	I	D
5.	Athletic director	L	I	D
6.	Auctioneer....................	L	I	D
7.	Author of novel	L	I	D
8.	Author of scientific book	L	I	D
9.	Auto sales representative	L	I	D
10.	Auto mechanic.................	L	I	D

* This shows the type of test items found on the Strong Vocational Interest Blank, a widely used interest test. In this section of the test, the subject indicates whether he or she would like (L), dislike (D), or be indifferent to (I) working in each occupation.

tivities, or hobbies. You might be presented three activities and asked to indicate which activity you like, and which one you dislike the most. A simpler approach is to ask you the extent to which you like or dislike the activity in questions. Representative interest test items are shown in Figures 15–3 and 15–4.

FIGURE 15–4
Sample interest test item*

		Most		Least
A.	Read a romantic story	_____	A.	_____
B.	Read a murder mystery	_____	B.	_____
C.	Read a science fiction story	_____	C.	_____
D.	Repair a broken bicycle	_____	D.	_____
E.	Cook a fine dinner	_____	E.	_____
F.	Refinish a piece of furniture	_____	F.	_____

* This shows the type of test items found on the Kuder Preference Record, another widely used interest test. The person taking the test is asked to indicate for each set of three activities the one he or she would most and least like to do.

Interest areas. One common feature of the scoring of interest tests is that they provide you with a rating or score on a number of basic interest scales. It is considered favorable when a job applicant has interests somewhat in line with experienced people in that type of job. The Strong Vocational Interest Blank (one of the most widely used interest inventories) has 21 basic scales, as follows:

Public speaking	Technical supervision	Medical service
Law/Politics	Mathematics	Social service
Business management	Science	Religious activities
Sales	Mechanical	Teaching
Merchandising	Nature	Music
Office practices	Agriculture	Art
Military activities	Recreational leadership	Writing

It would not be unusual for a manufacturing supervisor to score high on such scales as business management, technical supervision, mechanical, and teaching. However, the interpretation of interest tests is a complex, technical subject.

ASSESSMENT CENTERS

A comprehensive method of selecting people for supervisory and managerial positions is an assessment center evaluation.[11] (It should be noted that assessment centers are used more frequently for purposes of identifying the needs of individuals for training and development.) Some large organizations, such as Exxon and A.T.T., have assessment centers of their own. Many other organizations send job candidates to assessment centers serving a large number of organizations.

The evaluation taking place in an assessment center is based on a variety of information. Among the methods of assessment used are psychological tests, depth interviews with psychologists, interviews by personnel specialists and managers from other departments, small group problem-solving exercises, and in-basket tests.

While you are solving the problems placed in your in-basket, a group of trained observers judge your performance. Similar observations are made of your performance when placed in a problem-solving situation with five or six other job candidates. In one assessment center exercise, you are asked to handle this problem:

> You five people are office supervisors. All members of upper management are away on a management conference. Your responsibility is to make a tight deadline on a shipment. If you are late on this order, your firm will lose $100,000 in penalties. You are a nonunion organization. An employee, who claims he is the spokesperson for all the factory employees, comes to you with an urgent message: "Either we all get a $50 bonus, or we all walk off the job this evening." Take appropriate action.

Psychological evaluation. As part of the assessment center proceedings, a psychological evaluation of the job candidate is prepared. The evaluation is based on a combination of interview and test findings. Sometimes the report is filed separately, or its findings are incorporated into the assessment center report. A sample psychological evaluation of a supervisory candidate is presented in Figure 15–5.

---

[11] An illuminating description of the assessment center method is found in Douglas W. Bray, Richard J. Campbell, and Donald L. Grant, *Formative Years in Business* (New York: Wiley-Interscience, 1974), chap. 3.

FIGURE 15–5
A sample psychological evaluation for a supervisory candidate

```
                    PSYCHOLOGICAL EVALUATION


Name:  Gregory A. Falls                           Age: 25

Position:  Accounting Supervisor
           Home Office
           Metropolitan Corporation



Intellectual Functioning

He scores at the 15th percentile in intellectual ability among
a comparison group of managers.  His verbal score is at the
10th percentile and his numerical score at the 40th percentile.
His poor scores on these tests may reflect discomfort in
working under pressure.  His academic record, however, would
also suggest mediocre problem solving ability.  He shows satis-
factory communication skills both in speaking and writing.
Despite his accounting background, he dislikes paying close
attention to minute detail.  He is slow in coming to grips with
ambiguous problems.

Emotional Control and Stability

He has an average degree of psychological maturity.  He is a
relaxed individual with an apparently uncomplicated personality
make-up.  He is rarely tense or impatient and claims to have no
particular worries or concerns.  He displays a normal amount
of defensiveness when criticized.  He may respond to pressure
conditions by slowing down his work pace.  He is more lethargic
than enthusiastic in outward manner.  He is not a particularly
self-confident or self-assured person.

Motivation, Drive, and Ambition

He has manifested an average level of drive and ambition so far
in his career.  He is looking to enlarge his job opportunities.
He expresses an interest in becoming a small company controller
in about five years.  So far he has not established a pattern
of high success.  He appears to manage his personal and financial
life in a competent manner.  He is beginning to show signs of
more competitiveness than he displayed earlier in life.  He has
intense recreational interests that supplement his job interests.
```

PEER RATINGS

Another method of evaluating people for supervisory positions is to have them rated by co-workers who are familiar with their work. Such a procedure may sound highly subjective and laced with office politics. Nevertheless, it has merit. Input from

FIGURE 15-5 (continued)

Interpersonal Skill

He has average ability to relate to other people. His initial
impact is mediocre, but this is more impressive upon further
contact. He is effective in describing incidents and conducting
conversations with people. He does not possess unusually
negative personal characteristics that would detract from his
relating to people. But neither does he possess strong personal
leadership characteristics. He would not be seen by others as
threatening, and in this way could be effective in obtaining
information for making reports.

Insight Into Human Behavior

He has average perceptiveness about himself and other people.
He may miss the point of occasional subtle comments. He is
observant of other people and makes accurate comments about
them. He shows good insight into organizational problems. He
has taken very little constructive action about developing
himself for future managerial work. He perhaps has profited
from on-the-job development.

Leadership Style and Work Habits

He lacks formal supervisory experience except for some directions
giving to a department clerk. He scores at the 54th percentile
in Consideration and the 47th percentile on Structure on a
standardized leadership inventory. These scores suggest that,
as a supervisor, he would show a good balance between concern
for getting tasks accomplished and concern for people. He
appears to have average ability to organize his own work. He
may show occasional signs of carelessness with fine detail work.

Recommendation

He is not recommended for the position in question when psychological characteristics alone are given primary consideration.

Prognosis

Aside from his specialized knowledge and experience, he is
judged to be a mediocre candidate for a specialist or supervisory
position. His problem solving ability and his interpersonal
skills suggest that he will plateau early in his career in a
competitive corporate environment. He may show some weaknesses
in working with minute aspects of problems.

November 16, 19__

co-workers can be highly accurate because they are accustomed
to seeing you perform in instances where you are not trying hard
to impress people.

A realistic application of peer ratings is to use them as supplementary information, in combination with more conventional methods of evaluating people. A person considered for

promotion within a company should be evaluated by multiple approaches, including ratings by superiors, peer ratings, interviews, and tests.

WHAT CHARACTERISTICS SHOULD A CANDIDATE POSSESS?

No absolute answers are available to this important question. People who assess candidates for supervisory positions have different opinions about the characteristics required for success. Professionals in personnel selection also have varying viewpoints. Candidates who possessed most of these characteristics of effective supervisors described in Chapter 1 would usually receive a positive recommendation for a supervisor's job. In addition, they would also need to have appropriate job experience and a favorable reputation.

The characteristics sought after in a candidate for a supervisory position are summarized in Figure 15–6. In addition, the type of selection method or methods appropriate for measuring this aspect of behavior is listed to the right of each dimension.

FIGURE 15–6
Methods of measuring characteristics of effective supervisors

Characteristic of effective supervisor	Potential source of information about characteristic
Sound human relation skills	Interview, interest tests, group exercise, peer ratings reference check
Technical competence	Work sample tests, achievement tests, interview, reference checks, mechanical aptitude tests
Strong work motivation and high energy	Interview, job application form, personality test, reference check, peer ratings
Good problem-solving ability	Mental ability tests, interviews, group exercise, school records, peer ratings
Good work habits	Job application form (neatness), group exercise, reference checks, peer ratings
Ability to size up people and situations	Interviews, reference checks, personality tests, peer ratings
Self-confidence	Interviews, personality tests, group exercise, reference checks, peer ratings

Note: Group exercise refers to observing behavior while person is solving problem in assessment center exercise.

SUMMARY OF KEY POINTS

☐ Selection of employees and supervisors should be done in a systematic manner, using instruments developed by specialists in selection methods, particularly personnel psychologists. This chapter presents only the rudiments of personnel selection.

☐ In addition to providing basic biographical information used for record keeping, the job application form also includes information that could be related to job success. Weighted application blanks are those that are scored in a systematic manner as if they were tests.

☐ A job interview is an indispensable part of the selection process. Once applicants get through a brief screening interview, they qualify for a lengthier evaluation interview. Effective interviews usually follow a pattern. Standard areas of inquiry include: personal qualities, school achievement, work experience, skills in dealing with people, and orientation toward work and career.

☐ Strategies for conducting an employment interview include: Prepare in advance; Find a quiet place, Use a brief warm-up period; As open-ended questions; Use a few broad, general questions; Dig for additional details; Spend most of the time listening; Provide information about the organization; Have a wrap-up.

☐ Suggestions for being interviewed include: Do your homework about the employer; Have reasons to justify your plans; Focus on important aspects of the job; Do not be overly concerned about hidden meanings behind questions; Be nondefensive and straightforward; Ask a few intelligent questions; Show how you can help them.

☐ Reference checks are used as a follow-up to the application form and job interview. They are used to both verify factual information about the candidate (such as jobs held and schools attended) and learn about past job performance and behavior.

☐ Selection tests of job knowledge and special abilities include work sample tests, achievement tests, mechanical aptitude tests, and tests of psychomotor ability.

☐ Mental ability tests measure problem-solving ability or intelligence. At a minimum, intelligence has three components: (1) numerical comprehension, (2) verbal comprehension, and (3) inductive reasoning.

☐ Most on-the-job failures are not attributed to a person's intelligence or technical ability but to personality characteristics and job interests. Personality and interest thus have an important potential contribution in job selection. Interview observations and past behavior are often more accurate predictors of personality and interests than are standardized tests.

☐ The assessment center method is a comprehensive method of selecting people for supervisory and managerial positions. Assessment center evaluations are based on multiple sources of information, including psychological tests, depth interviews, observations of your behavior in small group exercises, and in-basket tests.

☐ Peer ratings (ratings by co-workers) are yet another method of selecting people for transfer or promotion. At best, they serve as supplementary information to other selection methods.

GUIDELINES FOR SUPERVISORY PRACTICE

1. Your input into the selection of employees can be quite valuable to the organization. In general, your evaluation is likely to concentrate on job competence and technical skill. Personnel specialists tend to concentrate their evaluations on general suitability for employment. This does not mean that your observations about the candidate's personal characteristics are not taken into consideration.

2. The most effective way of interviewing a job candidate is to follow a patterned interview which includes questions about important factors related to job performance. Take plentiful notes during the interview. Immediately after conducting the interview you should summarize your findings and observations in writing.

3. Knowing how to be interviewed is an important career skill. Simulated job interviews with friends are a useful way of improving such a skill. All information you provide in an interview should be accurate and capable of verification. Follow the suggestions for being interviewed presented earlier in this chapter.

QUESTIONS FOR DISCUSSION AND REVIEW

1. What about a job candidate's firmness of handshake as a predictor of job success? Or whether or not that candidate looks you square in the eye?

2. Describe any other selection method not mentioned in this chapter which you know is sometimes used by employers.

3. Do you think a person's job resume might be used as a substitute for an application blank? Why or why not?

4. What type of clothing would you wear to a job interview? Why?

5. Should a person smoke a cigar or cigarette during a job interview (assuming that individual were a smoker)? Why or why not?

368

6. One interviewer "accidentally" spills a glass of water on candidates for managerial positions. The interviewer claims that their reaction to the situation provides useful information about their personality. What do you think?

7. Some employment specialists claim that if you have a critical job opening in your department, you cannot be objective in evaluating candidates for that opening. What do you think?

8. Some interviewers begin the interview by saying nothing for the first ten minutes (not even asking a question). What do you think are the pros and cons of this approach?

9. Suppose an interviewer asked you how far you were in debt? What would be your answer?

10. In your opinion which are the three most valid selection tools described in this chapter? Explain.

11. In your opinion which are the three least valid selection tools described in this chapter? Explain.

12. Before the publisher of this book gave me the "job" of writing it, the company made me submit two sample chapters and an outline. What selection tool was he using?

13. Should supervisors be much more intelligent than their subordinates? Why or why not?

14. Do you think reference checking should be declared an illegal selection device? Explain.

A supervisory problem: The bogus engineering technologist

Harry, the supervisor of customer service engineering at the New Orleans branch of the company, received a surprise visit from Dexter, the regional personnel manager. Dexter explained why he was visiting the branch:

Dexter: Harry, I want to talk to you about Pete Flowers, the customer service engineer you hired eight months ago. I guess by now you've had some trouble with him?

Harry: Trouble, Dexter? Absolutely not. The kid has talent for fixing our machinery. It took him about three months to learn the machines he's responsible for inside and out. One of his biggest customers is Louisiana Foods. They swear by Flowers. They had a breakdown in the middle of the canning season. Flowers jumped into the project like he owned Louisiana Foods. I don't think it would be too far out of line to say Flowers is my best troubleshooter. You people in personnel sure helped me find a winner.

Dexter: Harry, that's why I'm down here today. We did a lousy job of selection. Flowers lied about his background when he applied for a job with us. He doesn't have a two-year degree in engineering technology. He's not even a high school graduate. Not only that. He didn't tell us that he's had a lot of trouble with bill collectors. I think we'll have to fire Flowers right away.

Harry: Fire him? I need the guy desperately. Don't even talk to me about taking away my best troubleshooter before you can give me a suitable replacement. Besides, give the kid a chance. He hasn't done us any wrong.

1. *Should Flowers be fired?*
2. *What would you do if you were Harry?*
3. *What mistake do you think the personnel department has made in the handling of this situation?*

SOME SUGGESTED READING

Adler, Seymour. "Using Assessment Centers in Smaller Organizations." *Personnel Journal,* September 1978, pp. 484–87, 516.

Anastasi, Anne. *Psychological Testing.* 4th ed. New York: The Macmillan Co., 1976.

Byham, William C. "Common Selection Problems Can Be Overcome." *The Personnel Administrator,* August 1978, pp. 42–47.

Dyer, Frank J. "An Alternative to Validating Selection Tests." *Personnel Journal,* April 1978, pp. 200–03.

Ebel, Robert L. "Comments on Some Problems of Employment Testing." *Personnel Psychology,* Spring 1977, pp. 55–64.

Famularo, Joseph J., ed.-in-chief. *Handbook of Modern Personnel Administration,* pt. 4. New York: McGraw-Hill, 1972.

Feild, Hubert; Bayley, Gerald A.; and Bayley, Susan. "Employment Test Validation for Minority and Nonminority Production Workers." *Personnel Psychology,* Spring 1977, pp. 37–48.

Grimsley, Glen, and Jarrett, Hilton F. "The Relation of Past Managerial Achievement to Test Measures Obtained in the Employment Situation: Methodology and Results—II." *Personnel Psychology,* Summer 1975, pp. 215–31.

Hinrichs, John R., and Haanpera, Seppo. "Reliability of Measurement in Situational Exercises: An Assessment of the Assessment Center Method." *Personnel Psychology,* Spring 1976, pp. 31–40.

Klimoski, Richard J., and Strickland, William J. "Assessment Centers—Valid or Merely Prescient." *Personnel Psychology,* Autumn 1977, pp. 353–62.

Ledvinka, James, and Schoenfeldt, Lyle F. "Legal Developments in Employment Testing: Albemarle and Beyond." *Personnel Psychology,* Spring 1978, pp. 1–14.

Moses, Joseph L., and Byham, William C., eds. *Applying the Assessment Center Method.* Elmsford, N.Y.: Pergamon, 1977.

Pace, Larry A., and Schoenfeldt, Lyle F. "Legal Concerns in the Use of Weighted Applications." *Personnel Psychology,* Summer 1977, pp. 159–66.

Rice, Berkeley. "Measuring Executive Muscle." *Psychology Today,* December 1978, pp. 94–96, 99, 100, 105–6, 109–10.

Schultz, Duane P. *Psychology and Industry Today.* 2d ed. New York: The Macmillan Co., 1978, chaps. 3, 4.

Wanous, John P. "Realistic Job Previews: Can a Procedure to Reduce Turnover Also Influence the Relationship between Abilities and Performance?" *Personnel Psychology,* Summer 1978, pp. 249–58.

Complying with regulations

LEARNING OBJECTIVES

After reading and working through the material in this chapter, you should be able to:

1. Understand how policies and rules help an organization reach its objectives.
2. Understand why a supervisor frequently has to interpret regulations to employees.
3. Be aware of a systematic plan for enforcing company policies and rules.
4. Avoid common pitfalls in using controls.
5. Know how to comply with cost-cutting measures.
6. Perform the calculations necessary for at least one method of justifying capital expenditures.

THE IMPORTANCE OF REGULATIONS

Imagine what would happen if your family life was conducted without regulations. People might broil steaks in the fire place at three in the morning. Any family member who wanted a material object at anytime would simply dip into the family savings account to obtain the money. A teenage member of the family might convert the family station wagon into a carnival float for the high school parade. A nursery school age child might decide when and if to take a bath.

Ideally, the family members described above would engage in self-regulation. They would choose courses of action that would be beneficial to themselves and to the family as a whole. Ideally, employees could function effectively by self-regulation alone. In practice, employees as well as family members need regulations to guide their actions. Regulations, if used properly, serve as guidelines in directing the effort of personnel toward achieving organizational goals.

A supervisor encounters regulations from several standpoints. Often the supervisor must interpret regulations to employees and see that such regulations are enforced. Equally important, supervisors must obtain a clear interpretation and learn how to comply with regulations for themselves.

DIFFERENT TYPES OF REGULATIONS

The term *regulation,* in general, refers to a rule or order prescribed by authority. Places of work are governed by a variety of regulations. In this book we are concerned primarily with four types of regulations: policies, rules, government laws, and controls.

Policies. A policy is a guide for carrying out action. It provides the basic framework or principles and rules to be used as reference information for making decisions. Policies enable supervisors and other managers to be consistent in making decisions about work-related matters.

Policies can be found to fit all the basic functions of an organization. A retail store might have a policy of standing behind any product they sell. In action, this would mean that the store will happily take back defective merchandise without hassling the customer. A manufacturer might have the following policy about overtime pay:[1]

> Overtime at the rate of time and a half will be paid for all hours in excess of 8 hours per day or 40 hours per week. In computing the hours over 40, paid holidays will be considered as having been worked if they fall within the normal workweek. The overtime premium will be calculated on the rate including applicable shift premiums.

Rules. A rule is a specific course of action or conduct that must be followed.[2] When rules are violated, corrective action

---

[1] Policy of Moore Business Forms, quoted in Maurice O. Beverly, "Establishing Policy," in *Handbook of Business Administration,* ed.-in-chief, H. B. Maynard (New York: McGraw-Hill, 1967), sec. 4, p. 11.

[2] Don Hellriegel and John W. Slocum, Jr., *Management: Contingency Approaches,* 2d ed. (Reading, Mass.: Addison-Wesley, 1978), p. 289.

should be taken, as described in Chapter 13. Here are a few miscellaneous company rules drawn from different companies:

> Any person spitting on the floor is subject to immediate dismissal. (From a newspaper pressroom in New York City.)
>
> All gifts over $5 in wholesale value must be returned to vendors. (From an insurance company in Toronto.)
>
> No help are allowed to drink alcoholic beverages while on duty. (From a restaurant in Ft. Lauderdale, Florida.)

Government laws. A useful definition of a government law is "any written or positive rule or collection of rules prescribed under the authority of the state or nation."[3] The next three chapters touch on laws governing relationships with the union, health and safety, and discrimination. Government laws weigh heavily on executive life. The president of a $400 million company told me in 1978, "I'm getting too old and tired to keep on fighting with all the laws that regulate business these days. I spend more time dealing with the government than with my own employees."

The Fair Labor Standards Act (FLSA) is one example of the many laws designed to protect the welfare of individuals.[4] It basically covers the employees of any work organization involved in interstate commerce and private household domestic workers. In 1978, the FLSA provided for a minimum wage of $2.30 per hour, a 40-hour week, and time and a half pay for overtime.

Controls. As used in organizations, controls are usually of the corrective type. The methods or mechanisms are designed to return the individual (or group of individuals) to an acceptable standard. In Chapter 13 we discussed a control model for dealing with ineffective performance. Its intent is to bring the ineffective employee back to an acceptable standard of behavior or performance.

We view controls as another type of regulatory mechanism that is essential for keeping employees and the department on

---

[3] From *The Random House Dictionary of the English Language,* unabridged ed. (New York: Random House, 1966).

[4] An excellent discussion of this law is Brent E. Zepke, "What the Supervisor Should Know About . . . the Fair Labor Standards Act," *Supervisory Management,* February 1977, pp. 30–36.

course. Many different controls are used on the job. Here are three everyday examples:

> One company weighs scrap at the end of each workweek to determine if the scrap rate is within acceptable limits.
>
> One hospital assigns two different people the identical task of taking inventory of drugs. The hospital is particularly concerned about preventing the misallocation of drugs.
>
> One company that manufactures small home appliances posts a security guard at the employee exit. Before the guard system was installed, employee theft had reached intolerable levels.

INTERPRETING COMPANY POLICY AND RULES

Company policies and rules are formulated at high levels of management. Middle management and supervision are usually left with the task of interpreting policies and rules to employees. A supervisor thus acts in the role of a judge or a lawyer. A policy may seem unambiguous as it stands on paper. Yet, in practice, it is subject to different interpretations. An important part of your job as a supervisor is to make sure that you understand a given policy, rule, or government regulation. It is worthwhile to assume that policies and rules will be often misinterpreted.

Laws, also, may require interpretation. For instance, an employee might use a chair as a ladder. You might have to explain that such an action violates a particular state safety law. (You might also add that using a chair for a ladder violates commonsense.)

Interpreting personnel policy. When a supervisor interprets policy to an employee, it frequently relates to personnel matters. Employees tend to be emotional about matters affecting them personally. Their judgments about personnel policies are thus likely to be highly subjective. Here is a seemingly straightforward policy about absence and tardiness: "An employee will be paid only for the hours he or she works. If an employee is late or absent, he or she will not be paid for the time lost."

Despite the apparent clarity of this statement, it may be subject to interpretations such as these:

> What do you mean I don't get paid for this morning? It wasn't my fault that I couldn't get my car started.

I couldn't shovel out my driveway. So I worked at home yesterday. I spent the whole day figuring out ways to improve the efficiency of the department. I think I should be paid.

I think I should be paid for the hour I was late this morning. At least four times during the last two months, I stayed at my desk an extra 15 minutes. I didn't get paid for those extra 60 minutes, so I think I should get paid for the hour I missed. What's fair is fair.

Faced with such subjective interpretations of policies or rules, the supervisor must display patience and firmness. Some of the techniques for managing gripes described in Chapter 11 would be particularly helpful in dealing with misinterpretations of company policy. If employees still feel that they have been mistreated, the problem should be referred to higher management or the personnel department.

ENFORCING COMPANY POLICIES AND RULES

Policies and rules that are written in company manuals but never enforced lose their effectiveness as guides to action. At the other extreme, policies and rules that are rigidly enforced may stifle initiative and discourage people. Suppose you were a supervisor in the pressroom, previously mentioned, that fires people for spitting on the floor. One employee hands another a peppermint which turns out to be laden with hot pepper. The surprised employee spits the spiced peppermint on the floor. Do you fire that employee?

Supervisors have to use judgment and compassion in enforcing policies and rules. They also have to be aware that policies and rules governing a particular matter even exist in the company. Figure 16–1 lists 23 areas in which most work organizations have policies and rules. You can assume that your place of work has some written statements governing employee behavior in these areas. Early in their history many small organizations do not have such regulations. As an organization grows, the development of such guidelines is almost inevitable.

In trying to enforce organizational regulations, it is helpful to recognize that such regulations are essentially expectations the company has of its employees. A policy might state: "Harmony will be maintained among co-workers." The expectation is therefore that loud verbal arguments and fisticuffs between em-

FIGURE 16–1
Topics of policies and rules in most places of work

Hours of work	Military service
Attendance	Hiring practices and probation
Adherence to company rules	Vacations and holidays
Demonstration of competency	Leave of absence
Maintenance of equipment	Sick leave
Relations with superiors	Benefits programs and retirement
Relations with co-workers	Wage and salary administration
Safety habits and housekeeping	Suspensions and dismissals
Overtime regulations	Promotions and transfers
Job training and qualifications	Personal use of company facilities
Self-development	and equipment
Membership in outside organizations	Prohibited activities such as use of drugs or alcohol, gambling, or buying or selling of goods on company premises

Source: Maurice O. Beverly, "Establishing Policy," in *Handbook of Business Administration,* ed.-in-chief, H. B. Maynard (New York: McGraw-Hill, 1967), sec. 4, p. 9.

ployees will be prohibited. A rule supporting this particular policy might state: "Any employee who engages in a physical fight with another employee on company premises will be suspended immediately."

The procedure recommended here for enforcing company policy and rules (or regulations in general) is progressive discipline.

FIGURE 16–2
Steps in the process of enforcing company regulations

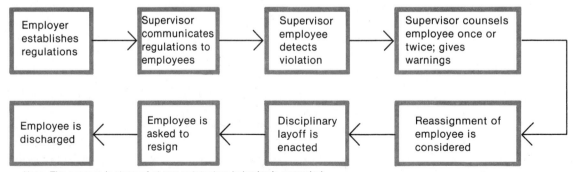

Note: The process is stopped at any point when behavior is corrected.
Source: Based on information in William F. Glueck, *Personnel: A Diagnostic Approach,* rev. ed. (Dallas: Business Publications, 1978), pp. 715–21. © 1978 by Business Publications, Inc.

The steps contained in this method have already been described in Chapter 13 in connection with managing ineffective performance. In essence, the supervisor first detects a violation and then uses the weakest reprimand (such as counseling or a warning) that will get the job done. If the violation of the regulation persists, the type of discipline is progressively increased. If the offending employee persists in disobeying regulations, the employee is ultimately recommended for discharge. The steps in progressive discipline are summarized in Figure 16–2.

THE EFFECTIVE USE OF CONTROLS

Controls are inevitable in any well-run organization. A supervisor has no alternative but to learn to make intelligent use of controls systems that are usually established at higher levels of management. Although managers below the executive level do not have the power to install or abandon control systems, they can still make recommendations about proper implementation of controls. The supervisor, for example, is in a good position to determine if the controls are working as planned. Six steps the supervisor might take to effectively implement controls will be highlighted here.[5]

Determine if the control measure is appropriate. In Chapter 6 we discussed the characteristics of effective objectives as used in a management-by-objectives system. Such objectives are in reality control measures. If control measures had such characteristics (for instance, relevance and clarity), they would generally be appropriate. Employee resistance to them would also be minimized. When it appears that a control measure is inappropriate for any reason, this observation should be passed on to higher management.

A police supervisor happened upon one such inappropriate control measure. Higher management decided that one measure of effective performance by a patrolman or patrolwoman would be the number of miles he or she traveled. Miles were measured by the police car odometer. The reasoning was that a large num-

---

[5] The information in this section is based somewhat on Ross A. Webber, *Management: Basic Elements of Managing Organizations* (Homewood, Ill.: Richard D. Irwin, 1975), chap. 15. © 1975 by Richard D. Irwin, Inc.

ber of miles would indicate that the police were not shirking duty by hanging out in coffee shops or the like. The control backfired. In order to turn in impressive results on the odometer, many of the patrol personnel stayed in continual motion, driving from one end of the city to another. Actual police coverage of the neighborhoods decreased with this new control measure. Instead of getting out of their cars and being visible on the street, the police spent more time in their cars than they had before the control was instituted.

High quantity standards (control measures) in general create problems. A supervisor should be alert to such unintended negative consequences of a quantity standard. As the push for productivity increases, quality may suffer. Equally significant, if quantity standards are too high, morale may decrease with a corresponding increase in absenteeism and turnover.

Determine if control measure is within control of employee. How would you like your performance downgraded because of something beyond your control? Suppose you were being held to a tight productivity standard and a sudden heat wave hit your city. The temperature in your department hit 120 degrees Fahrenheit (50 degrees Centigrade). All of a sudden productivity slows down, and absenteeism (along with beer drinking) increases dramatically. You failed to reach your objective, but an act of nature was responsible.

Employees sometimes fail to attain satisfactory performance as indicated by a control measure because of poor cooperation from others. A truck driver might be late with shipments because the shipping department did not have the packages ready in time. An orderly might fall behind on daily chores because the hospital laundry did not deliver bed linens on time.

Apply controls in a friendly manner. A commonsense approach to effectively using controls is to apply them in a friendly, or at least nonhostile, manner. One company embarked on a program of auditing hand tools on a monthly schedule. The reason for the control was a high incidence of disappearing hand tools. Plant management believed that employees were pocketing the tools. The audit system worked well in most departments. In one department, it met with immediate resistance. An angry, outspoken employee gave one version of the problem to the personnel department: "Ben has some nerve. Who does he think he is? Mr. Big Shot himself? He lays into us about the company finally putting an end to pilfering. He said if he had his way he would extend the audit right into our garages and basements. I don't have to take that kind of finger-pointing from any boss.

Be alert to contradictory control measures.   As pointed out by Ross A. Webber, a noted management professor, "One of the most difficult positions in life is when you can only look good on one performance criterion by sacrificing your evaluation on another criterion."[6] If employees are told to increase quantity *and* quality, the result may be confusion and chaos.

An automobile dealership decided to institute a set of controls for service department personnel. One objective related to increasing the number of cars serviced per week. Another objective related to decreasing the number of customer complaints about service. As you might suspect, these goals were somewhat incompatible. Only by taking more time with each automobile they serviced could the employees perform better service. Better service proved to be the one effective way of decreasing customer complaints.

Don't jump too soon.   An ineffective way of implementing a control system is to jump quickly at the first deviation from acceptable performance. A one-time substandard performance, or a one-time deviation from any control measure, may not indicate a genuine problem. It could simply be a random variation that will probably not be repeated for many years. Disciplinary action may not be warranted on the basis of this one-time departure from acceptable performance.

> A refuse collection supervisor cleverly averted a "jump too soon" problem. Higher management installed a new control system. Whenever it was discovered (usually through telephone calls from customers) that four or more garbage collections were not made on one route, the crew on that particular truck was handed a three-day suspension. Two weeks after the control was established, one of the most reliable crews failed to pick up the refuse of five customers.

---

[6] Ibid., p. 336.

The collection supervisor made note of the violation. Instead of telling the boss that the penalty should be imposed, the supervisor interviewed the crew to discover what might have caused the poor performance. The crew apologized to their supervisor and offered this explanation: One of the crew members was to be married next month. The night previous to their ragged performance, they held a bachelor party in his honor. The supervisor, recommending to the boss that the crew not be suspended, said, "We got a bunch of good boys here. I guess they are only human."

Don't spend too much time and money controlling. Controls become ineffective when the cost of control exceeds the money saved by their use. It may not be worth the supervisor's time to insure that nobody in the department is pocketing ballpoint pens, felt tip pens, or pencils. The money saved on a handful of misallocated writing instruments is a poor return on investment. A supervisor could better invest time in such matters as coaching employees on methods of improved performance.

Controls outside of employer-employee relationships can also be costly. An informal study conducted by a county welfare department determined that it would cost $8,000 in clerical and administrative salaries to uncover $4,000 in welfare fraud. It should be noted that the same agency already had a program to carefully screen welfare applicants. In addition, an attempt was made to regularly follow up on the current status of people receiving public assistance.

THE SUPERVISOR'S ROLE IN COST CONTROL

Another type of regulation periodically faced by plant, office, and laboratory supervisors is an order about cost control. Almost inevitably when budgets are tight, a cost-cutting program is announced from above. Almost all of a supervisor's responsibility for cost control lies within that supervisor's department. Supervisors would be going outside the bounds of a first-level manager's role if they recommended that the company close a plant that was losing money for the company. Even more out of keeping would be to recommend that one layer of middle management be eliminated.

Sufficient for the purposes of this chapter are four suggestions for ways in which a first-level manager can contribute to effective cost control. It should not be necessary to wait for a cost-cutting campaign to implement these ideas. Every dollar saved in costs contributes directly to making a profit or staying within budget.

Look for waste and excess.[7]   Unwarranted expenditures of this nature can occur in many forms. Idle workers, dripping pipes, drafty windows, reports received but never used, accumulating inventories of spare parts, lights left on in store rooms, and idle equipment are among the waste and excess widely found in work places. The supervisor should report such findings to higher management along with recommendations for taking care of such matters personally, or make appropriate recommendations to staff or line management.

Encourage a cost-trimming attitude among employees. Management alone cannot effectively control costs; cooperation of employees is needed at every level. The most effective single approach to reducing costs is the development of an efficiency-minded attitude. The supervisor should actively discuss the importance of cost savings other than methods of reducing personnel. Talk about the latter topic induces fears of layoff to many workers. Instead of becoming more efficient, they will often look for ways to make tasks take longer or "spread out the work."

Formal suggestion plans encourage a cost-cutting attitude among employees. But many cost-cutting ideas also emerge from departments where people are encouraged to be efficiency minded. The see-through envelope is a cost saver because of the clerical time saved in not typing names on envelopes. It was allegedly invented by a clerk who was looking for a way to trim the time it took to perform this job. Such time-savers, multiplied throughout the organization, reduce the amount of clerical overhead.

Evaluate equipment.   A mechanically minded supervisor who works with the equipment is often in a position to make dramatic strives forward in cost control. Harold E. Levenson, an instructor in mechanical technology, advises management to ask itself if less expensive equipment could perform the same

---

[7] Leonard R. Wass, "Controlling Costs: How to Cut Them in a Crunch," *Supervisory Management*, December 1976, pp. 7–8.

task. He supplies a checklist of questions management should ask:[8]

> Would a less accurate, smaller, or less sophisticated piece of equipment perform an adequate job?
>
> Are there other brands of equipment less expensive? Have lesser-known brands and foreign sources been considered? Has there been a thorough search of equipment catalogs, manufacturers' directories, and competitive sources?
>
> Can any items of equipment be built more economically in the company's own facilities?
>
> Can similar results be achieved by buying attachments for presently owned equipment?
>
> Can a different way be used to achieve organizational goals without buying the expensive items? (For example, could a different mode of production be substituted? Or could parts of the process be farmed out to a subcontractor?)
>
> Can any item of equipment be borrowed from another department?
>
> Are there any advantages to leasing the equipment?
>
> Can costs be shared with other activities by using the new facilities for additional uses?

Make more efficient use of space. A major business corporation recently embarked upon a cost-cutting campaign. One of the major strategies was to conduct a massive throwaway campaign. The company reasoned that if they threw away enough inactive files they would need at least one less warehouse for storage. The high cost of real estate purchase or rental makes such a savings substantial.

Since space costs money, it is to the company's advantage for employees to make more compact use of space. Lester Bittel observes, "Double- or triple-stacking pallet loads, for instance, cuts storage charges for space by a half or two thirds."[9] Similarly, if you threw out all the unwanted and unneeded items in your apartment or house, you probably would not need larger living quarters for a while longer than you thought.

---

[8] Harold E. Levenson, "A Basic Approach to Cutting Costs," *Supervisory Management,* April 1977, pp. 18–19. © 1977 by AMACOM, a division of American Management Associations. All rights reserved.

[9] Lester R. Bittel, *What Every Supervisor Should Know,* 3d ed. (New York: McGraw-Hill, 1974), p. 497.

An example of cost control: Justifying a capital expenditure

One of the many types of controls faced by supervisors is restrictions on expenditures. Managers who recommend acquiring a new machine, or replacing an old one, are usually asked to demonstrate the cost effectiveness of the purchase. Such acquisitions are included as part of the *capital budget,* a document that describes the alternative sources and use of funds.

A leading management text presents a concise analysis of three methods of demonstrating the anticipated value of making a given capital expenditure. Following is an excerpt of the description of these methods prepared by Donnelly, Gibson, and Ivancevich:[10]

The payback method.   The simplest and most widely used method is the payback method. This approach calculates the number of years needed for the proposed capital acquisition to repay its original cost out of future cash earnings. For example, a manager is considering a machine which will reduce labor costs by $4,000 per year for each of the four years of its estimated life. The cost of the machine is $8,000 and the tax rate is 50 percent. The additional after-tax cash inflow from which the machine cost must be paid is calculated in this way:

Additional cash inflow before taxes		
(labor cost savings)		$4,000
Less additional taxes:		
Additional income	$4,000	
Less depreciation ($8000 ÷ 4)	2,000	
Additional taxable income	$2,000	
Tax rate	0.50	
Additional tax payment		1,000
Additional cash flow after taxes		$3,000

After additional taxes are deducted from the labor savings, the payback period can be calculated this way:

———————
   [10] Reprinted with permission from James H. Donnelly, Jr., James L. Gibson, and John M. Ivancevich, *Fundamentals of Management: Functions, Behavior, Models,* rev. ed. (Dallas: Business Publications, 1978), pp. 136–38. © 1978 by Business Publications, Inc.

$$\frac{\$8,000}{\$3,000} = 2.67 \text{ years}$$

The proposed machine will repay its original cost in two and two-thirds years. If the standard imposed on managers requires a payback of at most three years, the machine would be deemed an appropriate investment.

Rate of return on investment. One alternative which produces a measure of profitability and which is consistent with methods ordinarily employed in accounting is the simple rate of return. Using the above example, the calculation would be as follows:

Additional gross income		$4,000
Less depreciation ($8,000 ÷ 4)	$2,000	
Less taxes	1,000	
Total additional expenses		3,000
Additional net income after taxes		$1,000

The rate of return is the ratio of additional net income to the original cost:

$$\frac{\$1,000}{\$8,000} = 12.5\%$$

The calculated rate of return would then be compared to some standard of minimum acceptability, and the decision to accept or reject would depend upon that comparison.

Discounted rate of return. A measurement of profitability which can be used as a standard for screening potential capital acquisitions and which takes into account the time value of money is the discounted rate of return. This method is similar to the payback method in that only cash inflows and outflows are considered. The method is widely used because it is considered the "correct" method for calculating the rate of return. It proceeds as follows, based upon the above example:

$$\$8,000 = \frac{\$3,000}{(1+r)} + \frac{\$3,000}{(1+r)^2} + \frac{\$3,000}{(1+r)^3} + \frac{\$3,000}{(1+r)^4}$$
$$r = 18\%$$

The discounted rate of return (r) is 18 percent, which is interpreted to mean that an $8,000 investment which repays $3,000
in cash at the end of each of four years yields a return of 18
percent.

The rationale of the method can be understood by thinking of
$3,000 inflows as cash payments received by the firm. In ex-
change for each of these four payments of $3,000, the firm must
pay $8,000. The rate of return, 18 percent, is the factor which
equates future cash inflows and present cash outflow.

SUMMARY OF KEY POINTS

☐ Regulations, if used properly, serve as guidelines in directing the
effort of personnel toward achieving organizational goals. Four
types of regulations studied here are policies, rules, government
laws, and controls. A policy is a general guide for carrying out
action. A rule is a specific course of action or conduct that must
be followed.

☐ Company policies and rules are formulated at high levels of
management. Middle- and first-level management are usually
left with the task of interpreting policies and rules to employees.
The supervisor must display patience and firmness in dealing
with the subjective interpretations of policies and rules often
made by employees.

☐ Enforcing company policies and rules is essentially a disciplinary
process. A system of progressive discipline is suggested in which
one infraction of rules or policy is met with counseling and
warning. If the infraction continues, despite corrective actions,
the employee must be discharged.

☐ Controls require careful implementation if they are to be effective. Six suggestions for implementing controls are: Determine
if the control measure is appropriate. Determine if the control
measure is within the control of the employee. Apply controls in
a friendly manner. Be alert to contradictory control measures.
Don't jump too soon at the first departure from standard. Don't
spend too much time and money controlling.

☐ Although cost control is not ordinarily thought of as a formal
regulation, it does fit into the policy area. A supervisor has an
active role to play in cost cutting and control. Four general sug-

gestions are: Look for waste and excess in your department. Encourage a cost trimming attitude among employees. Evaluate equipment for cost savings. Make more efficient use of space.

☐ Another form of cost control is justifying expenditures for capital equipment. Three methods of screening investment proposals described here are the payback method, rate of return on investment, and discounted rate of return.

GUIDELINES FOR SUPERVISORY PRACTICE

1. Many regulations actually simplify the job of a supervisor. Company policy serves as a guide to what should be done in a given situation. Rules help make discipline impersonal, thus aiding in the discipline process.

2. An important contribution a supervisor can make to the organization is to control costs. Cutting down on costs, other than during a cost-cutting campaign, will impress your superiors.

3. Managerial controls are inevitable in any large, modern organization. Instead of resisting them, you might improve your effectiveness by applying controls in a sensible manner. Often this means suggesting that controls with built-in flaws be modified.

QUESTIONS FOR DISCUSSION AND REVIEW

1. Some executives believe that government regulations drive many small businesses out of business. What do you think?

2. Give an example of a policy in relation to the course for which you are reading this book.

3. Give three examples of rules that govern a professional football game. What is the penalty for rule violation?

4. Make up a policy and a rule in relation to cigar smoking in passenger busses and airplanes.

5. A bank teller "turned in" another teller who borrowed $100 over lunch hour, even though the latter returned the money after lunch. Was the first teller justified? Would it matter to you what the teller used the money for?

6. One restaurant owner locks the meat refrigerator when he is away from the restaurant. Is this lock a control measure? Explain.

7. Are the metal detector devices used in airports control measures? Explain.

8. How does the purchasing function contribute to cost control?

9. Should supervisors recommend cost savings outside of their own department? What are some of the political considerations?

10. You are contemplating the purchase of a machine that costs $10,000. It will reduce labor costs by $2,500 per year for each of the five years of its estimated life. The tax rate is 50 percent. Calculate the rate of return on investment for this machine.

A supervisory problem: The ten percent solution

Bitsy, a payroll supervisor at Precision Machine Corporation, opened his morning mail. Of major importance was a directive from top management for every manager and supervisor to reduce operating costs by 10 percent. The memo concluded, "Unless we are successful in cutting costs using this method, more drastic actions will be taken."

Bitsy thought to himself, "Not a bad idea. We're being treated like mature, responsible adults. It's up to us to figure out how to trim expenses by 10 percent. If we fail, then top management will tell us how to do it." That morning, Bitsy worked out a plan for his department's contribution to cost cutting. He then scheduled a department meeting for the next morning at nine.

Bitsy opened the meeting: "I guess by now you've all heard rumors to the effect that costs will be trimmed 10 percent. Don't panic. Nobody in our department will lose their job. I have some ideas that will surely get the job done. I'll tell them to you now and follow it up with a written set of instructions.

"As I see it, the only fair thing to do is cut 10 percent across the board. We will try to reduce all costs by 10 percent. I'll give you a few of my specific suggestions now. You'll find the rest in the memo that I'm preparing:

Instead of buying a gross of ballpoint pens or pencils, we will order 11 dozen.

Salary increases will be cut by 10 percent this year. For example if somebody was going to receive a 7 percent increase, instead they would receive one for 6.3 percent.

Instead of taking one hour for lunch, I would like everybody to take 54 minutes. That way we can be 10 percent more productive.

I would like all typed reports to use 10 percent less paper. Please use 10 percent thinner margins. And keep your ribbons 10 percent longer.

"I trust everybody will agree with my recommendations. If we can't find ways to trim costs ourselves, higher management will do it for us."

1. *What do you think of Bitsy's methods for reducing costs?*
2. *How could you use the framework for accomplishing results to help Bitsy in his task?*
3. *Comment on the worthwhileness of each one of Bitsy's "10 percent solutions."*
4. *To what extent do you think Bitsy will be successful in reducing operating costs 10 percent?*

SOME SUGGESTED READING

Baum, John F. "Effectiveness of an Attendance Control Policy in Reducing Chronic Absenteeism." *Personnel Psychology,* Spring 1978, pp. 71–81.

Beverly, Maurice O. "Establishing Policy." In *Handbook of Business Administration,* ed.-in-chief, H. B. Maynard. New York: McGraw-Hill, 1967.

Hawk, Donald L. "Absenteeism and Turnover." *Personnel Journal,* June 1978, pp. 293–95.

Hellriegel, Don, and Slocum, John W., Jr. *Management: Contingency Approaches,* chap. 9. 2d ed. Reading, Mass.: Addison-Wesley, 1978.

Kress, Thomas G. "What the Supervisor Should Know about . . . Financial Control." *Supervisory Management,* January 1977, pp. 30–35.

Levenson, Harold E. "A Basic Approach to Cutting Costs." *Supervisory Management,* April 1977, pp. 16–20.

Myers, Edward A., Jr. "What the Supervisor Should Know about . . . Energy Conservation." *Supervisory Management,* October 1977, pp. 37–41.

Semradek, James J., Jr. "Nine Steps to Cost Control." *Supervisory Management,* April 1976, pp. 29–32.

Wass, Leonard R. "Controlling Costs: How to Cut Them in a Crunch." *Supervisory Management,* December 1976, pp. 6–10.

Zepke, Brent E. "What the Supervisor Should Know about . . . the Fair Labor Standards Act." *Supervisory Management,* February 1977, pp. 30–36.

Creating a safe
work environment

LEARNING OBJECTIVES

After reading and working through the material in this chapter, you should be able to:

1. Discuss a supervisor's role in creating a safe work environment.
2. Become a more safety-conscious person.
3. Understand the physical conditions under which accidents are the most likely to happen.
4. Understand how human factors such as morale, personal characteristics, and supervisory climate may influence accidents.
5. Be familiar with the purpose of OSHA and how these regulations influence a supervisor's job.
6. Be aware that a useful supervisory safety checklist is available for your use.

SAFETY AS A SUPERVISORY RESPONSIBILITY

The supervisor has primary responsibility for department safety in about the same way an automobile driver has primary responsibility for highway safety. Automotive engineers may design a safe car, highway engineers may design safe roads, but the driver has the primary role in accident prevention. Mechanical engineers may design safe equipment, architects and plant engineers may design safe work areas, but the supervisor is the person who creates an attitude of safety consciousness among employees and enforces safety rules.

389

When the term *work accident* is mentioned, people ordinarily think of mishaps in such places as factories, mills, refineries, and logging camps. But accidents also take place in offices, laboratories, retail stores, and medical offices. One unfortunate example: A medical technician disposed of a broken beaker by placing it in a refuse container with a metal lid. That evening a janitor tried to stuff some papers into that same refuse container. His wrist slammed against the broken beaker and he suffered a severed vein. Profusely bleeding and in shock, the man crawled to the sidewalk outside. A passerby administered first aid and summoned an ambulance. The janitor almost died as a result of this rare accident.

A supervisor should promote safety for several basic reasons. An obvious first is that work accidents cause human suffering and sometimes human lives. Second, good safety practices help productivity. Accidents result in considerable downtime among those employees not directly involved in the accident. One mutilated finger can shut down an entire production line.

Third, by preventing accidents, a supervisor can prevent a serious morale condition. Repeated accidents create an uncomfortable, discouraging atmosphere. An accidental death at the work site creates a sullen attitude among employees. Fourth, accidents are costly. Among the many direct and indirect costs are medical fees, increased insurance costs, decreased productivity, expenses involved in training a new employee, supervisory time, and compensation paid directly for the accident.

THE PHYSICAL ENVIRONMENT

A natural starting point in creating a safe working environment is to take whatever steps are necessary to insure that physical conditions are not hazardous. In all but the smallest companies, staff specialists such as safety, plant, or industrial engineers assist in designing relatively safe working conditions. A realistic strategy for a supervisor to use is to be alert to three general sets of physical factors that contribute to accidents: potentially hazardous locations, unsafe conditions, and potentially hazardous work schedules. Awareness of these factors as contributors to accidents will help you direct your efforts toward minimizing accidents due to physical causes.

Where accidents happen.   No work place is accident free, but four areas have the highest potential for accidents. They are listed in order, beginning with the place of highest accident frequency.[1]

> Wherever heavy, awkward material is handled, using hand trucks, forklift trucks, cranes, and hoists. About one third of industrial accidents are caused by handling and lifting material. Improper lifting by humans is also a frequent cause of accidents.
>
> Around any type of machinery that is used to produce something else. Among the more hazardous are metal and woodworking machines, power saws, and any machines with exposed gears, belts, chains, and the like. Even a paper cutter or an electronic pencil sharpener has a high accident potential.
>
> Wherever human beings walk or climb, including ladders, scaffolds, and narrow walkways. Falls are a major source of industrial and business accidents.
>
> Wherever people use hand tools, including chisels, screwdrivers, pliers, hammers, and axes. Hand tools also account for a good many household accidents.
>
> Wherever electricity is used in addition to usual lighting sources. Among the places where electrical accidents occur are near extension cords, loose wiring, and portable hand tools. Outdoor power lines have a high accident potential.

Unsafe conditions.   If you wanted to avoid an automobile accident, you would try to avoid driving on a crowded expressway during an ice storm. You should also be on the alert for unsafe conditions on the job. Aetna Life and Casualty Insurance Company makes note of the following work-related, accident-causing factors:[2]

> Improperly guarded equipment (such as a fender missing from a grindstone).
>
> Defective equipment such as a machine that overheats.
>
> Hazardous arrangements or procedures in, on, or around machines or equipment. A visitor to a company bent down to load one machine and injured his spine by ramming it into another machine.
>
> Unsafe storage including congestion, overloading, or the accumulation of rags with combustible vapors.

---

[1] This same information is cited in many places. A primary source is Aetna Life and Casualty Insurance Company, "A Safety Committee Man's Guide", cited in Gary Dessler, *Personnel Management: Modern Concepts and Techniques* (Reston, Va.: Reston, 1978), p. 426.

[2] Ibid., p. 423.

Improper illumination—glare or insufficient light.

Improper ventilation—insufficient air change or an impure air source.

In addition to this list, toxic chemicals are an ever-present danger. Protective clothing around such chemicals is an absolute must.

Potentially unsafe work schedules. Two noted industrial psychologists reviewed research suggesting that accident rates sometimes vary in relation to work schedules.[3] During the latter part of a day, when people tend to become distracted and fatigued, accident rates tend to increase. Long working hours, such as overtime conditions, also tend to increase the accident rate. Would you want to be operated on by a surgeon who has been working for 15 hours on one shift?

So far the matter has not been extensively researched, but the popular new four-day week, ten-hour day could be contributing to a higher accident rate. Whether this statement is true or false, it is worthwhile to be alert to potential accidents during the last two hours of the workday.

THE PSYCHOLOGICAL ENVIRONMENT

It is easy to understand that the physical working environment influences safety. Few people would argue, for example, that a noisy, poorly ventilated work area, accompanied by extremes in temperature and faulty equipment, would tend to increase accidents. The psychological environment, too, can have an important influence on accident frequency. Facts about how the psychological atmosphere influences accidents are not as easy to obtain as facts about the physical environment.

A note of caution: Few accidents are the result of purely physical or psychological factors. Most accidents stem from a combination of both. Put an untrained, inattentive person in front of an electric typewriter and the result could be a serious finger or arm laceration. If you are skeptical, here is a warning from the manufacturers of Smith-Corona typewriters. "If your typewriter is equipped with powered carriage return, you will find that the

---

[3] Ernest J. McCormick and Joseph Tiffin, *Industrial Psychology,* 6th ed. (Englewood Cliffs, N.J.: Prentice-Hall, 1974), p. 515. An early study of this problem is H. M. Vernon, "An Experience of Munitions Factories during the Great War," *Occupational Psychology,* vol. 14 (1940), pp. 1–14.

carriage moves quickly and forcefully back to the left margin. Keep your fingers out of its path to prevent injury."[4]

Furthermore, the naive typist might even suffer an electric shock from a brand new, fully inspected typewriter. Another warning from Smith-Corona: "Never insert metal objects, such as screwdrivers, paper clips, nail files, etc., inside a typewriter which is plugged in. An electrical shock may result."

Here we will examine three aspects of the human environment which can have a profound influence on accident severity and frequency: morale, accident proneness, and supervisory climate. The supervisor has some control over all three factors.

Safety and morale

A reasonable assumption to make about work-related accidents is that many of them are the product of low morale. When people are discouraged about their job, company, and supervisor, they are more liable to experience an accident. A psychological reason behind such accidents is that discouragement tends to take your attention away from the task at hand. Inattention, in turn, leads directly to accidents. Have you ever been thinking about an overdue bill while driving? Perhaps you recall not noticing the car pulling up short in front of you until the very last moment.

A number of years ago, a systematic study was made of the relationship between accidents and factors related to morale. Information was collected from 147 plants in the automotive and machine shop industry.[5] Separate statistics were collected for accident frequency, and accident severity.

Accident frequency was found to be highest in plants with conditions that breed low morale. Specifically, injury rates were the highest where employees had negative attitudes toward high-producing co-workers, where employees were required to engage in much heavy lifting, where living conditions were substandard, and where there was a record of many garnished wages.

---

[4] "Rules for Safe Operation," SCM Corporation, 200 Park Avenue, New York, N.Y. 10017.

[5] P. Slivnick, W. Kerr, and W. Kosinar, "A Study of Accidents in 147 Factories," *Personnel Psychology*, vol. 10 (1957), pp. 43–51; summarized in McCormick and Tiffin, *Industrial Psychology*, pp. 515–16.

Accident severity also seemed associated with low morale conditions, although the conditions reflected a different set of factors. Among the low morale conditions found were employees being required to eat in facilities separate from management, and no stated penalty for tardiness. (Some employees may have been discouraged because others were "getting away with murder.") Also related injury severity was associated with the absence of employee profit-sharing plans, extreme work temperatures, and places where the work could be characterized as dirty and sweaty. The presence of strong national unions (at the expense of strong local unions) was also related to severe injuries.

Many of the findings in these automotive plants and machine shops show a common theme of demoralization of the individual (for instance, seasonal layoffs, rivalries among employees, heavy and dirty work). The researchers involved in these studies believed that the loss of, or threat to, individuality produces preoccupation with personal problems which results in unsafe behavior. Poor living conditions, such as blighted neighborhoods, also demoralize workers and lead to accidents.

Accident proneness

A long-standing subject of debate among industrial psychologists and safety engineers is whether or not some people are accident prone. (Accident-prone persons have more than their share of accidents.) Although it is not easy to prove statistically, it is difficult to argue that certain personal traits and characteristics are not associated with being involved in work (or highway) accidents. People who have the following combination of characteristics would most probably be involved in accidents: carelessness, daydreaming, irresponsibility, poor coordination, and inattentiveness.

Some hard data have been collected relating certain personal characteristics to accident frequency. According to these studies, people with a high probability of having accidents:

Are usually under 30.

Have poor psychomotor (eye-hand coordination) and perceptual skills.

Are impulsive (they sometimes forget about safety cautions).
Are easily bored.[6]

A practical viewpoint for the supervisor to assume is that
anybody can be accident prone in a given situation. It is therefore
necessary to exert extra caution when a human situation arises
with high accident potential. One high school swimming coach
walked into the boy's locker room to discover that the team
members were whipping towels at each other. He regarded this
action as "healthy horseplay" among teenage boys. The healthy
horseplay resulted in one brain concussion and one severely
damaged cornea leading to permanent loss of vision. Horseplay
has an even higher accident potential in a work environment.

Another technique for counterbalancing accident proneness,
is to keep emotionally upset people away from work assignments that may lead to accidents. If one of your employees ar-
rives at work with bloodshot eyes and trembling hands, keep
this person away from the drill press or papercutter for the day.
On that given day, that particular employee is accident prone.

Supervisory climate and safety

In Chapter 10 we described various supervisory styles such as
authoritarian and participative. Differences in style contribute
to differences in climate or atmosphere within the department.
A supervisor who uses a democratic style often establishes a
warm, trusting, and supportive climate within the department.
Under these conditions, employees are likely to feel relaxed, or
at least not under heavy pressure. A relaxed, but not unalert or
unconcerned, attitude is conducive to good safety practices.

An extremely abrasive, insensitive, and intimidating approach to leading employees will, in some instances, precipitate
accidents. Many people become tense and fearful when the
supervisory climate is threatening. Employees who feel harassed
by their boss may also be so preoccupied with this harassment
that it will lead to unsafe acts. A bizarre example of how an
extremely threatening supervisor can precipitate an accident

---

[6] This information is summarized in William F. Glueck, *Personnel: A Diagnostic
Approach,* rev. ed. (Dallas: Business Publications, 1978), p. 558. © 1978 by Business
Publications Inc.

was reported by a plant physician. She told a management researcher:

> I remember the case well because it was the first accident I treated in my new position as plant physician. A young man was brought into the office by a co-worker. The patient was bleeding profusely from multiple cuts to the hand, wrist, and forearm. After applying appropriate medical procedures, I conducted my accident report interview. The patient told me his story in about these words:
>
> "This is the last . . . I'm going to take from that . . . boss of mine. He tells me that I'm the sorriest excuse for a set-up man he's ever seen. He said if I didn't stop bothering him with questions he was going to get me a job cleaning the restrooms. I got so mad I was going to punch him in the face. I swung. He ducked, and my hand went through the glass panelling around his desk."

Few supervisors are so insensitive that they would humiliate an employee to the extent of precipitating such a violent reaction. Nevertheless in the press of work demands it is not unusual for a supervisor to adapt an abrupt, harsh supervisory style. When carried to an extreme such a style may make employees anxious and tense. People who are operating under tension and anxiety are candidates for work-related accidents.

Age and length of service

We noted earlier that people under 30 tend to be involved in more work accidents than people over 30. A number of studies suggest a curious relationship between age and length of service in relation to accidents. People in their early 20s (mostly males have been studied) tend to be involved in many more work accidents than younger or older individuals. With increasing years, people become involved in fewer and fewer accidents. The accident rate continues to decline right up to retirement age.

The picture is much the same for experience in one job. When people first enter a job they are involved in relatively few accidents. After awhile their accident rate increases. After about six years of experience, the accident rates shows a steady decline.

Automobile insurance rates for young males take into account the fact that they have the highest accident rate of any group insured. With age, people become more cautious and careful—both on the job and highway. A counterargument is that older people are often assigned jobs with less accident potential!

SAFETY MANAGEMENT AND OSHA

In 1970, the U.S. Congress passed a law that has had a profound influence on safety-keeping practices in the United States. Almost every supervisor comes into contact with a regulation of the Occupational Safety and Health Act (OSHA).[7] Its basic purpose is to insure that every employee has a safe place to work, thus preserving human resources. Few supervisors would quibble with the purpose of OSHA. In order to accomplish its important mission, thousands of regulations governing safety and health have been written.

OSHA regulations. The employer is responsible for knowing the safety standards developed by OSHA. Glueck notes that this is an almost impossible task:[8] "The *initial* standards were published by *The Federal Register* in 350 pages of small print,[9] and interpretations of the standards are issued yearly *by volume;* one recent annual volume was 780 pages long! OSHA officers work with compliance operations manuals two inches thick.[10] Even the *checklist*[11] which summarizes the general industry standards is 11 pages long and lists 80 items."

OSHA regulations are quite specific, sometimes to the point of being picayune. At other times, the regulations follow good safety practice and commonsense. Here are two OSHA regulations covering quite different topics:

> All cracked saws shall be removed from service.
>
> Elevator signs warning they may be used by "authorized personnel only" must be printed only in block letters not less than two inches in height and shall be of a color offering high contrast with the background color.

The regulation governing letters on elevator doors is an example of "pickiness" on the part of OSHA regulations. In 1978 the U.S. Labor Department decided to discard 1,100 outmoded regulations governing such problems as the kinds of wood used in

---

[7] A good general reference about OSHA is "All about OSHA," rev. ed. U.S. Department of Labor, Occupational Safety and Health Administration, April 1976.

[8] Glueck, *Personnel,* p. 568.

[9] J. Wade Mitler, "OSHA: The Big Reach," *Personnel,* September–October 1976, pp. 45–53.

[10] "Occupational Safety and Health Standards," *Federal Register,* June 27, 1974.

[11] OSHA, *Compliance Operations Manual,* Washington D.C.: January 1976; OSHA, *General Industry Standards and Interpretations,* yearly volumes.

stepladders to construction requirements of portable toilets on building sites. Labor Secretary Ray Marshall said, "It is in the interest of business, American workers and OSHA to stop nit-picking and concentrate our efforts on the real hazards of life and limb."[12]

OSHA inspections. As a supervisor, you may have occasional contact with OSHA officials during a safety inspection. As a method of enforcing the law, OSHA inspectors visit work places according to their own schedule or by invitation from an employer, union, or employee. Penalties are quite stiff for OSHA violations. For instance, failure to correct a cited violation can result in a fine of $1,000 per day. If records are falsified to deceive OSHA officials, company officers are liable to jail sentences of six months.

During an OSHA inspection, it is within the best interests of the supervisor and the company for the former to be as open and cooperative as possible.

The supervisor's responsibility to OSHA. It would go far beyond the call of duty for supervisors to be conversant with every possible OSHA regulation governing their employer. It is usually beyond a supervisor's responsibility to make physical changes within the department to meet the government-imposed safety regulations. What supervisors can and should do, however, is to make sure that their employees are following the safety practices required by OSHA.

Many supervisors contend that OSHA regulations are difficult to enforce because employees are uncooperative. The company invests considerable time and money into meeting OSHA demands, but the system breaks down at the level of the individual worker. Here is a sampling of complaints:

> I can't get our fellows to keep those masks on. They say the darn things are too hot. Or that they don't want to look like an astronaut.
> This could be a stepladder factory and somebody in the office would still climb up on a chair to reach something on the shelf.
> The women tell me that if they wear the rubber gloves they're supposed to, it slows them down. Then their piece rate suffers. They act

---

[12] United Press International release, "1,100 OSHA Rules May Be Abolished," printed in Rochester, N.Y., *Democrat and Chronicle*, December 6, 1977, p. 6d.

like the company is taking bread from their table. We're only trying to obey the law.

What is a supervisor supposed to do about violators of safety rules? A safety rule violation is still a rule violation and should be treated as such. (See the relevant discussions in Chapters 13 and 15.) In addition, getting employees to comply with OSHA regulations is simply another case of overcoming resistance to change (see Chapter 12). Employees have to be sold on the tangible benefits from complying with safety regulations. One very tangible benefit is that a plant or office can be shut down if violations persist.

THE SUPERVISOR'S SAFETY CHECKLIST

A supervisor acting alone cannot create a safe working environment. You also need the commitment of top management toward making your company a safe place to work. In addition, you need good mechanical equipment, well-lit, well-ventilated work areas, well-trained employees, and a strong safety department. All the suggestions made so far in this chapter will also contribute to good safety practice.

One approach to improving the supervisory performance is to prepare a checklist of potential safety hazards and the appropriate remedial action for each one. As an example, to prevent accidents related to slipping and falling, the supervisor should "determine whether any hazardous location exists at which safeguards must be provided. Report any needs to the plant maintenance office and make certain corrective action is taken."[13]

Although a checklist of this nature has much to recommend it, it would have to include several hundred factors in order to cover every potential safety hazard at each place of work. Another checklist approach for supervisors is one developed at IBM. It lists 11 general suggestions that represent attitudes and practices designed to both prevent accidents and take care of them properly once they occur.

The 11 suggestions it contains can also be considered a

---

[13] Willie Hammer, *Occupational Safety Management and Engineering* (Englewood Cliffs, N.J.: Prentice-Hall, 1976), p. 105.

FIGURE 17–1
The supervisor's safety checklist

	My practice	
	Is adequate	*Needs attention*
1. I accept safety as just as much a part of my job as production, quality, and cost.	_____	_____
2. I recognize the relationship among good safety, good housekeeping, and good management.	_____	_____
3. I give adequate safety instruction to every new employee and to every old employee starting a new job.	_____	_____
4. I impart to all employees the understanding that the violation of standard safe work practices is just as serious as the violation of any other company rule. I am taking corrective action when safety rules are ignored.	_____	_____
5. I see that necessary personal protective equipment is provided.	_____	_____
6. I always set a good safety example myself.	_____	_____
7. By personal contact and group discussions, I make it possible for each employee to take part in the safety program.	_____	_____
8. I do not release new or relocated machines or equipment to an employee until I am satisfied that the necessary protective devices have been provided and the employees have received instructions regarding its safe operation.	_____	_____
9. I investigate and determine the cause of *all* injuries, even the minor cases.	_____	_____
10. I am constantly watchful for and I take immediate steps to correct unsafe work conditions and unsafe work procedures.	_____	_____
11. I see that all injuries are reported and promptly treated.	_____	_____

Source: Russel DeReamer, "Accident Prevention and Safety," in *Handbook of Business Administration* ed.-in-chief, H. B. Maynard (New York: McGraw-Hill, 1967), sec. 7, p. 168. Reprinted with permission.

method of measuring your own performance in the area of safety management. The supervisor's safety checklist is presented in Figure 17–1. Based on sound management principles, it is highly recommended for creating a safe working environment.

SUMMARY OF KEY POINTS

☐ Promoting safety is important in almost any work environment. Accidents cost human suffering, stop production, lower morale, and are quite expensive.

☐ A supervisor should take what steps are necessary to insure that physical conditions are not hazardous. A realistic strategy for a supervisor to use is to be alert to three general sets of physical factors that contribute to accidents: potentially hazardous locations such as where heavy material is handled, unsafe conditions such as improperly guarded equipment or the presence of toxic chemicals, potentially unsafe work schedules such as long hours.

☐ The psychological environment also influences accidents. Accidents usually take place because of the combined influence of physical and human factors. The psychological factors that can contribute to work-related accidents are low morale, accident-prone people, and an extremely unsettling supervisory style which creates a poor supervisory climate.

☐ The basic purpose of OSHA is to insure that every employee has a safe place to work, thus preserving human resources. In order to accomplish its purpose, thousands of regulations governing safety have been written. Many of these regulations have been criticized as being picayune.

☐ The supervisor's basic responsibility to OSHA is to make sure that employees are following the safety practices required by OSHA.

☐ A supervisor's safety checklist has been developed that summarizes most of the essentials of good safety management. It also serves as a good review of a supervisor's current safety practices.

GUIDELINES FOR SUPERVISORY PRACTICE

1. Aside from its value in reducing human suffering and saving money, good safety practice can also have a positive impact on your career. A supervisor who runs an accident-free or low-accident department tends to be well regarded by higher management.

2. There are basically four things a supervisor can do to help reduce accidents.[14] First, you can check for unsafe conditions, such as the ones described in this chapter. Second, you can ask staff specialists for help in selecting people who are unlikely to be accident prone for the particular job in question. Third, you can encourage and train your employees to be safety conscious. Fourth, you must enforce safety rules.

3. Unless you have another equally effective method of your own, your safety management practices are likely to be greatly enhanced by using the supervisor's safety checklist. Make it a part of your job as a supervisor.

QUESTIONS FOR DISCUSSION AND REVIEW

1. Now that you have read this chapter, what will you do differently with respect to safety practices?

2. Should every first-level supervisor in a mill, refinery, factory, or laboratory be trained in first aid? Why or why not?

3. Give two examples of how the ideas suggested in this chapter could be used to improve household safety.

4. Are you accident prone? Explain.

5. According to the *National Safety News,* March 1971, work fatalities number far less than fatalities at home or on the highway. (Specifically, 55,000 motor vehicle deaths; 27,000 at home; and 14,000 work-related deaths.) Explain these figures.

6. How do you think height and weight might influence your chances of being involved in work accidents?

7. According to your experience, what is the most frequent cause of accidents in an office?

8. Do you think OSHA should get involved in establishing safety regulations for professional athletics? Why or why not?

9. At what time of the day are you the most likely to be involved in an accident?

10. How might being too nice a guy or gal contribute to work accidents? Explain.

A supervisory problem: The attractive safety hazard

Brent, the safety manager, at Bartow Metal Stampings, walked over to Woody's office. The following discussion ensued:

[14] Gary Dessler, *Personnel Management: Modern Concepts and Techniques* (Reston, Virginia: Reston Publishing Company, 1978), p. 434.

Brent: Woody, we have something terribly important to discuss. But first of all, please don't think that I'm going to tell you how to run the production expediting department.

Woody: No, Brent, I know you too well for that. You probably have some very important safety statistics to hand me.

Brent: I wish it were that simple. It's about that beautiful new production expediter, Dottie. She's creating accidents out on the floor. We've all heard jokes about a woman being so good looking that other people turn around and look at her when she walks by. Dottie is so good looking that even many of our women employees feel impelled to glance at her.

Woody: I thought that after a month, the problem would resolve itself. I figured that people would get used to her lovely presence and would no longer be distracted by her. Just the other day one of our senior workers lost a tip of his finger when his eyes were following Dottie walking down the aisle.

Brent: Woody, the solution seems simple. Why don't you tell Dottie to wear drab, loose-fitting clothing to work? Tell her to also wear a scarf over her hair so she doesn't look so alluring.

Woody: Brent, don't you realize that would be discriminating against her because of her sex. I tried talking to Dottie about the subject one day. She accused me of being a sexist. She asked me if I told any of the physically attractive male production expediters to be careful what they wore on the shop floor.

Brent: OK, maybe it's my responsibility. Dottie is a darn good production expediter. But we can't have her creating accidents. I'll have a talk with her this afternoon. I'll let you know what happens.

1.   *What should Woody do about the situation of Dottie contributing to accidents?*
2.   *What steps should Brent take as safety manager?*
3.   *Is this incident more related to safety or discrimination?*
4.   *How might you apply the framework for accomplishing results to this problem?*

SOME SUGGESTED READING

Asher, Jules, and Asher, Janet. "Psychological Consequences of On-the-Job Inquiry." *Job Safety and Health,* March 1976, pp. 5–11.

Baldwin, Doris. "Industry's Secret Weapon: The Safety Committee." *Job Safety and Health,* July 1974, pp. 14–19.

Carvey, Davis W., and Nibler, Roger G. "Biorhythmic Cycles and the Incidence of Industrial Accidents." *Personnel Psychology,* Autumn 1977, pp. 447–54.

Ferry, Ted S., and Weaver, D. A., eds. *Directions in Safety.* Springfield, Ill.: Charles C Thomas, 1976.

Foulkes, Fred. "Learning to Live with OSHA." *Harvard Business Review,* November–December 1973, pp. 57–67.

Gardner, James. "Employee Safety." In *Handbook of Modern Personnel Administration,* chap. 48, edited by Joseph Famularo. New York: McGraw-Hill, 1972.

Mitler, J. Wade. "OSHA: The Big Reach." *Personnel,* September–October 1976, pp. 45–53.

National Safety Council. *Accident Prevention Manual for Industrial Operations.* 7th ed., 1974.

Peterson, Dan. "The Future of Safety Management." *Professional Safety,* January 1976, pp. 19–26.

Simonds, Rollin. "OSHA Compliance: Safety Is Good Business." *Personnel,* July–August 1973, pp. 30–38.

"Why Nobody Wants to Listen to OSHA." *Business Week,* June 14, 1976.

Relationships with the union

18

LEARNING OBJECTIVES

After reading and working through the material in this chapter, you should be able to:

1. Understand some of the ways in which a supervisor is involved in labor relations.
2. Understand why some employees prefer to belong to a labor union and others prefer not to belong.
3. Discuss the nature of a labor agreement or contract.
4. Describe a few approaches to handling complaints that will prevent them from becoming grievances.
5. Explain how the grievance process works in most unionized organizations.

About 24 million U.S. and Canadian workers belong to a labor union, representing about one quarter of the work force in these two countries. Union membership among manufacturing employees appears to have stabilized. In contrast, union growth within the ranks of public sector employees is growing rapidly. In addition, some higher-level occupational groups such as school teachers and engineers are growing in representation by employee associations.

Your work as a supervisor is therefore liable to involve direct contact with a labor union or similar association. Some people would argue that professional associations such as the American Management and American Bar associations also function as labor unions. Rational supervisors learn to work effectively with labor unions, just as they learn to work effectively with other forms of regulations.

406

Milestones in the American labor movement*

1636	A group of Maine fishermen engage in organized protest over the withholding of their wages.
1741	A group of bakers in New York City strike to protest a city regulation dealing with the price of bread.
1786	Philadelphia journeyman printers conduct strike against a wage cut. As a result, they attain a $6 per week salary.
1792	Philadelphia shoemakers form the first local craft union in the United States.
1825	Boston house carpenters, rebelling at their dawn-to-dusk working day, strike for ten-hour day and lose.
1829	*The Mechanic's Free Press* reports that hundreds of boys, age seven and older, are working from dawn until 8:00 P.M. in suburban Philadelphia factories. Children under age 16 comprise almost one half the New England factory labor force.
1834	A federation of local unions, the National Trades' Union, is founded. It is the first attempt at forming a national labor organization.
1842	The Massachusetts Supreme Court declares that unions are not illegal in the case of *Commonwealth* v. *Hunt*.
1852	The Typographical Union is formed, becoming the first national organization of workers that has continued to the present.
1869	A group of tailors form the Knights of Labor. They were interested in political reform and agitation and often sought political changes. By 1886 membership grew to 700,000 people. By 1893 they dissolved, due in part to their emphasis on social reform and a series of unsuccessful strikes.
1877	Strikes by railroad workers and clashes between strikers and federal troops result in the death of more than 100 people.
1886	Thousands of workers engage in nationwide strike demanding an eight-hour day. At a meeting in Haymarket Square, a bomb is hurled at police. Seven policemen and four workers are killed.
1890	United Mine Workers is organized.
1906	A strike by the International Typographical Union succeeds in establishing an eight-hour working day.
1914	Clayton Act is passed exempting unions from the provisions of the Sherman Act. Provisions of the Clayton Act limited the use of injunctions in labor disputes and gave legal sanction to picketing and other union activities.
1917	U.S. Supreme Court upholds the "yellow dog" contract whereby an employer could require nonunion membership as a condition of employment.
1932	Norris-LaGuardia Act is passed. "Yellow dog" contracts are outlawed and use of injunctions in labor disputes is made difficult.

Milestones in the American Labor movement (*continued*)

1933	The National Industrial Recovery Act (NIRA) is passed. Workers now have the right to organize and bargain collectively without interference from employers. (Act later declared unconstitutional.)
1935	The National Labor Relations (Wagner) Act is passed. Labor provisions of the NIRA are re-enacted and National Labor Relations Board (NLRB) is founded. Workers now have right to organize and elect representatives for collective bargaining.
1941	United States becomes embroiled in World War II. As a show of support of the war effort, unions give a no-strike pledge. After a ten-day strike, the United Auto Workers and Ford Motor Company sign a union-shop agreement.
1946	Immediately after the war, the most extensive wave of strikes in the nation's history erupts.
1947	The Labor Management Relations (Taft-Hartley) Act is passed. It amended the Wagner Act and declared certain union practices to be unfair labor practices. Outlawed were the closed shop, jurisdictional strike, and refusal to bargain. States now had the right to pass "right-to-work" laws, meaning that an employee does not have to belong to a union in order to be hired.
1959	Labor-Management Reporting and Disclosure Act (Landrum-Griffin) Act is passed. The act established certain rights of union members and required certain kinds of reports by both employers and labor unions.
	Longest major steel strike in history of labor takes place.
1962	President John F. Kennedy issues Executive Order 10988 which encouraged federal employees to unionize.
1965	Fifty thousand Philadelphia teachers ratify their first contract with the Board of Education.
1967	American Federation of Teachers and Chicago Board of Education agree on contract covering 23,000 teachers.
1974	NLRB jurisdiction is extended to nursing homes and not-for-profit hospitals.
1975	A group of medical doctors working at Chicago's Cook County Hospital engage in 18-day strike.
1976	Labor movement uses economic power for the first time. Ray Rogers of Amalgamated Clothing and Textile Workers Union pressures JP Stevens & Company's outside directors to quit its boards, and forces other companies to oust Stevens's officials who sit on their boards. Two Stevens's executives step down as directors of Manufacturers Hanover Trust Company after several unions threaten to withdraw their pension funds from the bank.
1979	American labor movement at a crossroads. Its membership as a percentage of the nonagricultural work force declines to 23.8

Milestones in the American labor movement (concluded)

> percent, a 41-year low. Growth of labor unions in the future appears to be among (a) public employees, (b) third sector (not-for-profit community organizations) personnel, and (c) technical, professional, and perhaps supervisory personnel.

* The milestones through 1975 closely follow those presented in Wendell L. French, *The Personnel Management Process: Human Resources Administration and Development*, 4th ed., Boston: Houghton Mifflin Company, 1978, Appendix. Additional information is based on John A. Fossum, *Labor Relations: Development, Structure, Process* (Dallas: Business Publications, 1979), chaps. 2, 3, 4. © 1979 Business Publications, Inc.; "Labor Comes to a Crossroads," *Time*, September 4, 1978, pp. 38–40.

THE SUPERVISOR'S ROLE IN LABOR RELATIONS

Much of the activities that fall under the label, *labor relations,* are activities carried out by supervisors and their employees. A supervisor's role in labor relations includes five tasks or expectations or obligations. The five overlap somewhat.

First, the supervisor's primary obligation is to protect the interests and rights of management. Just because a group of workers is represented by an outside organization, it does not mean that the employer must concede to every employee demand or whim. If management believes that good housekeeping helps productivity and improves safety, a supervisor can insist on high standards of housekeeping by employees. Management still has many prerogatives in a unionized organization.

Second, the supervisor is the linking pin between union and management and between the union steward and management. The supervisor communicates important messages back and forth between management and the union. As a linking pin, the effective supervisor keeps management informed about the quality of union-management relations.

Third, the supervisor is responsible for upholding the formal contract made between management and the union or other employee associations. Most labor contracts demand fair and equitable treatment of employees. A supervisor who allowed one clerk to work seated on a stool would thus have to allow all other clerks performing similar work the same privilege. No rational supervisor would object to such a doctrine of fairness.

Fourth, it is within the supervisor's role to establish a cordial relationship with the union steward. The steward is the front-line union official elected by the workers. Stewards do not have more formal power than the supervisor, but they can create problems for an unfriendly or hostile supervisor. A steward "bugged" by a supervisor might actively look for a chance to file a formal grievance. When a good relationship exists between the steward and the supervisor, the steward will take care of many employee problems. Stewards, for example, will sometimes encourage employees to obey company work rules, thus not damaging the reputation of the union.

Fifth, supervisors often function as paralegal technicians or lay lawyers. They make quick interpretations of the union-management contract to employees. When an interpretation seems complex, a supervisor should ordinarily consult the next level of management or labor relations specialist. A misinterpretation of the contract could result in a strike and cost the company millions of dollars. Sometimes contract interpretation can be an exercise in humor:

> Cindy asked her boss, Louise, for two hours off to visit the doctor. Under their particular union contract, employees could use this privilege twice a year. Before saying yes, Louise asked Cindy for the name of her doctor. Five minutes later Louise returned from her office, and told Cindy her request would be denied.
>
> Miffed, Cindy demanded an explanation. Louise replied, "Your doctor is Dr. Bertolli, a veterinarian. Our contract only allows for visits to medical doctors for people."

WHY EMPLOYEES JOIN OR DO NOT JOIN UNIONS

Many experienced supervisors were themselves once members of labor unions. To them it is understandable why many employees would voluntarily join a union. Supervisors who entered their positions without having been union members also need to understand the reasons underlying union membership. Such understanding helps facilitate empathy with union members. The general reason a person would join a union is to achieve personal gain. Among the many specific reasons people at different occupational levels join unions are these seven:[1]

---

[1] A summary discussion of this topic is William F. Glueck, *Personnel: A Diagnostic Approach*, rev. ed. (Dallas: Business Publications, 1978), pp. 641–43. © 1978 by Business Publications, Inc. See also V. Clayton Sherman, "Unionism and the Non-Union Company," *Personnel Journal*, June 1969, pp. 413–22; and Ross Stagner and Hjalmar Rosen, *Psychology of Union-Management Relations* (Belmont, Ca.: Wadsworth, 1965).

To achieve power. Many individuals feel powerless in comparison to their employer. "In union there is strength," cried the first union leaders. That organizing principle still makes sense today, even for professional athletes who are earning in excess of $200,000 per year. Various player's associations attest to this fact.

To improve their economic well being. Labor unions have always promised workers higher wages and other economic benefits such as medical insurance (and now dental insurance). It is often argued that many of the economic benefits received by nonunion workers stem from the efforts of labor unions. Many companies will grant employees all of the economic benefits they might achieve by unionization in order to keep away a union. In 1978 a machine tool company in Fort Worth, Texas, was on the verge of unionization. The company responded by offering the employees precisely those improvements in salary and working conditions the union thought they could obtain. A poster campaign (including derogatory cartoons about the union) was conducted indicating that the company was better than the union. The reason offered was that the company did not charge the worker union dues.

To achieve fairness and justice. A labor union offers formal mechanisms for resolving disputes with the employer. The union contract demands fairness in many aspects of employer-employee relationships. If a supervisor does something capricious, such as granting overtime assignments to a few favorite employees, a formal grievance can be filed. (It can be argued, of course, that nonunion organizations also have formal grievance channels.)

To achieve better working conditions. Physical working conditions in many companies throughout the United States and Canada are still shockingly poor in terms of ventilation, working space, restroom facilities, lighting, and the presence of poisonous substances in work areas. Before unionization (and government regulations) many more companies had such poor physical conditions.[2]

---

[2] The union view of why workers joined labor unions in their early days is expressed in Warner Pfluf, *The UAW in Pictures* (Detroit: Wayne State University Press, 1971), pp. 11–12; cited in Gary Dessler, *Personnel Management: Modern Concepts and Techniques* (Reston, Va.: Reston, 1978), p. 445.

Satisfaction of needs for affiliation.   As described in Chapter 3, groups offer people a chance to satisfy their natural desires to affiliate with other people. The more powerful the union, the more the need for affiliation is satisfied. Many union members say with pride, "I am a Teamster."

To avoid being an outcast.   People also join unions for defensive purposes. Imagine working in a plant of 1,000 employees where you were the only union "holdout." Or imagine being the only high school teacher out of 150 teachers who did not pay dues to the teacher association. In either case, you would have few friends at work or even luncheon companions. People often join unions out of subtle coercion.

It is also important to recognize that if given a choice, many people prefer not to join a labor union. Many employees identify with management. They want to climb the ladder and believe that union membership would make them an adversary of management. Many employees believe that unions are guilty of a wide range of practices that penalize initiative and protect mediocre workers. Seniority clauses lie at the top of this list.

A more emotional reason for avoiding union membership is that many workers want to remain independent and bargain for themselves. They feel that belonging to a union is beneath their dignity and a blow to their professional pride.

Finally, a number of workers see unions as a threat to their economic security. As one member of a steelworkers local union describes the situation, "One strike, and you would be in debt for ten years. The pay premium the union might be able to get you after the strike would never make up for your losses from a long strike. Besides, they take a big weekly chunk out of my paycheck.

HOW UNION AND MANAGEMENT VIEW EACH OTHER

A good deal of rivalry and conflict exists between labor and management. In the early days of the labor movement in the United States, union organizers were met by industrial "security squads" who battled them with fists, chains, knives, and guns. Unions, too, initiated many incidents of physical violence. Today the battleground between union and management is much like the battleground between political candidates. Beneath the former physical violence and today's verbal exchanges lie antagonistic perceptions management and labor have of each other.

Labor's perception of management

Union leaders and union members do not all share the same view about management. At one extreme, some union leaders view management as their partner in making the free enterprise system work. At the other extreme are representatives of labor who see management as the enemy. Despite these varied perceptions, a couple of stereotypes can be drawn of how labor views management.

Management is primarily interested in extracting as much profit as possible from their capital investment. They are more interested in profits than in the welfare of employees. To management, labor is a means to the end of making money.

Management is the beneficiary of the efforts of labor. Employees give forth effort, and management reaps the benefits. Jack London, a socialist writer, contends that working people furnish the labor and stockholders, the capital.[3] Stockholders are paid dividends for their efforts while labor receives wages.

The job of management is easier than the job of labor. Management should therefore not be paid so much more than non-management employees. At International Harvester, for example, the president is paid about 100 times as much as the average production worker (1978 figures).

Management's perception of the union

Managers, too, differ widely in their attitudes toward labor unions. Some liberal executives welcome unions and appreciate the union's effort in maintaining morale and discipline among its members. A more usual perception can be organized around three key points:[4]

---

[3] Jack London, *The Iron Heel* (New York: Bantam Books, 1971), p. 20; quoted in Jack Halloran, *Applied Human Relations: An Organizational Approach* (Englewood Cliffs, N.J.: Prentice-Hall, 1978), pp. 469–70.

[4] Stan Kossen, *The Human Side of Organizations,* 2d ed. (San Francisco: Canfield Press, 1978), p. 263.

1.   Labor unions are an outside group attempting to provide for the welfare of their members and themselves. In their efforts, they overstep their bounds and try to take over many management rights. Among these are making decisions about wages and working conditions.

2.   Labor unions are a force for increasing waste and inefficiency and lowering production. Without labor unions, profits would be much higher and business could expand more readily.

3.   Unions attempt to divide employee's loyalty between the company and the union. Without such divided loyalty, employees would be more company oriented.

As in most cases of prolonged conflict, both sides express some truth and some distorted perceptions. A supervisor is often caught in the middle between trying to satisfy the demands of the union and the employer. It is therefore helpful to understand both the management and the labor viewpoints.

SUPERVISING UNDER A LABOR AGREEMENT

A union's biggest impact on the work life of a supervisor stems from the labor agreement. After a union has been chosen to represent the employees of the organization, a labor agreement is drawn up. The process of drawing up the agreement is called *collective bargaining.* "Hammering out" the provisions of the contract is a long arduous process, often carried out round the clock and behind closed doors.

The labor agreement itself is essentially a contract. It might vary in length from 5 to 100 pages. Each contract is unique, but most labor contracts tend to have similar provisions. Every labor contract, for example, has something to say about holiday pay and grievance procedures. The contract is usually valid for one, two, or three years. It is renegotiated before its expiration date.

Typical sections of a labor agreement

An industrial relations vice president in a large industrial company has prepared a comprehensive list of the type of provisions found in most labor agreements or contracts.[5] A list of this

---

[5] C. W. Ufford, "Labor Relations: Collective Bargaining, Arbitration, and Mediation," in *Handbook of Business Administration* ed.-in-chief, H. B. Maynard (New York: McGraw-Hill, 1967), sec. 11, pp. 189–202. Our list is a paraphrasing of Ufford's list.

nature will help you appreciate the far-reaching impact a labor agreement has on a supervisor's job.

Intent, recognition, and representation. This section recognizes the union as the exclusive collective bargaining agent for the employees in the bargaining unit (the employee group represented by the union). It describes the bargaining unit in terms of the jobs included and excluded.

Membership requirements. The choice here is between a union shop and an open shop. A union shop requires all employees to join and remain members of the union. An open shop makes union membership voluntary. Closed shops are illegal according to the famous Taft-Hartley law. In a closed shop only members in good standing within the union can be employed by the company.

Wage rates and methods of pay. Actual wages for the various jobs are described here along with incentive plans and methods of job evaluation.

Management rights. In general, management tries to retain all rights which the union doesn't lay claim to in the contract. This is a particularly sticky area from a legal standpoint. What management thinks is its "right" may be subject to different interpretation by the union and the National Labor Relations Board.

Hours and overtime. Normally covered here are workweek and workday starting times, rest periods, coffee breaks, washup time, and similar topics.

Shift differential. Most contracts allow for higher rates for second and third shifts.

Seniority. The role of seniority in work assignments, layoffs, and transfers is a vital part of the labor agreement. "Seniority must be carefully defined and its application to operating conditions evaluated and carefully described."

Bereavement pay. Concrete provisions are specified as to how many, if any, days off employees may take to attend a funeral within the family. A provision might even be included as to whether or not you are entitled to additional time off on a working day if you attend a family funeral on a holiday.

Holiday pay. Included here are the specific holidays, the rate paid, and the rate of pay an employee receives who is required to work on a holiday.

Vacations. Among the items here are the seniority provisions for vacation and whether or not people can receive vacation pay instead of taking a vacation.

Grievance procedure.   No labor contract would be complete without specifying grievance matters. Among the topics described are what subjects are grievable, the specific steps within the grievance procedure, and the time allowed for each step. The procedure indicates the final disposition of the grievance by arbitration, strike, or other method. Often, a provision specifies whether or not stewards are paid for the time they spend handling grievances. Also, the extent to which stewards may leave their jobs to take care of grievance matters is specified.

Safety and health.   Provisions of this nature now overlap considerably with OSHA regulations. Also found here are the conditions under which (if any) production can be shut down for safety purposes, *and by whom.*

Apprentice programs.   This topic would include the nature and purpose of any apprentice programs; pay rates at successive stages of the program; and limits on the number, location, and utilization of apprentices.

Time off from work provisions.   Authorized leaves may include jury duty, court appearances, military leave, union duties, and perhaps time off to campaign for political office.

Strikes and lockouts.   This would specify when a strike can occur legally under the contract and the union's responsibility for an illegal strike. The provision describes what disciplinary action the company may take against employees or the union in case of an illegal strike.

Bulletin boards.   This would cover whether or not the union has its own bulletin boards; whether or not company boards will be shared by the union with or without approval, and for what type of information.

Term of the contract.   No contract is forever. When a contract lasts for more than a year, the date at which salary increases will be granted automatically is usually specified. Sometimes the contract may be reopened at a specific time to negotiate an important issue like wages.

Impact upon the supervisor's job

Similar to rules and regulations, in general, working under a formal labor agreement can simplify some aspects of the supervisor's job. If people know that wages have already been negotiated for the life of the contract, the supervisor does not have to worry about salary discussions with employees. If the contract specifies that employees can take off a day to attend divorce proceedings, the supervisor can grant a day off for such purposes with confidence. Upper management will not reverse this decision or criticize the supervisor's generosity.

Of fundamental importance, supervisors must *work within the framework of the contract.* They must use the many clauses of the contract as a specific guideline to supervisory practice—not to be violated except under very unusual circumstances. In a college library, all library personnel were asked to work one hour of uncompensated overtime to help save books from the ravages of a burst water pipe. Although a grievance could have been called, it was not. The supervisor believed that such an emergency warranted a small bending of the contract.

As a supervisor you should not actively look for ways to bend the contract. Such actions only create ill will between the union and management.

An obvious requirement of working under a labor agreement is that the supervisor must *carefully study the contract.* Although memorization may not be required, it is important to be aware that a provision exists for a particular issue. The contract can then be consulted to obtain the necessary details.

Consistency is important when it comes to interpreting provisions of the contract. Suppose you tell one woman in your department that she can have one extra day of vacation because she was ill during one of her vacation days. You have to treat the next similar request in the same manner. An office supervisor gave a black employee two hours off one afternoon to commemorate Martin Luther King Day. The supervisor believed that it fell within a provision for personal time off with pay. Next year another black employee made the same request. The supervisor denied the request, stating that it stretched the contract too far. Predictably, the second black employee threatened to file a grievance unless given equal treatment. Rather than dispute the matter, the supervisor conceded.

The above anecdote illustrates an important principle of supervising under a labor agreement. *Get help with difficult interpretations.* Consult with the next higher level of management or a labor relations specialist within the company. In some cases it might be helpful to discuss a difficult interpretation with the union steward before making a final ruling.

Motivating union employees

Supervisors frequently complain that it is difficult to motivate employees who belong to a labor union. Among their complaints are that the union controls everything: they determine wage rates, job rotation, and discipline. Such a view neglects some very important aspects of work motivation described in Chapter 8.

Many motivators exist that can be used without consulting the labor agreement. You can give praise and recognition for good performance; you can promise employees that they will be recommended for promotion to a job *outside the bargaining unit* if they keep up the good work; you can befriend an employee who does a particularly fine quality job; you can appeal to a person's "craft instinct."

If punishment is necessary in motivating an employee, the union usually allows for the use of some negative motivators under specified circumstances. Labor contracts typically specify what kinds of punishments are acceptable for lateness, tardiness, and substandard work. Before you use a particular sanction against an employee, it is important to consult your labor agreement and or the union steward.

HOW TO PREVENT COMPLAINTS FROM BECOMING GRIEVANCES

No labor agreement can be so complete that no disputes over interpretation of its provisions will ever arise. To deal with disputed issues relating to an interpretation of the labor agreement, the grievance procedure has been established. As a supervisor, you might dock the pay of a worker who reports late to work. He contends he is late because of severe weather conditions—specifically the wind was so strong he was afraid to drive his subcompact car down the highway until the wind subsided. You say that the phrase "severe weather conditions" was not intended to mean high winds. So he files a grievance, which is an orderly system for settling a dispute over contract interpretation.

Although grievance procedures make a contribution in providing a forum for solving problems, any grievance is disadvantageous to both parties.[6] Management and employees have their attention diverted from their jobs while a solution is being sought.

The proper handling of a complaint will often prevent a formal grievance from being filed. In a nonunion shop or office, it is also advantageous to prevent a minor complaint from becoming a major problem. Claude S. George, Jr., has assembled several helpful suggestions for the proper handling of gripes and complaints.[7] Supervisors who are able to behave in these ways when faced with a complaint will lower their grievance rates.

Never ignore a gripe or complaint. If you ignore the concern of an employee, it will not go away. Instead it may simmer into a major problem. The employee will often badmouth you to other employees because you took no action or did not listen to the gripe. Some people carry around unresolved gripes and complaints in their head for years.

Treat the employee and his or her complaint as being important. People are small-minded when it comes to their own complaint. One employee complained to her manager that her salary increase was $5 per month less than she had been promised. Her boss laughed, stating that she should take her case to the Salvation Army. The woman, in turn, complained to the union steward. A three-way conference was then called with his boss and the union steward. The boss was forced to defend his position. Perhaps if the boss had taken the woman seriously at first, he would not have been forced to defend himself to his boss and the steward.

Listen carefully to the employee's point of view. Gripe management is really a form of counseling. As you listen with care to complaints you may uncover the real problem annoying a person. A person who complains about a working area being too cold may really be looking for an excuse to avoid working with a particular co-worker.

Keep your temper under control. A characteristic of a suc-

---

[6] A useful reference here is Peter A. Veglahn, "Making the Grievance Procedure Work," *Personnel Journal*, March 1977, pp. 122–23, 150.

[7] Claude S. George, Jr., *Supervision in Action: The Art of Managing Others* (Reston, Va.: Reston, 1977), pp. 157–59.

cessful supervisor is remaining cool under pressure. Listening to an unfounded (in your perception) gripe tests your ability to remain composed under pressure.

Withhold your decision until you have collected the important facts.   When you receive a gripe, be sympathetic but avoid reaching a decision until you have heard both sides and gathered any other relevant information. A shipping clerk rushed over to the supervisor's desk and complained heatedly, "Joe just clobbered me for no reason at all. Look at my lip, it's bleeding." The supervisor replied, "We'll get that jerk fired." The employee ran back to the work area and told Joe he would be fired. An investigation of the fact revealed that the person who lodged the complaint struck the first blow!

Confront the problem.   Talking about a sensitive problem makes many supervisors tense. It is therefore a common practice to avoid speaking directly to the problem faced by the employee with a gripe. A better approach is to get to the heart of the matter rather than talking around the problem. If an employee objects to getting more than a fair share of dirty jobs, talk directly about how dirty jobs are distributed in the department. Do not engage in generalities about fair management practices.

Explain the reason for your decision.   An important supervisory principle is to explain why you made the decision you did. A logically based decision is easier to sell than one that seems arbitrary. If you refuse an employee a transfer because of a poor work performance, that fact should be explained. It is preferable to saying, "That's my decision, period."

Express confidence in the employee.   Often the gripe will be settled in such a manner that the employee does not get his or her way. Express confidence that the employee will be able to abide by the decision in a mature and responsible manner. The expression, "I know you can be a good soldier about this," still has merit in the modern world.

Fairness is all important.   Fairness boils down to looking at both sides of the gripe in an objective and open-minded manner. If the employee is right, admit it. Be willing to acknowledge the fact that you were wrong (if you were). Also be fair to yourself. If you and the company are right don't capitulate to the employee's side in a gripe session. Fairness works on both sides of a gripe.

HANDLING THE FORMAL GRIEVANCE

The employee grievance process is a formal way of handling an employee complaint. It can also be regarded as a formal method of resolving conflict, in which a series of third parties are brought into the picture. The number of steps in a grievance procedure varies from one to six, depending upon the particular

FIGURE 18–1
How a grievance is typically processed

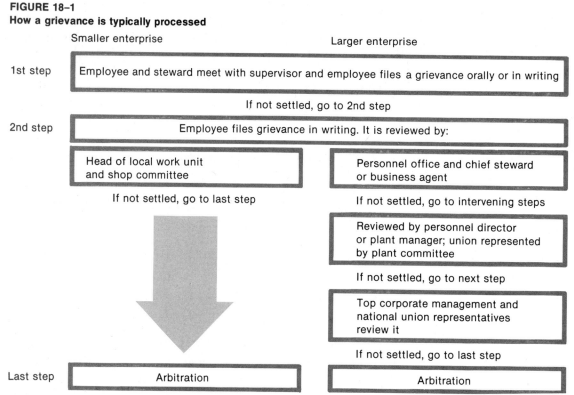

Source: William F. Glueck, *Personnel: A Diagnostic Approach* (Dallas: Business Publications, 1978), p. 682. © 1978 by Business Publications, Inc.

labor agreement. Glueck has provided an outline of the grievance procedure which reflects common practice in most unionized enterprises.[8] Figure 18–1 diagrams the grievance process for both large and small companies.

---

[8] Glueck, *Personnel,* pp. 681–83.

Step 1: Initiation of the formal grievance. Suppose an employee feels that he or she has been treated unfairly, or that his or her rights under the contract have been violated in some way. That employee then files a grievance with the supervisor. The grievance can be filed in writing or orally. Often the union steward is consulted to help file the grievance. Most grievances are settled at Step 1 by conversation among the employee, steward, and the supervisor.

The suggestions made in the previous section about handling complaints generally apply here. For example, the supervisor should listen carefully to the employee's complaint and maintain a controlled temper. A "hothead" is an easy mark for a union steward who wants to push a grievance up to a higher step.

Step 2: Department head or unit manager. If the steward, supervisor, and employee cannot reach a satisfactory solution to the problem, it goes to the next highest level in the organization. At this point, the grievance must be documented in writing by both sides. Which people are involved at this level depends on the size of the company or other enterprise. In small organizations it could be the head of the work unit, such as the general manager or deputy director. The union might be represented by a shop committee. In very large organizations the personnel or labor relations department and union business agent may participate in Step 2.

Step 3: The top manager of the employment unit and the local union president try to settle the grievance. If the grievance is not resolved at Step 2, higher-level officials from both the union and employer become involved in settling the dispute.

The following general principle applies: At each higher step in the grievance process, comparable levels of management from both company and union face each other: (a) supervisors and shop stewards meet; (b) middle management and the union committee or business agent meet; (c) top management and top union leadership face each other before resorting to arbitration or mediation.

Last step: Arbitration. If the grievance cannot be settled at lower steps, an independent arbitrator may be called in to settle the issue. Only about 1 percent of grievances go all the way to arbitration. Arbitration is often used as an alternative to a strike.

The arbitrator must be acceptable to both union and management. Arbitrators have decision-making authority. Once the decision of the arbitrator has been made, both parties must accept and abide by it. To do otherwise is to violate the contract.

Mediation is often confused with arbitration. The two processes are not the same.[9] A mediator is a third party who enters a controversy but holds no power of decision. Very few labor agreements (about 3 percent) allow for mediation. Yet mediation is widely used to settle strikes, often at the suggestion of some agency of the federal government.

A few sample grievances. The actual content of a grievance might take several thousand forms. Anytime employees think that they have been wronged in terms of the labor contract—and the issue is not 100 percent clear-cut—a grievance might be filed. Here is the basic issue contained in a few sample grievances from the files of a company with peaceful union-management relations.

> During the past four months I have not received my fair share of overtime assignments. I have the third highest seniority in the department, but I'm close to the bottom in terms of getting overtime work.
>
> I'm being deprived of my incentive pay. Once I get to making close to the top incentive pay on a particular job, the company transfers me to another job where I have to start all over.
>
> I arrived at my work station one hour late and I was docked one hour's pay. I shouldn't have been. I arrived at the plant on time, but because of all the snow in the parking lot, there was no space left for my car. It was the company's fault.

The proper conduct of the grievance procedure

Properly conducted, the grievance procedure will be an asset to the organization. It will efficiently and fairly resolve disputes at the bottom of the organization, thus preventing major disturbances such as strikes. It will help union and management to identify areas of ambiguity in the contract that should be

---

[9] Edwin B. Flippo, *Principles of Personnel Management,* 4th ed. (New York: McGraw-Hill, 1976), p. 535.

negotiated in the next contract. Finally, the grievance process is a useful communication channel between employees and management.

The President's National Labor-Management Conference of 1945 made certain recommendations regarding the grievance procedure that are still applicable today. If these recommendations are followed, the grievance process will benefit the organization. As recommended by the conference, a grievance procedure should emphasize the following:[10]

A. The basic objective of a grievance procedure should be sound and fair settlements, not winning.
B. The filing of a grievance should be considered as an aid to discovering and removing the causes of discontent.
C. Any tendency to support incorrect decisions made earlier in the grievance procedure should be discouraged.
D. Willingness to give adequate time and attention to grievances is necessary for effective functioning of the procedure.
E. For sound handling of grievances, familiarity with the contract is essential.

SUMMARY OF KEY POINTS

☐ The supervisor occupies a key role in labor relations. Among the supervisor's primary obligations are: Protect the interests and rights of management. Act as a linking pin between the union and management. Uphold the formal union contract. Establish a cordial working relationship with the union steward. Interpret the union contract to employees.

☐ Many workers choose to join labor unions in order to: achieve power, improve their economic well-being, achieve fairness and justice, achieve better working conditions, affiliate with a group, avoid becoming an outcast.

☐ Many other workers prefer not to belong to a labor union because they identify with management, prefer to remain independent and bargain for themselves, and believe they would be worse off financially.

☐ Union and management often conflict with one another due in part to the perceptions they hold of each other. Union leaders

---

[10] F. Elkourie and E. Elkourie, *How Arbitration Works*, rev. ed. (Washington, D.C.: *Bureau of National Affairs*, 1960), p. 50; quoted in Veglahn, "Making the Grievance," p. 150.

often perceive management as being primarily profit oriented, with very little genuine interest in the welfare of the worker. Management tends to view labor unions as outside influences trying to better their own cause. In the process of organizing workers, they promote waste and inefficiency, and divide worker's loyalties between the company and the union.

☐ The labor agreement or contract itself is an involved document, varying in length from 2 to 100 pages. It specifies a wide range of working conditions, salary matters, and the rights and privileges of the union. The contract is arrived at through the process of collective bargaining. The supervisor must work within the framework of the contract.

☐ Working under a union contract does not mean that a supervisor surrenders the ability to motivate workers. Praise, recognition, and the expression of appreciation are among the many possible ways a supervisor might use that are not tied in with the labor agreement.

☐ Disputes arising from interpretation of the contract are usually settled through grievance procedures. It is desirable for a supervisor to deal with a complaint before it becomes a formal grievance. Among the methods recommended for resolving complaints and gripes before they become grievances are: Never ignore a gripe or complaint. Treat the employee and the complaint as being important. Keep your temper under control.

☐ The grievance process involves a series of steps, following this general order: (1) Initiation of the formal grievance. (2) Discussion of the grievance among the employee, union steward, and supervisor. (3) Referral of the problem to higher levels of company management and union leadership. (4) Settlement of the dispute by calling in an outside arbitrator whose decision is binding.

GUIDELINES FOR SUPERVISORY PRACTICE

1. As a supervisor in a unionized enterprise, it is self-defeating for you to express antiunion sentiments to union members or to try to "beat the union." A more constructive approach is to work cooperatively with the union but at the same time protect the rights and prerogatives of management.

2. Having a large number of grievances filed against you not only wastes company resources, it can also damage your reputation as a supervisor. One way to prevent or decrease the number of grievances filed against you is to properly handle gripes and complaints. Follow the relevant suggestions presented in this chapter about handling gripes and complaints.

3. Another more fundamental reason that supervisors have a disproportionate number of grievances filed against them is due to a lack of familiarity or misunderstanding of the labor agreement. Should this be your situation, study the contract and consult with your company labor relations specialist.

QUESTIONS FOR DISCUSSION AND REVIEW

1. Do you think supervisors should have a union of their own? Why or why not?

2. In your opinion, why are so few agricultural workers unionized?

3. In what ways *does not* having a labor union present make it easier for a company to conduct business?

4. In what ways *does* having a labor union present make it easier for a company to conduct business?

5. Some companies purposely locate plants in areas where labor unions are weak or limited in number. What do you think of the ethics of such a practice?

6. What, if anything, do you think a first-level supervisor can do to prevent a strike within the plant or office?

7. In some South American and European countries, the president of the labor union often becomes the president of the company whose employees this union represents. Why is such a practice virtually unheard of in North America?

8. In your opinion, what advantage does the consumer receive when products are "union made"?

9. In your opinion, what disadvantages are forthcoming to the consumer when products are "union made"?

10. In one large industrial company it was observed that a small number of supervisors were the recipients of the vast majority of grievances. What about a supervisor who would make a person "grievance prone"?

11. What benefits do you think are forthcoming to students when high school teachers and guidance counselors are union members? Any disadvantages?

12. What are a few specific areas you feel quite strongly are management rights or prerogatives? In other words, what activities of management do you think should not be part of the labor agreement?

A supervisory problem: A question of seniority*

A company without enough work for all four of its keypunch operators decided to transfer one of them to a job in another classification. Gail H. had less seniority than the other operators, so she was transferred to an open job in the mailroom. However, the mailroom position was lower-rated than Gail's keypunch job had been.

The Saturday after Gail's transfer, the three keypunch operators were needed to work overtime on a special job. Gail thought she should have been invited to work the extra hours at her old classification, and she brought the matter to the attention of the union steward.

In studying the union contract, they thought they found the clause management had violated. The contract stated, "There shall be no work in excess of 40 hours per week while seniority employees are laid off due to no work being available."

Armed with this contract clause, Gail filed a grievance.

"We did nothing wrong," the personnel manager said during the grievance meeting. "If you had been on layoff, we would have had to call you back before we could let anyone in your classification work overtime. But you weren't laid off—you were permanently transferred to another job. So this clause has nothing to do with your situation."

Gail disagreed. "I didn't get transferred at my own request. I was transferred because of lack of keypunch work, which is the same as a layoff."

The case eventually went to arbitration.

1. Would you rule in favor of the union or company? Why?
2. Would you reach a compromise between the union and the company? Why?
3. In your opinion, should this grievance have gone all the way to arbitration? Explain.

SOME SUGGESTED READING

Bok, Derek, and Dunlop, John. *Collective Bargaining in the United States: An Overview.* New York: Simon & Schuster, 1970.

Brody, David, ed. *The American Labor Movement.* New York: Harper & Row, 1971.

Cohen, Sanford. *Labor in the United States.* 4th ed. Columbus, Ohio: Charles E. Merrill, 1975.

---

* Reprinted, by permission of the publisher, from, "If You Were the Arbitrator," by Morris Stone, *Supervisory Management,* April 1976, © 1976 by AMACOM, a division of American Management Associations, p. 23. All rights reserved.

Fossum, John A. *Labor Relations: Development, Structure, Process.* Dallas: Business Publications, Inc., 1979.

Hyatt, James. "Firms Learn Art of Keeping Unions Out." *The Wall Street Journal,* April 19, 1977.

Immundo, Louis. "Why Federal Government Employees Join Unions." *Public Personnel Management,* January–February 1973, pp. 23–28.

———. "Attitudes of Non-Union White Collar Federal Government Employees toward Unions." *Public Personnel Management,* January–February 1974, pp. 87–92.

Messick, David. "To Join or Not to Join." *Organizational Behavior and Human Performance,* vol. 10, 1975, pp. 145–56.

Mills, D. Quinn. "Managing Human Relationships among Organizations." *Organizational Dynamics,* Spring 1975, pp. 35–50.

Public Employee Unions: A Study of the Crisis in Public Sector Labor Relations. Institute for Contemporary Studies, 260 California St., San Francisco, CA. 94111.

Richardson, Reed. *Collective Bargaining by Objectives.* Englewood Cliffs, N.J.: Prentice-Hall, 1977.

Sloane, Arthur, and Whitney, Fred. *Labor Relations.* 3d ed. Englewood Cliffs, N.J.: Prentice-Hall, 1977.

"Unions Slip from Past Gains." *Business Week,* October 2, 1971.

Veglahn, Peter A. "Making the Grievance Procedure Work." *Personnel Journal,* March 1977, pp. 122–23, 150.

Dealing with job discrimination

19

LEARNING OBJECTIVES

After reading and working through the material in this chapter, you should be able to:

1. Become more aware of the types of discrimination practiced on the job.
2. Examine your own prejudices toward particular groups.
3. Be familiar with the major laws relating to job discrimination.
4. Develop a sound strategy for working under an EEO program.
5. Understand what actions to take when you think you are a victim of job discrimination.

The three statements below were made by three different supervisors. All three were committing acts of job discrimination despite the fact that they do not regard themselves as being prejudiced.

> Michelle, I don't think it would make much sense to recommend you for an outside sales job. What would your husband think if you were gone overnight on a business trip? Besides, who would take care of your kids when you were gone?

> Pedro, we have some pink paint left over from the model shop. Why don't you take it to paint your machine? I take it most of you guys like bright colors.

> Say "Shorty," don't be upset over not being considered for the assistant supervisor job. I just figured a guy your size wouldn't want to be a supervisor.

The first supervisor was discriminating against women. The prejudice is that women with family responsibilities are unwill-

428

ing to travel and that such travel would create family problems. The second supervisor gave leftover pink paint to an Hispanic because of a prejudiced belief that all Hispanics prefer bright colors. The third supervisor was discriminating against a male because of height. This prejudice was that males of below-average height are unsuited for leadership positions.

Contending with job discrimination has become an important part of a supervisor's job in recent times. Aside from being immoral and unfair, job discrimination in most of its forms is illegal today. Supervisors thus have to make sure they are not practicing discrimination in handling employees.

Job discrimination is an unfavorable action against another person because of a characteristic of that person which is not related to job performance. People are discriminated against for many reasons including their race, religion, sex, nationality, height, general appearance, and age. One supervisor attending a workshop claimed his company was discriminating against him because of his baldness.

Prejudice leads to discrimination. The term *prejudice* refers to an emotionally toned belief, favorable or unfavorable, to some person or group. When you are prejudiced for or against a group of people, you literally prejudge them. If you are prejudiced against gay people, you would prefer not to work for a gay boss. If you were not prejudiced toward gay people, you would welcome working for a gay person.

It is possible to be prejudiced without practicing discrimination. One white supervisor expressed it this way: "I'm not kidding myself. I'm prejudiced against black people. I was brought up that way. But on the job, a good worker is a good worker. I may not be personal friends with the black guys in my department, but it doesn't affect my evaluation of their work."

DELVING INTO YOUR OWN PREJUDICES

A good starting point in avoiding job discrimination is to understand your own prejudices. When you are aware of these prejudices and stereotypes, it can help you prevent turning them into action (discrimination). The process of examining your own prejudices may help you to question their validity. Unlike the supervisor just quoted, it is possible to gradually overcome prejudice directed against other groups of people.

Self-examination. Part of the work ethic training program described in Chapter 8 dealt with examining your own prejudices against people of work values radically different than your own. The same approach applies here.

At *step one* you write down all the prejudiced statements and negative stereotypes about that particular group. My personal preference is not to use the term *minority group* because many minorities are the subject of very little discrimination. The term *affected minority* is more accurate than minority. Swiss, Yugoslavians, and Asiatic Indians, for example, are certainly minorities in North America, yet they are rarely the victims of job discrimination.

Here is a portion of the "prejudice list" that a supervisor from a factory in the Bronx (part of New York City) prepared about Puerto Ricans:

> Prefer welfare to a regular job.
>
> Make a lot of noise on the subway.
>
> Forever looking to steal the silliest little things like apples or ballpoint pens.
>
> Laziest people in this country.

In *step two,* you examine each statement by asking yourself questions about its accuracy. The Bronx supervisor should ask these questions in relation to the comment about welfare:

> Suppose Puerto Ricans had a chance to work at jobs paying much more than welfare pays. Would they then prefer to work?
>
> If all Puerto Ricans want to be on welfare, how come there are so many Puerto Rican baseball players, singers, and skilled workers? What about Puerto Rican doctors and politicians? The facts don't completely square with my first thought.

Awareness training

Formal programs are sometimes conducted to help first-level supervisors become more aware of their attitudes toward a particular ethnic or racial group.[1] Most of the programs of this na-

---

[1] Chambers of commerce and industrial management clubs sometimes have information available about these types of awareness-training programs. Often they are called

ture have dealt with attitudes toward hard-core unemployed trainees who are black and toward women in general. The work ethic training program described in Chapter 8 represents the basic approach in these programs.

Awareness training helps supervisors become aware of their attitudes toward a particular group. Instead of making up a list of prejudices that only you see, you discuss these prejudices with other group members. By group discussion you become more aware of the fallacy in many of your prejudices. Participants in the program are encouraged by the group leader to "put on the table" their innermost fears and prejudices. A fear might be expressed in this form: "To tell you the truth, I'm afraid that someday I'll be working for a black woman. What would my wife think of me then?"

A dramatic feature of many of these supervisory awareness training programs is the presence of a staged black militant. The militant is trained to play the role of a particularly abusive black who is deeply prejudiced against white people. The "agitator's" role is to give you practice in being confronted with an extreme situation involving race relations. The purpose of such practice is to help you learn how to remain calm and cool under fire.

The black agitator does not only direct faked hostility against whites. If you are black and middle class, this individual has some abusive attitudes to express to you also. Expressed with powerful emotion and dramatic body language (including a glaring stare and a clenched fist), here is a sampling of statements the agitator uses in the training session:

> You honkey mother. . . . There's no way I'm going to pick that . . . up off the floor. You spilled it, you go pick it up.
> You Uncle Tom, pink. . . . Whose side are you on? Mine or the man's?

Reacting to statements such as these in role-playing sessions helps supervisors prepare for the worst they might encounter on the job with hard-core unemployed trainees. All hard-core unemployed trainees are culturally disadvantaged, lower-class individuals. Many of them have not learned how to constructively deal with their angry feelings. Instead, they will *sometimes* act

sensitivity training, which really is a misnomer. Mention of awareness training in relation to women is found in Andrew J. DuBrin, *Survival in the Sexist Jungle* (Chatsworth, Calif.: Books for Better Living, 1974), pp. 142–45.

in the manner of the "black agitator." Again, these training sessions exaggerate reality: They do not reflect the everyday life of the supervisor working with black, disadvantaged youths!

COMMON FORMS OF JOB DISCRIMINATION

Delving into your own prejudices could possibly uncover a number of different areas in which a person might harbor prejudices. As a supervisor, such prejudices are often translated into overt (open and obvious) or covert (hidden or indirect) discrimination. Here we will mention briefly six forms of discrimination often practiced on the job. Similar prejudices may show up in hiring people for jobs. You might use the following discussion as a checklist to ask yourself if you are practicing any of these forms of job discrimination.

Racism

When a supervisor treats another employee unfairly because of the latter's race, this person is practicing racism. The term *race* does not mean the same thing to everybody, here we are referring to the classification Caucasian, Negroid, and Oriental (white, black, or yellow). On one remote construction sight, a Chinese employee was asked to prepare dinner for the crew. When the employee asked why he was chosen, the supervisor replied, "Nothing personal, but I thought Chinamen liked to cook."

In recent years much effort has been directed toward overcoming antiblack discrimination. Although blacks have made considerable progress in being treated fairly, many would argue that they have yet to have achieved truly equal opportunity.[2] Much of the progress has been made at the individual worker and supervisory levels. A white supervisor still has a better chance of becoming a vice president than does a black counterpart. These odds are still true when the white and black person have similar experience, education, and skills.

---

[2] A look at this problem up to 1976 is "The Black on GM's Board," *Time,* September 6, 1976, pp. 54–55.

Ethnism

When a supervisor discriminates against a person because of national origin or religion, the supervisor is practicing ethnism—a coined word meaning unfair treatment of a particular ethnic group. Which group is likely to be discriminated against varies with such factors as geographic location, the particular industry, and the particular speciality within the industry.

For instance, in the past, Italians have been discriminated against in general. But Italians have been discriminated against less in the construction trades and in the manufacturing divisions of businesses. Today it would be difficult to document job discrimination against Italians.

In recent years, much effort has been directed toward overcoming discrimination against Hispanics (a wide variety of nationalities with Spanish or Latin origin, including Cubans, Puerto Ricans, Portuguese, and Costa Ricans).

Here is one of many thousands of possible examples of ethnism: A supervisor in an insurance agency does not recommend a Jew for a sales position. The reasoning used was, "I have no grudge against Jack. It's just that practically all our customers are Christians. They would prefer to buy insurance from another Christian."

Sexism

According to sexism, males and females should perform different kinds of activities both on and off the job.[3] Sexist beliefs often result in discrimination against females. Males, too, are sometimes the victim of sexist job discrimination. Females are still frequently given preference over males for jobs such as elementary school teachers, librarians, and nurses.

Since over one half the clerical and production work force is female, first-level supervisors may not be as guilty of sexism as are higher-ranking managers. Much of the legislation discussed in the previous section deals with combatting sexism. Few supervisors are thus likely to be guilty of overt sexism. The type of sexism practiced today against individual workers tends to be more subtle.

---

[3] One comprehensive look at sexism on the job is DuBrin, *Survival*.

"Can you type?"

Reprinted by permission The Wall Street Journal.

A supervisor in a large insurance company recommended a disproportionately high number of males for promotion into underwriting jobs. When confronted about this imbalance by the personnel manager, the supervisor replied: "Face it, the men employees need the money much more than the female employees. Most of the women have husbands who can contribute to their support." Even if this supervisor's statistics were correct (and they could be challenged), he would still be guilty of sexism. A fair promotion system recommends people on the basis of their job skills.

Ageism

When you discriminate against people because of their age, it is called ageism. The federal government so far has been concerned primarily against ageism against older people. Youths, too, are sometimes discriminated against because of their age. The government has been actively involved in recent years in prosecuting companies who discriminate against older people.

The first federal action against agism took place in 1974.[4] In that historic case the United States won an agreement from Standard Oil Company of California to award $2 million in back pay to 169 employees over age 40 it had laid off between 1971 and 1973.

Ageism is more likely to show up in laying off and hiring people than in dealing with them about work assignments. First-level supervisors tend to respect the stability and cooperativeness of older workers. A supervisor is more likely to discriminate against a young worker because of the youth's presumed unfavorable characteristics. A general feeling exists that young people have a weaker work ethic than older people. It is therefore easy to stereotype all young workers as uninterested in working hard.

Suppose a supervisor does not grant a particular 22-year-old his fair share of overtime work. The young worker complains. In response the supervisor offers this explanation: "We really need somebody dependable to work Saturday morning. Being single, you might decide to go off to the beach with your buddies rather than come in here on Saturday." The supervisor is guilty of practicing ageism (or perhaps youthism).

Heightism

Discriminating against males (and sometimes females) because of their height is a well-entrenched practice in North American society. Federal courts would generally declare heightism illegal, and it represents an unfair employment practice. Taller males tend to be paid more than their less tall counterparts. The average height of executives tends to be higher than the average height of men below them on the organizational ladder.[5] Some people would argue that taller people are

---

[4] "Age Discrimination Moves into the Limelight," *Business Week,* June 15, 1974, p. 104.

[5] A report of research on heightism is "Heightism," *Time,* October 4, 1971, p. 64.

more self-confident, therefore they deserve higher wages and higher-ranking positions.

If you are a supervisor, a good starting point in avoiding heightism is to cease making jokes or derogatory comments about a person's height. As implied at the outset of this chapter, nicknames such as "Shorty" or "Little Fellow" are a form of discrimination.

Gayism

A good deal of job discrimination still exists against homosexual males and females. Discrimination of this type can only be practiced when the person announces he or she is gay or he or she is presumed to be gay. Often the conclusion is reached that a male is gay because he exhibits effeminate mannerisms. Similarly, it is often assumed a woman is gay because she exhibits masculine mannerisms.

Such a conclusion can be ill-founded on two counts. First, displaying mannerisms of the opposite sex is not always a sign of gayness. Second, judgments about what characteristics are male or female are quite subjective.

Antihomosexual discrimination is practiced both in the hiring of people and in work assignments. People who admit their gayness or appear "unmistakably" gay are often denied jobs for which they are qualified. An overt homosexual male filed a formal complaint with the personnel department about the treatment he received in his department. He contended that his supervisor rated his performance low simply because he did not like gays. In addition, the man complained that he was asked to prepare coffee for the group. The personnel department resolved the problem by reassigning the man to another department.

DISCRIMINATION AND THE LAW

Hundreds of different laws and government regulations make it illegal to practice job discrimination for reasons such as race, sex, national origin, religion, and age. Some of the agencies established to enforce these laws, such as the Equal Employment Opportunity Commission, have thousands of specific regulations. Here we will summarize some of the major laws and constitutional amendments that prohibit discrimination. Taken together, they emphasize one key point: Job discrimination is illegal.

The Fourteenth Amendment. According to this amendment to the U.S. Constitution, no state shall "deny to any person within its jurisdiction the equal protection of the laws." The Fourteenth Amendment has been used to strike down state laws which discriminate on the basis of sex. As a case in point, state laws which deny women the right to practice certain occupations (such as telephone climber) have been declared unconstitutional.

State antidiscrimination laws. By 1979, about 40 states, the District of Columbia, and Puerto Rico had mandatory fair employment practices laws. Twenty-one of these states and the District of Columbia prohibit discrimination based on sex. In general the employment practices prohibited by state laws are the same as those prohibited by the federal law.

Sex as a bona fide occupational qualification is a major exception to fair employment practices laws in every state except Colorado, Maryland, and Wyoming. These three states have no exceptions of any kind. Among the bona fide occupational qualifications on the books of state and local laws are miners and smelters, and masseurs and masseuses (people who give body massages). This law is not interpreted to mean that a massage parlor is required to hire males to give massages to male customers.

The Equal Pay Act. This 1963 act prohibits discrimination on account of sex in the payment of wages by employers: "When male and female workers perform work requiring equal skills, effort, and responsibility, and performed under similar working conditions, they must receive equal pay." In 1972, coverage of this act was extended to an estimated 15 million administrative, professional, and salespeople.

Federal Civil Rights Act of 1964, Title VII. As powerful as its title implies, this act is extremely broad in scope, prohibiting discrimination in all phases of employment.[6] Title VII covers employers of 15 or more persons engaged in any industry affecting commerce. Among the employers included are employment agencies and labor unions, state and local governments, and educational institutions. Title VII declares that no employer subject to the provisions of the act "shall discriminate against any individual on the basis of race, color, religion, sex, or national origin."

Because of its complexity, covering both subtle and overt acts of discrimination, a special agency was created to administer this act. The Equal Employment Opportunity Commission (EEOC) both administers this law and investigates complaints about violations of the law. It also has the power to issue guidelines for interpretation of the act.

Despite its far-reaching provisions, there are exceptions to this law. As usual, if there is a bona fide occupational qualification, or when differentials in pay or privileges are based on geography, not sex, race, or national origin, the law does not apply. For instance, a white male supervisor, working and living in Los Angeles, California, will justifiably receive a higher salary than his black female counterpart in Lewiston, Maine. (We assume that the cost of living is higher in Los Angeles, than Lewiston.)

Also, if a scientifically validated test shows that a male is better qualified than a female (or vice versa), the more qualified person can receive the favorable employment decision.

Equal employment opportunity by federal contractors. Executive Order 11246, as amended, requires government contractors and subcontractors to institute an affirmative action program designed to insure hiring without regard to sex. Particular emphasis is placed upon programs for upgrading the status of the women in the organization. A supervisor might thus be asked to recommend a woman individual worker for promotion. Significant contracts have been withheld from companies that appeared to be holding back in insuring equal promotion and placement opportunities for women in all ranks.

Affirmative action programs differ in content from one com-

---

[6] A helpful overview of this act is Jerri D. Gilbreath, "Sex Discrimination and Title VII of the Civil Rights Act," *Personnel Journal*, January 1977, pp. 23–26.

pany to another, but they all are destined to show good faith in upgrading the status of women and selected minority groups. (Again, not all minorities are singled out for special attention.)

The Age Discrimination in Employment Act of 1967. Employers of 25 or more persons come under the jurisdiction of this act. Companies of this size are not allowed to discriminate against a person 40 to 65 in any area of employment because of age. It is likely that this act may apply to people both younger and older than these limits as attitudes toward age continue to become more flexible.

The Equal Rights Amendment (ERA). When and if the ERA is finally ratified by a sufficient number of states to become official, it will be one more force for fair treatment of everybody. When (or if) 38 of the 50 state legislative bodies ratify this amendment, virtually any form of discrimination against women will be unconstitutional.

Originally drafted in 1923 (not a typographical error), this amendment provides: "Equality of rights under the law shall not be denied or abridged by the United States or any state on account of sex."

Canadian human rights programs. As researched by Glueck,[7] "Canada's human rights programs in general have followed the lead of EEO programs in the United States. Federal and provincial governments have come to them later, and the statutes are only now (1978) beginning to be enforced." He notes that the results of Canadian human rights programs have not been as far reaching as those achieved by legislation in the states. Much of the Canadian emphasis has been placed on training programs designed to improve the positions of minorities.

SUPERVISING UNDER AN EEO PROGRAM

A supervisor is involved directly in the implementation of an EEO program. The equal employment opportunity manager in your company and related personnel are responsible for design-

---

[7] William F. Glueck, *Personnel: A Diagnostic Approach,* rev. ed. (Dallas: Business Publications, 1978), p. 623. © 1979 by Business Publications, Inc.

ing the program to insure that your organization is meeting federal standards in hiring and utilizing women and selected minorities. As a supervisor, your job will be to insure that people assigned to your department or chosen for upgrading are treated properly. For example, the EEO manager might inform you that you now have a Mexican-American male assigned to you as your assistant supervisor. Your job is to see that any training under you goes smoothly. Also, you are encouraged to do your best to see that he develops supervisory skills.

Three general strategies should be kept in mind for the supervisor working under an EEO program: Be on the side of the program. Recognize the problems of the affected minority person. Try to avoid reverse discrimination.

Be on the side of the EEO program. Complying with an EEO program is all part of obeying government regulations and practicing fairness in employee relations. Some employees will be suspicious of an affirmative action program (basically a plan for making sure that you are complying with EEO regulations). Among their fears will be that they will be replaced by a disadvantaged minority group member or they will be engaged in conflict with such individuals.

The supervisor should present a positive picture of the program pointing out that the company is only trying to live up to its responsibility in a democratic society. Employees will often ask if complying with EEO guidelines will result in financial losses for the company—which in turn will affect employee salaries. A sensible answer could be something to the effect: "Complying with EEO is good business. It allows the company to keep the federal government as a customer. It also means that we are eligible for other government business in the future."

Recognize the problems of the affected minority group member. Employees brought into your department on the basis of the affirmative action program have problems of their own. Some people think that they enjoy privileged status and should be grateful for what EEO has done for them. It will help you do a better job of supervising under EEO if you understand the point of view of people chosen for an affirmative action quota.

The problems of a black woman helped along in her career by

an affirmative action program are described by Marilyn Hubbard, a black woman herself: Her words probably illustrate the attitudes and feelings of many people helped by company compliance with EEO.[8]

> First, it's not true that companies are looking for blacks or women. If you are interviewed, that generally means there's a quota to be filled. If most companies had any choice, you would never be interviewed.
>
> A black woman may receive no support, either at work or at home. The black woman who was a secretary ten years ago, when her husband was a factory worker, may have moved up because of affirmative action programs. But she can't go home to talk to her husband about that, because he doesn't want to hear it. He's still where he was, and black men still tend to be very threatened if a black woman makes it.
>
> Instead of being pleased, the black community may say you're copping out to the whole white, middle class ethic. There's immediate hostility because you're succeeding. . . .
>
> You're on the defensive from day one, because the white men and women and black men are all going to assume you're a token. . . . She seems to be a threat to everyone. If she's promoted over white men or women, they're mad. And if she's promoted over a black man, he may be angriest of all!

Try to avoid reverse discrimination. A major battle faced by the supervisor trying to comply with an EEO program is to contend with shouts of "reverse discrimination" by employees who are not helped along by affirmative action. Unions too often complain about reverse discrimination against high seniority employees in favor of selected minorities. It is not uncommon these days for a white male to say, "Who's looking out for my interest? Just because I'm a male WASP nobody gives me a break."

One point of comfort is that Congress never intended reverse discrimination to take place when it passed equal opportunity and civil rights laws.[9] Complainers about reverse discrimination are not complaining about equal employment opportunity. As Gopal C. Pati observes: "They are complaining about the way the intent of the Congress and the spirit and letter of the law have been misinterpreted. The bureaucratic agencies and courts

---

[8] Nicki Scott, "Being Black: Female Path to Success," *Rochester Democrat and Chronicle,* November 19, 1978, p. 7c. © 1978 by Universal Press Syndicate.

[9] An excellent discussion of this topic is Gopal C. Pati, "Reverse Discrimination: What Can Managers Do?" *Personnel Journal,* July 1977, pp. 334–38.

now threaten a nonminority's basic right to work simply because he is not classified as a minority."[10]

For example, the EEO manager might inform you that a man or woman will be assigned to your department in a top-rated job. The employee so designated by EEO is automatically promoted over two other deserving, more senior employees. The best a supervisor can do in such a situation is to explain to complaining employees that the company is doing what it can to meet the demands of the affirmative action program.

What a supervisor *can* do about reverse discrimination is not to give preferential treatment to a selected minority individual once the person becomes a member of the department. All personnel decisions, to the fullest extent possible, should be based on objective standards of performance. All employees should be aware of these standards. Also, the same rules should apply to every employee in the department. If an affected minority group member neglects to punch the time clock, this worker must receive the same warning as the other members of your department.

DEALING WITH DISCRIMINATION AGAINST YOU

It is not inconceivable that you as an individual worker or as a supervisor could become the victim of job discrimination. To help you decide whether or not you are a victim of discrimination, ask yourself, "Would this be happening to me if I were not _____. If your answer is no, you have a basis for a complaint.

Step one in handling your complaint of discrimination would be to deal with people inside your own organization. You would begin by gently confronting your immediate superior. (The same method of conflict resolution described in Chapter 11.) If your complaint were not resolved at that point, you might discuss your problem with a member of the personnel department. If necessary, you might then go to your boss and take your complaint to successively higher levels of management.

Some companies have an "open-door" policy whereby anybody in the organization has the right to bring forth a complaint to the company president or chairman of the board. A risk in

---

[10] Ibid., p. 335.

exercising this option is that your immediate boss will become upset with you.

Step two is to take your complaint outside your organization to a state or federal government commission established for that purpose. Such a procedure should be regarded as a last resort for the employee who feels discriminated against. It is much preferable for you to first try to resolve your conflict inside the organization. An employee who uses an outside agency to resolve a discrimination problem is liable to be treated as a second-class citizen in the company from that point forward.

It is, of course, illegal for your organization to retaliate against you for having filed a complaint. But there is a big difference between treating you as a "second-class citizen" and retaliating against you in a formal manner. For those people who feel justice can best be served by using a governmental agency, the following procedure might be used.

In general, the swiftest approach to filing a complaint is to telephone both the U.S. and state departments of labor. A few brief inquiries will put you in touch with the right person to handle your complaint. If your complaint falls under the jurisdiction of the Wage and Hour Division of the Department of Labor, you can expect rapid action.

All complaints to this agency are held in strictest confidence. Usually the company being investigated is not aware whether the Wage and Hour Division is making a routine investigation or has been tipped off about a discriminatory practice. Once the investigation begins, the compliance officer investigates all the company records, including payroll information, job descriptions, and union agreements.

Frequently your complaint will be best suited for investigation by the Federal Equal Employment Opportunity Commission (EEOC). The EEOC should ordinarily be contacted in addition to filing your complaint with other federal or state agencies. Some paperwork will be necessary on your part, but the EEOC conducts the formal investigation.

File your complaint shortly after the alleged discriminatory practice takes place. Under some circumstances, your complaint needs to be filed within 180 days in order to be accepted. Speak to an EEOC representative to be certain of any time constraints on filing a complaint.

SUMMARY OF KEY POINTS

☐ Discrimination is an unfavorable action against another person because of a characteristic of that person unrelated to job performance. Prejudice leads to discrimination. It refers to an emotionally toned belief, favorable or unfavorable, to some person or groups.

☐ A good starting point in avoiding job discrimination is to delve into your own prejudices. One method is to simply write down all your negative feelings toward a particular group. Another method is to discuss your prejudices with other people in an awareness training program—a group discussion method that also involves playing the role of prejudiced people.

☐ Common forms of discrimination that might show up on the job include: racism; ethnism—discrimination against a particular ethnic group; sexism; agism—discrimination against older people; heightism—discrimination against people of well below average height; gayism—discrimination against gays.

☐ A wide range of national, state, and provincial laws prohibit job discrimination. Among the major national, state, and provincial laws prohibiting job discrimination are: the Fourteenth Amendment to the U.S. Constitution; state antidiscrimination laws; the Equal Pay Act of 1963; Federal Civil Rights Act of 1964, Title VII; Equal Employment Opportunity by Federal Contractors (Executive Order 11246); the Age Discrimination in Employment Act of 1967; the Equal Rights Amendment (when and if passed); Canadian human rights programs.

☐ A supervisor who works under an EEO program has day-by-day responsibility for seeing that it is implemented as intended. Three strategies for accomplishing this are: Be on the side of the EEO program. Recognize the problems of the affected minority group members. Try to avoid "reverse discrimination."

☐ If you think you are the victim of job discrimination in your organization, you should treat the situation as a case of conflict resolution. Gently confront the problem with your immediate boss. If not resolved, take your case to higher management. If your problem cannot be resolved internally, take your complaint to an appropriate state or federal agency established to deal with job discrimination.

GUIDELINES FOR SUPERVISORY PRACTICE

1. It may be difficult for you to overcome all of your deep-rooted prejudices toward particular groups of people. Nevertheless, it is crucial to your effectiveness as a modern supervisor to overcome any prejudiced behavior (job discrimination). For example, you may believe that women make poor mechanics. But if you supervise mechanical work, you must still give any woman in your department who so desires a fair chance at performing a mechanical job.

2. No supervisor can be expected to become familiar with all the legislation surrounding the issue of job discrimination. A general rule of thumb, however, is that all forms of job discrimination are illegal. Job discrimination that is not yet illegal (such as gayism) is still a violation of human rights.

3. If you are the victim of job discrimination, try to work at the problem within your organization before seeking the help of government agencies. Initiating a government investigation could possibly bring you into disfavor with higher management in your organization.

QUESTIONS FOR DISCUSSION AND REVIEW

1. Can you think of any form of job discrimination *not* mentioned in this chapter? Explain.

2. More than one half of the players in the National Basketball Association (NBA) are black males. To what extent do you think the NBA practices job discrimination against white males?

3. To what extent do you think professional baseball, basketball, football, hockey, and soccer teams discriminate against females?

4. Suppose a supervisor tells a "Polish joke" to an employee of Polish heritage. Is the supervisor practicing job discrimination? Is this an expression of prejudice?

5. In many companies you need at least a high school diploma to qualify for a supervisory position? Is this practice a form of job discrimination? Explain.

6. Do you think the "black agitator" in awareness training might actually be stirring up prejudice? Explain.

7. Do you think more job discrimination is practiced higher up in companies than at the first two levels? Explain.

8. Can you think of any job where being heterosexual would be a "bona fide occupational qualification"? Why or why not?

9. How can a supervisor avoid practicing "reverse discrimination"?

10. If the Equal Rights Amendment is finally passed, how do you think it will affect the life of the first-level supervisor?

11. In your opinion, should a textbook about supervision include a chapter on job discrimination? Why or why not?

A supervisory problem: Be nice to Maria

Sonya supervises the work of eight medical technicians in a laboratory that runs medical tests for physicians and small hospitals and a couple of government clinics. Quincy, one of the medical technologists, asks to see Sonya. With an exasperated expression on his face, he complains:

Quincy: I know you've heard this same complaint many times before from the group. You've got to do something about Maria. She's dragging down the performance of the group. When she's here and concentrating on the job, we can work with her. But about one fourth of the time, her mind is on something else or she's not here.

On a lot of the tests, we don't need her help. But we have to get her input to perform some of the other tests. Quite frankly, one of the "med techs" said she would resign unless you straighten out Maria.

Sonya: Okay, I'll level with you. I am aware of the problem. I've talked it over with Mr. Walters (the director of the clinic) several times. He knows it's a big problem. But he has a certain perspective you don't have. Maria is valuable to us for political reasons. On that basis I've been told to be nice to Maria.

Quincy: For what political reason do we have to be nice to Maria?

Sonya: Okay, Quincy, here are the facts of life. Maria is the only Puerto Rican medical technologist we have on the staff. If we want to retain our status as an equal opportunity employer, we must have at least one Puerto Rican medical technologist. Do you get the point?

1. *Should Sonya have been so frank with Quincy?*
2. *Is Walters right in insisting that Sonya be lenient with Maria?*
3. *How should Sonya deal with the complaints about Maria's performance?*
4. *How should Sonya deal with Maria, assuming the complaints are founded?*

SOME SUGGESTED READING

"Age Discrimination Moves into the Limelight." *Business Week*, June 15, 1974, p. 104.

Anthony, William P., and Bowen, Marshall. "Affirmative Action: Problems and Promises." *Personnel Journal*, December 1977, pp. 616–21.

DuBrin, Andrew J. *Survival in the Office.* New York: Van Nostrand Reinhold, 1977, chap. 7.

———. *Survival in the Sexist Jungle.* Chatsworth, Calif.: Books for Better Living, 1974.

Gilbreath, Jerri D. "Sex Discrimination and Title VII of the Civil Rights Act." *Personnel Journal,* January 1977, pp. 23–26.

Hall, Francine S. "Gaining EEO Compliance with a Stable Work Force." *Personnel Journal,* September 1977, pp. 454–57.

"Heightism." *Time,* October 4, 1971.

Jewell, Donald O., ed. *Women and Management: An Expanding Role.* Atlanta: Georgia State University, School of Business Administration, 1977.

Larwood, Laurie, and Wood, Marion M. *Women in Management.* Lexington, Mass.: Lexington Books, 1977.

Pati, Gopal C. "Reverse Discrimination: What Can Managers Do?" *Personnel Journal,* July 1977, pp. 334–37.

Robertson, David E. "New Directions in EEO Guidelines." *Personnel Journal,* July 1978, pp. 360–63, 394.

Schein, Virginia E. "Sex Role Stereotyping, Ability, and Performance: Prior Research and New Directions." *Personnel Psychology,* Summer 1978, pp. 259–68.

Wallace, Phyllis A., and LaMond, Annette, eds. *Women, Minorities, and Employment Discrimination.* Lexington, Mass.: Lexington Books, 1977.

part
six

**Helping yourself
succeed**

Managing yourself

20

LEARNING OBJECTIVES

After reading and working through the material in this chapter, you should be able to:

1. Understand how developing a set of ethics is part of self-management.
2. Identify a few useful strategies for improving your work habits (assuming they require improvement).
3. Identify a few useful strategies for advancing your career.
4. Be familiar with several techniques for managing your job-related tensions.
5. Know how to avoid becoming obsolete.

Much has been said in the previous 19 chapters about the supervisor's responsibility to the organization and to employees. As a supervisor, or prospective supervisor, you also have a responsibility to yourself to lead a satisfying and rewarding career. In this chapter we suggest strategies and techniques geared toward achieving such rewards.

Since self-development encompasses such a broad field of knowledge, it is particularly important that you delve into some of the suggested readings at the end of this chapter. One chapter in a book can, at best, give you a few workable guidelines for self-improvement and self-development. Only by diligent effort at putting them into practice will you derive any lasting benefit from such guidelines.

DEVELOPING YOUR OWN SET OF ETHICS

An often neglected part of self-development is developing an ethical code of business conduct. Many professional and business associations have elaborate codes of ethics incorporated into pamphlets. Among such groups are physicians, lawyers, psychologists, and life insurance sales representatives. If you were a member of one of these groups, you could use their set of ethics as guidelines to conducting yourself in your career.

Yet, even if you belonged to such a group, you would still need to develop an additional set of ethics that made sense to you in your everyday dealings. Unethical behavior can be defined as "the set of acts that the society thinks is right or wrong."[1] One way of grappling with the question of ethics is to look at what other people consider ethics to be. An interesting survey of this type was conducted in 1968. The results are summarized in Figure 20–1.

FIGURE 20–1
What "ethical" means to people

Most common	Percent who say
"What my feelings tell me is right."	50
"What is in accord with my religious beliefs."	25
"What conforms to 'the golden rule.' "	18
"What does the most good for the most people."	3
"What is customary behavior in our society."	3
"What is legal."	0

Source: Figure prepared by Ross A. Webber, *Management: Basic Elements of Managing Organizations* (Homewood, Ill.: Richard D. Irwin, 1975), p. 746. Webber's information is derived from R. Baumhart, *Ethics in Business* (New York; Holt, Rinehart & Winston, 1968), pp. 59–62.

In developing your own set of ethics, you could use Figure 20–1 as a guide. For instance following the approach suggested there, the best way of knowing if you are being ethical in a given situation is to be in touch with your own feelings. If you are about to blame a mistake of yours on one of your employees, ask yourself: "What do my feelings really say about such a trick?"

An even simpler way of developing your own ethical code is to

---

[1] William F. Glueck, *Management* (Hinsdale, Ill.: The Dryden Press, 1977), p. 580.

follow this doctrine: If you treat others the way you want to be treated, you will almost always behave ethically. If it were your company, would you want employees to walk out of the office with ballpoint pens stuffed in their pockets? Would you want a supervisor in a meat-packing company to fool the government inspectors about meat being fresh if you were going to eat that meat? The doctrine of "do unto others as you would like done to yourself" settles most issues of ethical conduct in a hurry.

IMPROVING YOUR WORK HABITS[2]

People with good work habits—those who organize their time well—tend to be much more successful in their careers than poorly organized individuals. Another major reason for having good work habits is that by doing so you will have more time to spend on personal life. You will also enjoy your personal life more if you are not preoccupied with unfinished tasks. Here we will discuss seven of the most important techniques and strategies for improving your work habits and thus becoming more efficient and effective.

Efficiency means that you accomplish tasks with a minimum of wasted time, material, and fanfare. If it takes you six hours to clean out your desk, you are not being very efficient. If you are a bill collector and you spend $75 collecting $70 from a delinquent customer, you are not being efficient.

Effectiveness refers to important results, or what you accomplish. You might be a tidy and efficient person, but the results you achieve might not be of significance. If you develop a highly efficient filing system for obsolete memos, you will probably make no particular impact on your company. If you developed a system of combing through the files to uncover a quality control problem, you would be considered effective.

A final point about this distinction: Being efficient often clears the way for being effective. If you are on top of your job, it gives you the time to work on the major tasks facing you.

Try work cost averaging. According to the stock investment strategy of dollar cost averaging, you invest the same amount of

---

[2] Much of this section is based on Andrew J. DuBrin, *Survival in the Office* (New York: Van Nostrand Reinhold, 1977), chap. 11.

money in a particular stock at different points in time. When the stock goes down in price, you get more shares for your money. When the stock rises in price, you get fewer shares for your money.

Similarly, in work cost averaging, you invest a constant expenditure of energy every working day. (As one woman describes this strategy, "Everyday is Monday.") The payoff is that you develop a precious supply of bonus time that you can use for forward planning and thinking creatively about your job. If you find yourself with an afternoon of discretionary time, you can figure out ways of doing your job more effectively. Such improvements should ultimately enhance your reputation wherever you work.

Maintain an updated list of chores (and rate them A, B, or C). The essence of this strategy has already been described in Chapter 6 about goal setting. Few people are so innately well organized that they can make good use of time without preparing a list of activities that need doing. In other words, most of us need to plan ahead. The supervisory planners commercially available are basically orderly systems of allocating your time among various activities. Many of these planners suggest apportioning your time into 30-minute chunks. In addition to time allocation, such planners serve as convenient record-keeping devices for luncheon engagements, expense account items, and important dates.

Alan Lakein, a noted time management consultant, advocates assigning an A, B, and C rating to each item on your list.[3] "A" items have the highest value; "B" items have medium value; "C" items have the lowest value. A list of chores using the ABC valuation technique might look like this:

B   Ask boss about rearranging office layout.
A   Ask for promotional opportunity in new division.
C   Clean out basement.
C   Rotate tires on car.
A   Have broken tooth fixed.

---

[3] Alan Lakein, *How to Get Control of Your Time and Your Life* (Wyden, 1973), pp. 21–22.

Concentrate on important tasks. In order to become more effective in your job, you have to concentrate on tasks where superior performance could have a big payoff for your department or company.[4] For example, no matter how quickly you took care of making sure that your department was clear of debris, it would not make your department an outstanding success. However, if you concentrated your efforts on bringing unique and desirable merchandise into the store, it could have a big impact on your business success.

Identify and plug time leaks. Many a landlord or homeowner has scurried around in recent years to identify and plug water or heat leaks. In years past the money saved from stopping drips or drafts was rarely worth the effort. With the substantially increased cost of energy and water in recent years, plugging leaks

Reprinted by permission The Wall Street Journal.

has become more profitable. The cost of wasted time has also been inflated enough to justify your identifying and plugging time leaks. By putting more of normal working hours to good use, you can increase your output without increasing your number of hours worked.

---

[4] The person most responsible for advocating effectiveness as applied to the job is Peter Drucker. See Peter Drucker, *The Effective Executive* (New York: Harper & Row, 1966).

Common time leaks worth plugging include: socializing on the job; 90-minute lunch breaks; excessive time spent in warming up to get started working; too much time spent winding down to stop working; visiting other people in the plant or office instead of phoning them to discuss a work problem.

Learn to say no. "Of all the time-saving techniques ever developed, perhaps the most effective is the frequent use of the word *no*," points out Edwin C. Bliss.[5] You cannot take care of your own priorities unless you learn to tactfully decline requests from other people that interfere with your work.

Bliss suggests that if your boss interrupts your work with an added assignment, "Point out to your boss how the new task will conflict with higher-priority ones and suggest alternatives."[6] When your boss recognizes that you are motivated to get your major tasks accomplished and not to avoid work, you'll have a good chance of avoiding unproductive tasks.

A word of caution. Do not turn down your boss too frequently. Much discretion and tact is needed in using this approach to work efficiency.

Guard against procrastination. A major time waster for many people is procrastination. Recognizing that you are procrastinating can sometimes help you remedy the situation. Procrastination is such a widespread human phenomenon, it is useful to speculate about its cause. One possibility is that people worry that they will perform poorly on the task being delayed: You cannot receive a poor grade on a paper until after it has been submitted. You cannot incur a large dental bill (and discover that your teeth are in poor health) until you actually visit the dentist. You cannot be turned down for a job until you are interviewed.

Lakein believes that you can reduce the extent of your procrastination by calculating its price.[7] Suppose you delay adding two quarts of oil to your car—an expenditure of less than two dollars (1979 U.S. dollars). The total cost of this procrastination

[5] Edwin Bliss, *Getting Things Done: The ABC's of Time Management* (New York: Scribner's, 1976). Excerpts of this book are found in Edwin C. Bliss, "Give Yourself the Luxury of Time," *Mainliner*, December 1976, pp. 53–55, 75.

[6] Ibid., p. 55.

[7] Lakein, *How to Get Control*, pp. 144–51.

might be over $400—the price of having your engine rebuilt. By not having your resume prepared and printed on time, you might miss out on a high-paying job that you really wanted. Your cost of procrastination would include the difference in salary between the job you do find and the job you really wanted. Another cost would be the loss of potential job satisfaction.

Avoid perfectionism.   Thoroughness is a virtue on most jobs until it reaches the point of diminishing returns. If every typographical error were removed from a newspaper, the price of the paper would have to be increased to an unrealistic level. Even worse, the paper would usually be late. Striving for excellence is certainly worthwhile. Striving for perfection is often self-defeating. Bliss provides a telling anecdote about the place of perfectionism in business:[8]

> Sir Simon Marks, who was chairman of the consistently profitable Marks & Spencer retailing chain in Great Britain, maintained that those who make a fetish of perfection are wasting time and money that could be allocated elsewhere. Hence his system of "sensible approximation" in inventory procedures. His motto: "The price of perfection is prohibitive."

ADVANCING YOUR CAREER[9]

The strategies of office politics described in Part IV of this book can be regarded as ways of advancing your career. The person who cultivates higher ups, co-workers, and subordinates and who gains power is in essence making plans for career advancement. Here we will examine several career advancement strategies that have withstood the test of time. However, indiscriminate use of any of these tactics may backfire. For example, if you overdo the strategy of achieving broad experience, you may be seen as a job hopper. Also you might be leaving jobs before you have learned them well.

Stay tuned to the outside world.   The most general suggestion for career management is for you to heighten your sensitiv-

---

[8] Bliss, "Luxury of Time," p. 55.

[9] The information in this section is based on Andrew J. DuBrin, *Winning at Office Politics* (New York: Van Nostrand Reinhold, 1978), chap. 9; and Andrew J. DuBrin, *Fundamentals of Organizational Behavior,* 2d ed. (Elmsford, N.Y.: Pergamon, 1978), pp. 159–70.

ity to the external environment. Organizations must adapt to their external environment in order to survive, and so must individuals. Since the external environment is usually unstable, prescriptions of what you should do right now to cope with the environment are of temporary value. Yet the general principle of being aware of the external environment is valid.

Geographic shifts in areas of economic prosperity must be taken into account in career planning. During the present decade the Southeast and Southwest portions of the United States (and parts of Alaska) are on the economic upswing. So is Alberta, Canada. All things being equal, a person has a better chance for career advancement by gravitating toward a growth industry in a growth area. Only by carefully studying basic sources (government reports) or objective secondary sources (for instance, *The Wall Street Journal*) can such external forces and movements be understood.

Another important aspect of the external environment that could affect your career is the relative prosperity of a particular industry. If you find a job in a rapidly growing industry, your chances for rapid advancement would be better than in a stable or declining industry. Among the predicted growth industries for the early 1980s are those that deal in lightweight metals or metal substitutes, leisure products and services, and fuel conservation devices.

Make an accurate self-appraisal. The most important ingredient in mature career planning is to have an accurate picture of your strengths, areas for improvement, and preferences. Feedback about the self can be obtained professionally through career counselors, through performance appraisal review sessions, or by obtaining peer evaluations. The latter type of information can be obtained in personal growth groups or more informally through asking significant people their opinion of you.

One supervisor constructed a brief form asking questions such as, "What have I done that displeased you this year?" He gave this form to other supervisors in his division, his boss, and the clerical staff in his office. The information he received helped him become more effective with others. In this regard he learned that he was standing too close to people (violating their *personal space*) when he talked to them.

Set realistic goals.   Setting goals is useful in managing your career, but the goals you set should be realistic or *meaningful.* Chris Argyris observes that goals which lead to personal growth are (1) challenging or stretching, (2) relevant to a person's self-image, (3) set by the person independently or in collaboration with another individual, and (4) implemented by the person's independent effort.[10]

A note of caution is in order: occasionally people do reach seemingly unattainable goals. Robert J. Ringer, author of *Winning through Intimidation,* contends that one year he made close to $850,000 in real estate commissions. Establishing realistic goals does not preclude such activity. Each time you achieve one set of goals, adjust your sights upward.

Outperform the competition.   Above all else, career advancement is contingent upon good performance. As described in a career management book:

> Job competence and talent are still the number one success ingredients in all but the most pathologically political organizations. All other talk about success strategies is fanciful without first assuming that the person on the make is competent in his or her specialty. Before anybody is promoted in any big organization, the prospective new boss asks, "How well did he (or she) perform for you?" Even if you become the most adept office politician (including cavorting with people in power), you still have to exhibit job competence to be assigned more responsibility. I know of no woman manager who, prior to becoming a manager, was not skillful at something specific, be it computer programming, bookkeeping, writing, editing, nursing, or welding.[11]

Achieve broad experience.   A widely accepted strategy for advancing in responsibility is to strengthen your credentials by broadening your experience. Broadening can come about by performing a variety of jobs, or sometimes by performing essentially the same job in different organizations. Two specific suggestions for attaining breadth should be kept in mind.

Don't be blocked by an immobile superior.   If you work for a boss whom the organization thinks is unpromotable, try to get

---

[10] Quoted in Douglas T. Hall, *Careers in Organizations* (Pacific Palisades, Calif.: Goodyear, 1976), pp. 183–84.

[11] Andrew J. DuBrin, *Survival in the Sexist Jungle:* A Psychologist's Program for Combatting Job Discrimination against Women, Copyright © 1974, Chatsworth, Calif.: Books for Better Living, p. 30. Reprinted with permission.

from under that boss. That manager is probably not a good model and will block your upward progress. Tactfully ask for a transfer, or look around the organization for an opening for which you feel you could qualify. If these maneuvers fail, your career progress may be contingent upon finding a job in another organization.

Be prepared to practice self-nomination. Have the courage and aggressiveness to ask for a promotion or a transfer. Your boss may not believe that you are actually seeking more responsibility. An effective method of convincing your boss is to volunteer yourself for specific job openings or for challenging assignments. A boss may need convincing because many more people claim to be seeking advancement than the number who will actually accept more responsibility. Verne Walter, a career counseling practitioner, provides this anecdote about the importance of self-nomination:[12]

> A general foreman in a heavy-equipment manufacturing company held hopes for broader and more responsible management experience. He had been a general foreman for approximately five years when he heard of the general manager's plan to create a new position—Manager, Planning and Control. He strongly desired to be considered for it.
>
> However, he believed it would be presumptuous of him to express his feelings to his superior. He was apprehensive about being perceived as overstepping his bounds. He rationalized that both his superior and the general manager knew him well, and that undoubtedly the administrative and planning ability he had shown on projects over the past would be recognized by them. As a consequence, he did nothing to convey his desires to management.
>
> Unknown to the foreman, the general manager, in answer to the question, "Had he thought of this man as a prospect," said, "Heavens no. I wouldn't think of it. His strength is in line operations. We'll be expanding his operation within the next three years, and he's looking forward to the added responsibility our expansion plans entail."

Find a sponsor. A swift route to career progress is to find a sponsor—somebody at a high place in the organization who is impressed with your capabilities.[13] Such a person can even be a blood relative or one by marriage. One reason that taskforce

---

[12] Verne Walter, "Self-Motivated Career Planning: A Breakthrough in Human Resource Management," *Personnel Journal,* March 1975, p. 115.

[13] The modern concept of finding a sponsor should be credited to Eugene E. Jennings, *Routes to the Executive Suite* (New York: McGraw-Hill, 1971).

assignments are helpful to career progress is that they provide you with the opportunity to be seen by a variety of high-ranking people in your organization. Many an individual who performed well in an activity such as the Community Chest has found a bigger job in the process.

Grab a shooting star.   A rebuttal to the find a sponsor technique might be that it is often difficult to cultivate a higher-up from a low vantage point in the organization. If you are typing invoices, it can be difficult to be discovered by the vice president of finance. However, it might be possible to cultivate somebody who does have a sponsor. The trick is to find somebody who appears to be headed for big things in his or her career and to develop a good relationship with that person. As the individual climbs the organizational ladder, you will follow. Val provides an apt example:[14]

> I work for the city. In my department, the head of the internal audit section of the finance division was the protege of the Director of Finance. An individual in the internal audit section, because of family ties, became the protege of the internal auditor. When the position of assistant to the Director of Finance opened up, the internal auditor's protege was chosen over five senior members of the department. People sometimes think office politics doesn't apply to civil service jobs so a lot of people were surprised when this young man from another department was selected for the assistant position.

Document your accomplishments.   Keeping an accurate record of what you have accomplished in your career can be valuable when being considered for promotion. Astute career people can point specifically to what they have accomplished in each position. Here are two examples from different types of jobs:

> A ski shop store manager increased sales to deaf skiers by 338 percent in one year by hiring a deaf interpreter to work in the shop on Saturday mornings.

> An assembly supervisor saved my company $36,000 in one year by suggesting we switch from steel to nylon ball bearings in our line of bicycles and baby carriages.

Manage luck.   Good fortune weighs heavily in most successful careers. Without one or two good breaks along the way (such

---

[14] This anecdote was researched by Mark Kindig.

as your company suddenly expanding and being in need of people for key jobs), it is difficult to go far in your career. The effective strategist to some extent *manages luck* by being prepared for the big break. Douglas T. Hall offers two suggestions about dealing with chance events:

> First, you can anticipate what conditions might arise and develop *contingency plans* for them (e.g., "If we have a recession, I'll go back to school"). Ask yourself, "What are all the things that could go wrong?" And "How would I respond to each course of events?" Second, you can prepare yourself to be ready to take advantage of opportunities when they come along. (A colleague of mine recently said, "Luck is the reward of the diligent."[15]

Hitch your wagon to yourself. The ultimate career-boosting strategy is to have faith in what you are doing and persist in doing it well. If you hitch your wagon to yourself, you will not be bothered by your detractors. Eventually, your contributions will be recognized because what you are doing is worthwhile and of value to the world. Hitching your wagon to yourself is your career foundation. Other strategies of career planning and office politics are designed to supplement this basic strategy. If you lack technical, clerical, or administrative skills and ideas of your own, you are lacking the basis for a successful career.

MANAGING YOUR JOB-RELATED TENSIONS[16]

No matter what the source of your job-related stress and frustration it will probably create internal tension. Unless this tension is managed properly it may lead to harmful consequences such as intestinal disorders or irrational behavior (as described in Chapter 2). Eight time-tested suggestions should be kept in mind in waging your battle against the potentially harmful effects of tension. No one tension-reducing technique is best for everybody. You should choose the one that works best for you. For instance, some people are far too impatient to be bothered with a technique such as transcendental meditation which requires sitting still for 2, 20-minute periods per day.

---

[15] Hall, *Careers,* p. 188.

[16] This section is generally based on a similar discussion in DuBrin, *Survival in the Office,* chap. 4.

Another vital consideration is that your tensions might be so overwhelming that do-it-yourself techniques will not work. In that case, you should seek the help of a mental health professional such as a psychiatrist, clinical psychologist, or psychiatric social worker. Your family doctor might be a good starting point for such a referral.

Take constructive action about your problem. My number one recommendation about coping with job-related stress (or stress of any kind) is to take constructive action. Your problem will never be resolved until you take the first step of doing something positive about your problem. Your first step in a positive direction can be likened to the first tablespoon of warm soup to a disaster victim: It won't cure your problem, but it's a welcome start. Assume you are frustrated because your boss will not make decisions of any significance. Until you take the first step of discussing that problem with your boss, your tension about the situation will persist.

Attack the cause, not the symptoms. Your job-related tension will continue to gnaw at you unless you modify the conditions that underly your problem. Hank, a production supervisor for a commercial printer, noticed that his smoking and drinking were approaching the danger level. With the encouragement of his wife, Hank enrolled in separate clinics for smokers and drinkers. He was able to stop smoking and control his drinking, but he still felt that too much stress existed in his job. His tension level remained annoyingly high.

What Hank needed to do was to confront management about the fact that he did not have enough authority to carry out his responsibility—the true cause of his stress. For instance, one time he was told to accomplish a major printing job in one week's less time than it ordinarily took, but he was not authorized to use overtime help. Until Hank's underlying job problems were solved, he could not reduce his job-related tension.

Strengthen your personal qualifications. Many of the stresses people experience in their careers stem from the fact that they can readily be replaced. A statement familiar to many people at all job levels is, "If you dislike things around here, move on.

There are many people with qualifications as good as yours who would be willing to do your job for less money than you are making."

The more unique you are in a positive sense, the less your concern about job security. Personal qualifications can be strengthened in a formal way (credentials such as education and specialized training) or in an informal way (for example, good reputation or valuable job experiences).

Talk out your problems. Strain, the adverse effects of stress, is reduced somewhat by the mere process of talking about the problem bothering you. Almost everybody familiar with human behavior recognizes this adage, but few people put it to good use. Talking about your problem with a sympathetic listener is a good start toward dissipating stress. An important by-product of talking about your problems is that it may lead to constructive action that contributes to their resolution.

Have your job redesigned. Many of the stresses that take place in organizations are caused more by situations than by people. In other words, some jobs are inherently stressful and frustrating. An accurate clue to this phenomenon is when several consecutive people fail in a given position. One example of such a job is being a collection agent in a high crime area. All examples of poorly designed jobs, however, are not so obvious.

Barry, a credit supervisor, absorbed a good deal of hostility from the sales department when he was forced to disallow an order written by a company sales representative. His cancellations only came about when his research showed the customer to be a bad credit risk. In conference with the sales manager, the controller, and the president, Barry made a suggestion for easing his conflict with the sales department:

> Sales people often blast us for throwing cold water on their hot customers. The problem, as I see it, is that the sales people are committing the company to shipping new customer equipment before we have cleared their credit ratings. We are sent sales contracts to approve. It would be much wiser for us to get involved before the new customer actually signs a contract. It would make sense for the salesman to say that he needs two signatures to approve a capital purchase of the magnitude of our drill presses. With repeat business, the salesman can do whatever they want. But I still think that checking with the credit department first is a financially sound idea.

Get ample physical exercise. It is well known that being in good physical shape helps you to cope with job-related stress. A person with a cardiac system beautifully toned by constant exercise is less likely to have a heart attack when overworked than a person whose heart is already weak from lack of exercise. It is also well accepted by many people that physical exercise helps prepare your mind for taking on tough mental tasks. Finally, being in good physical shape makes you more resistant to fatigue; thus you can handle a bigger mental or physical work load.

Physical exercise is now also considered an effective way of dissipating tension. In a *Psychology Today* survey answered by 23,000 people, physical exercise was listed as their number one constructive method of reducing job tensions.[17] Jogging is also known to reduce mental depression.

Learn to relax on your own. Tense, overworked people continue to be urged by their physicians, friends, spouses, and gurus to relax. The simple expedient of learning to relax is apparently still an important method of reducing the tensions brought about by stress. Ten everyday suggestions for learning how to relax are presented in Figure 20–2. If you can accomplish these, you may not need formal methods of tension reduction such as psychotherapy or tranquilizing medication.

Try TM and related techniques. Transcendental meditation (TM) is officially defined as a process of establishing a physiological state of deep rest. TM researchers contend that during meditation, the mind—although awake and able to respond to stimuli—is in a unique state of restful alertness. This state has been described as a fourth major state of consciousness. The other three are wakefulness, dreaming, and deep sleep.

The TM technique is relatively simple once learned.[18] It consists of getting into a comfortable upright position, closing the eyes, and relaxing 20 minutes in the morning and evening. The mind is allowed to drift with no effort or control required. Dur-

[17] Patricia A. Renwick and Edward E. Lawler, "What Do You Really Want from Your Job?" *Psychology Today*, May 1978, p. 54.

[18] Most bookstores and libraries now carry several books about TM. One comprehensive recent book is Jay B. Marcus, *TM and Business: Personal and Corporate Benefits of Inner Development* (New York: McGraw-Hill, 1978).

FIGURE 20–2
Ten suggestions for relaxation and tension reduction

1. Plan to have at least one idle period every day.
2. Learn to listen to others without interrupting them.
3. Read books and articles that demand concentration, rather than trying to speed-read everything.
4. Learn how savor food by taking your time when eating pleasant food.
5. Have a quiet place for retreat at home.
6. Plan leisurely vacations where virtually every moment is not programmed.
7. Concentrate on enriching yourself in at least one area other than work.
8. Live by the calendar, not by the stop watch.
9. Concentrate on one task at a time rather than thinking of what assignment you will be tackling next.
10. Avoid irritating, overly competitive people; they tend to bring out the worst in another competitive person.

Source: Based on information found in Meyer Friedman and Ray H. Rosenman, *Type A Behavior and Your Heart* (Greenwich, Conn.: Fawcett Crest, 1975), pp. 207–71.

ing TM the mind focuses on what is known as a mantra, a meaningless sound assigned to the meditator by the teacher. It is considered taboo for people to reveal their mantras. Also, somebody else's mantra supposedly will not help you.

At its best, TM produces deep rest and relaxation with the meditator showing such distinct physiological changes as a decrease in heart and respiratory rate and lower bodily metabolism. Meditators frequently note that they feel more relaxed or less hurried than before they began to meditate.

Dr. Herbert Benson, a cardiologist from Harvard, is one of many researchers and practitioners who question the claim of exclusivity made for TM. His best-selling book during the mid-1970s, *The Relaxation Response,* offers a simple and workable method of relieving stress.[19] By getting yourself quietly comfortable and thinking of the word *one* (or any simple prayer) with every breath, you can duplicate the tension-reducing effects of TM.

---

[19] Herbert Benson, *The Relaxation Response* (Morrow, 1975).

Concentrate on your work or hobby. For those individuals who feel uncomfortable about joining what appears to them to be a religious cult (TM) or even going through formal exercises to relieve stress, an alternative exists. Learning to concentrate on a meaningful activity for 30-minute periods can be stress reducing. For example, you might concentrate so hard on what you are studying that the book in front of you (and its contents) is your only touch with reality. Should you prefer tennis as a way of practicing concentration, stare so hard at the ball that it appears to be grapefruit sized. Furthermore, you should be able to read the trademark with clarity—even while playing.[20]

The principle underlying concentration as a method of tension reduction is probably similar to the underlying principle behind other relaxation approaches. Your muscles and brain seem to be energized by carefully focusing them on something quite specific. Even if tension is not reduced, performance in the task at hand is improved!

HOW TO AVOID GOING OUT OF STYLE[21]

"Why bother asking Herman anything anymore?," said one lab technician to another. "He'll only tell us that, as supervisor of the photolab, he's not supposed to be up on technical details. I think poor old Herman stopped learning anything new about the time color processing became popular."

Herman exhibits a behavior pattern that seems to afflict about 10 percent of all people in technical, professional, managerial, and supervisory jobs. For a variety of reasons, they have lost some of their former effectiveness and are, therefore, classified as suffering from obsolescence.[22]

A number of successful people prevent their own obsolescence in an automatic, intuitive fashion. The majority of people would do well to develop a specific program or embark upon

---

[20] A thorough description of how concentration can improve performance in sports is W. Timothy Gallwey, *The Inner Game of Tennis* (New York: Random House, 1974). Gallwey has become a national celebrity who has established clinics to help people improve their concentration in tennis, skiing, and in life in general.

[21] This section of the chapter is based on DuBrin, *Survival in the Office*, chap. 18.

[22] The most comprehensive discussion of obsolescence related to the job currently available is H. G. Kaufman, *Obsolescence and Professional Career Development* (New York: AMACOM, 1974). See also, Andrew J. DuBrin, *The Practice of Managerial Psychology* (Elmsford, N.Y.: Pergamon, 1972), chap. 6.

certain courses of action to avoid becoming obsolete. It could have a big impact on your career. The five suggestions offered in this final section of the chapter should prove helpful in combatting obsolescence.

Determine what else you could do for a living besides your present job.   Finding a good answer to this question is an effective way of preventing obsolescence (and reducing worries about job security). In recent years an increasing number of people have answered this question by developing a secondary occupational speciality (S.O.S.). An ideal S.O.S. should be one that represents a logical transition from what you are doing now to another type of job for which there might be equal or greater demand. Sometimes an S.O.S. can be a different type of work or the expansion of a hobby into a full-time paid job. It is not uncommon for production supervisors to gradually develop a business of their own such as home improvement, automobile repair, or landscaping. If necessary, these supervisors could earn a living by performing these activities full time.

To increase your value to your current employer, develop an S.O.S. that you could perform in your own company if necessary. One office supervisor decided to learn about quality control by taking night courses and visiting the quality control department on occasional lunch breaks. When her job was abolished due to a company relocation, she qualified for a job as an inspection supervisor.

Ask for a demotion.   Many people in our society fall victim to the Peter Principle. They are promoted to a position that they cannot handle properly. Because of being promoted once too often, they become ineffective and therefore obsolete. Should you become placed in such a position, there is no disgrace in asking to be demoted back to a position that you can comfortably handle.

Most people balk at the idea of a demotion because of our strong cultural value that; in organizational life, "higher is better." It is also important to realize that a person's reputation in any work organization is enhanced when that person performs a job well. It is much better to function as an able maintenance technician than to be an obsolete maintenance supervisor.

Engage in personal long-range forecasting. An effective way to prevent becoming obsolete is to figure out what kinds of knowledge and skills you will need to handle your job in the future. In essence, the person who wards off obsolescence does so by developing a leading-edge orientation in a particular field.

Unless you are clairvoyant, it is difficult to figure out what skills and knowledge you will need in the future. Nevertheless, there are ways of determining what kinds of skills and knowledge are in the forefront of your field before too many others make the discovery. Check carefully into trade journals in your field such as *American Machinist, Purchasing Week,* or *Industry Week* for articles about new developments that could influence your job. Reading want ads in local or national newspapers may also provide valuable clues as to what skills within your field are in demand.

A careful reading of the magazine *Supervisory Management* will help you discover what kind of information the modern supervisor is supposed to know. An approach of this nature will keep you at least a step ahead of others in your line of work. Such an individual is much less likely to become obsolete.

Receive continuous feedback. One reason many people become obsolete is that they perpetuate the same old errors. Honest feedback from others can help an individual prevent repeating the same mistakes year after year. Feedback of this nature should be part of a performance review system. Effective managers tend to give this kind of feedback spontaneously as the need arises.

> Mack, an administrative assistant, had not received a promotion in three years. His newest assignment was a lateral transfer, working for Bud, manager of systems and procedures. Bud called Mack into his office one month after his starting date. "Mack, I have something sensitive to tell you, but I think it will help you. I've noticed that you touch people too much when you are talking to them. As an outside observer, I can see that people wince when you put your arm around them, males and females included." Shocked at first, Mack quickly changed his touching behavior. Gradually, he was better accepted by people he worked with and received a promotion to supervisor one year later.

Develop a lifelong positive attitude toward self-development. By far the most effective method of preventing going out of style is to develop a lifelong positive attitude toward self-development and self-improvement. The habitual self-developer recognizes that personal growth and knowledge acquisition are possible in almost every experience. With a positive attitude toward development, you can acquire valuable insight in situations that at first seem hopeless. You stand an excellent chance of becoming obsolete if you fail to profit from comfortable and/or frustrating work situations.

Scott, an inventory control specialist, was assigned to Greg, a supervisor with a legendary reputation for poor management practices. After working for this autocratic, defensive, highly suspicious manager for six months, Scott was asked by a personnel specialist how he liked his new assignment. Scott thought for a moment and then replied:

> I assume what I say will go no further than this room. To tell you the truth, I'm learning quite a bit from Greg. He is considered to be a basket case as a supervisor by many people. A lot of it isn't his fault. Management made the error a long time ago of making him a supervisor when he just wasn't supervisory material.
>
> I want to be a manager someday. Greg serves as a model of what a manager should not do. You could almost make up a checklist of how not to supervise people by following Greg around for a week. I wouldn't want to work under him for more than a year, but in the interim, he's an excellent negative model.

What about you? It's your choice. With an optimistic and positive attitude, you, too, will keep from going out of style. With a pessimistic and dour attitude toward work situations that don't go your way, you may never achieve success in the practice of supervision.

SUMMARY OF KEY POINTS

☐ Part of self-development is developing an ethical code of business conduct. A simple way of developing your own ethical code is to treat others the way in which you want to be treated.

☐ An important success factor for a supervisor is to practice good work habits. Such habits help you become both efficient and effective. The suggestions offered here are: Try work cost averaging. Maintain an updated list of chores. Concentrate on important tasks. Identify and plug time leaks. Learn to say no. Guard against procrastination. Avoid perfectionism.

☐ Much is known about the area of advancing your career. Eight key strategies summarized here are: Stay tuned to the outside world. Make an accurate self-appraisal. Outperform the competition. Achieve broad experience. Find a sponsor. Document your accomplishments. Manage luck. Hitch your wagon to yourself.

☐ Tension is almost inevitable in a competitive job environment. Proper management of your tensions prevent much discomfort and illness and keep you productive on and off the job. Nine strategies for managing or coping with your tension discussed in this chapter are: Take constructive action about your problem. Attack the cause of your tensions, not the symptoms. Strengthen your personal qualifications. Talk out your problems. Have your job redesigned (to reduce the most stressful element). Get ample physical exercise. Learn to relax on your own. Try TM and related techniques. Concentrate on your work or hobby.

☐ A major problem facing many supervisors (and workers at other levels) is obsolescence—the general condition of losing some of your former effectiveness for any of a number of reasons. Five strategies particularly helpful in preventing obsolescence are: Figure out what you could do for a living besides your present job. Ask for a demotion back to a job that you can comfortably handle. Engage in personal long-range forecasting. Receive continuous feedback about your job performance and capabilities. Develop a lifelong positive attitude toward self-development.

GUIDELINES FOR SUPERVISORY EFFECTIVENESS

1. You should not leave your career development to somebody else. Many large business and governmental organizations have formal programs of career development open to supervisors. Yet even in these situations, it is your responsibility to make sure that the organization understands your capabilities and goals. If you passively sit back and wait to be developed, you may wind up becoming obsolete. Personal and career development requires active participation on your part.

2. Assume you understood all the information presented in the previous 19 chapters and you also possessed all the other skills and knowledges required of a modern supervisor. You might still fail as a supervisor if you did not practice good work habits and cope with your tensions.

3. If you improve your work habits, an important side benefit is that you will probably decrease a substantial portion of your job-related tensions. One reason many supervisors (and other employees) are tense is that they feel overwhelmed by their job.

**QUESTIONS FOR
DISCUSSION AND
REVIEW**

1. Why do you think a chapter on self-management was included in this textbook about supervision?
2. Give a specific example of unethical conduct in business that you are familiar with. Why do you consider this conduct to be unethical?
3. What do you see as the potential dangers in being too well organized?
4. Which techniques of improving your work habits described in this chapter are you the most likely to use? Why?
5. Successful business executives usually have neat and orderly desks. In what way do you think neat and orderly desks contribute to their success?
6. Suppose a supervisor's day is consumed up with personnel problems. How can this supervisor then use the principle "concentrate on important tasks"?
7. What are some time leaks in your day?
8. Which of the career advancement strategies described in this chapter are you the *most* likely to use? Why?
9. Which of the career advancement strategies described in this chapter are you the *least* likely to use? Why?
10. Which of these career advancement strategies has apparently been used by the current president of the United States or prime minister of Canada?
11. In addition to the techniques mentioned in this chapter, how might you document your accomplishments?
12. What technique or techniques have you found particularly helpful in reducing your job-related tensions?
13. Do you think supervisors should be given 20 minutes to meditate during their working day? Why or why not?
14. Is an immediate superior a good person to talk over your problems with? Why or why not?
15. What are you doing these days to prevent becoming obsolete?

A supervisory problem: What do you do when everybody wants to see the boss?

Lloyd Bartow, a management consultant, was conducting a workshop about time management at a newspaper. Midway through the presentation, Spike Meadows, head of the machine maintenance department, said, "Oh sure, your idea about spending one hour per day on paperwork or planning sounds great in theory. But in my line of work, I don't even have five spare minutes to myself. The job of my department is to make sure the presses keep running. We're hit with requests all day. When somebody has a problem they insist on speaking to me. If I'm out to lunch or on vacation, they say, 'Well, I'll speak to Spike when he gets back.' I'm in a time trap and there is no way out.''

Bartow replied, "But there must be some way you can appoint an acting department head for the times when you are taking care of paperwork or planning."

"That's what you as an outsider might think," answered Meadows. "But everybody in this newspaper wants to see the boss when they have a machine problem."

1. *How might you use the first Framework for Accomplishing Results in helping Meadows get better control of his job?*
2. *What should Bartow tell Meadows?*
3. *Do you think it might be true that a fire-fighter's job such as Meadow's might not leave room for planning or doing paperwork during normal working hours?*

SOME SUGGESTED READING

Bliss, Edwin C. *Getting Things Done: The ABC's of Time Management.* New York: Scribner's, 1976.

Briggs, Dorothy Corkille. *Celebrate Yourself: Making Life Work for You.* New York: Doubleday, 1977

Figler, Homer R. *Overcoming Executive Mid-life Crisis.* New York: Wiley, 1978.

Ginsburg, Lee R. "Career Planning: Steps You Can Take for Yourself." *Supervisory Management,* May 1977, pp. 2–10.

Haldane, Bernard. *Career Satisfaction and Success: A Guide to Job Freedom.* New York: AMACOM, 1974.

Hibbard, Janet G., and Landrum, Robert K. "How to Fight Time (and Win)." *Personnel Journal,* May 1978, pp. 256–59.

Lakein, Alan. *How to Get Control of Your Time and Your Life.* New York: Wyden, 1973.

Levinson, Daniel J. *The Seasons of a Man's Life.* New York: Knopf, 1978.

Miller, Donald B. *Personal Vitality.* (Plus *Personal Vitality Workbook.*) Reading: Mass.: Addison-Wesley, 1977.

Rummel, Rose Mary, and Rader, John W. "Coping with Executive Stress." *Personnel Journal,* June 1978, pp. 305–7, 332.

Stockard, James G. *Career Development and Job Training: A Manager's Handbook.* New York: AMACOM, 1978.

Sunshine, John. *How to Enjoy Your Retirement.* New York: AMACOM, 1975.

Thornton, George C., III. "Differential Effects of Career Planning on Internals and Externals." *Personnel Psychology,* Autumn 1978, pp. 471–76.

Van Maanen, John, and Katz, Ralph. "Individuals and Their Careers: Some Temporal Considerations for Work Satisfaction." *Personnel Psychology,* Winter 1976, pp. 601–16.

Zenger, John H. et al. *How to Work for a Living and Like It: A Career Planning Workbook.* Reading, Mass.: Addison-Wesley, 1977.

Glossary

accident proneness. A behavior pattern in which an individual is involved in more than an average share of accidents.

action plan. A description of what needs to be done to achieve an objective or bring performance back to an acceptable level or standard.

anxiety. Generalized feelings of fear and apprehension that usually result from a perceived threat. Feelings of uneasiness and tension usually accompany anxiety.

appropriate reward or punishment. A positive or negative motivator that produces results with a given individual in a given situation.

authority. The right to control the actions of others. Also, control that is sanctioned by the organization or society.

autocratic leadership. A leadership style in which the leader attempts to retain most of the authority. The autocratic leader typically makes a decision and then announces it to subordinates.

awareness training. An intense group discussion method, conducted by a human relations trainer, designed to make people more aware of their attitudes and prejudices about a particular group. Often used in overcoming prejudice toward selected minority groups and females.

behavior modification. A system of motivation that intends to change the behavior of people by manipulating incentives (thus changing the person's environment). Desired responses are rewarded while undesired responses are ignored or punished. Also referred to as reinforcement theory.

behavioral objective. An objective expressed in terms of the actual actions to be accomplished such as "clean all the office windows, inside and out, by January 15th."

brainstorming. A conference technique of solving specific problems, amassing information, and stimulating creative thinking. The basic technique is to encourage unrestrained and spontaneous participation by group members. Also called *group brainstorming,* it can be practiced by yourself.

bureaucracy. A rational, systematic, and precise form of organization in which rules, regulations, and techniques of control are precisely defined. A typical bureaucracy has many layers of management and many specialists.

career advancement strategy. Any systematic plan, ethical or unethical, aimed at improving your chances for success at work over the long range. Documenting your accomplishments is one such strategy.

career development. The process of creating a pattern of jobs in a series of steps from the initial job to retirement.

case. An involved description, usually based on reality, that is useful in illustrating or studying a phenomenon. This book uses very brief cases to illustrate many of the concepts and ideas discussed.

classical conditioning. A basic form of learning in which a stimulus that usually brings forth a given response is repeatedly paired with a neutral stimulus (one that does not typically evoke the response). Eventually the neutral stimulus will bring forth the response when presented by itself (such as feeling hunger pangs when the factory lunch whistle blows).

coaching. Helping an individual overcome a specific, immediate problem by giving advice and encouragement.

commonsense. Sound practical judgment that is independent of specialized knowledge, training, or the like. Natural wisdom, not based on formal knowledge.

communication. The passage of information between or among people by the use of words, letters, symbols, or body language.

conflict. A hostile or antagonistic relationship between people. Also, simultaneous arousal of two or more incompatible goals or motives. Often accompanied by tension, anxiety, or frustration.

conformity. To behave similarly in form, nature, or character to other people in a group. Conformity can be helpful or harmful.

confrontation. Bringing forth a controversial topic or contradictory material with which the other party is emotionally involved. To say to an employee, "Your performance is unacceptable," is to initiate a confrontation.

control. A measure taken to see that things are actually going according to plan. Used in the controlling function of supervision or management.

coping. To contend with something or somebody on even terms with success, such as coping with tension or irrational people.

creativity. The ability to process information in such a way that the result is new, original, and meaningful.

crucial subordinate. An individual who performs well in an assignment upon which the superior's performance is dependent. A "troubleshooter" often becomes a crucial subordinate.

decision. The passing of judgment upon an issue under consideration. Arriving at a choice among alternatives.

delegation. The process by which authority and work assignments are distributed downward in an organization.

disarm the opposition. A technique of conflict resolution in which you disarm the other person by agreeing with his or her criticism of you.

discipline. Training people to act in accordance with rules and regulations, or punishment inflicted by way of correction and training. Also, to bring a state of order and obedience by training and control.

emotion. Any strong agitation of the feelings triggered by experiencing love, hate, fear, joy, and the like.

emotional insecurity. A feeling of lack of self-confidence and uncertainty and a concern about your chances of succeeding in a variety of situations.

ethics. The body of moral principles or values governing a particular culture or group. Ethical behavior is what society thinks fits in with these moral principles and values.

eustress. An amount of stress that makes you come alive. A positive force in the lives of people.

feedback. Information that tells you how well or poorly you have performed. Also, knowledge of results about one's behavior that helps you judge the appropriateness of your responses and make corrections where indicated.

fifth freedom. A new ethic that has gradually developed in North America whose basic premise is that not being supervised is preferable to being supervised. Or simply, the freedom from supervision.

flextime. A method of organizing the hours of work in which employees have flexibility in choosing their own hours. People working under flextime are required to work certain core hours, such as 11:00 A.M. to 3:00 P.M., but they have flexibility in which hours they choose to work for the rest of the day.

fogging. A way of responding to manipulative criticism by openly accepting the criticism. Such as, "Yes, it's true I was one hour late for work today."

forecast. A projection about the future from

which management derives budgets and plans.

formal group. A group that forms in response to the demands and processes of the formal organization. An officially sanctioned group.

formal organization. The organization as it is supposed to be or as it is written on paper. It is the official, sanctioned way of doing things.

frame of reference. A standard we use against which to judge other things, people, or ideas. What an employee thinks is a "good" or "bad" job depends a lot upon the worker's frame of reference.

framework. A basic system or design for understanding something. A framework serves as a basic outline or mode.

frustration. Thwarting or blocking of a need, wish, or desire.

frustration tolerance. The amount of frustration a given individual can handle without suffering adverse consequences. When a person is fatigued, frustration tolerance decreases.

functional organization. The traditional organization in which departments are arranged according to the activity or process they perform, such as accounting or purchasing.

game. A repeated series of exchanges between people which appears different on the surface than its true underlying motive.

gentle confrontation. A method of conflict resolution in which the person with a gripe openly, but tactfully, brings the problem to the attention of the person involved in the dispute.

goal. An event, circumstance, object, or condition for which a person or animal strives.

grapevine. The major informal communication network in an organization. Used in both the transmission of rumors and true information.

group. A collection of individuals who regularly interact with each other, who are psychologically aware of each other, and who think of themselves as a group.

group cohesiveness. The attractiveness of the group to its members, which leads to a feeling of unity and "stick-togetherness."

Herzberg's two-factor theory of motivation. The view advanced by psychologist Herzberg that the factors leading to satisfaction and motivation are not the same as those leading to dissatisfaction or low motivation. In general, factors that give you a chance to satisfy your higher-level needs lead to job satisfaction and motivation.

human behavior. Any actions or activities engaged in by people including both external (such as movement) and internal activities (such as thinking and feeling).

human relations. The art and practice of using systematic knowledge about human behavior to achieve organizational and/or personal objectives. Similar to organizational behavior.

human relations skills. A loose term generally meaning the ability to get along with and work well with people.

individual differences. The basic concept of psychology that human beings show variation on almost every trait and characteristic. For instance, people have individual differences in height, intelligence, hearing ability, and aggressiveness.

informal communication pathway. A communication route that develops spontaneously in an organization, such as the grapevine.

informal group. Natural grouping of people in a work situation that evolves to take care of people's desire for friendship and companionship.

informal organization. A pattern of relationships that develops to both satisfy people's social needs and get work accomplished. It is not written down and includes informal groups.

intelligence. The capacity to acquire and apply knowledge, including solving problems. Technically, intelligence refers to the capacity to learn, the ability to deal with abstractions, the ability to manipulate symbols, and the ability to handle new situations.

intuition. Direct perception of truth or fact that seems to be independent of any reasoning process. A keen and quick insight that can be helpful to solving complex problems.

job design. The basic way in which a job is set up or designed. Job design can be an influential factor in employee motivation and satisfaction.

job enlargement. A method of increasing worker satisfaction by increasing the number of tasks for which the worker is responsible.

job enrichment. A system of job design that attempts to increase worker motivation and satisfaction by making the nature of the job more exciting, rewarding, challenging, or creative. Or building into the job more decision making, planning, and controlling.

job rotation. A method of increasing worker satisfaction and motivation by rotating a person through different assignments.

job satisfaction. The amount of pleasure or contentment associated with a job. In contrast, job *motivation* refers to the effort directed toward achieving job goals.

labor relations. That aspect of personnel management that deals specifically with relationships between management and a labor union or association.

law of the situation. Something logical about a given situation that indicates to people what actions should be taken. Orders stem logically from this "law."

leadership. The process of influencing other people to achieve certain objectives.

leadership style. The characteristic manner or typical approach a particular person uses in leading people. Many different leadership styles are possible, including participative, autocratic, and free rein. Sometimes referred to as supervisory style.

line responsibility or authority. The activities of departments or other units of the organization which contribute directly to the organization's production of goods or services.

management by objectives (MBO). A system of management in which people are held accountable for reaching objectives they usually set jointly with their superiors. Objectives at lower levels within the organization contribute to the attainment of goals set at the top of the organization.

Maslow's need hierarchy. A widely quoted and accepted theory of human motivation developed by Maslow, emphasizing that people strive to fulfill needs. These needs are arranged in a hierarchy of importance—physiological, safety, belongingness, esteem, and self-actualization. People tend to strive for satisfaction of needs at one level only after satisfaction has been achieved at the previous level.

matrix organization. An organizational design that combines the functional organization with the project organization. A person working in a matrix organization reports to both a project head and a functional (departmental) head.

mid-career crisis. A general concern that career-minded people have between the ages of 35 and 55 about their level of accomplishment, usually associated with the mid-life crisis. The symptoms of the mid-career crisis include feelings of dissatisfaction, boredom, and restlessness.

middle manager. Manager or supervisor whose place in the organization lies between first-level management and top-level management (board of directors, president, vice presidents). The middle manager's job involves considerable coordination of the work of others.

morale. The general satisfaction level of a group. It is the composite of feelings, attitudes, and sentiments that contributes to a general feeling of satisfaction.

motivation. The "why" of behavior. All those inner striving conditions described as wishes, desires, and drives. It is an inner state that activates or moves a person towards a goal.

motivator. Job elements or incentives that energize you to action (exert a motivational impact on you).

motive. A need or desire coupled with the intention to attain an appropriate goal. Your motive in attending school might be to secure a better job for yourself.

negative reinforcement. Similar to positive reinforcement, negative reinforcement attempts to reinforce the desired behavior. Instead of providing a positive reward, the person is allowed to avoid something negative (such as a penalty) when making the desired response.

objective. A specific end state or condition

aimed for that contributes to a larger goal. Your objective might be to perform well in your job this month to help you reach your goal of having a successful career.

obsolescence. A condition in which a worker at any level loses some of his or her former effectiveness to the point where the person does not meet current job standards.

office politics. Any method of gaining advantage for yourself in a job environment that is not strictly related to merit. For example, finding a sponsor or complimenting your boss.

ombudsman. In a job environment, an individual who listens to the problems of an employee and then acts as a spokesperson for getting that problem resolved at a higher organizational level. Or any official who investigates complaints.

operant conditioning. A form of conditioning in which certain of the person's spontaneous actions or responses are rewarded, ignored, or punished, resulting in a strengthening or weakening of that response. Also known as behavior modification or reinforcement theory.

organization design. The way in which an organization is laid out with a purpose in mind. For example, if you wanted to manufacture a product, you would have to design an organization to accomplish that end.

organizational unit. A subpart of an organization such as a department or division.

participative leadership. An approach to leading others in which subordinates share decision making with the leader. Emphasized by the human relations or behavioral school of management thought.

perceptual defense. A general tendency in perception to see things in such a way that our view of the world remains consistent. Perceptual defense is also used to deny events that we consider unpleasant for whatever reason.

perfectionism. A propensity for setting extremely high standards along with a displeasure at achieving anything less. A perfectionistic person is often obsessed with details.

performance appraisal. A formal system of measuring, evaluating, and reviewing employee performance.

personality. Those persistent and enduring behavior patterns of an individual that tend to be expressed in a wide variety of situations.

personal development. A general (and loose) term for almost any type of self-improvement or self-development. Also, development more related to the individual than to the organization.

positive reinforcement. Receiving a reward for making a desired response, such as getting approval from a boss for being prompt. Also, considered a system of motivating people. See also behavior modification, operant conditioning, and reinforcement theory.

power. The ability to control others by a variety of means, including your personality characteristics and formal position in the organization.

power motive. A desire for control over people and other resources. The power motive can be directed at helping yourself or others.

problem-solving ability. Essentially mental ability or intelligence used for the purpose of solving problems.

procrastination. A tendency to delay taking action or making decisions. Often displayed when an important change faces an individual.

productivity. Those behaviors related to achieving work output or job performance.

progressive discipline. Administering punishments or sanctions in increasing order of severity until the person being disciplined improves (or is terminated).

project management. A way of organizing work according to a particular purpose or mission. It involves a temporary group of specialists from diverse disciplines working together under the same manager to accomplish a fixed objective or purpose.

Pygmalion effect. The tendency for employees to work up to the expectations of their boss. If you are confident of an employee's ability, the person will often justify your confidence.

realistic goal. A goal that a person finds challenging but not one so difficult that it usually results in failure and frustration.

reciprocity. A form of work motivation in which the superior and the subordinate exchange favors. If the subordinate shows good work motivation, the superior grants a favor in exchange.

role. Behavior, or a sequence of behaviors, expected of an individual occupying a given position within a group. It is within the role of a supervisor to administer discipline to subordinates.

role ambiguity. A condition that exists when you are uncertain of your true responsibilities. Often accompanied by a feeling of uneasiness.

role conflict. Anxiety generated in a person when people have incompatible expectations of you or when two or more of your roles conflict with each other.

schmoozing. The act or process of engaging in social interaction with other individuals during normal working hours. It includes such activities as "chit-chatting" and making telephone calls for social purposes.

selective perception. Perceiving things that you want to perceive, or not perceiving things that you do not want to perceive. An employee thus might not hear that he or she has been given a poor performance review.

self-actualization. Making maximum use of your potential. Similar to self-fulfillment.

self-appraisal. Making an evaluation of your own strengths, weaknesses, capabilities, interests, and so forth. Useful in managing your career.

self-concept. The way in which a person views himself or herself. Also, your knowledge and understanding about yourself or your identity.

self-confidence. The extent to which a person has a positive attitude toward his or her own capabilities.

self-discipline. Disciplining or training oneself, usually for purposes of self-improvement.

self-nomination. Naming yourself as a contender for transfers, promotions, and special assignments.

serendipity. The gift of unintentionally finding valuable things while you are looking for something else.

setup questions. Asking another person a question designed to make that person look good or bad. A technique of office politics.

shaping of behavior. Inducing somebody to achieve the desired response by first rewarding any action in the right direction, and then rewarding only the closest approximation. Using this approach, the desired response is finally attained.

shared decision making. A situation in which a manager allows and encourages subordinates to participate in (provide inputs to) the decision-making process. An important aspect of participative management.

staff function or responsibility. The activities of departments or other subunits of the organization which contribute indirectly to the production of goods and services. Staff personnel generally advise line personnel.

stimulus. Physical energy, or anything else, that arouses an individual and produces an effect on that person. A noise could be a stimulus and so could a safety poster.

strain. A reaction to stress implying an unfavorable reaction to the individual or group; a change in the state of the internal system.

stress. Any demand outside or inside the person that requires the person to cope with the demand. Groups and organizations also experience stress.

stressor. A source of stress acting on the individual or group.

supervisor. A first-level manager responsible for directing the work activities of one or more subordinates. Some writers call any manager a supervisor.

supervisory climate. The working atmosphere or psychological climate governed by the leadership style of a particular supervisor.

supervisory effectiveness. The extent to which a supervisor accomplishes results that are desired by the organization.

supervisory practice. The actual conduct of a supervisor's job. You are practicing supervision when you help an employee with a work-related problem.

symptom. A sign or indicator that a particular condition is taking place. A fever is a symptom of bodily infection; a high accident rate may be a symptom of low morale.

synergy. The action of two or more people to

achieve an effect that none of the people could achieve individually. The whole is greater than the sum of the parts.

task force. A small group of individuals called together to solve a problem or explore and develop a new idea for an organization. Members are usually picked on the basis of their potential contribution or knowledge rather than on the basis of rank.

tension. Mental or emotional strain; a feeling of internal uneasiness that is usually associated with stress or an unsatisfied need.

Theory X. McGregor's famous statement of the traditional management view that considers people as usually lazy and needing prodding by external rewards.

Theory Y. McGregor's famous statement of an alternative to traditional management thinking. It emphasizes that people seek to fulfill higher level needs on the job and that management must be flexible and human relations oriented.

training. Teaching people a particular skill so that they can put that skill to practice.

transactional analysis (TA). A technique for improving interpersonal relationships that looks upon every human relationship as a transaction between the ego states (parent, adult, child) of people.

transcendental meditation (TM). A system of almost total relaxation involving the achievement of a physiological state of deep rest. Meditation involves sitting quietly alone.

type A behavior. A behavior pattern characterized by impatience, compulsiveness, high tension, high energy, and a constant striving for success.

value. The importance a person attaches to something such as education, religion, sports, or high-quality products.

workaholic (work addict). A person addicted to work to the extent that it has adverse consequences for family and personal life. The condition may also interfere with job effectiveness as the person often loses perspective and objectivity.

work cost averaging. A method of improving your efficiency in which you invest about the same amount of time and energy into your work everyday. By the end of the year you will have increased your productivity and avoided many instances of cramming.

work ethic. The belief that hard work is a good thing in itself.

work habits. A person's characteristic approach to work, including such things as organization, handling of paperwork, and the setting of priorities.

work motivation. The expenditure of effort toward the accomplishment of department or organizational goals. Work motivation is but one aspect of human motivation in general.

Name index

Subject index

This book has been set VIP in 11 point and 9 point Trump Mediaeval, leaded 2 points. Part numbers and titles are 36 and 24 point Trump Mediaeval. Chapter numbers are 54 point Palatino and chapter titles are 18 point Trump Mediaeval. The size of the type page is 36 by 45½ picas.